LONG IS THE WAY AND HARD

Long Is the Way and Hard

One Hundred Years of the National
Association for the Advancement of
Colored People (NAACP)

*Edited by Kevern Verney
and Lee Sartain*

Foreword by Adam Fairclough

The University of Arkansas Press
Fayetteville
2009

ISBN-10: (cloth) 1-555728-908-5
ISBN-13: (cloth) 978-1-555728-908-8
ISBN-10: (paper) 1-555728-909-3
ISBN-13: (paper) 978-1-555728-909-8

13   12   11   10   09   5   4   3   2   1

Designed by Liz Lester

⊛ The paper used in this publication meets the minimum requirements of the
American National Standard for Permanence of Paper for Printed Library
Materials Z39.48-1984.

LIBRARY OF CONGRESS CATALOGING-IN-PUBLICATION DATA

Long is the way and hard : one hundred years of the National Association for the
    Advancement of Colored People (NAACP) / edited by Kevern Verney and
    Lee Sartain.
        p.   cm.
    Includes bibliographical references and index.
    ISBN 978-1-55728-908-7 (clothbound : alk. paper) —
ISBN 978-1-55728-909-4 (pbk. : alk. paper)
        1. National Association for the Advancement of Colored People—History—
20th century. 2. African Americans—Civil rights—History—20th century.
3. Civil rights movements—United States—History—20th century. 4. African
Americans—Politics and government—20th century. 5. United States—Race
relations. I. Verney, Kevern, 1960–   II. Sartain, Lee.
        E185.5.N276L66   2009
        973'.0496073—dc22
                                                    2009021913

CONTENTS

FOREWORD

Adam Fairclough

The National Association for the Advancement of Colored People is the oldest, largest, and most influential civil rights organization in the United States. For one hundred years, it has pursued a straightforward yet exceedingly difficult goal: to ensure that African Americans are treated as equal citizens. This goal was straightforward in the sense that the NAACP simply demanded the "strict and impartial" enforcement of the Constitution, which had been amended after the Civil War to abolish slavery and outlaw racial discrimination. The Thirteenth Amendment had outlawed slavery and "involuntary servitude." According to the Fourteenth Amendment, blacks were full citizens of the United States, and all citizens were entitled to "equal protection of the law." The Fifteenth Amendment established equal political rights, making it illegal for a state to deny the right to vote on the grounds of "race, color, or previous condition of servitude."

When the NAACP was founded in 1909, however, the prospects for enforcing these constitutional provisions could hardly have been less encouraging. "Often plundered of their just share of the public funds, robbed of nearly all part in government, segregated by common carriers, some murdered with impunity, and all treated with open contempt by officials, they are held in some States in practical slavery." This declaration by the National Conference on the Negro, which launched the NAACP in New York City on May 31, 1909, did not exaggerate. An upsurge in lynching—the open, brazen, killing of blacks by whites, often in public spectacles of revolting sadism—symbolized just how far African Americans had been written out of the Constitution.

The men and women who founded the NAACP believed that only

a new organization with a new strategy could reverse this situation. Since the Civil War blacks had looked to the Republican Party—the party of emancipation and equal rights—to protect them. But after the collapse of Radical Reconstruction (1867–1877), the Republican Party abandoned its role as the champion of racial equality. By 1909, when the black vote in the South had been almost entirely suppressed, the Republican Party saw no political advantage whatsoever in defending the interests of African Americans or protecting blacks against white aggression. In the North, the Republicans' base, most whites believed that Radical Reconstruction had been a blunder: race relations in the South should be treated as a local matter to be decided within the South itself. The status of black southerners would, in effect, be decided by white southerners. With what amounted to a pledge of nonintervention from the North, whites in the South, acting through the Democratic Party, constructed a system of white supremacy that was buttressed by legislation, law, custom, and violence. The aim of this system—often dubbed "Jim Crow," a synonym for segregation—was quite clear. The South's white leaders openly acknowledged that they intended to keep the black population permanently disfranchised, permanently segregated, and permanently subservient.

The rest of the nation was more than a passive spectator, however, when it came to racial discrimination. The Congress, the Supreme Court, and presidents from both political parties acquiesced in, and even approved, the South's new racial order. Moreover, even though nine-tenths of the black population still resided in the former Confederacy, antiblack prejudice was rampant in the North as well. Northern states for the most part rejected the legalized forms of segregation favored in the South. Nevertheless, the actions of public officials and private citizens reflected a commitment to preserving white racial privilege. Housing discrimination produced segregated black ghettos. School boards fostered racially segregated schools. Public accommodations often enforced a color bar. Employers and unions colluded to exclude blacks from skilled jobs, and sometimes from entire industries. Opportunities for white-collar employment were slim to nonexistent: the occupational ceiling for the vast majority of black men was that of factory worker, postal worker, Pullman car porter, or longshoreman. Black women were largely confined to domestic work; the only "middle-class" occupation open to them was that of schoolteacher. Although blacks in the North could usually vote, they lacked political influence: in 1909 the Congress did not contain a single African American. Virtually everywhere they went, blacks could anticipate contempt, hostility, and even violence from whites. Some of the nation's most serious race riots took place in northern cities. In short, the founders of the NAACP believed that the two main political parties were complicit in the oppression of blacks, just as the pre-1850 Whigs and Democrats had colluded to protect slavery. The NAACP would be to the twentieth century what the abolitionist movement had been to the nineteenth, a movement of uncompromising principle that would challenge the political establishment and force the nation to confront its greatest evil.

The founders of the NAACP also believed that their new movement, although nationwide in scope and ambition, must be anchored in the North. In the southern states, conditions for blacks had become so oppressive that to denounce racial injustice was to risk life and limb. The Memphis teacher and journalist Ida B. Wells, for example, found herself fleeing the South, one step ahead of a mob baying for her blood, after she had condemned lynching in uncompromising terms. Even whites who offered polite criticisms of the South's racial order ran the risk of political and social isolation. The men who enforced Jim Crow not only demanded obedience, they also demanded conformity. In short, no overt movement against white supremacy could be launched from within the South: it had to be organized from the North. In the North, blacks were at least permitted freedom of expression. In the North, too, blacks could find white allies who, although small in numbers, commanded money, political connections, and legal skills. From the outset, therefore, the NAACP was interracial in its membership and leadership—something that would have been impossible in the South, where Jim Crow laws and social conventions forbade blacks and whites from associating on a basis of equality. The NAACP opened a national office in New York City, and W. E. B. Du Bois moved there from Atlanta to edit the organization's monthly magazine, the *Crisis*.

The northern-based NAACP represented a decisive rejection of the South's conservative black leadership. For a decade after 1895,

Booker T. Washington, a former slave from Virginia, had been the best-known face of black America and the most influential African American in the land. A man of indefatigable drive and determination, as well as a masterful diplomat, Washington made a humble school in Alabama, Tuskegee Institute, the symbol of a new approach to race relations. Decrying Radical Reconstruction as a mistake, Washington urged blacks to eschew politics, avoid "rights" agitation, and devote their energies to practical education, moral improvement, and the acquisition of property. Coupled with a plea for friendly relations with whites in the South, Washington believed that his conservative policy would take the sting out of southern racism, facilitating black economic progress and paving the way for the eventual restoration of civil and political rights, only this time with the acceptance of the white population. Dubbed the "Wizard of Tuskegee" for his ability to conjure up financial and political support, Washington forged strong personal ties with northern philanthropists and industrialists, enabling him to channel outside money to black schools and colleges in the South. Through his relationship with President Theodore Roosevelt (1901–1909), Washington also acquired a degree of behind-the-scenes political influence.

By 1909, however, it had became painfully clear that Washington's strategy of conciliating white southern leaders, and downplaying of constitutional rights in favor of self-improvement, had failed to halt the relentless decline in the status of blacks in the South. Two of the most influential founders and early leaders of the NAACP, W. E. B. Du Bois and Oswald Garrison Villard, were both former supporters of Washington who had concluded that his appeasement of the white South had become self-defeating. The foundation of the NAACP thus moved the center of black leadership from the South to the North. Before his death in 1915 Washington—who kept a wary eye on the NAACP's rapid growth—seemed to recognize that fact himself. For decades, the NAACP suffered from its perception in the South as an "outside" organization, and its branches in the South proved highly vulnerable to threats and violence from whites. Yet the NAACP never gave up on the South: on the contrary, the formation of southern branches was always a top priority. Its northern base enabled the NAACP to survive as a national organization and to maintain an organizational presence in the South despite everything that white southerners could throw at it. The NAACP directly challenged the notion that the South's "race question" was a regional, rather than a national, concern.

The NAACP's founders invoked the moral passion of the abolitionist movement—some were the descendants of abolitionists—and vowed to be "as harsh as truth, and as uncompromising as justice." They warned that "the systematic persecution" of law-abiding black citizens threatened the very existence of the United States as a democratic nation. Rejecting all theories of racial hierarchy, and denouncing racial segregation as wrong in principle as well as practice, they unveiled an "organized and aggressive movement on behalf of the Negro's rights." The NAACP promised to investigate lynching, publicize other injustices, and combat racial stereotypes by advertising the "marvelous achievements of the colored people." It undertook to mobilize public opinion and to lobby Congress. Above all, it planned a systematic campaign of litigation, using the best lawyers in the land, in order to force the Supreme Court to confront the issue of racial discrimination. The NAACP's deceptively simple demands—strict enforcement of the Constitution and "equal educational opportunities for all"—were enough to keep the organization occupied for the next hundred years.

The NAACP's activities and achievements have been so wide-ranging that they defy a simple summary. NAACP lawyers represented black defendants and saved many from the gallows, gas chamber, and electric chair, sometimes appealing convictions all the way to the Supreme Court. Although the Association never achieved its goal of making lynching a federal crime, its dogged campaigning contributed to the rapid decline of lynching after 1920. The NAACP launched legal challenges against the "white primary" and other forms of disfranchisement, a campaign for universal suffrage that lasted fifty years. It protested against discrimination in federal programs and opposed segregation in the armed services. At the end of the 1930s it joined hands with the labor movement to further the interests of black workers. Its alliance with labor, however, never inhibited the NAACP from criticizing racism in the unions. Documenting and attacking employment discrimination was a constant, whether it occurred on the railroads, in the shipyards, or in the post office. The NAACP challenged segregation in public transport and in housing. It used its political clout to scuttle the appointment of a white supremacist to the Supreme Court. It brought court cases to stop southern school boards from paying black teachers less than white teachers. It got black students into the graduate schools of the South's top universities. And, of course, it campaigned to equalize public schools and then to integrate them. All the while, the NAACP also pursued a double-sided cultural agenda, on the one hand attacking racist depictions of blacks in films, books, and newspapers, and on the other hand showcasing the common humanity and positive achievements of African Americans. Such was the NAACP's influence that, by the 1930s, its leaders had easy access to the White House. When Lyndon Johnson acceded to the presidency, the first black leader he contacted was the head of the NAACP.

As this collection of essays makes clear, however, the NAACP was far more than the small group of national officials who set the organization's official agenda. The NAACP was a membership organization and, by the Second World War, half a million people had joined. Organized into local branches, which were grouped in state "conferences," the members not only supported the national organization but also supplied much of the organization's drive. There was always a tension between the national office in New York and the local branches. Like all organizations that employ the elective principle—labor unions, for example—the NAACP's democracy looked more impressive on paper than it did in practice. The small cadre of full-time officials exercised enormous influence, and they became adept at manipulating elections, stage-managing conventions, and creatively interpreting the rule book. Nevertheless, the branches often kicked back, defying or simply ignoring New York. Moreover, the officials in New York acknowledged that the success of the NAACP's national strategy depended upon local initiative; its court cases and legal challenges had to bubble up from below. Although often portrayed as a top-down bureaucracy, the NAACP was in fact fairly democratic— certainly when compared to other civil rights organizations—and local activists enjoyed a wide degree of autonomy.

Internal politics was often the NAACP's bane. The handful of top officials constantly quarreled, plotted, and maneuvered for position. But under normal conditions these leaders could at least—even if not on speaking terms—work together. At the branch level the frictions could be far worse. Factional conflicts, which were often based on little more than personality clashes, could paralyze a branch and even destroy it. In one sense, internal politicking is the price that any organization pays for having a democratic structure. In the case of the NAACP, however, the exclusion of African Americans from *actual* politics, and the fact that blacks had so few other outlets for their abilities and ambitions, made the organization's internal politics especially intense. Nevertheless, although factionalism sometimes threatened to overwhelm the organization, it never did. The integrity of its leaders and its commitment to democratic procedures served the NAACP well.

The NAACP never lacked for critics in the black community or for white critics who claimed to share the same commitment to racial equality. Black nationalists have been especially hostile to the Association. From Marcus Garvey in the 1920s to Malcolm X in the 1960s, advocates of black separatism decried the organization's commitment to interracialism. The NAACP's obsession with integration, they charged, stemmed from the fact that well-educated, light-colored mulattoes ran the organization, and that white people—especially Jews—exercised far too much influence. More plausibly, blacks and whites who were inclined to Marxist and socialist ideas faulted the NAACP for neglecting the economic basis of racism. Integration appealed to the small black middle class, they argued, but it offered little prospect of improving the lives of most blacks, who were desperately poor. The NAACP's emphasis upon constitutional rights was simply too abstract and remote. These same radicals argued that the interests of black workers could be better served in the labor movement, especially within the interracial unions of the Congress of Industrial Organizations. Both black nationalists and left-wing critics faulted the NAACP for its trust in institutions—the courts, the Congress—that were controlled by white people. From the 1930s to the present day, critics have also assailed the NAACP for its aversion to public protest—what the civil rights movement called "non-violent direct action"—arguing that although the organization had a mass membership it failed to utilize it effectively. Although many of these criticisms were overdrawn, top-ranking NAACP officials often privately questioned their organization's effectiveness. However, economic inequality proved easier to identify than to attack. Although the NAACP *did* develop an economic agenda, it continued to focus on legal redress against discrimination—constitutional and legal inequalities were always clearer to define and easier to tackle. Besides, the middle-class bias of the NAACP's membership—although not nearly as pronounced as some critics charged—did not incline it toward political or economic radicalism.

The NAACP's virtues often reflected its faults. Its unswerving commitment to legalism could be rigid, but it gave blacks a means of forcing change, through the federal judiciary, at a time when the executive and legislative branches were deaf to African Americans. Its reluctance to cooperate with other organizations sometimes betrayed narrow self-interest, as well as arrogance, but it also expressed the NAACP's steadfast refusal to compromise its ideals—it had no truck with communists, who lacked commitment to democracy, or with black nationalists, who mimicked America's racism. If the NAACP often seemed slow moving and bureaucratic, that was because a large, complex organization that abided by the rules moved deliberately. If the NAACP failed to produce a charismatic leader like Marcus Garvey or Martin Luther King, that fact reflected, in part, its commitment to internal democracy. Charismatic leaders tended to be authoritarian leaders, and organizations built around such leaders failed to last. The NAACP had—still has—staying power. Indeed, the record of the NAACP is so long and varied that no general history of the organization can hope to do it justice. There is enough in that record to keep many historians fully occupied for years to come. The essays in this magnificent collection reflect some of the best work on the NAACP, written by a generation of historians who came of age after the heyday of the civil rights movement. This fascinating collection offers fresh insights into both the strengths and weaknesses of this hugely important organization on the hundredth anniversary of its birth.

THE NAACP IN HISTORIOGRAPHICAL PERSPECTIVE

Kevern Verney and Lee Sartain

If the spirits of the 1909 founders of the NAACP were able to look down on the Association in its centenary year they would have found much to celebrate. From humble beginnings in the early 1900s, by the start of the twenty-first century the Association embraced a nation-wide network of members and branches, and in presidential election years aspiring occupants of the White House routinely addressed its national gatherings. Internationally, the NAACP commanded instant recognition and respect from any right-minded journalist or scholar with a serious interest in U.S. race relations, an accolade that reflected the tireless campaigning of innumerable NAACP activists in the cause of black civil rights over the course of almost a century. In short, the Association commanded enviable status and respect.

This was not always the case. When the NAACP was founded the prospects for a pressure group striving to protect and advance the citizenship rights of African Americans could hardly have seemed more bleak. The end of the nineteenth century and early years of the twentieth century constituted the lowest point in the African American experience since the end of the Civil War in 1865. Indeed, race relations in that era is now generally perceived by historians as being so depressing that it is referred to simply as the "nadir."

It was a time when a majority of white Americans generally thought of nonwhite peoples, and those of African descent in particular, as being innately inferior to those of Anglo-Saxon ancestry. Reflecting this prejudiced perspective, mainstream historians and other scholars of the period showed little interest in either the work of the NAACP or African American history as a whole. This was even the case when the subject matter of their research would seem to have positively required it.

In his influential study *American Negro Slavery* (1918) the historian Ulrich Bonnell Phillips, himself descended from a slave-owning family, examined the institution of slavery almost exclusively from the perspective of white slaveholders. Such an omission notwithstanding, scholars of the day hailed Phillips's tome as a definitive work in the field. The African American scholar Carter Woodson provided a rare dissenting voice. In a wry review of Phillips's *magnum opus* Woodson, a descendant of former slaves, tellingly noted "in just the same way as a writer of the history of New England in describing the fisheries of that section would have little to say about the species figuring conspicuously in that industry so the author treated the Negro in his work."[1]

Now revered as one of the founding fathers of African American historiography the passage of time has brought vindication for Woodson, but in his day his voice was as a lone cry in the wilderness, unheard by the ears of the scholarly establishment. Before the 1950s African American history was regarded as being a matter of concern only to African Americans themselves or the occasional white scholar, such as August Meier, with an eccentric preoccupation with the subject.

In the absence of interest by mainstream historians early publications on the NAACP were, for the most part, comprised of memoirs by leading members of the organization. W. E. B. Du Bois, the Association's head of research and editor of its journal, the *Crisis,* contributed *Darkwater: Voices From Within the Veil* (1920), followed by the more-detailed *Dusk of Dawn: An Essay Toward an Autobiography of a Race Concept* (1940). In the intervening years James Weldon Johnson, NAACP national secretary from 1920 to 1930, and the first African American to occupy that position, added his autobiography, *Along This Way* (1933). A founder member of the Association and longstanding senior office-holder and member of the national board of directors, Mary White Ovington, published her reminiscences *The Walls Came Tumbling Down* in 1947. The next year this was followed by *A Man Called White,* the memoirs of Walter White, Johnson's successor as secretary.[2]

Collectively, these works were invaluable in providing insider insights and in highlighting the Association's achievements and the adverse racial climate in which it was forced to operate. At the same time they had limitations. Historians are inclined to be wary of a biography-centered approach to the past, and for good reason. Biographies tend to place emphasis on the experiences of one individual at the expense of others. They also tend to neglect broader political, social, and economic developments, which, arguably more than any individual, are the prime movers of historical change.

The problems of autobiographies are even greater. Authors, either consciously or unconsciously, are likely to present their own role in events in a positive light. They may use their reminiscences to vilify perceived enemies or to omit information that might embarrass friends or colleagues. Albeit for the best of motives the works by Du Bois, Johnson, Ovington, and White thus played down internal divisions within the NAACP for fear of damaging the work of the Association. In particular they contained little or no references to the longstanding conflict between Du Bois and White in the late 1920s and early 1930s that, at times, diverted the attention of members of the NAACP secretariat and board of directors away from confronting the pressing social and economic problems that confronted African Americans at the height of the Great Depression.

In a broader context the autobiographies of early NAACP leaders tended to focus attention on national events and the work of the national office in New York rather than the activities of the Association at the state level. This encouraged what the British historian Peter Ling has described as a "Russian Doll" kind of perspective.[3] In short the public perception of the NAACP was often confined to the view of the large outer doll, embodied in the Association's best-known national spokespersons. However, this concealed the complex and diverse character of the NAACP, as manifested in the series of increasingly smaller dolls contained within, that represented the organization and activity of the Association at state, city, and local levels.

By the mid-1950s the NAACP was experiencing generational change as early leaders, such as Du Bois, Johnson, Ovington, and White, either passed away or retired from active work in the Association. In this vein Assistant Secretary Roy Wilkins succeeded White as secretary following the death of his erstwhile boss in 1955. These years were also marked by increasing political and social upheaval in the wider United States, reflected in the rise of the postwar civil rights movement, and, by the mid-1960s, antiwar protests and the emergence of Black Power. Simply put, it was a time when the United States was at unease with itself.

The changing times also prompted important, if less dramatic, developments within the historical profession. From the late 1950s, and increasingly in the 1960s and early 1970s, the academic community showed unprecedented interest in African American history. A number of scholars combined academic research with active involvement in civil rights protests, having what the historian August Meier described as a "participant-observer" relationship with the civil rights movement. Meier himself joined the NAACP, attended meetings of the Congress of Racial Equality (CORE) and the Student Nonviolent Coordinating Committee (SNCC), and took part in desegregation protests in Baltimore.[4] Similarly, in the late 1950s and early 1960s the historian Howard Zinn not only authored a full-length study of the SNCC but lived and worked in the black community in Atlanta, Georgia, participating in the campaign for desegregation in the city. In 1965 over forty American historians, including Richard Hofstadter, C. Vann Woodward, John Hope Franklin, and Kenneth Stampp, showed their support for black civil rights by joining Martin Luther King in the march from Selma to Montgomery.[5]

In historiographical terms the 1960s and 1970s were also notable for seeing the emergence of what became known as the "New Social History." Reflecting the mood of the time historians researching diverse chronological periods and geographical areas began to study the past from the perspective of the poor and dispossessed rather than the wealthy and privileged. Scholars like Rodney Hilton, Christopher Hill, and E. P. Thomson enriched the study of English history from the medieval period up to the present.[6] Some fifty years after the heyday of Ulrich Bonnell Phillips historians researching antebellum slavery finally heeded Carter Woodson's advice. In an outpouring of new works scholars like Kenneth Stampp, John Blassingame, Herbert Gutman, George Rawick, and Eugene Genovese examined the "peculiar institution" from the viewpoint of the slaves rather than their masters.[7]

Surprisingly, researchers on African American history in the twentieth century though radical in their choice of subject were generally more conservative in their methodology, adopting a leader-centered, rather than a "bottom-up" approach. Early studies on the postwar civil rights movement thus focused on the policies of presidential administrations, the actions of nationally known civil rights leaders, and the organizations they headed. Martin Luther King attracted special attention, resulting in what is now recognized to be a "King-centric" approach to the study of the civil rights struggle and overemphasis on the "Montgomery to Memphis" timeline that marked the period of his leadership.

This paradox can be explained by a number of factors. The political climate of the time in the United States encouraged a "Great Man" view of history. The 1950s and 1960s were notable for the emergence of a number of youthful charismatic individuals—John F. Kennedy, Robert Kennedy, Martin Luther King, and Malcolm X—who featured prominently on the still comparatively new medium of television. The subsequent tragic martyrdom of all of these figures only served to reinforce their iconic status.

In the academic community practitioners of the "New Social History" were motivated not just by idealism but also by the need for originality, a search to find new perspectives on well-worn historiographical debates. Civil rights scholars, however, were not in this position. The very nature of their research meant that, with a few exceptions, they *were* the pioneers in their field. The advantage of this situation was that they were not under the same pressure to come up with original ideas. The disadvantage was that they did not have a familiar and well-used body of primary source materials to utilize in their research. They had to discover these for themselves. Faced with this challenge, as the historian Charles Eagles has observed, it was natural for scholars to turn to the kinds of primary sources with which they were most familiar, such as political archives, the writings of leading individuals and the records of national organizations.[8]

In respect to the NAACP it is thus not surprising that although the 1950s and 1960s resulted in a proliferation of new studies many of these were notable for a continuation of the biography-centered "Russian Doll" approach. In 1959 and 1960 Francis Broderick and Elliott Rudwick provided the first full-length scholarly biographies of W. E. B. Du Bois. In the 1960s Du Bois's final, and most forthright, autobiography, *A Soliloquy on Viewing My Life from the Last Decade of Its First Century,* provided further insights into his life and career.[9] In the early 1970s Walter Hixson, B. Joyce Ross, and Eugene Levy provided valuable biographical studies on Moorfield Storey, Joel Spingarn, and James Weldon Johnson, respectively.[10]

Studies by Clement Vose, Charles Flint Kellogg, and Elliott Rudwick and August Meier deepened scholarly understanding of the NAACP's national organization and legal work.[11] In the late 1960s and early 1970s Black Power radicals attached great importance to the need for African Americans to assume leadership responsibilities in civil rights organizations. This concern was reflected in the work of Kellogg, Meier, and Rudwick, who focused attention on the development of the NAACP from being a white-run to a black-run organization in the early 1920s. This line of inquiry was further prompted by claims made by Marcus Garvey and his Universal Negro Improvement Association (UNIA) in the 1920s that whites dominated the NAACP. Garvey and his supporters alleged that leading African American spokespersons in the Association sought to secure their own advancement in white society rather than the larger goal of racial uplift. This selfish preoccupation reflected their own mixed race ancestry and devalued the role of the NAACP to the point where it became little more than the "National Association for the Advancement of Certain People."

The studies by Kellogg, Meier, and Rudwick were important in correcting such unjust and caricatured perceptions. At the same time emphasis on the changing balance between white and black leadership arguably led to a skewed understanding of the history of the Association. The transition from white to black leadership in the NAACP was a process, not an event. The earlier white founders of the Association were not expelled overnight, but rather continued to exercise significant influence in the NAACP throughout the 1920s and into the early 1930s. Moreover, important as it was symbolically, the growth of African American leadership in the Association during this period had only limited impact in terms of policymaking. There is little or no evidence of any racial divisions between white and black members on the NAACP board of directors during the 1920s, or between white board members and salaried African American officeholders in the NAACP's New York secretariat.[12]

At the same time preoccupation with the racial composition of the Association's leadership risked neglecting other factors, such as class, that were potentially a source of weakness and disunity. Both whites and blacks in the NAACP's national office came predominantly from well-educated middle-class backgrounds. In part, this helps to explain the preference of the national leadership for courtroom based actions rather than grassroots protests, and also the problems experienced by the Association in developing an economic agenda during the early years of the Great Depression.

Similarly, the focus on the NAACP's board of directors and its New York secretariat diverted attention away from the need to analyze the relationship between the national office and its local branches. In this context it is important to bear in mind that the NAACP was founded from the "top down." The national office of the NAACP came into existence before local branches of the Association had been organized. This meant that from the outset control over key decisions on policy and the day-to-day running of the Association were centered on its New York headquarters. In the early years, when even the very survival of the NAACP seemed at times to be in doubt, this was probably an advantage. Over time, however, this concentration of power at the center increasingly became a source of tension.

It was inevitable that as the number of local branches grew, and local officers of the NAACP gained in confidence and experience, that they would seek to have a greater say in the running of the Association. Despite some efforts by the national leadership to address this concern, for example the expansion of the NAACP's board of directors to include some grassroots organizers, this issue continued to be a problem into the 1950s and 1960s, as is highlighted by a number of essays in this volume.[13] The Association continued to be hierarchical in structure with the national office inclined to view local branches primarily as sources of revenue. Grassroots activists were expected to implement and support policy decisions made in New York rather than develop initiatives of their own. Moreover, funds raised by the branches were used largely to finance work at the national level rather than in developing the administrative and organizational support structure needed to manage relations between the New York headquarters and the nationwide network of branches. In consequence there were never adequate numbers of staff employed in the national office to deal with branch work. From the 1930s onward, if not earlier, local leaders of the Association thus complained regularly of the failure of national officers to respond promptly to their inquiries and of lengthy delays even in respect to routine matters, such as the posting out of membership certificates.

The 1980s onward through to the early years of the twenty-first century predictably saw the continuing publication of important biographical and autobiographical studies of leading NAACP figures. In 1982 *Standing Fast: The Autobiography of Roy Wilkins* provided significant insights into the thoughts of the former Association executive director and assistant secretary on developments in the civil rights struggle over the course of the twentieth century.[14] In common with other autobiographies by leading NAACP organizers it was, however, less revealing about the internal working of the Association, as Yvonne Ryan notes in her essay. It is thus surprising, as she observes, that there continues to be no full-length biographical study of Wilkins more than twenty-five years after his death.

Fortunately, other key NAACP figures fared better. In the 1980s Genna Rae McNeil and Sheldon Avery provided much needed scholarly studies on the legendary NAACP legal counsel Charles Hamilton Houston and national field secretary William Pickens. Manning Marable added to the growing body of scholarship on W. E. B. Du Bois and in 1993 and 2000 David Levering Lewis's magisterial two-volume study of the iconic NAACP founder came close to providing the definitive account of the life of his subject, if such an achievement can ever be possible.[15]

In 1998 Carolyn Wedin provided fresh insights on the life of another founding member of the Association, Mary White Ovington. In 2002 Mark Robert Schneider contributed the first detailed study of the Association in the 1920s, and the following year Kenneth Janken added a seminal study on Walter White, NAACP assistant secretary of the 1920s and national secretary of the Association from 1930 until his death in 1955. Janken's impressive work was also notable as the first full-length scholarly biography of the NAACP leader.[16] This omission, as Simon Topping observes, can be attributed to a number of factors. White, in common with Wilkins, was an able and tireless administrator but cautious and conservative in outlook. Both men also lacked the personal charisma and inspirational public-speaking skills of other leading figures in the twentieth century civil rights struggle, most notably Martin Luther King. Moreover, by the 1950s and 1960s, when African American history finally achieved mainstream scholarly recognition White, born in 1893, and Wilkins, born in 1901, appeared to be the outdated spokespersons of an older generation compared to more radical younger activists.

The important contributions of Lewis, Janken, and others notwithstanding, the most significant development in the study of the NAACP since the 1980s has been the ongoing microfilm publication of *The NAACP Papers* by an eminent editorial team of historians led by the late August Meier.[17] An extensive, but by no means complete, selection of documents from the full collection of the NAACP papers housed in the Library of Congress, this initiative has opened up to scholars an unprecedented volume of primary sources on the NAACP. Ironically, historians who have often been critical of the Association's national office for its excessively bureaucratic tendencies have been the principal beneficiaries of such practices. The diligence and efficiency of successive generations of workers in the NAACP's New York headquarters in maintaining files of correspondence, committee minutes, and other written records of the Association's activities have resulted in a body of records that, in terms of both quality and quantity, easily surpasses those available for almost every other area of African American history.[18] Indeed, a principal dilemma for researchers has been the fact that the papers are simply *so* extensive. A detailed scholarly history of the Association derived from a thorough examination of all the available material would require several lengthy volumes of published work and as many decades of archival research by any historian brave enough to undertake the task.

Understandably, scholars have been wary of embarking on a venture of such Homeric proportions. Instead the last years of the twentieth century saw a proliferation of studies on specific aspects of the NAACP's history, making selective use of the files available. In 1980 Robert Zangrando penned a study of the Association's longstanding campaign for a federal antilynching law. Over the course of the next two decades Dan Carter, Robert Cortner, Kenneth Goings, and Grif Stockley added case studies on the Association's activities ranging from the 1910s through to the 1930s.[19] Denton Watson, Jack Greenberg, and Mark Tushnet contributed seminal works on the Association's congressional and courtroom battles against segregation. In 2004 and 2005 Charles Zelden and Manfred Berg added an important new dimension with studies on the NAACP's voting rights campaigns, a subject that Charles Zelden explores further in his essay for this volume.[20]

Notable developments in the writing of civil rights history in works published since the 1980s included more emphasis on the organization of protests at local level, greater recognition of the role played by women activists, and a better appreciation of the importance of class. Publications on the NAACP in this period also reflected these broader trends. Beth Tompkins Bates and Christopher Robert Reed published influential, groundbreaking studies on the Association in Detroit and Chicago. The autobiography of Aaron Henry, NAACP organizer in Mississippi, and works by Ben Green and Merline Pitre, on Florida and Texas, provided equally valuable insights into the activities of the Association in the South.[21]

Pitre's study, centered on the life and career of the Lone Star activist Lulu B. White, together with Barbara Ransby's 2003 biography of Ella Baker and Caroyln Wedin's earlier biography of Mary White Ovington, provided much-needed accounts on the contribution of women organizers in the Association.[22] This important development in correcting the gender imbalance in many existing studies of the NAACP was continued in coeditor Lee Sartain's work on the NAACP in Louisiana. Sartain's prize-winning monograph argued that in the Pelican State women were "invisible activists," quietly taking on much of the crucial day-to-day work of the Association while their male counterparts in more high-profile, but less-active, positions within local branches received much of the credit for their achievements.[23]

Despite the growing number of scholarly publications on the NAACP there were still many aspects of its history that required further exploration as the Association approached its 2008–2009 centenary. Notwithstanding the 2005 publication, *Freedom's Sword,* by the journalist and NAACP insider Gilbert Jonas, there continued to be no authoritative scholarly history of the NAACP from its formation in 1909 to the end of the twentieth century.[24] This doubtless reflects the fact, as has been indicated earlier, that it is a near impossible task to provide a detailed history of the NAACP within the confines of just one volume.

Similarly, despite the work of Pitre, Ransby, Sartain, Wedin, and others there was, as August Meier and John H. Bracey pointed out, still a need for more work on women activists in the Association.[25] In particular there was as yet no full-length biography of the legendary national field secretary of the 1930s and 1940s, Daisy Lampkin. Indeed, she received not even so much as a solitary mention in the index of Jonas's history of the Association. Equally, the achievement of Pitre and Sartain in highlighting the work of women NAACP activists in Texas and Louisiana raised the question of how many others remained still as yet unrecognized for their equally important contributions in other states.

In a different vein, the Second World War may no longer have been what historian Richard Dalfiume once called the "forgotten years of the Negro Revolution," but they arguably continued to be the forgotten years of the NAACP.[26] The war years saw a ten fold rise in NAACP membership, from 50,000 in 1940 to some 500,000 by the end of 1945.[27] Moreover, the conflict prompted a radical shift in the thinking of the Association secretary Walter White, who came to view civil rights as less a domestic American issue than part of a wider global struggle against racial injustice and colonialism.[28] Paradoxically, there was no detailed monograph on the national organization and policy of the NAACP during the war and even in terms of journal articles and essays the number of publications on the work of the Association in this period remained limited.

The essays in part 1 of this volume shed new light on a variety of underexplored topics in the historiography of the NAACP. Simon Topping assesses the contribution of Walter White as a race leader in the light of Kenneth Janken's recent groundbreaking biography of the NAACP leader. Yvonne Ryan continues this theme, analyzing the quiet, but often effective, diplomacy of White's underrated successor, Roy Wilkins. In a similar vein Simon Hall reexamines the policies of the NAACP in the late 1960s. Questioning the image of the Association in these years as a conservative organization in an era of political radicalization, he argues that the NAACP's national leadership did not just persist with traditional strategies because they were unable to adopt a new mindset. A no less important consideration was that such tried and tested initiatives had proven to be effective over many years. Given this there was a justifiable reluctance on the part of Wilkins and other leading NAACP figures to abandon them in favor of other less-proven methods.

Jenny Woodley and George Lewis consider aspects of NAACP policy that have been largely ignored by scholars, the Association's cultural campaigns, 1910–1950, and the propaganda war of the late 1950s as the NAACP vied with southern segregationists to win over the hearts and minds of the American people in the aftermath of the 1954 *Brown* decision. Focusing on the late 1950s and the 1960s Peter Ling examines the complex and often-strained relationship between Martin Luther King and the NAACP national leadership as well as the links between NAACP and SCLC activists at the local level.

Although wider civil rights scholarship since the 1980s has been rich in detailed studies of local protest movements the same is not yet true of the NAACP. There is clearly a need for more full-length monographs on the grassroots organization of the Association. Moreover, much of the best work on the NAACP at the local level remains scattered in diverse journals and essay collections, or is embedded in wider state studies on civil rights. Valuable as such individual accounts are they provide little in the way of comparative analysis on the differences and similarities between the way branches of the Association developed in diverse geographical settings. Indeed, there is not even so much as a single volume of writings that brings together studies on the NAACP in different regional locations.

The essays in part 2 of this volume begin the process of remedying this omission, seeking, as Beth Tomkins Bates has advised, to connect the national agenda of the NAACP with local protest networks.[29] Beverly Bunch-Lyons and Nakeina Douglas highlight the development of one of the first rural southern branches of the Association, in Tinner Hill, Virginia. Kevern Verney and Lee Sartain examine the difficulties in establishing effective NAACP branches in the Deep South, in Alabama and Louisiana, respectively.

Focusing on the struggle against the all-white primary in Texas, Charles Zelden demonstrates the tensions that often resulted between the Association's national office and its grassroots leaders in the Lone

Star State. Pursuing a similar theme, but in a different geographical setting, Patrick Flack and Andrew Fearnley consider national-local tensions in two northern branches of the Association, Detroit and Cleveland. Examining another northern city, Chicago, Christopher Robert Reed highlights the ideological and class divisions that hampered the development of the NAACP in the "Black Metropolis."

In another change of location Jonathan Watson provides a welcome contribution on the NAACP in California, 1914–1950, a region in which, as he points out, the work and organization of the Association has all but been ignored by historians. Returning to the South John Kirk analyses the fluctuating fortunes of the NAACP in Arkansas from its early organization in the state to the dramatic confrontations of the 1950s and 1960s.

Although, as Andrew Fearnley prudently observes, there is no such thing as a typical NAACP branch, a number of common themes emerge in the essays in part 2. In addition to the recurring issue of national-local tensions in the Association that has already been highlighted Verney, Sartain, and Reed demonstrate the significance of class divisions as a barrier to developing an effective grassroots organization of the Association in the interwar years. A key factor in overcoming this obstacle was the efforts by local leaders to develop an economic-orientated agenda in response to the challenges of the Great Depression and the Second World War.

In recent years the issue of class divisions within the civil rights movement has been of increasing interest to historians, as reflected in groundbreaking studies by scholars such as Andrew Manis and Robin D. G. Kelley.[30] Generally perceived by both contemporaries and later academic researchers as overly conservative and middle class, the historical reputation of the NAACP has suffered as a result. The role and significance of class is, however, a complex one. It is easy to argue that leaders in the NAACP's national office, like former diplomat and novelist James Weldon Johnson and the cerebral W. E. B. Du Bois, enjoyed a privileged status within African American society. Charges of elitism against NAACP activists at grassroots level are more open to debate. Local Association officials may have often worked in a job—such as a mail carrier or a railroad porter—that commanded status and respect within African American communities. At the same time these occupations were hardly elitist in the way the term would be understood in wider U.S. society. At the very least the lifestyle of such activists was very different to that enjoyed by the likes of Johnson and Du Bois, yet they continue to be categorized by scholars with the common label of "middle class."

On other occasions, as Jenny Woodley and Simon Hall observe, the conservative image of NAACP spokespersons is, on closer examination, more a reflection of cultural outlook or generational differences than social status. The concept of class, both in studies on the NAACP and the wider civil rights struggle, continues to be loosely defined by scholars. Further research in this area, and a clearer understanding of exactly what is meant by the term class, would be welcome.

Adopting a different perspective, Reed and Fearnley point out the importance of the Great Migration of 1915–1925 as another formative experience in the lives of African Americans that had a profound impact on the development of early NAACP branches. African American migrants who joined the NAACP in the north often retained strong links with family and friends in the south. They also maintained a keen interest in NAACP initiatives and developments in race relations in the region, raising the intriguing question as to the exact meaning of the term "local" in respect to grassroots NAACP organization in the interwar years.

PART ONE

The NAACP
at the National Level

CHAPTER ONE

"All Shadows Are Dark"

Walter White, Racial Identity, and National Politics

SIMON TOPPING

WHEN WALTER WHITE died in 1955 after twenty-five years as executive secretary of the NAACP, commentators both within and outside the African American community reflected upon his career and speculated about his legacy. The *Chicago Defender* went so far as to say, "Fifty years from today . . . men the world over will still be acknowledging Walter White as a poet of freedom, an author of justice."[1] Yet within a few years he would be a largely forgotten figure even among African Americans, and while the legacies and influence of his predecessors as the community's ostensive leaders, Frederick Douglass, Booker T. Washington, Marcus Garvey, and W. E. B. Du Bois, were acknowledged, revised, cited, and re-revised, White was very much overlooked. Even the NAACP, the organization he molded, quickly forgot the architect of its campaigns for antilynching legislation, school equality, fair employment, and military desegregation. It quickly forgot the man who had held the Association together during the grimmest days of the Depression and made the NAACP a force on the national political stage. The activists of the 1960s seemed only dimly aware, if they were aware at all, of the man whose battles they were continuing and even concluding. Yet such was White's contemporary fame, within days of his death the Association was contacted by Oxford University Press about publishing his biography, while Universal Studios quickly sounded out his widow regarding a film of his life.[2]

Until relatively recently, the historiography of the civil rights movement had been no kinder to White; historians of civil rights in the New Deal era all recognize his role in establishing the NAACP as part of the "Roosevelt Coalition," even if none dwells particularly on his importance to the nascent civil rights movement.[3] More generally, he has been overlooked in studies of African American leadership and even failed to make a list of the top one hundred African American figures of the twentieth century.[4] This neglect has been comprehensively redressed by Kenneth Janken, but it is still worth asking why the pivotal figure in African American political life, "the president of the Negroes," for a quarter of a century was so routinely bypassed.[5] The obvious answer is that White was simply a product of his time and his death coincided with a sea change in American race relations and black activism. The NAACP's last major victory in White's lifetime was, of course, the *Brown* decision of 1954, and this fatally undermined the Jim Crow system he had spent his life fighting. As a result of *Brown*, the civil rights struggle moved both southward and onto the streets, away from White's natural environment, lobbying in the corridors of power. White's approach may seem hopelessly old-fashioned in retrospect, but he employed the tactics he regarded as the most effective at a time when Jim Crow remained deeply entrenched. During White's reign the black community, particularly in the South, was simply not strong enough to take its grievances onto the streets or to engage in the mass, grassroots action that would characterize the later struggle. In White's era lynch mobs often awaited those who dared defy segregation, the courts were largely unsympathetic to African Americans, and the federal government was seemingly permanently in thrall to southern reactionaries.

There is also an underlying sense that White does not belong in the pantheon of great African American leaders because he was a "voluntary Negro." White had blond hair and blue eyes and was perhaps only ½₂ black; he could have easily "passed" as white, and did so on occasions when investigating lynchings.[6] Yet White chose to live his life as an African American and suffer the indignities that this entailed, but this commitment was called into question and there was a perception among some African Americans that he was merely playing at being black and happily moved between the two worlds. W. E. B. Du

Bois, his greatest rival and critic in the NAACP, viewed White with barely restrained contempt.[7] In 1934, at the height of one of their many feuds, Du Bois told the readers of the *Crisis,* the Association's own journal, that "Walter White is white. He has more white companions and friends than colored. He goes where he will in New York City and naturally meets no Color Line, for the simple and sufficient reason that he isn't 'colored.'"[8] While traveling in England during the Second World War to analyze racial tensions in the U.S. military, White met the white Virginia-born Lady Astor, who exclaimed: "You are an idiot, calling yourself a Negro when you're whiter than I am, with blue eyes and blond hair."[9] Upon his death, NAACP colleague and Eleanor Roosevelt confidante Mary McLeod Bethune remarked that he "chose to be the champion of minority rights by identifying himself with the Negro, insisting that he had Negro blood."[10]

There is no doubt that White often reveled in his liminal status, using it to disarm both domestic white bigotry and foreign assumptions about race relations in America.[11] He, nevertheless, bristled when his race was questioned: "I am a Negro. My skin is white, my eyes are blue, my hair is blond. The traits of my race are nowhere visible upon me . . . [but] I am not white."[12] He did, however, recognize his dual heritage: "I am white and I am black and know that there is no difference. Each casts a shadow, and all shadows are dark."[13] White knew the precariousness of African American life as well as anyone and his light skin did not necessarily provide protection from the threat of racist violence. Indeed, he traced his personal radicalization to the riot that engulfed his hometown of Atlanta in 1906, when he, aged only thirteen, and his father armed themselves to protect their home from a white mob. He recalled that "in that instant there opened up in me a great awareness; I knew who I was. I was a Negro, a human being with an invisible pigmentation which marked me as a person to be hunted, hanged, abused."[14]

White seemed to be courting controversy when he divorced Gladys, his African American wife, to marry the white divorcée, Poppy Cannon, in 1949. Although he postponed this action for many years to protect the NAACP from the inevitable fallout, to his African American critics his remarriage seemed to validate their accusations that he aspired to whiteness.[15] The final collapse of White's marriage coincided with his failed attempt to resign from the Association due to his heart condition. The board of directors, with no inkling of White's plans, refused to accept his resignation and offered him a year's leave of absence instead, and they were taken aback when he duly married Cannon. The newly-weds quickly left the country, ostensibly so that White could participate in an international version of the popular radio show *Town Hall of the Air*, but the anticipated furor surrounding their marriage was also clearly a factor.[16]

White's marriage to Cannon was extraordinarily controversial. His sister Helen, for example, told him that it would ruin his legacy, warning: "your name will be mud."[17] Many in the NAACP wanted him sacked, notably board member Carl Murphy, the managing editor of the *Afro-American* newspaper, who confided that despite White's many achievements, his actions had "so weakened his usefulness that the Association will assume a grave risk in attempting to keep him in office." Indeed, the *Afro-American*'s reporters had polled the black community and most people, particularly women, were against the marriage.[18] In the *Afro-American* Murphy had already declared that White had "tossed away" his thirty-five-year career, harshly asserting that "the race itself is to blame for permitting a man who wanted to be white so bad to be their spokesman for so long. This error should not be repeated."[19]

The *Chicago Defender*, which published a weekly column by White, opposed the marriage, claiming that his actions reinforced the white perception that African American men wanted to marry outside their race.[20] The *Charlotte Post* added that it would "give added ammunition to the southern whites who long have asserted the NAACP . . . merely seek[s] social equality of colored Americans."[21] J. Robert Smith in the *Los Angeles Sentinel* had reached a devastating conclusion: "talking of race pride, Walt has shown that he has none. He merely used the race to get where he wanted."[22] The implication that White had used "the race" rather than his *own* race reinforced the underlying sense that he was not truly an African American.

The controversy surrounding White's marriage was compounded by an article he wrote for *Look* magazine about a chemical that could change skin color from black to white. This, to Janken, was an endorsement of passing, a view many of White's contemporaries and even close allies shared, being insulted by the implication that they should change their skin color to appease white racists.[23] The *Afro-American* was again the most caustic voice in the African American press.[24] White professed himself surprised by the fuss. He vigorously and unconvincingly tried to defend himself, claiming that it was satire, something neither he nor *Look* employed; once again White's racial commitment and blackness had been called into question.[25] White and Cannon faced a maelstrom on returning from their international trip in September 1949. Association publicity director Henry Lee Moon counseled White on dealing with "unfriendly" journalists, arguing that he should plead that his marriage was a "personal matter," defense of which "will inevitably be interpreted as [an] apology." Regarding the *Look* fiasco, Moon suggested that White stress he was in no way recommending the bleaching agent and his comments should be viewed in the same context as George Schuyler's novel *Black No More*.[26]

Cannon claimed that the original draft of the *Look* article was supposed to include a picture of a Harlem drugstore where various hair straightening and skin lightening products were on sale, juxtaposed with a picture of a tanning store with its sun lamps and skin lotions. She said that White was making an ironic comment on those people of both races who wanted to change the hue of their complexion, but the pictures that would have illustrated White's key point were omitted from the final piece. As a result, "editorial writers shrieked that Walter White advocated the bleaching of the whole colored race" and "was anti-Negro."[27] White's reaction in his *Chicago Defender* column was, according to Cannon, "partly in fun, but mostly out of exasperation," as apparently many of those African Americans who had written to him were actually inquiring where they could buy the chemical.[28] White clearly did not deserve the opprobrium heaped upon him, but his reputation barely survived the *Look* episode and he was only offered his old job back, with reduced responsibility, in May 1950 after a prolonged and stormy meeting of the board of directors.[29]

Despite this mauling, White had always been hugely popular among African Americans. For example, his sister Madeline told him how poor southern African Americans often had his picture on display in their homes: "for many of them you are all that they have. You and the NAACP . . . [and] so often to them you are the NAACP."[30]

While this was not veneration on the scale enjoyed by Franklin Roosevelt or later by Martin Luther King Jr., it does give a sense of White's contemporary fame and the high esteem in which he was held by many ordinary African Americans. This was especially true of African Americans in the military.[31] At the outbreak of the Second World War, White pointed out the discrepancy between the rhetorical purposes of the conflict and the reality of American segregation, especially in the military. White fought tirelessly for African Americans in uniform, visiting Britain, North Africa, and the Pacific to hear their grievances and even acted as defense counsel in Guam in the court-martial of African Americans troops.[32] An African American officer recalled a surprise visit from White in the Philippines: "the crowd went wild, they stomped the earth, they whistled, they threw their hats into the air; . . . [when] Walter White, the War correspondent, . . . the voice of thirteen million, stepped upon the stage."[33]

White is probably most famous for his investigations of lynchings in the South in the 1920s, culminating in his book *Rope and Faggot* published in 1929, and his leadership of the NAACP's campaign for a federal antilynching law in the 1930s, the former securing his reputation as an energetic campaigner and the latter leadership of the Association.[34] He investigated as many as forty-one lynchings and eight race riots between 1918 and 1930 and was able to use his fair complexion to visit and interview members of mobs.[35] Tales of his brushes with death became legend and he regaled his audiences and readers with stories of leaving the town of Elaine, Arkansas, one step ahead of the mob.[36]

There was more to White's investigations than mere derring-do and publicity; White offered sophisticated analysis of the reasons behind lynching and of mob behavior. What White discovered was that the traditional justification of lynching, the defense of white womanhood against sexual violence by African American men, was a myth. In fewer than one in six cases was rape given as the pretext for lynching.[37] White noted ruefully that as the price of cotton fell the number of lynchings rose and that lynching was a result of the vicissitudes of the rural economy.[38] He concluded that lynching was rooted in a combination of white supremacy and economic jealousy, noting: "it is not difficult to imagine the inner thoughts of the poor white as he sees members of a race he has been taught by tradition . . . to believe inferior making greater progress than his own."[39] When he died many of the tributes paid to White credited him with the virtual elimination of lynching in the United States. *Time*, for example, declared: "if there's any single monument to Walter White it's the record wiped clean of lynchings."[40] While this is certainly an overstatement, White nevertheless played a key role. He kept the issue in the public spotlight, and he noted that the number of lynchings always fell when bills to tackle the crime were inching through Congress.[41] Moreover, the antilynching campaigns also raised the public profile of the NAACP and enabled it to raise desperately needed funds during the lean years of the Great Depression.

The antilynching campaign also helped White to assume greater and greater control of the NAACP. The Great Depression made the Association's militant elements more assertive, making calls for economic reform as an agency of racial uplift, demands culminating in the report of the Committee on Future Program in 1934. This advocated the most fundamental overhaul of NAACP policy since its foundation in 1909, including a radical economic program, strengthening links with labor and turning the Association into a mass movement.[42] White paid tribute to the work of the committee but, predictably, objected to the plan and ensured that it was not implemented.[43] Indeed, in thwarting the plan White, in effect, removed all his critics and rivals from the upper echelons of the Association. Wolters comments that White "was dominant and virtually unchallenged. The militants were convinced that their demise was largely the result of White's devious and unscrupulous tactics."[44]

As White tightened his grip on the NAACP during the 1930s, its policies increasingly began to reflect his personal politics. White was unusual for an African American in the 1920s as he saw beyond the bigotry of the Democratic Party's southern powerbase to its growing northern liberal wing; moreover, he wanted to cure African Americans of what he saw as their "chronic Republicanism," instinctive, ineffectual support for the party of Lincoln, despite its extraordinarily poor record since the Civil War.[45] White, therefore, was a Democrat at the head of an officially nonpartisan organization.[46] In 1928 he seriously toyed with joining Al Smith's campaign for the presidency and consistently and bitterly opposed Herbert Hoover whom he disdainfully dubbed "the man in the Lily-White House."[47]

Franklin Roosevelt's New Deal made African Americans, especially in the North, the unintended beneficiaries of federal munificence and persuaded White to re-launch the decade-dormant antilynching drive. Moreover, key New Dealers such as Harold Ickes, Robert Wagner, and Eleanor Roosevelt, in particular, were sympathetic to African American needs. This gave White an unprecedented level of access to the corridors of power, as Bates notes: "White became a major resource within the Roosevelt administration for advice on the welfare of black Americans."[48] Yet White's influence was essentially superficial, and he would find himself constantly frustrated by the recalcitrance of Franklin Roosevelt together with professional southerners' domination of American political life. Dray believes that he may have been "black America's representative to the White House during the 1930s" but "he and many of his demands were kept at arms' length."[49] Janken makes the noteworthy observation that "White confused his influence and access to power, which was considerable and important, with power itself."[50] White, Kirby agrees, "did not represent a serious political threat to the administration."[51] Moreover, "because he had a voice within the Roosevelt administration did not mean that most black Americans did."[52]

Although painfully frustrated by his lack of progress, White was pragmatic enough to recognize that whatever the very serious limitations of Roosevelt and his party, they still offered the best opportunity of advancement, and he would consistently align himself and by definition the (nonpartisan) Association with the emerging New Deal coalition.[53] White's influence was limited, but not entirely negligible. A good example of this came when Roosevelt was coerced by White, the trade unionist A. Philip Randolph, and the latter's March on Washington Movement (MOWM) into creating a Fair Employment Practices Commission (FEPC) in 1941. White lent his support to Randolph despite being distrustful of mass action, but the MOWM was, in effect, a monumental bluff that dragged only partial concessions from a reluctant president (desegregation of the military had also been demanded). White knew that his claim that 100,000 African Americans would take to the streets of Washington, D.C., unless their demands were met was, to put it mildly, exaggerated, but the threat had the desired effect on Roosevelt. It was White who then wrote

Executive Order 8802 creating the agency. Similarly, in 1946 White led the Emergency Committee on Mob Violence which met President Truman in the wake of an upsurge in racist violence and although he declined the chairmanship of the soon to be created President's Commission on Civil Rights (PCCR), he was able to virtually pick and choose the members who would publish their groundbreaking report *To Secure These Rights* a year later.[54]

Another key characteristic of White's reign was the NAACP's involvement in political campaigns. White's strategy was based on "supporting our friends and defeating our enemies,"[55] supposedly regardless of political allegiance, using the real or potential threat of the black vote as leverage against politicians, invariably northern and usually Republican, who acted against the interests of the black community. Unsubtle, the policy often alienated the politicians whose goodwill he most needed. His mentor and predecessor as executive secretary James Weldon Johnson warned him during efforts to pass the Dyer antilynching bill in the early 1920s that simply threatening politicians with the loss of the African American vote was potentially counterproductive.[56]

What White's tactics lacked in diplomacy, they often made up for in their publicity value. Like the antilynching campaign, they generated considerable exposure for the Association and it could take partial credit for some high-profile victories. The apex of this occurred in 1930 when, under White's dynamic leadership, the NAACP helped to prevent the nomination of Republican John J. Parker to the Supreme Court. Parker had run for the governorship of North Carolina in the early 1920s and repeatedly made racist remarks about African Americans and their fitness to vote.[57] White's intensive lobbying and a barrage of telegrams from Association members in marginal states convinced enough senators to vote against President Hoover's nominee, leaving his "Southern Strategy" in tatters in the process, and this approach of selective targeting of elected officials would become a template for future campaigns.[58]

No other campaign achieved the coverage or success of the Parker fight, but in its immediate aftermath the NAACP claimed credit for the defeats of Senators Roscoe McCullough in Ohio and Henry Allen in Kansas, while Du Bois claimed in 1934 that "all the Senators who voted for Parker who could be reached by the colored voter have been defeated."[59] Du Bois was, of course, exaggerating, but this bold claim served the broader purpose of letting politicians know that African Americans were no longer prepared to be taken for granted. A situation analogous to the Parker case arose in 1937 when Roosevelt nominated Alabama senator Hugo Black to the Supreme Court, but the response of White and, by definition, the Association was very different. Black, like Parker, had made racist statements earlier in his career and had even been a member of the Ku Klux Klan.[60] White took the matter to the White House, noting the Klan allegations, the ignoring of the NAACP's inquiries about the senator, and the lack of open hearings on, and speed of, the appointment. White certainly had a point about the haste in which the hearings and confirmation were concluded, but there is a real sense, compared to the energetic campaign conducted against Parker, of simply going through the motions regarding Black.[61] White's confession that "strictly as a matter of principle, this Association could not afford not to express itself" indicates a lack of real enthusiasm for the fight.[62]

This lack of enthusiasm was because White correctly saw in Black a potential ally on the Supreme Court who, although he had played to the southern galleries to secure his political career, rose above the professional bigots of the South.[63] White also recognized that a vigorous campaign against Black could harm hard-earned links to the White House and the New Deal, in contrast with the Parker case where relations between the African American community and the president had long since broken down and the nomination was part of a wider, lily-white political strategy. White's response to the Black nomination demonstrates, therefore, that he was nothing if not pragmatic, adopting the expedient, practical course, rather than the consistent, principled option, putting up token resistance in the hope that Black would prove a sympathetic appointee, while also maintaining that he and the Association had been blindsided by the speed of the nomination and confirmation process.[64]

There is no doubt that White saw himself as the focal point of the Association. Du Bois declared: "He seemed really to believe that his personal interests and the interests of his race and organization were identical."[65] White privately conceded as much to Poppy Cannon: "They are right in charging that I dominate the Association. But if I hadn't done so there would be no NAACP. I kept it alive during the terrible days of the Depression when nearly everyone else was ready to surrender in despair. I have built it up (only to you would I say this) to its present power."[66] This sense that he was the heart and soul of the NAACP led him to rule the Association somewhat autocratically and to constantly seek the limelight, most embarrassingly in the aftermath of the *Brown* decision when he tried to upstage Association legal counsel Thurgood Marshall and his team. Marshall, in front of the assembled press, lost patience with White and asked him where he acquired his law degree.[67] White would doubtless have claimed that he had earned the right to be present for the Association's greatest triumph.

Nor was White afraid of attacking or offending the political establishment. He was convinced that the vote gave his people a power they had always previously lacked. This became the cornerstone of White's political philosophy, but it was a dangerous tactic. He believed that African Americans would see progress through voting, rather than mass action, because the African American vote in key northern states could decide a close presidential election. Furthermore, their political power far outweighed the lily-white southern vote in the electoral college.[68] Paradoxically, he maintained that he wanted the African American vote to be fluid and independent, while realizing that if African Americans were to have influence they had to vote as a block for the winning candidate in a close election. When this strategy paid off in 1948, White felt that Truman was less appreciative than he ought to have been.[69] The new president talked a good game on civil rights but was, ultimately, hamstrung by a slender victory margin and the need to reunite his seriously divided party. Moreover, the rebellious Dixiecrats were welcomed back to Congress by friend and foe alike; White noted ruefully, "both Democrats and Republicans were as deferential to the southerners as though the Dixiecrats had won the election."[70] The situation was worse after the election of 1952 when African Americans had again voted *en masse* for the Democrats, only for the party to end up on the wrong side of a landslide and be saddled with a disinterested president and a conservative Congress.[71]

White was both an instinctive and a pragmatic anticommunist. He had tangled with communists on numerous occasions in his career, most disastrously in the Scottsboro case of 1931 when he and the

Association had been utterly outmaneuvered.[72] As the cold war began and its attendant anticommunist hysteria gripped the nation, it was imperative for the NAACP not to be seen as a communist front, an accusation made by conservatives, and especially southern Democrats, who equated civil rights with subversion. White, along with assistant secretary Roy Wilkins, ensured that what little communist influence within the Association was rooted out and put it on record as being anticommunist, but the most important aspect of this process was that it was done, despite the hysteria of the era, without a witch-hunt against Association members.[73] Once again White had steered the NAACP successfully through potentially very tricky waters, and in doing so had kept the civil rights struggle and the Association respectable and loyal, essential on the eve of the *Brown* decision.

White's legacy must be viewed positively. To be sure his tactics, his management style and his sense of his own central importance to the NAACP can all be questioned, but even his harshest critics conceded that he turned the Association into a mass movement, raised its public profile, oversaw its switch to a largely African American senior staff, and firmly established it as the key voice of African Americans.[74] Those in the 1930s, and beyond, who viewed White's leadership as conservative and cautious when radicalism was required, failed to understand, as White did, that the precarious nature of the modest gains achieved by African Americans had to first be consolidated within the American political mainstream. It was all very well to envision a grand alliance of labor and African Americans as the Committee on Future Plan did, but it was hopelessly idealistic even within the context of the radical experimentation of the New Deal. Upon his death, White was seen as "the nearest approach to a national leader of American Negroes since Booker T. Washington," a not necessarily flattering comparison.[75] Although, arguably, a gradualist, he was clearly not an accommodationist in the public manner of the man from Tuskegee. White may have viewed the struggle for equality as an incremental process, but he retained a militant streak and a genuine outrage against racism in all its forms. Yet, throughout his career, despite innumerable hardships, frustrations, and setbacks, White never lost faith in the ideals of America or the righteousness of his cause.

CHAPTER TWO

In Harlem and Hollywood

The NAACP's Cultural
Campaigns, 1910–1950

JENNY WOODLEY

A 1925 PRESS RELEASE for the National Association for the Advancement of Colored People outlined the organization's main activities for that year. They were listed under the following headings: "Segregation, Legal Defense, Lynching, Disenfranchisement, Discrimination, and [the] Cultural and Artistic Development of the Negro."[1] This last activity—the "Cultural and Artistic Development of the Negro"—may appear out of place alongside the NAACP's better-known areas of concern such as segregation or lynching. Indeed, one of the NAACP's most-renowned members, W. E. B. Du Bois, rhetorically asked, "how is it that an organization of this kind can turn aside to talk about Art?"[2] This essay sets out to answer this question. It examines the NAACP's cultural campaigns during the Harlem Renaissance of the 1920s and in Hollywood, first in 1915 and again from the end of the 1930s. Although these were two very different sites of artistic production the NAACP applied a broad cultural policy to both. This essay considers what this policy was and what it sought to achieve. It also explores the construction of racism and how to fight it, the relationship between art and propaganda, the Association's appropriation of middle-class values and its strategy of assimilation.[3]

The cultural campaigns in Harlem and Hollywood may seem far removed from the legislative and legal battles for which the NAACP is more commonly known. However, those campaigns were grounded in the basic principles that informed all of its work. A brief examination of these principles demonstrates why the NAACP followed a cultural strategy and what it hoped to achieve. August Meier identified the original goal of the NAACP, to which it adhered from its founding until the 1960s, as "securing the basic citizenship rights guaranteed by the Fourteenth and Fifteenth Amendments of the Constitution."[4] The NAACP believed that the Constitution, if properly applied, would grant African Americans equality. It did not call for a radical overhaul of society or its institutions. This was because the NAACP believed that inequality was an anomaly and that the American system could and would correct it. Inequality was caused by racism and racism was a mental attitude. This attitude was born of ignorance and perpetuated by misunderstanding and misinformation. James Weldon Johnson summed up the NAACP's position when he wrote, "The status of the Negro in the United States is more a question of national mental attitude toward the race than of actual conditions."[5] He argued that white America's opinion about African Americans needed changing, not the system itself.

The "national mental attitude" that restricted the advancement of African Americans was formed, in large part, by the images of the race that appeared in American culture. In literature, art, music, and film African Americans were portrayed as little more than stereotypes, used to introduce sentimentality, humor, or primitiveness. The NAACP believed that one way to change racial perceptions, therefore, was to create a more accurate picture of black life. It sought to provide examples of cultural achievement and to eliminate negative stereotypes, replacing them with positive images. It hoped that in doing so it would change white attitudes toward black Americans, which would, in turn, open the door to greater racial equality.

The NAACP's involvement with the Harlem Renaissance marked its first attempt to challenge opinions about African Americans through the arts. James Weldon Johnson argued, "nothing will do more to change [the national] mental attitude and raise his status than a demonstration of intellectual parity by the Negro through the production of literature and art."[6] He believed that cultural achievement was the ultimate marker of success and that if African Americans could demonstrate their artistic abilities then the white world would no longer be able to deny them equal rights. The NAACP encouraged and promoted black authors, poets, painters, playwrights, and other creative individuals. These artists were to be shining examples of what the race could achieve. This emphasis on cultural prowess began with the organization's inception and continued through the years of the Harlem Renaissance. The NAACP followed a policy of, in David Levering Lewis's phrase, "civil rights by copyright."[7]

The two NAACP officials who probably did the most to mentor the "New Negroes" of the Renaissance were James Weldon Johnson and Walter White. As well as producing their own literary work, they encouraged and advised younger artists and established links with publishers. They formed personal relationships with key Renaissance figures such as Countee Cullen, Claude McKay, and Langston Hughes, and were often instrumental in helping to have their work published and then publicized. Johnson and White brought together the businessmen of the Renaissance and an African American book buying public. For men like Johnson and White, the Renaissance was not just about creating literature but about getting people to buy and read it. They helped create examples of black artistic achievement and made them visible to white America because they believed that art could only change attitudes if the public was exposed to it.

While the work of individual NAACP officers was significant, it was the *Crisis* magazine that was the NAACP's primary tool in facilitating the artistic outpouring of the 1920s. It was edited by W. E. B. Du Bois, the Association's director of publicity and research, and from the first issue he included discussions about and reproduction of the arts. With the assistance of his literary editor, Jessie Fauset,[8] Du Bois published work by leading black artists such as Langston Hughes, Claude McKay, Jean Toomer, Countee Cullen, Aaron Douglas, Laura Wheeler, and Addison Scurlock. According to Jean Yellin's index, almost a thousand original poems, songs, short stories, and dramas were published between 1910 and 1934 (the years of Du Bois's editorship).[9] The most notable absence from the pages of the *Crisis* was jazz. The Association was suspicious of this distinctly African American music because of its connection to working-class blacks and the scandalous excesses of Harlem nightlife. Instead, it emphasized "high" cultural forms that were associated with refinement and education.

Du Bois published much of the work in the *Crisis* with the magazine's predominantly black readership in mind.[10] He wanted African Americans to learn about the vibrancy of their culture and to develop an "intelligent appreciation" of art.[11] He knew that black artists needed financial support and so he encouraged blacks to become patrons of the arts by going to the theater or buying books. "Only in this way," he wrote, "can we give to the world a new Negro American art."[12] Du Bois believed African Americans should be the critics of black artistic endeavor, not whites. He told an audience of NAACP members in 1926, "The ultimate judge has got to be you."[13] Furthermore, the arts were given a prominent place in the *Crisis* in order to inspire racial pride. African Americans themselves needed to be aware of the accomplishments of their race.

Du Bois was also aware of the potential effect of racial representations on the white public. Indeed, he became increasingly concerned with how novels, poems, and artwork could influence white opinions. By the mid-1920s he had become disillusioned with the Harlem Renaissance. He thought white artists were exploiting their relationship with Harlem's African Americans and were distorting black life in their work. He was particularly disappointed in Carl Van Vechten's *Nigger Heaven* (1926), which he described as being like a "blow in the face."[14] Worse still was the use of these debauched images by black artists. He wrote of Claude McKay's *Home to Harlem* (1928), "for the most part [it] nauseates me, and after reading the dirtier parts of its filth I feel distinctly like taking a bath."[15] Du Bois called for a change in the way the race was represented in art. In June 1926 he gave a speech at the NAACP conference in Chicago in which he laid out his manifesto. He argued that depictions of degenerate, immoral blacks were forced upon African American culture by a racist society and that continuing to use them perpetuated white supremacy. Thus to be truly free the artist must tell his own race's truth as opposed to white American perceptions of it. The speech continued with his most decisive statement: "all Art is propaganda and ever must be, despite the wailing of the purists . . . I do not care a damn for any art that is not propaganda."[16] Du Bois advocated African American art and literature that showed the respectable, hardworking, and moral side of black life. This was the "truth" that black artists should tell. Du Bois stressed the political over the aesthetic value of the arts: he wanted work that would help the cause of racial advancement.

There were those within the Renaissance who disagreed with Du Bois's interpretation of the role of art. Many of the artists themselves rejected the notion that their art must contain only images of middle-class black life in order to advance the race. The younger generation such as Wallace Thurman, Zora Neale Hurston, and Langston Hughes incorporated folk dialect and primitivism into their art; elements at odds with Du Bois's genteel images. Furthermore, they believed that artistic standards were more important than political messages. Nevertheless, there were many intellectuals and artists who shared the NAACP's conviction that the arts could be used as a weapon in the fight for civil rights. Indeed, this belief was a key principle behind much of the work of the Renaissance.[17]

During the first half of the twentieth century a new battleground of cultural representation emerged: the American film industry. The NAACP used the same principle that guided its work during the Renaissance—the idea that racism could be affected by cultural representations—and modified it for a different context. Rather than encouraging a body of black cultural work the NAACP concentrated on challenging the racial stereotypes so prevalent in American films. In the earliest films of the twentieth century, African Americans appeared as the "Tom," the "Coon," the "Mammy," and the black rapist. In the 1920s the "Jester" was the dominant type and in the following decade it was the "Servant."[18] Such stereotypes reflected and reinforced white perceptions of African Americans as lazy and stupid, loyal and docile, or dangerous and violent. The preponderance of such demeaning portrayals of the race greatly concerned the NAACP. It feared that this new and powerful medium would have a profound impact on racial prejudices. As Walter White wrote in his autobiography, "the most widely circulated medium yet devised to reach the minds and emotions of people all over America and the world was perpetuating and spreading dangerous and harmful stereotypes of the Negro."[19] Film was particularly powerful because, to quote White again, it appealed to "both the visual and auditory senses."[20] This gave the images a reality and vibrancy that no previous medium had been able to offer. It made the racial stereotypes more "real" than ever before.

The NAACP's solution was to try to persuade moviemakers to remove such images and replace them with more positive depictions of African Americans. It had clear ideas about what the alternative should look like. "There are Negro sharecroppers and there is no reason why . . . their existence should not be acknowledged," White argued. "But there are also Negro artists, doctors, lawyers, scientists, teachers, business men, and others who have made and are making very material contributions to their own and the country's advancement. We contend that these others should be shown in the films as well as sharecroppers, the comedians and the menials."[21] The NAACP wanted respectable, hard-working black characters in order to show white America the "material contributions" they were making to the country. Cultural representations, as during the Renaissance, would be used to demonstrate African Americans' eligibility for full citizenship.

The first example of the power of film to impact on race relations came with the release of *The Birth of a Nation* in 1915. To NAACP members, D. W. Griffith's film glorified the antebellum South and vilified Reconstruction. The Association argued the film represented the African American as an "ignorant fool, a vicious rapist, a venal and unscrupulous politician, or a faithful but doddering idiot."[22] The head office was alerted to the potential harm of the film by its Los Angeles branch and it quickly launched an unprecedented national campaign that lasted over three decades.[23] Association staff questioned *Birth of a Nation's* historical accuracy and warned that screenings would provoke racial violence. The NAACP had limited success in its campaign, with some of the most offensive scenes cut (including the most explicit images of the rape scene) and bans at state and city level. In many ways the publicity it generated about the film was counterproductive and by 1924 the national office acknowledged it had "been forced to spend far more money on this film than it could really afford."[24] Despite this admission, the film continued to overshadow all others for the Association for over a decade as it obsessed over revivals and rumors of remakes.

The NAACP learned an important lesson from its largely unsuccessful campaign against *The Birth of the Nation:* it could not just rely on publicity and protests after a film was released; it had to go to the filmmakers themselves and lobby for change at the point of production. The NAACP launched a new campaign directed at the heart of American filmmaking: Hollywood. This coincided, significantly, with the outbreak of war in Europe and America's entry into the conflict. The United States Government became increasingly concerned about the effects of low black morale on the war effort. The Office of War Information attempted to improve morale, and it put pressure on Hollywood to produce films that featured positive depictions of black participation in the war.[25] The NAACP seized the opportunity that this convergence of interests offered and Walter White headed to Hollywood.

White made a number of trips to the West Coast in the first half of the 1940s. He lobbied whomever he could reach, from the writers, actors, and directors to the powerful producers and studio heads. He had an important ally in the shape of former presidential candidate and chairman of the board at Twentieth Century Fox, Wendell Willkie. It was Willkie who became White's pass into a world usually closed to African Americans. He helped the NAACP secretary organize trips to Hollywood in February and July 1942, and he introduced him to the key men from the studios. The highpoint was a lunch on July 18 given in White's and Willkie's honor and hosted by producers Daryl Zanuck and Walter Wagner. White explained to the assembled producers and executives the effect their films were having on race relations. "Restriction of Negroes to roles with rolling eyes, chattering teeth, always scared of ghosts, or to portrayals of none-too-bright servants perpetuates a stereotype which is doing the Negro infinite harm." Moreover, "showing him always as a mentally inferior creature, lacking in ambition, is one of the reasons for the denial to the Negro of opportunities and for low morale . . . as it constantly holds the Negro up to ridicule and disparagement."[26]

White believed he was educating Hollywood's most powerful individuals and opening their eyes to the problem. He claimed Zanuck had told him, "I make one-sixth of the pictures made in Hollywood and I never thought of this until you presented the facts."[27] The NAACP hoped that if it could only highlight the problem then Hollywood would feel compelled to change. However, White was not naïve. He knew the film industry was a business and that profit would always be the motivating factor. He told the executives that "Negroes wanted no propaganda films" and that they "did not ask motion picture companies to lose money to satisfy a minority because to remain in business the companies had to make pictures that will sell."[28] White was not asking for a radical overhaul of the film industry but for a change in tone and content when it came to African American characters. With vague promises from the studios that they would "find ways and means of helping to put into effect some of the suggestions offered," White returned to the East Coast confidently declaring, "Negroes will hereafter no longer be restricted to comic or menial roles in motion pictures."[29]

However, despite the promise of films such as *Crash Dive, Bataan,* and *Sahara* (all 1943), progress was painfully slow.[30] Increasingly frustrated with the studios' reticence to make good on their promises, particularly after the death of Willkie in 1944, White formulated a new plan. He developed the idea of an "information bureau in Hollywood to which producers, directors, writers and others could turn for guidance."[31] The bureau would have been an extension of the policy of publicity and education that White had been employing for the previous five years, but he was never able to muster enough support or money for his venture.[32] He continued to monitor Hollywood's output until his death in 1955, writing letters of praise or condemnation and reminding the studios of their promises.[33] Walter White's forays into Hollywood, though frustrating, were significant. He was one of the few African Americans to lobby America's film industry on behalf of the race during this period. More important, the NAACP was one of the first civil rights organizations to make the link between motion pictures and race relations.

A study of the NAACP's cultural work is useful not only in itself but also for assessing some of the assumptions and claims that have been made about it as a civil rights organization. Megan Williams writes, "Historically, the NAACP has worked to gain civil rights and achieve integration by . . . adopting the dominant culture's values of middle-class respectability and morality."[34] The Association encouraged the depiction of decent and reputable African Americans in art and films. It realized that many whites felt the privilege of equal rights, if it were to be granted at all, should only be extended to educated and economically successful blacks. Therefore films, literature, and art should show black life at its best. In Hollywood, White lobbied for the inclusion of black doctors, lawyers, and teachers in motion pictures. During the Harlem Renaissance Du Bois called for artists to embrace representations of respectability. African Americans were to be presented as industrious, hardworking, pious, and educated. The black sociologist E. Franklin Frazier in his scathing indictment of the "Black Bourgeoisie" argued that African Americans created the illusion of a prosperous middle class in order to be accepted by the white world. He claimed that in the segregated cities after World War I, "a class structure emerged which was based upon social distinctions such as education and conventional behavior, rather than upon occupation and income."[35] Frazier suggested that African Americans could attain middle-class status by *appearing* middle class. The NAACP, which was preoccupied with the *image* of the race, wanted to show whites that African Americans could embody middle-class values and behavior. In other words, even if they were not economically middle class they should be presented as educated, professional, moral, and hardworking in order to be accepted by white America.

The NAACP's cultural campaigns could be seen as reflecting a broader policy of assimilation. Although there were some differences of opinion between individual officials, the Association rejected the separation of the races socially, economically, and politically, and it promoted an integrated society. David Levering Lewis argues that the NAACP, as "Talented Tenth" African Americans, "embraced an ideology of extreme cultural assimilationism."[36] Certainly, Walter White promoted assimilation when he was in Hollywood. He worked with the white film industry, and he wanted black characters to be incorporated into mainstream pictures. They should appear alongside white characters and thus depict the integrated American society for which the NAACP was striving. White told a friend that when he and Willkie went to Hollywood they made it clear "neither of us favored the all-Negro picture," their reasoning being that "90 percent of movie goers in the United States are white and they will just not go to see an all Negro picture unless it has some unusual merit."[37] This reflected White's pragmatism—he knew that Hollywood was unlikely to make such pictures—but his stance also reflected a desire for racial assimilation both on and off the screen.

This desire could explain the NAACP's decision to ignore black

Hollywood. Walter White was critical of black actors who took what he considered to be demeaning roles, and he was willing to sacrifice their careers in order to achieve the NAACP's goals. He wrote, "What is more important—jobs for a handful of Negroes playing so called 'Uncle Tom' roles or the welfare of Negroes as a whole? If a choice has to be made, the NAACP will fight for the welfare of all Negroes instead of a few."[38] This stance inevitably led to tension with a number of Hollywood's black stars. They resented White's interference, were angered that he had bypassed them and gone straight to the white producers, and feared for their livelihoods if he got his way. Hattie McDaniel, in particular, saw White's campaign as a personal attack.[39] The NAACP also ignored the work of black filmmakers such as Oscar Micheaux. It could have collaborated with them and helped develop race films with strong political messages. But, at a time when the concept itself was disgraced, White was not interested in "propaganda" films. The NAACP believed a more subtle approach would have a great effect on people's attitudes. According to a report in *Variety*, "Just as Hollywood now puts one out of each fifteen persons in a crowd scene in uniform . . . so White desires that one out of ten persons be a Negro in normal pursuits."[40] White hoped such small adjustments would have a cumulative effect on white attitudes. He wanted black inclusion to become the norm in cultural representations in order to facilitate actual integration in everyday life.

If there was a strong link between the NAACP's aims in Hollywood and its integrationist agenda then the issue became more complicated when it was applied to the Harlem Renaissance. There were those in the Association who celebrated the uniqueness of black talent. Indeed, they recognized that "without distinct Negro character, there could be no Negro genius."[41] James Weldon Johnson argued that what was distinctive in American culture was African American in origin: "[The Negro is] the creator of the only things artistic that have yet sprung from American soil and been universally acknowledged as distinctive American products."[42] He edited an anthology of "American Negro Poetry" and with his brother published a collection of Negro spirituals.[43] The spiritual had its roots in Africa and slavery and therefore could be celebrated as a black creation. The *Crisis* frequently featured work by Aaron Douglas, who was an "artist concerned with black life" and whose work incorporated elements of the "folk" and images from Africa.[44] It was the "folk" which was most commonly identified as being the truest source of black expression. On these occasions the NAACP actively encouraged the creation of a distinct black culture.

This policy, however, was only taken so far. According to some scholars, while the Renaissance may have reflected what was distinctively black, it was refracted through the prism of white cultural values. Harold Cruse argues the Renaissance failed largely because of its attempts to integrate and appropriate middle-class values. This led to the dominance of white middle-class standards and a "cultural paternalism" that created a barrier to true black artistic expression.[45] Henry Louis Gates Jr. is similarly critical of the "New Negroes" for trying to become "'just like' every other American [by] imitating those they least resembled." They used Western (white) forms of "high" culture at the expense of the "folk." Indeed, Gates argues it was jazz, not literature, which was black America's most profound contribution to art in this era.[46] This interpretation suggests the NAACP followed a policy of cultural assimilation and that this had a detrimental effect on the work created during the Renaissance. George Hutchinson offers a different interpretation. He argues the Harlem Renaissance was a "striking experiment in cultural pluralism." In other words, its participants attempted to incorporate their work into a wider culture but without losing its distinctive racial character. Hutchinson sees the NAACP as part of this process. Its "idea of assimilation entailed the 'blackening' of the national culture."[47] The Association accepted those dominant, white artistic values and aesthetics but it wanted black artists and their work to be accepted within these criteria.

The NAACP aimed for something more significant than simply influencing the representation of African Americans; it hoped that cultural changes would precipitate greater racial equality. In this way the NAACP could be guilty of overvaluing cultural attainment. It put too much emphasis on the arts as the marker of civilization and too much hope in the idea that racist whites would be dragged out of their ignorance by artistic talent. There is no evidence from the NAACP records to suggest that its cultural campaigns directly improved the status of African Americans. Furthermore, its emphasis on promoting middle-class values and its policy of cultural assimilation meant the NAACP neglected some forms of black culture. It did not engage with jazz nor with some of the younger artists of the Renaissance. Its refusal or inability to cooperate with black filmmakers and actors meant it had to rely on white benevolence and left it unable to challenge Hollywood on its own terms. While many individual members had flexible attitudes toward cultural forms, as an institution the NAACP approached culture in a narrow and potentially limiting way.

The greatest flaw in the NAACP's cultural policy was the way in which it conceived of racism. It believed racism was an anomaly that existed principally in people's minds. In fact, racism is also structural and it exists in the institutions of society. This is what African Americans came to realize during the civil rights movement and why they struck at these institutions to bring about racial equality. Nevertheless, the continued use of a cultural approach during this period suggests that it had some merits. As Joe Street's study has shown, civil rights activists during the sixties used black cultural forms as part of the political struggle. They used different forms and in different ways—for example, there was more emphasis on black empowerment through culture and little interest in using the arts to affect white opinion—but they continued a tradition that saw the political in the cultural.[48]

It is important to recognize that the cultural campaigns were not the only, or even the principal, focus of the NAACP's attention and efforts during its first forty years. The fight for an antilynching law, numerous court cases, the campaign for voting rights and the battle for equal education took up more of its time and money. Indeed, members of the NAACP recognized there were dangers if cultural attainment was given too much prominence. Du Bois was concerned that acknowledging black artistic talent could be used to pacify racial agitation: "there are today a surprising number of people who are getting great satisfaction out of these younger Negro writers because they think it is going to stop agitation of the Negro question." He warned that African Americans could not rest on their artistic laurels, they had to keep fighting for equality.[49] The cultural campaigns were thus part of a larger strategy that confronted racial inequality on a number of fronts.

The continued agitation in the twenty-first century by the NAACP and other African Americans for greater access to and inclusion in popular culture suggests the cultural battle is one that still needs fighting.

There has been a slight shift in emphasis, with greater focus on encouraging diversity within the entertainment industry. The NAACP realized the most effective way of changing racial representation was for African Americans to participate at all stages of production. Nevertheless, the basic principles which guided the NAACP's work in 1910 remain largely the same today. In April 2007 it launched the STOP campaign to end demeaning images of African Americans in the media, particularly those of women. According to a press release, the NAACP believes "racism is taught" and that "when it comes to forming ideas and establishing norms, nothing is more influential than the images and concepts delivered into our lives on a daily basis by radio, television, film and the Internet."[50] A century after it first published the work of black poets, picketed cinemas, and educated movie moguls, the NAACP continues to fight racism with culture.

CHAPTER THREE

"A Gigantic Battle to Win Men's Minds"

The NAACP's Public Relations Department and Post-*Brown* Propaganda

GEORGE LEWIS

O N FEBRUARY 1, 1959, NBC-TV anchorman Chester "Chet" Huntley went on air to make a series of startling comments on the state of southern race relations. "The NAACP may have outlived itself," he pronounced. Believing that "never in history has society been changed by law," Huntley argued that a solution to the school desegregation crisis besetting the South could only be found "by taking the issue away from the unyielding elements which have taken control on both sides." One of the United States' most popular and trusted television anchormen was suggesting live on a network broadcast that the school crisis had transformed the NAACP into one of those "unyielding elements," and that as a result the Association had become "an unacceptable symbol" for both moderate and conservative southern whites. Huntley did concede that the NAACP and its followers were likely to win the *de jure* battle over schools, but believed that it would be no more than a pyrrhic victory, for its price "will be a heritage of distrust and conflict that may last as long as the bitterness following Reconstruction."[1]

What made Huntley's remarks all the more surprising were contemporary perceptions of him as an advocate of racial equality. He had previously spoken out against both racism abroad, in South Africa, and discrimination at home, against Mexican Americans, and as one recent chronicler of NAACP activities has described him, he was one of a handful of news anchors who "generally sympathized with the civil rights struggle" and who "buttressed the public's regard for [Roy] Wilkins and therefore for the NAACP."[2] Huntley's characterization of the NAACP as in some ways "unacceptable" is also at odds with the Association's image as a mainstream organization that preferred its reform to be magisterial rather than radical. Indeed, contemporary activists were fond of characterizing the NAACP as a slow-paced administrative behemoth, and historians have often portrayed it as a blinkered organization that adhered to a rigidly legalistic approach to enduring problems of racial inequality in an era in which other organizations, notably the Fellowship of Reconciliation and the Congress of Racial Equality in the 1940s, and the Montgomery Improvement Association in 1955–1956, were experimenting with direct-action protest techniques.[3]

In stark contrast to its established reputation, the collective response of the NAACP's executive officers to the Huntley affair was immediate, quick-witted, and forceful. It was orchestrated by the NAACP's Department of Public Relations, which was based in New York City and operated under the close oversight of the Cleveland-born journalist Henry Lee Moon. Within twenty minutes of Huntley's program going on air, the PR department notified the press that 250 telephone calls had been made to NBC, 225 of which had protested Huntley's views. Working with only one full-time assistant, Moon concentrated the department's energies on the Huntley affair for a week after the broadcast, drawing upon the Federal Communication Commission's "Fairness Doctrine" to negotiate equal broadcast time for the NAACP to answer Huntley's assertions. A series of meetings with NBC officials led to the scheduling of a second program, on February 8, in which Huntley was given exactly ten minutes to reiterate his point of view, Roy Wilkins was given the same amount of time to provide the NAACP's rejoinder, and Tom Waring, a prolific disseminator of segregationist material and editor of the Charleston, South Carolina, News and Courier, was given equal time to defend southern segregationists. Wilkins, who appeared last on the program, ably knitted together a carefully prepared text with *ad hoc* rebuttals of Waring's accusations, quoting from J. Edgar Hoover's

Masters of Deceit to deflect Waring's insinuations of the NAACP's subversive background, and using Channing Tobias's policy statement that "calm reasonableness [should]prevail" after *Brown* to answer Huntley directly. The PR department's internal report on the saga suggested that Wilkins's performance "met with nationwide approval, as indicated by many communications extolling the brilliant and effective manner in which the executive secretary set forth the NAACP position."[4] Moon was not one to let the opportunity of pressing home an advantage slip by. He organized the hasty reproduction of Wilkins's words as a published pamphlet, *Roy Wilkins Answers Chet Huntley,* for which the "popular demand" was so great that the original stock of five thousand was already severely depleted by the end of March.[5]

Despite the high profile of all three protagonists on the February 8 program, and the fact that the episode stands at the confluence of a number of separate historiographical traditions, the Huntley affair remains a notable omission from the historical record.[6] That omission is symptomatic of the treatment that the work of Moon and his PR department has received more generally in what is an otherwise rich and diverse record of NAACP activity. The department's work was an integral part of the NAACP's tactical approach to overcoming racial inequality, not only while Moon was at its helm from 1948 to 1974, but from the Association's very inception.[7] Even when the Association's funding was running at a deficit after the Second World War, a premium was placed on public relations work. Walter White, for example, wrote in 1952 of the need to "constantly use the newspapers, radio, television and public platform" to remind the public of the changes that the NAACP had wrought on U.S. society. When Roy Wilkins acceded to the leadership, he was impatient to discuss improvements to the NAACP's public relations program, both internally with local branch presidents in 1956 and externally, where twice in one year he employed the high-profile firm of Elmo Roper Associates and "a dozen of the country's top public relations experts" to discuss "public relations problems confronting the Association."[8] When Gloster B. Current ran NAACP Leadership Training Workshops throughout the 1960s, he had a simple message for his assembled audiences: "Image-making is one of the most important functions in America. The Association's image is set forth by its Public Relations Department."[9]

For too long, historians have ignored the impact that the Association's myriad public relations activities have had on the success of its wider campaigns. A number of innovative recent studies have drawn attention to the NAACP's attempts to maximize the potential of radio, from Wilkins's appearance on a Washington, D.C., station just after Pearl Harbor to the groundbreaking syndication of *The Walter White Show,* but beyond that historians have failed to appreciate the extent to which the PR department's work remained central to the Association's activities.[10] Given the iconic work that the NAACP carried out in the nation's courts, as well as its broader attempts to politicize the United States' black population, it might be argued that the PR department's work was an inconsequential sideshow. Such an analysis would, however, be deeply misleading, for it misses the essence of Moon's work: this was a means to an end, not an end in itself. PR campaigns and daily press releases were primarily designed to bring attention to the work that other sections of the NAACP were already undertaking, and to highlight the continuing circumstances of inequity and oppression under which the vast majority of African Americans were forced to live.

There were three mainstays of the department's activities. On a daily basis, Moon and his team oversaw a continuous sequence of processes by which they sought to promote the Association's work, protect the NAACP's image, and control the accurate flow of relevant information to the media. That work included the design and distribution of publicity posters and pamphlets, some of which were completed in house, such as promotional materials to accompany the publication of Langston Hughes's *Fight for Freedom: The Story of the NAACP* which were developed by Moon's assistant, Jesse DeVore, in summer 1962.[11] For other more-complex and higher-profile campaigns, the department showed a keen awareness of its own professional limitations and often turned to freelance copywriters including New York–based Edwin Hanft, who designed a campaign to run in the *New York Times* to highlight the detrimental effects of continuing school segregation more than five years after *Brown.*[12] News sources were constantly trawled to monitor the Association's representation in the press, which proved to be an awesome task requiring great diligence. In one month alone, for example, NAACP employee Julia E.

Baxter confirmed to Moon that 250 newspapers had been scoured and 1,650 news clips had been processed.[13]

Controlling the information that reached the news media on issues pertinent to civil rights was more hazardous, and the extent to which the NAACP sought to do so exemplifies the swiftly changing context in which the battle for civil rights was being played out. A year after *Brown*, 70 percent of all U.S. homes boasted television sets, and segregationists quickly revealed themselves to be canny operators of this new propaganda medium, which in turn forced the NAACP to pay ever closer attention to media sources and to foster good working relationships with news networks.[14] Gaining coverage for the Association's work and promoting its views soon became such a dominant part of its activities that, in one month alone, eight officers were called upon to appear on five television programs and three radio broadcasts, in order to present facts, analysis, and argument in support of the NAACP's position.[15] Moon saw to it that each local branch was furnished with a twenty-page dossier that detailed the various ways in which press releases should be assembled and disseminated at a local level, too, including advice on adopting a writing style that would catch an editor's eye and the differences between hitting deadlines for daily and weekly newspapers.[16] When the forces of lawful desegregation collided with southern resisters intent upon preserving segregated public schools, the PR department worked hard to ensure that it was the NAACP's version of the ensuing events, rather than that of southern resisters, that was disseminated to newsrooms.

The department's bid to position itself as a fulcrum for information at times of racial crisis was eased by the careful long-term process of what it termed "the routine dispatch of press releases and other public information to the media of mass communication," which ensured that reporters looked upon the NAACP as a credible news source as a matter of habit.[17] Years of meticulous groundwork reaped handsome rewards. As the Little Rock schools situation spiraled into chaos in September 1957, for example, the PR department began to collate a printed chronology of the events that led to the standoff between Orval Faubus and federal forces in the Arkansas capital which could be easily distributed to reporters. As Moon had anticipated, members of the media came to his department rather than *vice versa,* which saved precious time and resources. They were "besieged throughout September by reporters, magazine writers, radio and television commentators and foreign correspondents seeking background information, contacts and guidance in covering the Little Rock tragedy," Moon reported. There were few spare moments, but if he did find time Moon used it to offer public relations counseling to Daisy Bates, president of the Arkansas State Conference, and Clarence Laws, the NAACP's southwest regional field secretary.[18]

The NAACP's public relations operation was most comfortable, and most effective, when it was specifically deployed to counter the claims of the South's most vocal opponents of racial change in the post-*Brown* era. The slew of published and reprinted works produced by massive resisters has long been acknowledged as a fundamental part of a southern strategy that one contemporary newspaper editor referred to as an "offensive by duplicating machines."[19] Although it has received little credit for doing so, the NAACP was at the vanguard of attempts to counter the South's post-*Brown* segregationist literature. Other organizations also contributed, notably the Southern Regional Council (SRC) through its *New South* periodical, but it was the NAACP that proved to be by far the most energetic and consistently imaginative counter-campaigner.[20] As the Association's own guidance notes made perfectly clear to each of its local branches after the *Brown* decision, "Segregation, in the main, is dead from a legal point of view. Our Association is now engaged in a gigantic battle to win men's minds."[21]

The NAACP's response to massive resistance propagandists is as important in terms of its mechanics as it is in terms of its content. On one level, for example, analysis of the techniques that Moon and his small team employed necessitates a subtle shift in the broader historical understanding of the dynamics of the post-*Brown* South. The prevailing historiographical view is one of "call and response," whereby, having successfully questioned the constitutionality of separate but equal education in the Supreme Court, the NAACP instituted local desegregation suits or petitions across the South, to which segregationists responded by ratcheting up the volume and vehemence of their actions and rhetoric. Looking in particular at the fact that segregationist Citizens' Councils were often founded as a direct riposte to local

NAACP activity, and that Councils that were already in existence increased the volume and sharpened the content of their members' activities in response to NAACP drives, historians have surmised that the Association was primarily a proactive force in the resistance years while segregationists were reactive.[22] The methods that Moon's department employed suggest a very different form of events, however, for this was very much responsive and reactive campaigning. Branch PR officers were warned specifically to maintain a state of "constant alertness" to segregationists' ploys in their local communities and to counteract them swiftly. Indeed, a fundamental part of their organizational role was explained to them as the need to "answer NAACP attackers in your community. You must do it immediately (not next week or month, for the damage will have been done by then)."[23]

In terms of content, this responsive mode offered Moon an unexpected bonus, for it allowed his office to use segregationists' own utterances as the central building blocks of NAACP campaigns. It soon became apparent, for example, that speeches which were specifically designed by segregationists to appeal to local gatherings of likeminded southerners could be reprinted in a different context and exposed to a national audience for positive effect. The technique was best exemplified by two otherwise contrasting pamphlets that formed the centerpiece of much of the NAACP's southern propaganda effort, the first of which dealt with accusations of communist infiltration that had long dogged the Association. While debate continues to rage between historians over the extent to which the pervasive domestic anticommunism of the early cold war forced the NAACP into physical purges of its own membership, the Association's literary response to accusations of communist infiltration has again commanded little attention. Red-baiting the NAACP was a staple of massive resistance rhetoric, but it was not until the accusatory remarks of a segregationist holding legal office in a southern state appeared in print that the Association's officers were spurred into producing a meaningful, published counteraction. In 1955, a number of Citizens' Council groups reprinted a speech by Georgia's attorney general, Eugene Cook, entitled *The Ugly Truth about the NAACP*, which claimed to rely upon "one hundred and twenty-one pages of single-spaced, typewritten copy" drawn up by the House un-American Activities Committee, purporting to show that the NAACP was riddled with communists and fellow travelers.[24] While the responses of Roy Wilkins, who wrote reassuringly to all branch and youth council officers to deny communist influence, and Thurgood Marshall, who contacted J. Edgar Hoover for advice in implementing plans to militate against future communist infiltration, have been well chronicled, the PR department's response has not.[25] In January 1957 the NAACP published a direct rejoinder to *The Ugly Truth about the NAACP,* unambiguously titled *The Truth Versus Ugly Lies about the NAACP,* which not only played upon Cook's words for its title but also reproduced ten "lies" from Cook's piece and answered them, one by one, in adjacent columns. "The NAACP has stood the test of time," the pamphlet concluded testily. "Despite the angry attacks of the white supremacists, the Association continues to grow stronger and stronger"; it was the Association's "enemies" who were being "exposed for their un-American acts and lies."[26]

A second campaign was far snappier and less densely worded, but nevertheless still managed to showcase the success that the NAACP gleaned from adroitly reproducing segregationists' pronouncements in different contexts, both to draw attention to their absurdity and to highlight the essentially parochial nature of much of their content and concerns. On August 12, 1955, Senator James O. Eastland, who was one of the major architects of southern white resistance, addressed an audience in Senatobia, Mississippi.[27] With the *Brown* decision at the forefront of his mind, Eastland declared that "you are not required to obey any court which passes out such a ruling. In fact, you are obliged to defy it." When the NAACP released a four-page pamphlet with Eastland's remarks on the front cover, there was a pointed reference to him as chairman of the Senate Judiciary Committee. Following a double-page spread of thirty newspaper cuttings reflecting "Violence . . . terror . . . and Death in the South," the back cover boasted a carefully selected quotation designed to isolate Eastland and his supporters: "There can be only one law," President Eisenhower had said on November 1, 1956, "or there will be no peace." The insinuation was clear. By refusing to be bound by a proclamation of the U.S. Supreme Court, Eastland was himself helping to create an un-American climate in which violence and terror could flourish. A leading figure of the segregationist cause was not simply being pitted against its great nemesis, the NAACP, but also against a U.S. president. Eisenhower might have lost all but two southern states in his successful 1952 campaign, but he pointedly never publicly voiced support for *Brown,* and counted southern states' rights stalwart James F. "Jimmy" Byrnes among his advisers and confidants.[28]

Massive resistance propaganda fell into two broad categories, that which was designed to garner national support for southern racial practices, and that which was intended to solidify the South into a dissent-free, homogeneous bloc. While resisters were trying to heal internal divisions, the NAACP was at the forefront of civil rights groups aiming to exacerbate them. The Eastland pamphlet's significant potential in that regard so excited Moon that he complicated his normal distribution procedures—which involved the simple mailing of the Association's publications to an eclectic distribution list—to maximize its impact. Each copy of the Eastland pamphlet that was sent out was accompanied by what appeared to be a hand-signed cover slip from Wilkins, noting that the executive secretary would "appreciate any comment you may wish to make." The juxtaposition of Eastland's open lawlessness with Eisenhower's careful constitutionalism skillfully exposed the variance that existed in the extent to which southerners were willing to cling to segregation. Where, for example, Florida-based attorney W. H. Adams III was moved by the Eastland pamphlet to write to Eisenhower to advise him that he was "one of the growing number of people in the southern part of the United States who feel whether or not we as individuals personally agree with the segregation decisions of the Supreme Court, they are the law and as such all of us should comply with them in good faith," an attorney from Pollocksville, North Carolina, informed his president that the pamphlet "only gives one side of the picture." Typed in a manner unlikely to gain him new clients, he went on to proclaim that it "makes no reference to the mess we have in our Capitol city brought about by intigration [*sic*] that you urges [*sic*]," which led to a situation in which "white people are leaving the city and integration has made it unfit for both white and Negros [*sic*]."[29]

From 1956 until the end of the decade, while Eisenhower continued to prevaricate over federal support for desegregation and student-centered direct action remained in its infancy, massive resistance was at its height. Moon's department faced it head on, and actively campaigned against resisters' propaganda schemes with verve, skill, and considerable tactical acumen. In autumn 1956, for example, the Mississippi State Sovereignty Commission (MSSC) a propaganda agency set up and sponsored by the Magnolia state's segregationist legislature in March 1956, began a public relations charm offensive that was specifically designed to court support for southern segregation beyond the Mason-Dixon line. The MSSC had taken the unprecedented step for a state-sponsored resistance organization of appointing its own public relations director, Hal C. DeCell, who invited the editors of twenty-one New England newspapers to Mississippi in October 1956. DeCell's plan was to allow them to see segregation at work firsthand, and was predicated on the deeply flawed and highly paternalistic assumption that north-erners opposed segregation only because their view of it was colored by misrepresentation and inaccurate reportage, and that personal experi-ence of the situation in the South would at the very least soften their opposition to the region's racial mores, and very likely overturn it altogether.

Any objective analysis of DeCell's proposal would have exposed its inherent weaknesses and limitations, but the NAACP's executive offi-cers were unwilling to risk the damage that a successful segregationist propaganda coup might inflict. In testament to the premium that both sides were now placing on winning over public opinion, the NAACP and the MSSC joined battle. On Moon's suggestion, Wilkins wrote per-sonally to each of the New England editors before their due departure dates, explaining that he was glad that each would "get a first-hand view of what goes on in Mississippi" while warning them to remember that "the sponsors of conducted tours show to the visitors only those aspects of the community which they wish tourists to see." To complete the Association's targeted intervention against the MSSC's campaign, Wilkins's letter urged the editors to find ways to "try to talk freely with some Negro citizens of Mississippi," and offered seven questions for the editors to ask their hosts that would highlight racial inequalities in Mississippi. Finally, Wilkins enclosed three NAACP pamphlets with his letters, M is for Mississippi and Murder, A Southerner Looks at Moderation, and The NAACP: An American Organization.[30]

The pamphlets were carefully selected, for each performed a differ-ent task: the first highlighted the lawless brutality that characterized black-white relations in the Delta; the second suggested that segregation was neither inevitable nor the only way in which southern society could feasibly exist, despite segregationists' dogmatic claims to the contrary; and the third was a preemptive strike aimed at disarming any claims that the MSSC might make in reference to the subversive nature of the NAACP. The first, known internally as the "three Ms" pamphlet, had already caused a stir when it was sent in January 1956 to each member of the House of Representatives and Senate, as well as the NAACP's regular mailing list. It presented a potent mixture of newspaper accounts of the racially motivated murder of African Americans in Mississippi, including Emmet Till and the Reverend George W. Lee, and further examples of re-contextualized segregationist remarks, the most notable of which were those made by the executive secretary of the Mississippi Citizens' Council to reporter Homer Bigart that "Sir, this is not the United States. This is Sunflower County, Mississippi." The pamphlet infuriated segregationists. Many conveniently turned a blind eye to the increasingly sophisticated propaganda efforts of their own side to castigate the NAACP for going beyond its legal remit to indulge in such pamphleteering. Mississippi native John Bell Williams, for example, theatrically waived aloft what he termed this "filthy little document" on the floor of the House, calling it the "latest shot to be fired in this libel campaign." A Texan attorney on the NAACP's mailing list was blunter still: "I assume from your propaganda," he wrote to Wilkins, "that you aspire to be the Dr. Goebbels of America."[31]

The majority of the New England editors responded healthily to Moon's and Wilkins's attempts to undermine the MSSC's planned junket. A number of them did indeed manage to slip away from their official hosts to talk to black Mississippians, whose version of local conditions would most certainly not have chimed with those of the MSSC's members and supporters, and many wrote in disparaging terms of both Mississippi's race relations and the MSSC's conceit. The editor of Milford, New Haven's *Cabinet Press*, for example, later told Wilkins that he and his colleagues were indeed told "that 'all' the Negroes we managed to speak to alone were 'NAACP radicals.'" Using a language and style heavily redolent of a number of the NAACP's own publications, he explained that his only reply to the MSSC's message was "a fact is a fact, whether repeated by a radical or a conservative. It doesn't seem to matter who tells us the Negroes don't vote in Hattiesburg; the important question is: Do they?"[32] To the evident joy of the NAACP's PR department, and no doubt much to the chagrin of their Mississippian hosts, many of the New Englanders published articles that pointed to the brutality of black life in the Delta, not just in terms of the region's "dramatic injustices" that grabbed headlines across the nation, but also for the "thousands of tiny indignities that add up," in one editor's view, "to something far worse."[33]

While it would be disingenuous to claim that the NAACP's propaganda campaign was the sole deciding factor in the New England editors' collective dismissal of the MSSC's abortive public relations stunt, the Association certainly contributed to the Mississippi segregationists' failure. They were greatly helped by the editors' own existing views on the situation, and the MSSC's richly paternalistic reading of southern race relations and clear misunderstanding of the national mood. The fact that the MSSC had been so thoroughly outmaneuvered did not, however, mark the end of massive resisters' attempts to court national public opinion. In fact, it signaled the start of a series of such segregationist campaigns, as resisters made increasingly desperate efforts to garner northern support, and with it a chance of long-term victory. As those campaigns became more sophisticated, so the NAACP was forced to respond with increasing vigor. In effect, massive resisters had opened up a new front in the battle to retain segregation, and it was one that stretched the resources of the NAACP considerably. By 1958, segregation's propagandists were no longer content to confine themselves to the southern states. Where previously they had lured northern newspapermen into the South as conduits for the dissemination of their ideas, they now took their arguments to the newspapers of the North directly.

The most notable of the campaigns in northern newspapers, which included the publication of the two Putnam Letters of 1959, was a full-length advertisement placed in the *New York Herald Tribune* by Louisiana's Joint Legislative Committee to Maintain Segregation (JLC). A staunchly segregationist organization dominated by state senator and Associated White Citizens' Councils of Louisiana chairman William M. "Willie" Rainach, the JLC had begun to stretch the resources of Moon's department in early February 1958. The Citizens' Council of Louisiana had broadcast a series of television programs on local station WJMR-TV extolling segregation and denouncing the work of the NAACP. Fearing the impact that those programs might have on civil rights activity in the state if left unanswered, Moon, Wilkins, and Morsell carefully prepared two scripts for the New Orleans NAACP branch to use as televised rebuttals, which were aired by WJMR-TV on February 9 and 16, respectively. All three men were clearly beginning to feel the strain. As Wilkins later candidly admitted to P. L. Prattis, editor of the *Pittsburgh Courier,* "These days, between trips and speeches, staff and outside conferences, Board committee work, telephone and correspondence, I sometimes meet myself along about midnight with last week's work still undone." It was no coincidence—and offered no respite for the PR department's workload—when the JLC's advertisement appeared in the *Herald Tribune* the day after the second program had aired. Outlining the "Position of the South on Race Relations" for the "People of New York City," it forced Moon, Wilkins, and Morsell into hasty collaboration once more, this time to draft an internal memorandum to be circulated to all NAACP officers to outline the deficiencies in the JLC's claims. The success of the PR department's deliberate attempts to position itself as a source of information for media outlets led Moon to rush out an internal memorandum advising his fellow officers on how best to respond to the anticipated flurry of press interest. The tone and content of the JLC's message, however, posed significant problems, for it not only reiterated longstanding segregationist claims—that racial segregation was a sound basis for society that led to "normally cordial relationships between Southern white and colored people," and that subversion lurked menacingly behind organized calls for civil rights reform—but also carefully omitted equally longstanding references to racial inferiority. There were soothing palliatives specifically designed to appeal to the *Herald Tribune*'s East Coast readership, most notably a reference to "the establishment of workable race relations" North and South, and further references to "recent tragic events" in desegregating cities such as New York that were carefully designed to raise that readership's fears. Moon spent considerable time formulating a response to the JLC's claims that segregation was the most salient way to deal with "more than one-half of the Negroes in this country who will live in the North by 1980," and it finally took him over 2,000 words to dismantle the advertisement—which was less than half that length—paragraph by paragraph.[34]

By the close of the decade, even that noted apologist for southern segregation, *News and Courier* editor Thomas R. Waring, had conceded in writing that he had to "yield to the NAACP" where "propagandistic argument" was concerned. That was testament not only to the considerable acumen and energy with which Moon ran the PR department, but also to his early realization that the department had to be involved in a broad panoply of activities. Responses to Eastland's remarks and the JLC's letter were necessarily high profile, yet much of the department's work was more mundane if no less important: having to write to the *New York Herald Tribune* in 1957 to point out that it was offensive to use the term "Negress" in a newspaper headline may not have been essential to the greater cause of racial equality, but altering the perception of an editor who "did not realize that it was regarded as objectionable," while simultaneously seeing fit to boast that his was "among the first papers to drop the offensive use of 'Negro' in crime stories," made more of a mark. Clearly, even in liberal East Coast communities, there was much work to be done.[35]

The specific, reactive campaigns that were designed to neuter the efficacy of massive resistance propaganda deserve more intense scrutiny. The NAACP's response to that propaganda has been as thoroughly ignored by historians as the propaganda itself, whether it appeared in print or on television. Understanding the ways in which Moon, his PR department, and very often his fellow executive officers coordinated those campaigns also adds essential depth to the collective historical understanding of the NAACP in a number of ways. In general terms, it reveals yet more of the difficulties that beset civil rights advocates throughout the 1950s, for the NAACP's executive officers endured great stresses and strains in their attempts to protect the Association's image and promote its agenda; more specifically, much of the Association's PR work highlights the increasing skill and sophistication with which certain segregationists sought to preserve their way of life in the post-*Brown* South, and also, crucially, the lengths to which the Association itself had to go in order to counter those campaigns effectively. Finally, and perhaps most important of all, the PR department's work reinforces the fact that the NAACP viewed the problems presented by southern segregation holistically, for the resources that were poured into negating segregationist propaganda serve as an acknowledgment that long-term success in the fight for racial equality required more than winning important legal battles, overturning de jure segregation, and politicizing potential African American voters.

CHAPTER FOUR

Leading from the Back

Roy Wilkins's Leadership of the NAACP

YVONNE RYAN

A NUMBER OF RECENT works have begun to reassess the contribution of the National Association for the Advancement of Colored People to the civil rights movement in a more positive light than the impression left by its critics, particularly during the late 1960s, would suggest.[1] However, the contribution of the leader who steered the organization through its most dramatic years, Roy Wilkins, has been almost ignored. Wilkins led the Association from 1955 to 1977 and his position at the head of the NAACP places him at the heart of the civil rights struggle. He appears in the index of every study of the movement published in recent years but, while most of the other civil rights leaders have been studied at length, the only record we have of Wilkins's life and work is his own autobiography, posthumously published in 1982 and which he had promised "would set the record straight." Sadly, while this book offers Wilkins's view of some key events in the struggle for civil rights, it gives little insight into the inner workings of the Association and even less about its subject, "the model bureaucrat and organization man . . . the extraordinary tactician and strategist."[2]

His conservatism, his public, although not private, reticence, and his pragmatism combine to form a less-than-compelling subject. However, by failing to examine Wilkins's position it is impossible to build a complete picture of this period and of the part played by the NAACP, the largest and arguably most important black civil rights group. His absence is particularly surprising in light of the increasing amount of attention paid to the NAACP's contribution to the movement.[3] Wilkins's advocacy of process rather than protest suggests that more charismatic or dramatic peers have overshadowed his role in the historiography of the movement. Although his position as head of the NAACP and therefore one of the most powerful African Americans in the United States was unambiguous, his contribution to the civil rights movement has been less clearly defined in scholarly examination of the period. Therefore, several questions remain to be answered: Was Wilkins simply a bureaucrat who stifled his organization, or, did his political skill help consolidate the emotional impetus provoked by events such as at Selma and Birmingham into solid legislative achievements?

While Wilkins had a finely honed ego, and made many public appearances, he was extremely reticent about his private life and beliefs, and so little personal information is available. His archival papers yield few consistent insights into his thinking. He was married to Aminda Badeau, a social worker, for over fifty years but kept his distance from other personal relationships: in one magazine interview he claimed to have not one close personal friend and had little interest in activities outside of the Association.[4] He read the occasional detective novel and was an avid collector of railway timetables, a legacy from the profession of his Uncle Sam and also from his own time spent as a railway porter. Arguably his most rebellious vice was a passion for sports cars. In the 1960s he had a black TR-3 that he polished on Saturday mornings when at home, then drove out on Saturday afternoons, occasionally in the company of his nephew Roger.[5]

Wilkins's mother died when he was five years old, and his father left Wilkins and his two younger siblings in the care of Wilkins's maternal aunt Elizabeth and her husband, Sam, in St. Paul, Minnesota. Uncle Sam worked for the president of the Northern Pacific Railroad in his private railroad car and as such was a proud member of the black middle class who owned his own home and sent all three children to college. His uncle taught Wilkins that, to be successful, "he had to be educated and neat, have learning and clean fingernails."[6] Uncle Sam's self-reliance and economic independence informed Wilkins's lifelong belief in the American way of life and forged his identification with the black middle class and the NAACP, which, despite accusations from some quarters in his later career that he and the Association were too distant from ordinary blacks, made him popular with the organization's membership to the end of his life.

The neighborhood in which he grew up had a profound influence on his views on racial integration. Wilkins's was one of only three black families in an area populated with Swedish, Norwegian, Polish, German, and Irish immigrants. He wrote of this experience, "For me integration is not an abstraction constructed on dusty eighteenth-century notions of democracy. I believe in it not only because it is right but because I have lived it all my life."[7] His first significant brush with racism came when Wilkins moved to Kansas City to edit the *Kansas City Call*, one of the country's leading black newspapers. "Kansas City ate my heart out," he later said. "It wasn't any one melodramatic thing. It was a slow accumulation of humiliations and grievances. I was constantly exposed to Jim Crow in the schools, movies, downtown hotels and restaurants."[8] However, despite this late epiphany, his childhood experiences informed Wilkins's more dispassionate approach to the fight for freedom.

Wilkins liked to claim that he and his family were "entwined" with the Association almost from its beginning. His Uncle Sam was the forty-second member of the St. Paul branch when it received its charter in 1913 and, for a short period in his early twenties, Wilkins was secretary of the St. Paul chapter of the NAACP.[9] He spent almost all his adult life working for the Association, first as assistant secretary to the flamboyant Walter White, then, in 1955, after twenty-four years in the national office he became executive director and de facto representative of America's ten million blacks, leading the Association for twenty-two years and finally retiring at the age of seventy-six after a protracted and increasingly bitter reluctance to leave the post. In fact, he was so entrenched within the organization that, even as his retirement was debated, no succession plan was in place, thus weakening the NAACP for some years following his departure.

Although a journalist by profession, Wilkins joined the Association in 1931 because it offered, "the opportunity to acquire more than a local reputation, and, perhaps most significant of all, the opportunity to share in the crusading for a great cause."[10] But it was also a place where "the pall of office politics and intrigue was thicker than the smog in Los Angeles."[11] Wilkins's relationship with White was difficult almost from the start of his career with the NAACP. Within six months of joining the organization he became embroiled in a Du Bois–led attempt to oust White but hastily withdrew his support when the rebellion failed.[12] White and Wilkins continued to work together for almost quarter of a century but, while relations always remained publicly loyal and cordial, it is clear that suspicion and jealously governed their working relationship.[13]

The Second World War boosted the Association with a dramatic rise in membership. By 1946, the NAACP had approximately 420,000 members, a significant increase from the 250,000 members it had in 1943.[14] While Detroit remained the biggest branch by far, southern branches, in particular, showed a surprising vigor. In South Carolina, for example, membership grew from 800 in 1939 to 14,000 in 1948. On the way, through its alliance with labor groups, the Association had broadened its base to include blue-collar workers, and moved away from its traditionally middle-class roots to establish itself as the principal voice for a broader group of black interests.[15] But, Wilkins argued, the NAACP was unprepared for such dramatic growth: "We had a big membership —500,000 members and 1,200 branches—and a large income, but we didn't know how to use them."[16]

Wilkins laid the blame for this situation, in part, on weaknesses in the branch structure with resources put into opening offices in Washington and Hollywood, and hiring a labor secretary rather than more regional secretaries and field workers.[17] Such problems were long-standing. When Wilkins was offered the editorship of the *Amsterdam News* in 1941, he took the offer seriously, not just because, as he wrote to White, he was concerned about the financial stability of the organization, but also because of its "muddling of the vitally necessary reorganization of our branch structure."[18] A study commissioned by the NAACP's Committee on Administration that same year confirmed Wilkins's fears when it found that the structure of the national office was not conducive to either closer involvement with branches or for providing a simple conduit of information from headquarters to branches.

At the same time rumors persisted that communists had infiltrated some of the NAACP's larger branches despite little evidence to support the allegations.[19] One of the attacks made upon Wilkins centered on his attitude to the role of communists within the Association. As cold war rhetoric intensified during the late 1940s, waves of anticommunist sentiment led to an erosion of civil liberties and a widespread suspicion of liberals of all persuasions, and particularly organizations that criticized any aspect of the American way of life. This was clearly a difficult predicament for the NAACP. Wilkins certainly had no sympathies with communism, rejecting it on the grounds of both patriotism and pragmatism.[20] The NAACP membership appeared to agree with Wilkins. A resolution passed at the Association's annual convention in 1950 gave the board of directors authority to suspend, reorganize, or expel any branches that were controlled by communists.[21] Those branches that were supposedly infiltrated by communists were few, with the Richmond and San Francisco branches in California and several branches in Boston, Philadelphia, New York, and Long Island cited as having previously been connected with the communist party or other left-wing or labor groups, an accusation that could be leveled at many who sympathized with the left during the Depression.[22]

While the NAACP was fending off accusations that it was a communist organization, the Supreme Court handed black Americans the victory they had long been waiting for with the Supreme Court's ruling in *Brown v. Board of Education*, "one of life's sweetest days" as Wilkins later called it.[23] However, the NAACP's faith in judicial rulings, even as sweeping as *Brown*, would soon be tested. The ruling triggered a wave of white resistance, which the Association significantly underestimated. A successful attempt by Alabama to close the Association's operations in the state for several years created a vacuum that would be filled by the Southern Christian Leadership Conference (SCLC), and in Louisiana, for example, the Association was severely limited in its activities for several years, allowing most branches in the state to fall into decline.[24] The verdict also had an impact on the NAACP's strategy. Wilkins acknowledged at a congressional hearing several years later that the decision shifted the Association's emphasis from defensive to offensive in that, with no legal basis for segregation left, the NAACP had to fight public attitudes, emotions, and traditions to win support for equal rights legislation and litigation.[25] Against this background, when White died suddenly in 1955, Wilkins was quickly and unanimously appointed as his successor, a move that was generally approved by the Association's members and by the black press.[26]

Clarence Mitchell and Thurgood Marshall had both been unofficially suggested as potential leaders. One recent study of the NAACP claimed that competition between Marshall and Wilkins for the position of executive director led to an escalation of tension between the two men and within the organization at large, but there is little evidence in the archives to support this assertion.[27] On the contrary, several episodes cited by Marshall's biographers and correspondence between the two men suggest a mutual liking and professional respect.[28] Wilkins's belief in the power of legislation to help dismantle segregation also meant working closely with Mitchell, who, as Washington director of the NAACP, was highly regarded on Capitol Hill. Despite earlier difficulties, by 1957 the two, according to Mitchell's biographer "displayed considerable respect for each other and worked closely as a team."[29]

As leader of the NAACP, Wilkins's main objective was to prod the three branches of government to work together, but he had little faith in either the executive or congressional branches, saying of Eisenhower, "if he had fought World War II the way he fought for civil rights, we would all be speaking German today."[30] Wilkins was initially tentative in imposing any organizational changes. In a memo to the board six months into his new role, he proposed that the pre-1950 organization plan, where all responsibility for administration and staff fell under the executive director's rule, be restored. He also said that the branch, public relations, and accounting departments were not functioning properly and needed to be improved. Finally, Wilkins requested time to confer with department heads and present more-detailed recommendations at the January 1956 board meeting.[31] But, by that time, the black citizens of Montgomery had taken to the street, forcing the "wiliest and best organized" civil rights group in the country to fight for its position.[32]

The Montgomery bus boycott took the NAACP completely by surprise. The legal challenge to the city's segregated public transport system prompted by Rosa Parks's arrest should have ideally suited the Association. However, the speed with which the boycott was arranged, without waiting for the judicial outcome, was a departure from the Association's preferred order. Mrs. Parks and some of the boycott's organizers had had long connections with the NAACP, which the Association was quick to note, but it was unable to dictate the pace of events. The rapid speed with which the boycott took hold also highlighted the extent to which black Americans were ready for action.

Wilkins had strong misgivings about the use of boycotts as a weapon but, nevertheless, could see that the Montgomery activists had quickly captured national attention and that the NAACP, already committed to helping the boycott leaders, had to play a more prominent role in events. He sent a telegram to branch leaders across the South urging their cooperation with local ministers and groups to raise funds that should be sent either to Martin Luther King Jr. or to the NAACP's national office "to be used for Montgomery victims since NAACP is behind the legal action now pending in court challenging segregation statutes."[33] In a letter to King, he also reassured him that the Association would continue to support the protest by taking on all the legal costs for those arrested, including Mrs. Parks, and put the NAACP's legal staff at their disposal. Wilkins also promised the Association would assume the majority of costs associated with the legal challenge against Montgomery's segregated buses and, if necessary, extend emergency financial aid for weekly expenses.[34]

The success of the Montgomery boycott, Wilkins argued, was a "happy combination of elements that would make a boycott successful [but] such a combination does not exist everywhere."[35] His response to the main example of nonviolent direct-action, used by Gandhi in India, was that in that country, Indians comprised 99 percent of the population and therefore could wield some economic power by withdrawing labor or custom. That was not the case in the United States where black Americans made up approximately 11 percent of the population. The Montgomery protest, he argued, was successful only because it was a purely local protest motivated by purely local conditions.[36] His great fear was that the tactics used in Montgomery would encourage similar but much less successful protests that would deflect the Association from its more profitable strategy of litigation and lobbying, and fuel white resistance even further.[37] Wilkins also argued that the NAACP's participation in boycotts could leave the Association "in such a vulnerable position that we be damaged to the point of ineffectiveness in carrying out our general program."[38]

No matter what Wilkins's views on the tactics, the success of the Montgomery boycott posed serious challenges for the NAACP. Mass action instigated at a grassroots level began to shift the locus of power, the popularity of Martin Luther King deflected attention of the media, politicians, and black Americans away from the NAACP and the boycott's success fed the growing criticism of the NAACP's reliance on legalism. Most seriously, the emergence of new groups such as King's Southern Christian Leadership Conference heightened competition for funds and power. Stanley Levison, King's adviser, challenged the NAACP's ability to harness the masses, those who, as Levison said, "[haven't] $15, $50 or $100 for a ticket or a tuxedo, but who [have] zeal, energy and native talent which cannot be bought, but can be given without cost if we ask for it."[39]

When King addressed the NAACP's annual convention in San Francisco at the end of June 1956, he electrified the audience with a call to protest "courageously" against segregation "even if it means going to jail. If such is the case we must honorably fill up the jailhouses of the South. It might even lead to physical death."[40] Wilkins, by contrast, challenged President Eisenhower and Congress to act more directly in support for desegregation, suggesting a conference to discuss the problem of noncompliance with the *Brown* ruling.[41] Wilkins also suffered by comparison with Walter White. In an article published in 1956 the *Amsterdam News,* a frequent critic of Wilkins, damned him with faint praise in an article asking why all was not well for the new leader, "Wilkins, unlike the late Walter White, is not the take-charge type of leader, who within himself would be a dynamic figure. He has been the methodic kind of workman who handles the administrative details, and has done an excellent job at this."[42] Unfortunately, the paper said, rising domestic tensions had placed him in a position that forced him into the spotlight where "his every word and action in public are a matter of national concern."[43]

The actions of Montgomery's black citizens were the main talking point in the convention halls and the issue of mass action was brought to the floor. A resolution was passed to "broaden the NAACP's program by all lawful means and recommend that the board of directors give careful consideration to the Montgomery model," with Wilkins firmly convinced that the Association should remain focused on pressing the three pillars of government on desegregation and leave direct-action protest to King, albeit with financial and rhetorical support from the NAACP.[44] For all its sedateness, Wilkins's 1956 convention speech symbolized an approach that was grounded in the political reality of an ongoing presidential campaign and the belief that civil rights must be included in the manifestos of both main political parties if any meaningful action by the executive or legislative branches was to be secured in the next session of Congress. Such political support would also serve to bolster the Association's apparently pedestrian strategy of congressional lobbying in the face of the more dramatic actions of the newer civil rights groups.

The four years following the Montgomery boycott saw little or no major civil rights demonstrations, lulling Wilkins and the NAACP into a false sense of security. However, he had underestimated the frustration of black Americans with the painfully slow implementation of the Supreme Court's decision in *Brown*. The wave of protest sparked by the sit-in demonstrations in North Carolina in February 1960 presented Wilkins with some of the greatest challenges in all his years with the NAACP. Although the tactics of the protesters failed to convince Wilkins, he appears to have been genuinely moved by the courage of the students and young protestors who braved violent crowds, physical attacks, and jail sentences in some of the harshest prisons in the country. The new groups and their leaders now drove the pace of change, at least publicly. Wilkins, however, increasingly became the link between the civil rights movement and the establishment in Washington, which was uncomfortable dealing with the more militant leaders. Wilkins, it seemed, could speak the language of power.

In a profile of Wilkins, published in the *New York Times* in March 1965, he described his "blueprint" for civil rights leadership: "The Negro has to be a superb diplomat and a great strategist, He has to parlay what actual power he has along with the goodwill of the white majority. He has to devise and pursue those philosophies and activities which will least alienate the white majority opinion. And that doesn't mean that the Negro has to indulge in bootlicking. But he must gain the sympathy of the large majority of the American public. He must also seek to make an identification with the American tradition."[45] For Wilkins, this meant, in large part, negotiation with the white power structure. His role as conduit between the civil rights groups and Capitol Hill elite was probably his most significant contribution to the civil rights movement, bridging the divide between ordinary black Americans and their representatives in Washington. Wilkins had forged beneficial working relationships with those members of Congress most sympathetic to civil rights both through his work at the NAACP and through his chairmanship of the Leadership Conference on Civil Rights (LCCR). In working with A. Philip Randolph to lobby for a permanent Federal Employment Practices Committee, the breadth of organizations that comprised the LCCR enabled Wilkins to position himself as spokesperson for a much broader group than black Americans.

As the wave of demonstrations spread across the South, Wilkins expended much of his energy in ensuring the passage of the landmark civil rights bills of 1957 and 1964 and the Voting Rights Act of 1965. However, rather than lobbying for the legislation simply through the NAACP, Wilkins used the LCCR to maintain pressure on wavering congressmen. In both the House and Senate battles for the 1964 Act, for example, representatives of the LCCR were paired with a maximum of two congressmen in teams who then met with Mitchell on a regular basis to share information on the progress of the legislation.[46] Wilkins also made full use of his access to the highest reaches of political power.

Although the NAACP had dealings with both Kennedy and Johnson during the 1950s, Wilkins's first contact with both came during the battle to pass the 1957 Civil Rights Act. When Kennedy took office, Wilkins had been assured that he would have access to the president "if he had a pressing matter" that warranted discussion, and the president's aides responsible for civil rights certainly recognized that any friendliness on Wilkins's part toward the administration had to be maintained if there was to be any progress on this front.[47] The aides similarly realized that his position was under pressure from the newer civil rights leaders and were keen to bolster his standing, particularly in his capacity as influential leader of the NAACP's membership.[48] Kennedy's aides were also sufficiently aware of the dynamics at work among the civil rights leaders and were careful to advise the president on how each leader should be approached. In Wilkins's case, they suggested that, when meeting with the president in the company of the other black leaders, he was more constrained in his ability to compromise than might be the case when meeting with the president alone. In one instance, they suggested pursuing the opportunity for a "frank discussion" on Kennedy's civil rights program, "with one who will have considerable influence in determining the reaction of the Negro community."[49]

Wilkins attended a meeting at the White House early in Kennedy's term of office to discuss a potential federal civil rights program that he developed with Arnold Aronson, secretary of the LCCR, but, to Wilkins's disappointment, the issue did not fully engage the administration's attention until James Meredith attempted to register at the University of Mississippi. The case for a comprehensive civil rights package became imperative when water cannons and dogs were turned on demonstrators in Birmingham, Alabama, in April 1963. The incident, which was broadcast on national television and detailed in the world's press, encouraged the administration to craft civil rights legislation, which Kennedy presented to the nation two months later, in an emotional speech, giving Wilkins a feeling of "new confidence."[50]

It was not until Johnson became president, however, that Wilkins's political expertise could be fully exercised. The two men shared a pragmatic view of the world and a conviction that the political process was the only way to secure equal rights. The rise of the young, rebellious civil rights leaders, with whom Johnson had little in common, suggests that the president would have had little choice but to engage the older, more moderate elements of the movement, namely Wilkins and Whitney Young, of the Urban League, even if he had not respected or even liked them. The choice of Johnson as vice president was an unpromising one in Wilkins's view. Although the senate leader who guided the 1957 Civil Rights Act through congress, and whose political pragmatism was in part responsible for the amended legislation that finally appeared on the statute books, Johnson was a southerner and the much-weakened bill that was finally passed disappointed many blacks. Johnson had done little during his time in Kennedy's shadow to dispel black suspicions of his southern background. However, despite these doubts, the new president and Wilkins quickly found common ground on which the Civil Rights and Voting Rights acts were built.[51]

When Johnson took office, he made it clear that his legislative priorities would be the passage of Kennedy's civil rights and tax bills. The president quickly met with the main civil rights leaders during his first weeks in office but saw Wilkins first. The fact that his initial meeting was with Wilkins gave the NAACP leader political capital both inside and outside the organization. When the Association was undergoing a survey by a management consultant company, hired to oversee a reorganization, Johnson's recognition of Wilkins as one of, if not the, principal black leader he wanted to deal with, was put forward in his defense when criticized about his national image.[52] For the remainder of his term, Johnson used Wilkins as counsel when he wanted to make black appointments within his administration. He called him numerous times and encouraged Wilkins to call him at any time. He also played host to Wilkins and his wife at his ranch in Texas. And, as with Kennedy's aides, some of whom remained in the Johnson White House, the president's civil rights advisers were at pains to ensure that Wilkins's position within the NAACP and among the other civil rights leaders remained strong. In one example, Jack Valenti advised the president not to attend a dinner celebrating Martin Luther King because "King and Wilkins are locked in a power struggle. If you go to the dinner, (you) elevate King over Wilkins, and probably demean Wilkins who is having his problems with the leadership of the NAACP."[53]

In much the same way as Johnson was able to make full use of his prodigious political skills and his knowledge of the congressional process—and personalities—to help ensure passage of the civil rights bill, Wilkins was able to make use of his influence over the NAACP's members and the organizations that comprised the LCCR to exert pressure on Congress. Wilkins summoned NAACP delegates to Washington shortly before the House began debating the bill in February 1964, stipulating that only those branch leaders who knew their congressman should attend.[54] Ensuring the successful passage of the bill dominated Wilkins's life for much of the first half of 1964. He traveled from Florida to California to bolster support for the bill, appearing at rallies and on television, speaking to students, religious, civic, and business groups, and of course, NAACP branches.

Many factors contributed to the 73–27 Senate vote in favor of the bill. However, the efforts of Wilkins and Mitchell, in shoring up support from wavering allies, and through Wilkins's mobilization of the NAACP membership and, possibly more important, the LCCR, in waging a sustained and credible campaign of pressure were crucial in capitalizing on the wave of emotion following Kennedy's death, and the outrage much of America felt when faced with the images of southern belligerence. As *Brown* proved only too bitterly, securing legislation, or a favorable court ruling, was only half the battle. Wilkins told delegates at the NAACP's annual convention in 1965 that it was the "Association's job to help the government in these circumstances to enforce all the civil rights laws. This is the direction we will take in the coming year."[55] However, Wilkins's close relationship with the Johnson administration was beginning to attract criticism within the organization.[56] It was even rumored that Johnson had offered Wilkins a post in his administration, which Wilkins strenuously denied at the NAACP's annual convention in Denver, and there is no direct evidence that such an offer was made.[57]

That criticism grew louder as the United States' involvement in Vietnam began to divert government attention and money away from civil rights issues. However, for Wilkins the Meredith March of 1966, in which James Meredith planned to march through Mississippi, in part to highlight voter registration, was the "turning point" in destroying the tenuous coalition of civil rights groups.[58] When a sniper shot Meredith during the walk, an emergency meeting comprising the new, militant, leaders of the SNCC and the Congress of Racial Equality (CORE), as well as Whitney Young, Martin Luther King, and Wilkins, was convened at Meredith's hospital bed to decide what should be done next. But, the discussion soon disintegrated into internecine bickering about the purpose of a renewed march. Among several militant demands Stokely Carmichael listed in a draft manifesto, was that the march be an indictment of the Johnson administration and "put President Johnson on the spot."[59] True to form, Wilkins argued that the march should be a show of support for the 1964 Civil Rights Act and was opposed to any public criticism of Johnson. Wilkins was also disturbed at SNCC's insistence that white participation be drastically reduced and that the black self-defense group, Deacons for Defense, be used to protect marchers along the route.

Carmichael finally suggested that it was time for Wilkins to retire and write his memoirs. His aim, Carmichael admitted later, was to dis-suade Wilkins and Young from taking part in the march—which would have undoubtedly diluted its militancy. King's participation was vital, however, in part because of the media attention he attracted, but also because Carmichael felt King's involvement would pull King inevitably to the left of the movement. [60] The split was irrevocable and destroyed what was left of the fragile civil rights coalition. The con-tradictory aims of the left and right wings of the movement, which had previously been able to coexist, however uncomfortably, in a wide common ground, were pulled irreparably apart and eradicated any possibility of compromise, forcing the SNCC and the NAACP in par-ticular to declare their allegiance to separatism or integration, nonvi-olence or violent retaliation, and, within twelve months, whether to fall in step behind or against the president's foreign policy in Vietnam.

Wilkins's fury at the outcome of the meeting in Memphis was still evident in a memorandum to delegates of the annual convention a month later in which he warned of the problems that were likely to come from dealing with the other civil rights groups.[61] He listed a series of incidents that highlighted the financial exploitation and deceit inflicted upon the NAACP by groups that not only did not share the Association's commitments but could even be "pursuing certain goals that have nothing to do with civil rights at all."[62] The separation between the young militants and the NAACP was finally severed when the SNCC embraced "Black Power." The term Black Power had an immediate and electrifying impact on the civil rights movement and would rapidly define the public vocabulary about race relations. But, even proponents of Black Power found it difficult to define the term. For the most part, Black Power, as embraced by the SNCC, was a rhetorical construct. Nevertheless, the very image of militant and charismatic young black men championing the cause of separatism and black nationalism became a prism through which commentators could view their own ideas of which direction the civil rights move-ment, the fight for equality, and the very notion of what constituted equality should take.

For Carmichael the fundamental concept of Black Power rested on one premise: "Before a group can enter the open society, it must first close ranks," a concept that was anathema to Wilkins. [63] Wilkins, and therefore by definition the NAACP, had historically been the staunchest advocates of racial integration. As one of the basic tenets of the organization's principles, it was inconceivable to him to have invested so much in the battle to destroy segregation only to see the next wave of civil rights activists reject white society and advocate black economic institutions, black schools, and black college courses. The NAACP's annual convention in Los Angeles that June would be the battleground on which Wilkins would choose to face down not only Black Power but also challenges to his leadership from within the NAACP and the Association's relationships with other civil rights groups.

Wilkins went on to define in the harshest, most uncompromising way his response to Black Power. "No matter how endlessly they try to explain it, the term 'black power' means anti-white power. In a racially pluralistic society, the concept, the formation and the exercise of an ethnically-tagged power means opposition to other ethnic powers, just as the term 'white supremacy' means subjection of all non-white people. In the black-white relationship, it has to mean that every other ethnic power is the rival and the antagonist of 'black power.' It has to mean 'going-it-alone.' It has to mean separatism." And separatism, he argued, offered little to the disadvantaged but the chance to "shrivel and die." In a statement that embodied Wilkins's equally militant opposition to Carmichael and his followers, the NAACP leader told delegates, "It is a reverse Mississippi, a reverse Hitler, a reverse Ku Klux Klan. Black power . . . can mean in the end only black death."[64]

While Black Power was never a serious threat to the Association, Wilkins's overstated response and his insistence that "in this unsettled time when shifts are the order of the day and when change is in the air, we can sail our NAACP ship 'steady as she goes,' with more drive to the turbines, more skill at the wheel" suggested his talent for reading the mood of the NAACP's membership was no longer as acute as it had been.[65] Although the Association remained resolutely conservative, there was a growing frustration at the lack of economic progress among black Americans. The war in Vietnam, and the disproportionate number of black casualties was also becoming a cause for dissent and Wilkins's adamant refusal to protest the loss of black lives and the devastating effect the foreign war had on the domestic War on Poverty was viewed as a consequence of his closeness to the Johnson administration.[66]

Wilkins retired in 1977, after forty-six years with the organization. His last years were spent defending his decision to stay on, despite considerable pressure to pass the baton to a successor. When he left, the *Washington Post* praised his achievements and his "methodical, low-key ... philosophy of quiet persuasion."[67] However, while his survival in the face of numerous internal and external challenges was notable, it was hardly surprising for one as politically shrewd as Wilkins. Using his position as leader of the NAACP and the LCCR, he guided, persuaded, and navigated legislation that finally enshrined equal rights for black Americans. His ability, albeit possibly unconscious, to act as the conduit between the protesters on the streets of Alabama and the white power structure in Washington was an essential component in translating the emotional impetus arising from Selma, Birmingham, and other cities into effective legislation. However, the efficacy of the major civil rights acts, and the question of whether longer-term benefits for black Americans could have been accrued, had Wilkins focused on economic equality as intensely as equal civic rights is the subject for a wider debate, as is Wilkins's failure during the 1960s to inspire and engage young activists and so set the NAACP on course for a stronger future. For all that Wilkins was a "professional bureaucrat," lacking in charisma and vision, he was "the man who kept things together," the man who led from the back.[68]

CHAPTER FIVE

Uneasy Alliance

The NAACP and
Martin Luther King

PETER J. LING

T HE NAACP HAS never worked comfortably with charismatic figures. It feuded with Marcus Garvey in the Association's early
years, and in the 1940s, it was worried first about A. Philip
Randolph's all-black March on Washington Movement and then, about
the impact of both Paul Robeson's and W. E. B. Du Bois's communism
on the NAACP's ability to operate under the Red scare. As the 1960s
dawned, it was watching the career of Harlem congressman Adam
Clayton Powell warily and listening to the fulminations of Minister
Malcolm X of the Nation of Islam with concern. If Martin Luther King
Jr. found it difficult to keep his relations with the Association cordial,
he was in memorable company.

Nevertheless, King came from a loyal NAACP household. His
maternal grandfather, the Reverend Adam D. Williams, had helped to
establish the Atlanta branch, and his father, the formidable Daddy
King, was a very active and prominent local member pushing voter
registration and equalization suits in the 1940s. King joined the
NAACP in Montgomery shortly after his arrival and took out a lifetime membership. Once the Montgomery bus boycott was successfully concluded in December 1956, the NAACP signaled that he was
expected to become one of its leading supporters by awarding him its
highest honor, the Spingarn Medal. During his early years on the

national stage King largely deferred to more experienced figures, like the NAACP's Roy Wilkins, in joint efforts to lobby the Eisenhower administration. He supported Wilkins and the national executive when they expelled maverick branch leader Robert Williams of Monroe, North Carolina, over the issue of African American recourse to violent retaliation, and he gave his support to national rallies in support of school desegregation and in protest against escalating segregationist terrorism.

In this essay, the focus will be on two periods when tensions between King and the NAACP had a significant bearing on the course of the movement. The first of these will be 1960–1963 when the NAACP struggled to come to terms with an explosion of nonviolent direct-action campaigns. Much of the resentment was excited not by King but by others, although the NAACP could not shed the feeling that money that went to King's Southern Christian Leadership Conference would otherwise have gone to the Association. It also felt that King pursued short-term publicity rather than long-term development and that this was part of a broader political naïveté on his part. King also seemed ready to exploit local contexts in which the national NAACP had disappointed local militants. This was certainly the case in St. Augustine, Florida, in 1964.

In contrast, the rift that was evident in the second period, 1966–1968, although sharpened by King's refusal to join the NAACP leadership in wholesale denunciations of Black Power, was very much the product of King's own decisions: to campaign outside the South against ghetto poverty and to denounce the Johnson administration's policy on Vietnam. At the time of his death in April 1968, King was arguably more alienated from the NAACP leadership, both local and national, than at any other time of his career.

To be fair to the Association, during King's civil rights career (1955–1968), it faced multiple challenges. His emergence coincided with the segregationist backlash against the organization in the wake of the *Brown* school desegregation decisions (1954 and 1955). The Association had enough challenges to its survival without a rival organization emerging to compete for funds. Resentment was stoked by the fact that King's Montgomery protest movement was built on NAACP foundations. Rosa Parks was the city branch's secretary and youth leader, and black labor leader E. D. Nixon had been branch chairman. "Nixon," in Roy Wilkins's words, "was the true godfather of the boycott; through him all the years of fighting and organizing done by the Brotherhood of Sleeping Car Porters and the N.A.A.C.P. came to fruition in Montgomery."[1] Wilkins's account of the Montgomery campaign sets the tone for his treatment of King and other rivals: namely, guarded praise accompanied by criticism and a zealous recounting of the NAACP's role.

A relative newcomer to the Alabama capital, King had declined an executive position with the NAACP branch only months before Parks's arrest, citing the pressure of work and family commitments. It is entirely understandable therefore that when the boycott ended and King agreed to head a new organization, the SCLC in early 1957, the NAACP regarded this initiative as opportunistic and potentially damaging. In the *Pittsburgh Courier*, Gloster Current, NAACP director of branches, complained about the creation of "two organizations with the same goal when one has been doing such an effective job."[2]

The involvement of Ella Baker in the early management of the SCLC probably did not foster trust, given the enemies she had left behind at the NAACP national office after her departure as director of branches in May 1946. On the contrary, Baker's rich network of contacts with local NAACP branches across the South threatened to give the SCLC a further means of siphoning NAACP support. Long after she left her position, she received a steady flow of invitations to speak at NAACP branch events in the South, and her vigorous leadership of the New York City NAACP branch ensured that Wilkins and Gloster Current remained well aware of her capabilities and independent inclinations. They warily watched her school integration work through the group Parents in Action and remained fearful that militant action in New York City might alienate moderate liberal supporters of efforts to desegregate southern schools. At the same time, Wilkins and others knew firsthand that Baker was neither deferential nor easily contained by organizational loyalties; they rightly suspected that she would prove a difficult asset for the SCLC to exploit. Nevertheless, the limited success of the SCLC's 1958 Crusade for Citizenship was largely due to Baker.[3]

King strove to mollify NAACP fears, in public at least. Privately, he complained in 1959 that there was an orchestrated attempt to criticize the SCLC's voter registration efforts and that this was driving a wedge between his organization and the NAACP. Candidly, he conceded that neither organization had done enough in this field, but he insisted: "The job of registration and voting is so big that it will take the concerted efforts of every organization."[4] A deeper level of NAACP disaffection was evident in the aftermath of the SCLC-sponsored conference for students active in the sit-in movement, which was held at Raleigh, North Carolina, in April 1960. The sit-ins, far more than the Montgomery bus boycott, established nonviolence rather than legalism at the vanguard of racial protest, and they drew recruits especially from NAACP youth councils. Once again the NAACP feared that other organizations were encroaching on its turf.

In general, its misgivings fell into three categories. First, there was the fear that the new direct-action groupings would drain membership from the NAACP. Second, there was a concern that, since these protests attracted greater media attention than did litigation, donations that might otherwise have gone to the NAACP would flow instead to the students, or to the SCLC, or to a revitalized Congress of Racial Equality, now headed by former NAACP program director James Farmer. CORE's Freedom Rides drew widespread press coverage in 1961 and the protracted legal cases that followed the arrest of Freedom Riders in Mississippi provided a further ground for concern within the NAACP. Both CORE and the Student Nonviolent Coordinating Committee (SNCC) were heavily reliant on the NAACP and the Legal Defense and Education Fund for legal aid. Their adoption of a "jail, not bail" principle may have vexed the Association's eminent attorney Thurgood Marshall, who was accustomed to fighting to secure bail for African American defendants facing southern justice, but the NAACP was more troubled in practice by the protesters' failure to abide by their avowed principle. The bonds set for their release by southern judges were deliberately excessive. This tied up vital cash, some of which was lost entirely when out-of-state defendants failed to return for their trials. "If we are expected to pay the bills," Roy Wilkins informed the SNCC activist Ed King in September 1961, "we must be in on the planning and launching, otherwise the bills will have to be paid by those who plan and launch."[5]

At what proved to be the SNCC's founding conference in Raleigh, the Nashville-based minister James Lawson's calls for a nonviolent army excited the student activists far more than did King, whose actions since Montgomery (albeit unavoidably limited by his recuperation from a near-fatal stabbing in 1958) seemed weak and ineffectual to the sit-in students. Lawson's speech at the conference was particularly dismissive of the NAACP's faith in litigation. The *New York Times* quoted him as saying that the Association had become little more than "a fund-raising agency" and "had neglected the major resource we have—a disciplined, free people who would be able to work unanimously to implement the ideals of justice and freedom." According to an SNCC report Lawson remarked that "the legal question is not central. There has been a failure to implement legal changes and custom remains unchanged. Unless we are prepared to change the climate . . . the law can never bring victory."[6]

Lawson's preference for direct action over legalism might have mattered little had it remained unreported. Unfortunately, it received such prominent coverage that when Roy Wilkins picked up his newspaper he "read that Reverend King had said that the sit-in demonstrators were 'moving away from tactics which are suitable merely for gradual and long-term change.'"[7] When King appeared on *Meet the Press* on April 17, 1960, the same day that the *Times* reported Lawson's hostile remarks, he was asked to explain why the NAACP was now dismissed as too conservative and too slow. King tried to finesse the question by stating that he did not hear Lawson make any such comments, while simultaneously insisting that any complaint about slowness was not aimed at the NAACP but at those "agencies and the courts that will use the law to delay and get it bogged down in complex litigation processes."[8]

King's public distancing of himself from Lawson's remarks was judged by Wilkins to be too little, too late, and he wrote to King expressing his distress and disappointment on April 27, 1960. Reporters at the Raleigh meeting had observed that Lawson's critique had not been rejected by King himself. Wilkins pointed out to King that it was Ella Baker, SCLC's departing executive director, not King, who had felt compelled to clarify that Lawson's views were no more than a personal opinion. Given Baker's considerable disenchantment with King by this stage and her eagerness for the students to form an independent continuing organization of their own, her comments were more protective of the event and her SNCC protégés than they were of King's relations with the NAACP. Certainly, Wilkins was convinced that King himself had genuinely welcomed a move away from tactics that were allegedly "suitable merely for gradual and long-term change." In his memoirs, the NAACP leader remarked that "to equate our faith in law with gradualism, the South's main device for resisting change, was a very low blow."[9]

Memoirs written after the fact frequently adopt a coded language. Wilkins writes: "The air cleared afterward, and my admiration for Dr. King remained as great as ever, but from then on, whenever we had disagreements among ourselves, we tried very hard to keep them in the family."[10] The level of Wilkins's admiration for King probably did not vary from this point onward, and a better gauge of that esteem might well be the NAACP leader's collaboration with the Federal Bureau of Investigation. Regarded by the FBI as part of the black community's "responsible leadership," Wilkins met regularly with senior bureau officials. In November 1964 Cartha "Deke" Deloach, top aide to FBI director J. Edgar Hoover, informed Wilkins that King was known to have expressed his dislike and disregard for the FBI's leader. According to Deloach, Wilkins responded that this upsetting information made him "all the more determined to initiate action to remove King as soon as possible."[11] FBI records are certainly as self-serving as any memoir, but there is ample evidence that Wilkins envied and resented King's stellar status and sincerely believed that King remained a political *ingénue,* whose conduct exposed the movement to unnecessary risks.

As the SCLC, the SNCC, and the CORE worked across the South in the fight against Jim Crow, it was readily apparent that the only civil rights organization at the start of the 1960s with an active structure in place was the NAACP. Relations between the Association's New York–based national office and its local branches had never been devoid of disagreement. While some branches in the 1960s, such as Mobile, Alabama, and Columbia, South Carolina, proved their loyalty by assiduously working to limit or prevent King's involvement in their community, others expressed their disaffection and independence by courting Dr. King. The Albany campaign of 1961–1962 was noted at the time for the way it revealed internal divisions within the black community of that southwest Georgia cotton town. King's failure there had multiple causes, but clearly the misgivings of NAACP stalwarts like Marion Page about the militancy of relative newcomers like William Anderson and their external allies, both the SNCC and the SCLC, played their part. Anderson and others had been energized by the wave of direct-action campaigns sweeping the South, but to more conservative voices in the NAACP, their Albany movement showed the naïveté of believing that such tactics were universally applicable. The campaign could only be deemed a success, one NAACP official commented, "if the goal was to go to jail." [12]

Years later, Wilkins essentially affirmed this criticism in his memoirs. Commenting on the Montgomery example, he wrote:

> My own view was that the particular form of direct action used in Montgomery was effective only for certain kinds of local problems and could not be applied safely on a national scale . . . the America of the Eisenhower era and the Silent Generation was not the India of Gandhi and the Salt March. When Gandhi led his people against the British, Indians made up the vast majority of the population; non-cooperation could wreck a national economy. Such actions could work in the South, but only in cities like Montgomery, where Negroes were in the majority or in sufficient numbers to make their weight felt . . . The danger I feared was that the Montgomery model would lead to a string of unsuccessful boycotts where conditions were not so favorable at a time when defeats could only encourage the white supremacists to fight all the harder. [13]

In this sense the NAACP's misgivings about Dr. King were fundamental. They felt that he used tactics that were only truly effective in extracting local concessions under a limited set of conditions to excite expectations at a national level. African Americans rarely possessed the economic leverage to force concessions in this view so their non-cooperation might work to deepen lines of division, particularly if the failure of such tactics encouraged white resistance and bred a sense of frustration among African Americans that erupted into violence. Such an outcome could easily fuel a conservative backlash, once the media began portraying African Americans as villains rather than victims.

As the crisis in Albany resurfaced in the summer of 1962 with King once more in jail, the level of antipathy between the NAACP and the

SCLC was captured by an FBI intercept on the home phone of King's adviser, Stanley Levison. To the joy of FBI eavesdroppers who delighted in recounting movement dissension, Levison told a friend that "the NAACP and the Administration would like to see Martin King kill himself. And the tactic [to prompt this] is to let him languish in jail." Levison also detected the NAACP's hand in media reports decrying King's efforts to escalate the Albany protests. *Time* magazine had reported that King had "failed to convince Albany's Negroes" of the value of nonviolent protest. It quoted an anonymous local black figure as saying: "Some of us think we can do the job less wastefully." Such skepticism of the value of street demonstrations was certainly echoed at NAACP headquarters.[14]

An instructive defeat, the Albany campaign was inspired more by the recent Freedom Rides and sit-ins than by the fading memory of the 1950s bus boycotts. CORE's James Farmer had devised the Freedom Rides precisely to raise the movement's agenda from the local level of the lunch counter sit-ins to the national level of interstate transportation, correctly calculating that this was more likely to trigger federal intervention. In a rare negative assessment of his beloved Association, Wilkins had confessed to Farmer when the latter moved to head CORE that in some ways he envied him. "You're going to be riding a mustang pony, while I'm riding a dinosaur," Wilkins declared.[15] More commonly, Wilkins defended the careful NAACP approach. Once the initial Freedom Rides had elicited segregationist attacks that compelled Attorney General Robert Kennedy to press the Interstate Commerce Commission (ICC) to enforce desegregation of terminal facilities as required by the *Boynton* decision, Wilkins saw no need for their continuance since ultimately the issue's resolution had to come via the courts.

In Albany, the city's failure to comply with the ICC ruling should have been addressed through litigation. The staging of mass marches and picketing of segregated facilities that ensued clearly sought to focus national attention on segregationist defiance, and King's involvement was consistent with that strategy. But the strategy failed so long as local sheriff Laurie Pritchett managed the policing of the movement's actions circumspectly and ensured that his resources in terms of jail space were greater than the movement's resources in terms of individuals willing to go to jail. In this sense, the NAACP saw the Albany campaign as wasteful, a view that was actually less sharply at odds with King's still developing strategic vision than with that espoused by SNCC workers like Charles Sherrod. Sherrod was convinced that confronting the segregationist order broke particularly potent constraints of fear that were vital in the maintenance of white supremacy. King shared this belief insofar as he saw "standing up" as fundamental to the task of getting the oppressor off your back but, after Albany, his successful campaigns were more targeted. Ironically, at the time, both the SNCC and the NAACP criticized King for trying to exploit Albany for his own national media-orientated agenda. The SNCC believed the priority should be nurturing the local insurgency and the NAACP believed the priority should be establishing better structures for interracial dialogue and legal redress. Both believed that King's involvement damaged the local community.

Criticizing a setback is always easier that criticizing a victory. The 1963 Birmingham campaign seemed to restore faith in King's nonviolent tactics. Birmingham white leaders made concessions in the June accord that went beyond what they had previously contemplated, and far more important, the clashes in Birmingham and many other cities prompted President Kennedy to call on Congress to pass comprehensive civil rights legislation, a move that he had hitherto discounted. Nevertheless, even during the Birmingham campaign, the black critics of King's methods, notably his use of child demonstrators, reflected partly the character of many NAACP branches in the Deep South. Middle-class figures like John and Deenie Drew had never really warmed to the relentlessly confrontational approach of Fred Shuttlesworth's Alabama Christian Movement for Human Rights, and they welcomed the restoration of NAACP operations in Alabama in 1964. Figures like A. G. Gaston, Birmingham's leading local black businessman, initially sympathized with the white moderate belief that the municipal reforms that had made public safety commissioner Eugene "Bull" Connor a lame duck in the spring of 1963 could ameliorate Birmingham's race relations quietly and gradually, if given time. By May, Gaston accepted that the nonviolent protests had made local whites more amenable to moderate demands, but the deterioration of race relations in the Magic City by the fall of 1963 rekindled his doubts. Such individuals belonged to a tradition of racial diplomacy and pragmatic accommodation among the small southern black upper class that was well represented in the NAACP. In the plantation districts of the Deep South, simply belonging to the NAACP was an act of defiance, but in the growing cities, NAACP membership often signaled a commitment to racial uplift where militancy was tempered by the knowledge that as members of the black elite, they had something to lose. The anxiety that King's high-risk tactics could easily do more harm than good deepened after the violent scenes and innocent deaths that wracked Birmingham during 1963.

Nevertheless, by the late spring of 1963, direct action had become such a dominant feature of the movement that even the NAACP had to be seen to be committed to protest. The most conspicuous example of this was the desegregation campaign in Jackson, Mississippi. Wilkins himself cites it as proof that the NAACP did not work exclusively through the courts. On June 1, 1963, Wilkins and the NAACP state president Medgar Evers were arrested with a group of picketers outside the segregated Capitol Street stores. Talking to Levison, King reportedly laughed at Wilkins's conversion to direct action, saying, "We've baptized brother Wilkins."[16] Wilkins's memoirs show that he was well aware of the positive public relations effect of his arrest and he very deliberately placed it in the context of previous arrests to show how he had been misjudged. But while declaring that en route to jail he knew that he "was once again where [he] belonged," he remained intent on reiterating his concern over the "distorting aspects" of the "more mediagenic" direct action. He was seeking "a real legislative program from Kennedy, not a stretch in a Southern hoosegow." In an obvious reference to King's pursuit of media attention, he added: "New laws would make a difference; nothing is deader than last week's newscast or headlines."[17]

This overriding concern for the practical formal outcomes of campaigns was equally evident in the NAACP's reaction to the proposed March on Washington. As street protests erupted in communities across the South and tensions intensified in major northern centers such as Boston, Chicago, Detroit, and Harlem, the NAACP shared official misgivings about plans to stage mass demonstrations in the nation's capital. Such moves were as likely to consolidate conservative opposition to racial reforms as they were to galvanize a bipartisan liberal coalition. With characteristic condescension, Wilkins recalls: "Dr. King, who had no real legislative experience, was thinking of applying direct action and the tactics of Birmingham to the capital, a line of thought I considered disastrous."[18] The subsequent march might well be identified with King because of his unforgettable address, but Wilkins clearly implies that its success in wooing public opinion was due to the abandonment of King's original militant protest plans.

Significantly, Wilkins gives no mention in his memoirs to King's St. Augustine campaign. In 1964 when King was seeking a protest center from which to publicize the need for a civil rights bill that would eliminate segregation in public accommodation, he settled on the Florida resort town of St. Augustine. Militancy there largely dated from the arrival of dentist Robert Hayling, who had taken charge of the NAACP Youth Council in 1963. A Korean War veteran, Hayling resembled his fellow maverick NAACP branch leader Robert Williams. Following the murder of Medgar Evers in Mississippi, he stated that he and his NAACP colleagues would "shoot first and ask questions later." Reprimanded by the national NAACP for being needlessly provocative, Hayling turned to Martin Luther King for support in his efforts to challenge the virulent racism of one of America's oldest cities. With the help of a headline-grabbing campaign of interracial sit-ins over Easter 1964, Hayling exposed the tourist resort as a Ku Klux Klan stronghold in the national media. King's SCLC escalated the campaign during May and June, and then suspended it once national gains—passage of the civil rights bill on June 20—were secured. Given the scant and uncertain character of local gains, the historian David Colburn has concluded that St. Augustine's black community "paid a heavy price for inviting King into their community."[19] Local branches who felt neglected by the national leadership and who fell temporarily under militant influence recognized King as an alternate source of national resources, but the legacy of his campaigns made the majority of branches mistrustful of his objectives. Like their counterparts in the National Baptist Convention, they sometimes saw King as someone selfishly in search of the limelight.

King's recklessness in the eyes of the NAACP was confirmed once his activities visibly expanded their scope in 1965. In mid-June 1965, SCLC staff had debated the case for a northern campaign. King was convinced that he could not ignore the mounting signs of racial conflagration in metropolitan areas outside the South. The five days of destruction that began on August 11 in the Watts district of Los Angeles precipitated his intervention, despite the hostile reception he experienced when he visited Watts six days later. Unsurprisingly, Roy Wilkins recounts King's difficulties with alacrity. "Those folks in the ghetto," he observes, "didn't need his dream—they wanted jobs, a decent place to live." In Wilkins's view, the entire movement was ill prepared for the opening up of another front in the fight for racial justice.[20]

Many of the NAACP's largest branches—such as Chicago, Detroit, Los Angeles, New York, and Philadelphia—were located in metropolitan communities that might serve as King's northern beachhead. Each of these cities had NAACP branches that had restive relationships with the national office, but at the same time, they all shared a predisposition to resent an "outsider" like King coming into *their* city and claiming a leadership role. In New York and Philadelphia in particular, local black leaders let King know in no uncertain terms that he was not welcome. Philadelphia branch president Cecil Moore had already responded to ghetto discontent following a three-day racial disturbance in late August 1964. Realizing that what would become known as Black Power elements threatened the NAACP's community leadership position, Moore became more assertive of black independence through his campaign against employment discrimination and segregated and inadequate welfare provision. Moore ran against incumbent black congressman Robert Nix in 1965 and drew Black Power support to his mayoral campaign of 1967. He represented a type of local black leader who strengthened his local status by outflanking King and other civil rights groups.[21]

When King selected Chicago for his northern protest campaign, he was primarily attracted by the emergence of a mass movement among black Chicagoans around a classic NAACP issue: inequality of schools. The NAACP had been one of several local organizations that had called for the dismissal of Chicago school superintendent Benjamin Willis for his failure to provide equally for African American children in his management of the city school system. However, the branch's ability to challenge local conditions was limited by its ties to local African American congressman William Dawson, who in turn had ties to Mayor Richard Daley Sr.'s formidable political machine. Consequently, the schools' fight was primarily led by a consortium known as the Coordinating Council of Community Organizations under Al Raby.[22]

By the time King launched his Chicago campaign, Daley's political influence had blocked efforts to remove Willis, and when King raised a number of other issues related to deprivation in ghetto districts, Daley proved similarly adept at defusing the issue through token actions. King's lack of success undoubtedly confirmed doubts about his political judgment in NAACP circles. Only when the movement began its marches into white neighborhoods to protest housing discrimination did the campaign gather momentum. By that stage (August 1966), King's position had been damaged by the emergence of a new battle cry for African American liberation: "Black Power." First popularized by the new chairman of the SNCC, Stokely Carmichael, at a rally in Mississippi on June 17, 1966, the slogan confirmed the schism between the direct-action groups, SNCC and CORE, on the one hand, and the more moderate NAACP and the National Urban League on the other. This further complicated King's position as he strove to appeal to both sides and to resist demands that he condemn both "Black Power" and the ghetto disturbances that so colored its media reception. Beginning July 12, Chicago witnessed three days of widespread violence, which Mayor Daley was able to portray as a byproduct of King's protest campaign. A visibly shaken King told a press conference that he needed victories if he was to continue to provide an alternative to violence.

Judging by the remarks of its executive director Roy Wilkins, the NAACP was unequivocal in its condemnation of Black Power. He told the Association's annual convention on July 5 that no matter how its advocates tried to explain it, Black Power was "a reverse Mississippi, a reverse Hitler, a reverse Ku Klux Klan." It was a *go-it-alone* strategy that set race against race and as such it would prove "the father of hatred and the mother of violence." Yet as the historian Simon Hall has recently reminded us, Wilkins did not speak for all 500,000 members of the NAACP. Addressing the convention's Los Angeles audience after Wilkins, Watts preacher James E. Jones urged the NAACP not to be "scared into a position of defense by the power structure" but instead to take up the challenge of making Black Power an "honorable and a factual part of the total power spectrum in America." Many delegates applauded Jones's speech as loudly as they had Wilkins's keynote address. In the aftermath of the convention, which had also heard Wilkins's hostile remarks echoed strongly by Vice President Hubert Humphrey, the national office received letters reiterating Jones's criticisms and even terminating membership unless the Association recognized that Black Power meant nothing more than "the self-determination, self-respect and self-protection for Black people."[23]

Wilkins was equally forthright in his refusal to disavow President Lyndon Johnson's policy in Vietnam. As early as July 1965, he had warned colleagues that critical comments on foreign policy would simply weaken "the civil rights drive." Predictably, therefore, when King emerged as a leading critic of the war in April 1967, the NAACP board voted unanimously to "stick to the job for which [the Association] was organized," and repudiated any proposed merger of peace and civil rights movements as "a serious tactical mistake." Such a position was consistent with the NAACP's tradition of stressing African American patriotism in its fight for equal citizenship and more specifically with the cold war liberalism that had been the Association's defensive posture since the Red scare. This anticommunism was bolstered further by the NAACP's leadership's close alliance with the Johnson administration. Whereas the SNCC and CORE had become alienated from the liberal wing of the Democratic Party by 1966, the NAACP regarded the legislative gains of 1964 and 1965 and the programmatic initiatives of the War on Poverty as proof that the current administration was an ally in the struggle for racial equality unparalleled in American history. Certainly, Roy Wilkins regarded Johnson as a personal friend and was flattered by his attention.

King's public stance against the administration over Vietnam was seen by Johnson insiders as an attempt to curry favor with white radicals and black militants. His position certainly underlined the extent to which Wilkins and the national NAACP remained loyal to the president and detached from the new radicalized elements of the movement. Within the NAACP, this stance, like the denunciation of Black Power, provoked grassroots criticism and especially the charge that Wilkins was a presidential puppet. In May 1967 Gloster Current reported that several New York City branches were united in their complaint that the organization was too supportive of the administration and the national board, which had always contained critics of Wilkins, had voices that echoed that view.

At the same time, some local NAACP branches adopted an anti-administration position at odds with the national leadership's tacit support. Often there was a generational element to the emergence of anti-war opinion. By early 1967, the NAACP's Youth and College Division was calling for a system of voluntary national service as an alternative to the military draft. While such local sentiments placed some members of the NAACP on the same side as Martin Luther King over the war, this sympathy did not translate into strong support for King's efforts to generate a nonviolent crusade against militarism and economic injustice. Those members who were sympathetic to King's stance over the war were in many instances also sympathetic with the harsher rhetoric of Black Power and unconvinced that nonviolence was a viable strategy for tackling ghetto problems. Those members who were hostile to King's stance over the war because of its damaging political effects were sometimes equally anxious over his efforts to broaden the movement's agenda by fomenting street protests in metropolitan communities. The violence that erupted in Memphis as King tried to lead a protest march there in support of striking sanitation workers was seized upon by such critics as further evidence that King's ego-driven actions were likely to make a bad situation worse by fueling a conservative backlash. It was from this perspective that they viewed King's proposed Poor People's Campaign in the nation's capital.

Thus, the Martin Luther King who was slain on the balcony of the Lorraine Motel on April 4, 1968, was more mistrusted than venerated by the NAACP. Over a two-year period, he had taken an increasingly radical public position on both domestic and foreign policy and had alienated the Johnson administration. In doing so, he had epitomized the contrasting styles of charismatic and bureaucratic leadership. By this stage, King was in his own words, "going for broke," acting from personal moral imperatives rather than political calculations. He had come to believe that he did indeed have a prophetic role. Although it was always a more complex institution than its critics claimed, the NAACP was the exemplary model of bureaucratic leadership within the civil rights movement. It valued self-preservation and continuity and operated more from a secular faith in education and systemic juridical processes than from a religious commitment to the transcendental attainment of justice. Its home was the court and the committee room rather than the pulpit or the sacrificial altar. Ironically, as King became increasingly the prophetic voice that frightened mainstream America in the late 1960s, he inadvertently channeled donations toward the NAACP enabling it to carry forward the vital work of litigation that fleshed out the legislative measures of the Johnson years. The subsequent fruits of integration enjoyed by black professionals from lawyers to newscasters flowed as much from the NAACP's legalism as from Dr. King's words and witness. The movement needed both despite their fundamental contradictions.

CHAPTER SIX

The NAACP
and the Challenges of
1960s Radicalism

SIMON HALL

D URING THE SECOND half of the 1960s the national leadership of the NAACP had to contend with mounting opposition to the war in Vietnam and growing calls for "Black Power" from within the civil rights movement. Their response was to seek to distance the Association from those organizations, most notably the Student Nonviolent Coordinating Committee and the Congress of Racial Equality, which adopted antiwar positions and advocated Black Power. This has typically been viewed as evidence of the Association's conservative, reactionary tendencies.[1] However, the NAACP's stance should be seen primarily as a logical product of its own experiences of working within the civil rights movement during the early 1960s. Providing a more nuanced and sympathetic treatment of the Association's relationship with the radical firmament of the late 1960s helps rescue the organization's leadership from what E. P. Thompson termed the "enormous condescension of posterity."[2]

The war in Vietnam first emerged as a serious national political issue during 1965, when President Lyndon Johnson precipitously increased the number of U.S. combat troops in South Vietnam and ordered Operation Rolling Thunder, a massive bombing campaign against the communist North. These developments energized the domestic peace movement and made the war a topic of discussion, debate, and activism within the civil rights movement.[3] In January 1966 the SNCC became the first civil rights organization to take an official position against the war in Vietnam, accusing the U.S. Government of being "deceptive in its claims of concern for the freedom of the Vietnamese people."[4] In July, CORE's national convention passed a strong antiwar resolution.[5] Then, in April 1967, the Reverend Dr. Martin Luther King Jr., who had first raised concerns about the war in the spring of 1965, finally made his position regarding America's military involvement in Southeast Asia unequivocal. In a powerful speech delivered at New York's historic Riverside Church, King condemned the U.S. Government as the "greatest purveyor of violence in the world today," and called for a negotiated settlement with the communist National Liberation Front.[6]

Until 1969 the NAACP's official position on the war in Vietnam was, in essence, to have no position: it claimed that the war was an issue entirely separate from civil rights concerns, and that therefore civil rights organizations should not be expected to take a stand one way or the other.[7] As NAACP executive director Roy Wilkins explained, the Association had no right to assume that members who had signed up for the civil rights fight would "want their civil rights organization to commit them to a stand on the Vietnamese War."[8] The NAACP leadership was also determined that the focus on civil rights should not be dissipated by other concerns. Writing in his syndicated newspaper column in July 1965, Wilkins argued that if the movement went "off on a foreign policy kick" it would "weaken its effectiveness in discharging its major responsibility here at home."[9] On April 10, 1967, in the aftermath of King's antiwar speech, the NAACP board of directors unanimously passed a resolution stating that any attempt to merge the peace and civil rights movement was "a serious tactical mistake." They also pledged that the NAACP would "stick to the job for which it was organized."[10] It was a theme that Wilkins reprised that August when he accused those black leaders who were "moaning" about the war of neglecting the fight for civil rights at home and giving too much attention to "Asia, Africa, and the islands of the sea."[11]

The war in Vietnam was not the only radical challenge that the leaders of the NAACP encountered during the late 1960s—they were also faced with the dramatic emergence of Black Power.[12] On the evening of June 17, 1966, SNCC chairman Stokely Carmichael addressed a rally in

Greenwood, Mississippi. Carmichael, who had just been released from jail, acknowledged the "roar" of the angry crowd with a "raised arm and a clenched fist" as he moved forward to speak. "This is the 27th time I have been arrested—and I ain't going to jail no more," he told the several hundred mostly local African Americans. "The only way we gonna stop them white men from whuppin' us is to take over. We been saying freedom for six years and we ain't got nothin'. What we gonna start saying now is Black Power!" [13] Within a few months the SNCC and CORE had dropped their commitments to nonviolent tactics and integration as an immediate goal and had become all-black organizations. A host of new Black Power groups and activists emerged, too, most notably the Black Panther Party, which was founded in Oakland, California, in October 1966.

The NAACP leadership was unambiguous in its public opposition to the Black Power slogan. On July 5, 1966 Wilkins addressed the NAACP's fifty-seventh annual convention in Los Angeles. The veteran civil rights leader used the opportunity to tell the 1,500 delegates and watching journalists that "no matter how endlessly they try to explain it . . . the term 'Black Power' means anti-white power . . . it has to mean 'going-it-alone.' It has to mean separatism." For the NAACP chief Black Power was a "reverse Mississippi, a reverse Hitler, a reverse Ku Klux Klan" that could result only in "black death." [14] Black Power militants, meanwhile, were dismissed by Association officials as "preachers of hate" and "hell-raising opportunists" who wished to "plunge" African Americans "back behind the barbed wire of restriction, inferiority, persecution and death to both the spirit and the body." [15]

In explaining the NAACP's response to Black Power and the war in Vietnam historians have tended to emphasize the conservatism of figures such as Roy Wilkins and Gloster Current, the director of branches; the national leadership's closeness to the Johnson administration; and the caution and conformism that was encouraged by the organization's bureaucratic structures. While there is much value in these arguments, it is enlightening to explore the NAACP's reaction to the radicalism of the late 1960s in relation to its own experiences of movement activism. One of the most important developments in recent civil rights historiography has been to focus on local organizing and the role played by ordinary people in the struggle for racial justice. Much of this scholarship has shown how the "radical turn" within the civil rights movement—which manifested itself most visibly in opposition to the war in Vietnam and support for Black Power—grew directly from the experiences of activists themselves.

In their organizing work in the Deep South, civil rights activists encountered what the historian Hasan Kwame Jeffries has described as "self-determinist cultural practices" among black southerners—most notably an abiding commitment to armed self-defense and the prevalence of Washingtonian strategies of self-help.[16] In their interactions with local blacks, these young grassroots organizers came to appreciate the importance of independent black political organizing and self-reliance. They also realized that the tradition of self-defense was, in the words of Bob Moses, so "deeply engrained in rural southern America" that little could be done to affect it, and so began the move away from a strict adherence to nonviolent methods.[17] The SNCC's adoption of Black Power in the summer of 1966 was to a considerable degree both congruent with, and a product of, its longstanding commitment to working with local people to challenge white supremacy, open up economic opportunities, and build political power. As former SNCC field secretary Jean Wiley recalled, Black Power "was really what we were trying to do anyway, we just didn't call it that. Get people registered, get the numbers in so that they can start changing the sheriff and the county government."[18] This, of course, was exactly what the SNCC attempted to do in Alabama's Black Belt in 1965 by founding the Lowndes County Freedom Organization (LCFO)—an independent political party with a Black Panther emblem.[19]

In addition to being inspired by their encounters with local African American southerners to explore black nationalist ideology and develop independent black political action, those working on the front lines of the civil rights struggle in the early 1960s were also often radicalized by their experiences.[20] The failure of the federal government to adequately protect civil rights organizers from white racist violence featured prominently in this process, as did the lessons that were learned about the harsh realities of political power. The 1964 Democratic Party national convention in Atlantic City, where the Mississippi Freedom Democrats failed in their bid to unseat the racist state regulars, was particularly galling for many.[21] Black activist Zoharah Simmons recalled how "there's nothing like being dragged into a paddy wagon and thrown into the lock-up[,] you know . . . this stuff changes you . . . and I guess I do think it was a radicalizing process because it changed my life completely."[22] As SNCC leader James Forman explained, five years of struggle had changed many activists from "idealistic reformers" to "full-time revolutionaries. And the change had come through direct experience."[23]

All this helps us to understand why many civil rights workers who cut their teeth at the grassroots level, working for the SNCC and CORE in particular, became so critical of America's military involvement in Vietnam and were willing to embrace or advocate Black Power.[24] SNCC's Bob Moses, for example, explained that "our criticism of Vietnam policy does not come from what we know of Vietnam, but from what we know of America."[25] Indeed, the SNCC's January 1966 statement against the war in Vietnam made an explicit link between its antiwar position and its previous experiences of working for justice in the South.[26] As activist-historian Howard Zinn said in 1965, opposition to the war among southern black activists came "from the cotton fields, the country roads, the jails of the Deep South, where these young people have spent much of their time."[27] Moreover, activists, their idealism tempered by the experience of organizing, began to question both the primacy of nonviolence and the value of interracial organizing. Increasingly, southern field workers accepted the need for armed self-defense and came to believe that the leadership skills and intellectual self-confidence of white activists actually reinforced racial stereotypes and contributed to a culture of dependency.[28] As Stokely Carmichael put it, Black Power was something that had "grown out of the ferment of agitation and activity by different people and organizations in many black communities over the years."[29] Historians have often agreed with Clayborne Carson—arguing that "the new black consciousness . . . grew out of the experiences of activists in the southern struggle."[30]

The experience of Wilkins and his colleagues in the NAACP national secretariat, however, was markedly different. From their perspective, a combination of nonviolent mass protest, targeted litigation, and deft political lobbying had helped shatter the southern caste system. The Civil Rights Act of 1964 and the Voting Rights Act of 1965 dismantled the legal framework for segregation and facilitated black enfranchisement, while the liberal policies of Lyndon Johnson's administration promised tangible economic gains for African Americans through the Great Society and War on Poverty programs. Rather than growing disillusioned and embittered with a system that seemed unresponsive, the experiences of Wilkins and his colleagues during the first half of the 1960s seemed to show that not only could the system work, but that it actually was. Speaking in 1969, Roy Wilkins stated that President Johnson had "committed the White House and the Administration to the involvement of government in getting rid of the inequalities between people solely on the basis of race. And he did this to a greater extent than any other President in our history ... when the chips were down he used the great powers of the presidency on the side of the people who were deprived."[31]

In part, of course, the view of the NAACP's leaders reflected their own approach to working for civil rights. Roy Wilkins had always been ambivalent about nonviolent direct action—which he once described as "blowing off steam."[32] Moreover, while the SNCC sought to foster indigenous leadership and empower local African Americans, the NAACP leadership preferred to focus on winning support for progressive legislation by lobbying congressmen and by using litigation to strike down segregation laws.[33] The NAACP's stance also reflected an understanding of America's political topography. The urban unrest, seen in the long, hot summers of rioting between 1965–1968, the growing polarization over the war in Vietnam, and the emerging countercultural and student protest movements all helped to fuel a conservative backlash against the liberal politics of the postwar era and contributed to a decline in public support for the civil rights movement.[34] With liberals struggling to hold the line against the rise of the New Right, civil rights groups that opposed the war in Vietnam or offered support for Black Power risked isolating themselves from potential allies and leaving themselves exposed to a damaging conservative counterattack.[35]

All this cemented the NAACP's belief that coalition with liberal Democrats, organized labor, and other progressive forces was the only realistic means to secure further gains—an approach advocated most notably by civil rights strategist Bayard Rustin.[36] The success of this "coalition strategy" during the second half of the 1960s was, however, dependent on maintaining good relations with Lyndon Johnson. Roy Wilkins, a regular guest for barbecue at the LBJ ranch in Texas, had developed a very strong friendship with the thirty-sixth president.[37] Indeed, NAACP labor secretary Herbert Hill believed that there had never been "such a close personal relationship" between a president and an NAACP chief.[38] It is, therefore, hardly surprising that Wilkins was keen to distance himself, and his organization, from antiwar critics and Black Power advocates who were not shy of making brutally personal attacks on LBJ.[39]

The success of the "coalition strategy" also relied on the civil rights movement using rhetoric and tactics that were rooted in mainstream notions of respectability in order to win, and retain, the support of white allies and the broader public. During the 1950s and early 1960s civil rights organizations had gone to great lengths to ensure that the "whole style, tenor and symbolism of black protest was carefully orchestrated to appeal to mainstream white sensibilities about proper behavior in pursuit of legitimate goals." Activists had, for example, dressed smartly, acted with dignity and decorum, and grounded their demands firmly within America's Republican-Democratic tradition. This approach had helped the movement secure public support and political influence.[40] Concern over image played a key role in shaping the NAACP's response both to opposition to the war in Vietnam and Black Power, with the Association's leaders keen to avoid being associated with what were often seen as disreputable and un-American forces.

Although the vast majority of those who marched against the war in Vietnam were ordinary, respectable, patriotic citizens, the public perception of the antiwar movement was quite different. The media focused, understandably, on its more outrageous and colorful elements —with the carrying of National Liberation Front flags, the burning of draft cards, the wearing of long hair and countercultural dress, and militant rhetoric featuring prominently in the accounts of news and television journalists.[41] Sometimes, as in the October 1967 attempt to levitate the Pentagon—replete with witches, diggers, and hippies—the peace movement was itself culpable for the negative image in which it was portrayed.[42] The NAACP's leaders were also concerned about the perceived anti-Americanism of the peace movement. As early as August 1965 Roy Wilkins had argued that civil rights activists should "not tinker with patriotism at a time when their country is engaged in armed conflict,"[43] and he later suggested that the antiwar movement aided

America's "ideological enemies."[44] Wilkins's patriotism is revealed in comments that he made in the spring of 1967—"I don't speak as a hawk or a dove . . . But, is it wrong for people to be patriotic? Is it wrong for us to back up our boys in the field . . . They're dying while we're knifing them in the back at home." He continued, "Maybe I'm a bit old fashioned . . . maybe we are wrong, maybe we shouldn't be in Vietnam. But when you're out there in the trenches being fired at, you have to fight back."[45]

For the NAACP leadership, issues of respectability were linked intimately with the question of anticommunism. In the early postwar period the Association had adopted the central tenets of cold war liberalism and, as Herbert Hill explained, his colleagues in the national office "were Cold Warriors."[46] In December 1965, for example, NAACP assistant executive director John Morsell wrote one antiwar critic explaining that he was "thoroughly convinced of the righteousness of the objective" in Vietnam and pointing out that many liberals believed that "a free and stable world" was "incompatible with Communist aggression."[47] The NAACP leadership also believed that antiwar agitation was fomented by communist agitators, and director of branches Gloster Current interpreted antiwar sentiment at the local level of the Association as a product of "left-wing shenanigans." As he explained, the "left-wing . . . is having a field day! Its most recent project is to create problems over our country's Vietnam policy."[48] Roy Wilkins shared this concern—in a newspaper column warning against the civil rights movement involving itself in debates over the war he explained that there were "of course, many kibitzers in the civil rights campaign whose No. 1 objective is not the attainment of the civil rights of Negro citizens."[49]

In 1969, with a Republican in the White House, opposition to the war widespread among liberal Democrats, and an emergent "respectable" peace movement centered on the Vietnam Moratorium Committee, Wilkins and the NAACP finally took a position against the war in Vietnam. At the annual convention in July, delegates adopted a strongly worded resolution that condemned the war as "cruel, inhuman, and unjust," and called upon the United States to withdraw quickly and "concentrate our wealth and skills on peaceful measures to prosecute our own domestic war on poverty."[50]

In explaining the NAACP's opposition to Black Power, historians have tended to emphasize fundamental ideological differences.[51] Certainly areas of disagreement existed, most notably regarding the NAACP's continued commitment to integration and support for inter-racialism. In private, however, the Association's leaders acknowledged that they actually *agreed* with much of Black Power, at least when it came to the pluralistic version as defined by Stokely Carmichael and the political scientist Charles Hamilton during 1966–1967. Armed self-defense, the mobilization of black voting strength, calls for economic empowerment, and the fostering of racial pride were all things that the nation's oldest civil rights organization could endorse.[52] In September 1966, for example, John Morsell explained that "by and large there is no disagreement with most of the specific objectives" outlined by Black Power leaders.[53] Two months later Morsell wrote that "all of the goals which Mr. Carmichael . . . asserts to be comprehended in the phrase 'Black Power' turn out, on inspection, to be merely restatements of goals pursued by the NAACP since its founding."[54]

Nevertheless, the NAACP leadership sought to distance itself from Black Power, and their public criticisms remained robust. To a considerable extent, however, this appears to have owed more to concerns about image than to ideological conviction. A central characteristic of Black Power was its militant, uncompromising, sometimes anti-American rhetoric. Stokely Carmichael, for example, urged blacks to "take over," told whites to "Move on over, or we'll move on over you," and declared that Black Power meant "bringing this country to its knees . . . smash[ing] everything Western civilization has created."[55] CORE leader Floyd McKissick, an early advocate of Black Power, told reporters that "the greatest hypocrisy we have is the Statue of Liberty. We ought to break the young lady's legs and point her to Mississippi."[56] The fiery rhetoric may have been designed to "rouse the slumbering masses—not . . . promote riots," as historian William Van Deburg has pointed out, but this distinction was lost on most observers.[57] "Happily or unhappily," wrote John Morsell, "the extreme statements" made by Black Power advocates "when they are carried away on the waves of demagoguery have rendered the slogan useless as a constructive symbol." This, he explained, was "the *essence* of our position in regard to the 'black power' slogan."[58] Indeed, the NAACP's leaders were profoundly concerned about the "emotional" rhetoric that Black Power advocates used—rhetoric that caused "alarm and confusion" among the public and harmed the cause for civil rights.[59] They believed that it was the "requirement of realistic and responsible leadership" to use language designed "to advance rather than retard" the civil rights cause.[60]

There are many reasons why, during the second half of the 1960s, the leaders of the NAACP sought to distance the Association from the growing opposition to the war in Vietnam and the emergent Black Power movement.[61] In part, it reflected their own sense of patriotism and commitment to liberal politics and anticommunism. As Herbert Hill explained, "the leaders of the NAACP were . . . not radicals, [were] not revolutionary. I think for the most part we accepted the assumptions about American society, with the reservation that we ought to get rid of racial discrimination." While "radicals on the subject of race," the Association's leaders "identified with [American] society."[62] Their decision was also, perhaps, illustrative of the generation gap. Roy Wilkins, born in 1901, had always been somewhat dismissive of the sixties generation of activists, describing them as "young squirts" and "smart-alecks" who had "been straining every nerve in order not to appear to be like the old folks."[63] Interestingly, a good deal of the antiwar and pro–Black Power sentiment within the NAACP membership was centered on youth chapters. In October 1967, for instance, a dramatic protest by a youth contingent helped force the adoption of an antiwar resolution by the New York State Conference; while youth chapters in Milwaukee, Shreveport, and New Orleans were especially prominent in their enthusiasm for Black Power.[64] It was also true that the NAACP's leaders (and much of its grassroots membership, too) felt strongly that the struggle for civil rights should take precedence over issues such as the war in Vietnam, and they remained steadfast in their support for both integration and interracialism.[65] There was also a strong desire to maintain the organizational integrity and cohesion of the Association by avoiding controversial and potentially divisive issues.[66] And, of course, the political strategy to which the Association was committed proscribed associating with causes, organizations, or activists that were, rightly or wrongly, viewed by much of the American public as disreputable and anti-American.

Ultimately, however, the NAACP's response is best understood when placed in the broader context. During the first half of the 1960s activists working with groups like the SNCC had their faith in the underlying goodness of America's social, economic, and political system shaken. They became disillusioned and radicalized by their experiences of organizing, and came to question many of their original assumptions, tactics, and goals. Ultimately, this led them to embrace more militant tactics in pursuit of more radical ends. The emergence within the civil rights movement of opposition to the war in Vietnam and support for Black Power was, to a large extent, a consequence of this process. The leaders of the NAACP, however, had not shared in a similar experience. If anything, their civil rights work during the same period had served to reaffirm their faith in the American system and it convinced them that coalition with mainstream liberalism remained by far the best way to secure further progress for the Republic's black citizenry. In short, they had not been given good reason to embrace the new radicalism. Indeed, from the perspective of NAACP headquarters in New York City, it appeared that there was little to gain, and a great deal to lose, by associating with the antiwar and Black Power movements.

PART TWO

The NAACP at the State, City, and Local Levels

CHAPTER SEVEN

The Falls Church Colored Citizens Protective League and the Establishment of Virginia's First Rural Branch of the NAACP

BEVERLY BUNCH-LYONS
AND NAKEINA DOUGLAS

FALLS CHURCH IS located in Fairfax County, Virginia, a county recognized today as one of the wealthiest in the country. According to census reports for 2003, the median household income in the county was over $80,000.00, nearly double the national median income for that same year.[1] Geographically, Falls Church is located approximately eleven miles from Washington, D.C., and less than ten miles from Alexandria, Virginia. It is part of the Washington Metropolitan area.

From its earliest beginnings as a town, there existed a free black population living within the boundaries of Falls Church in Fairfax County. From the middle of the 1850s until the end of slavery as much as one-fifth of the black population was comprised of free blacks. Virginia lawmakers maintained control over the free black population through legislation. One particularly harsh proposal put forth by two Virginia governors required all free blacks to leave the state or be forcibly removed. A second proposal, which eventually became law, allowed whites to enslave free blacks if convicted of certain crimes. As evidenced by such legal maneuvers, status as a free black person did not guarantee protection from the Black Codes that characterized practices in the state of Virginia during this period.[2] As the nineteenth century drew to an end, many laws governing blacks in the state grew more restrictive in response to social, economic, and political gains made during the period of Reconstruction. Blacks continued to settle throughout Falls Church, many in the area that was commonly referred to as the "Early Black Suburbia," known today as Baileys Crossroads. As the population increased, blacks built churches, stores, and other facilities to accommodate their growing community.[3] Economic progress was steady, yet as the twentieth century approached, a stagnant ideology of race relations based on patronizing and patriarchal attitudes clung to the air in Falls Church. The passage below, though written well into the twentieth century, is reminiscent of the environment that blacks living in Falls Church during the early twentieth century inhabited.

> There was a special place at the fireside for Mammy. She was an institution: life did not function without her. In the corner by the fire, in the best spot, was Mammy's chair. Here in slave times she nursed her "white children," gave them a growing philosophy of life, and prepared them for their place in society—a place she usually determined. The negro Mammy of yesterday was a basic influence on the everyday life of Falls Church. She held a respected place in the family, and her word was law. Usually a woman of superior intelligence and character, Mammy was chief among the servants (they were called slaves in legal documents).[4]

The remnants of this racial milieu created the backdrop for race relations in Falls Church during the early twentieth century. Blacks and whites often peacefully coexisted in Falls Church as long as blacks, those living within the town and those passing through, did not attempt to change the racial landscape in the town. When they did, they met with strong resistance both within and outside the legal system.[5] One example is a 1907 case involving Barbara Pope, a black woman from Washington, D.C., who refused to ride in the "colored" section of the trolley on her trip to Falls Church. Once Pope arrived in Falls Church she was arrested, detained for almost twenty-four hours, and fined. Her violation was cited as "breaking the Jim Crow" law. Pope filed a suit for $10,000 for the violent manner in which she was removed from the train. She was awarded one cent in damage as a way of mocking her efforts and as evidence that her suit was not taken seriously. Furthermore, the case demonstrated that local officials had no intention of voluntarily succumbing to African American demands for equality.[6] One of the local newspapers blamed the newly created trolley for bringing "undesirables" to the county and cited the Pope incident as the perfect example.

Only a year later in 1908 another trolley car incident occurred in Falls Church, further highlighting growing racial tensions. This incident involved Sandy James and Lee Gaskins, two black men who were forcibly removed from the trolley for alleged drunkenness. The two were later accused of derailing the trolley as it made its way to a subsequent stop. They were believed to have piled stones on the rail line. Local whites gathered to search for the two. Gaskins was located, tried, and convicted. He served a ten-year sentence, a fate that was likely better than that of Sandy James, who was never found, but was rumored to have been bludgeoned on the head twenty-five times by the local sheriff.[7]

Falls Church residents publicly voiced theirs concerns that the new trolley system would provide undesirables (namely, blacks from other areas) with transportation into their communities. They feared that the trolley provided easy access to those wanting to work in the District, and live in communities such as Falls Church. As these concerns mounted, law officials actively began creating legislation to bar blacks from living in certain areas of Falls Church. In 1912 the Virginia Legislature passed a law entitled "An Act to provide for designation by cities and towns of segregation districts for residences of White and colored persons, for the adoption of this act by such cities and towns, and for providing penalties for violation of its terms."[8] This law legalized residential segregation which gave cities and towns the right to racially segregate. Virginia and its towns and cities were no different than many other southern towns and cities during the early 1900s where residential segregation was actively pursued and practiced.[9] The scholar Roger Rice writes, "Race segregation by custom dated back to the ante-bellum period. Segregation by law, however, had been a somewhat less constant fact of life for Negroes immediately after the Civil War. Nonetheless, the legal status of the Negro had diminished as Jim Crow legislation rose throughout the South during the years 1890–1910."[10]

Once the Virginia Legislature passed its law allowing for segregation, local legislators in Falls Church wasted little time before enacting measures that restricted black residents to a small section of town. Other cities and towns in Virginia—for example, Ashland and Richmond—had already passed residential segregation ordinances before the statewide legislation was passed.[11]

In November 1914, Mayor John Herndon of Falls Church encouraged council members to adopt a segregation ordinance after it was rumored that a black person intended to live in West Falls Church. The ordinance was introduced by two council members, Reginald Munson and Samuel Styles. According to the ordinance, it would be unlawful for "any person to sell or rent land or dwellings to the negro race" within certain areas of Falls Church. Legislators in Virginia, as well as those in other states who supported residential segregation, argued that it was a public health and safety issue. Furthermore, it was suggested that segregating the races reduced the potential for hostility and curbed the possibility of racial violence. Many of these statutes allowed exceptions in the case of servants or other blacks deemed to be critical to the daily routine of white families. Such exceptions demonstrated that arguments often used to support residential segregation served as a ruse for the racist ideology that permeated the court system at the local and state levels.[12] Leon Higginbotham writes:

> During the early 1900s, most American state courts located in southern and borderline states interpreted the Constitution in a racist manner. Not only did these state courts permit *de jure* urban racial housing segregation, but they encouraged its application in the broadest and most pervasive context. Moreover, in upholding such segregation, these courts used judicial reasoning that was analytically inconsistent and philosophically biased. Their reasoning, which this article refers to as the reincarnation of "slavery jurisprudence," reflected the values and personal prejudices of some judges who viewed black Americans as different from and inferior to whites. Thus, state and city governments could do to blacks what they could not do to other Americans.[13]

Early legal attempts to force blacks to live in segregated communities corresponded with the mass migration of blacks into urban areas in both the North and South. Pushed by the lack of job opportunities, a failing cotton industry, growing racial violence, and disfranchisement, while pulled by industrial employment, greater autonomy, and more social outlets, many of those seeking to improve their economic and social circumstances left rural communities in the Deep South and began pouring into cities and towns in search of opportunities. For example, historians Meier and Rudwick write, "Between 1900 and 1910 large percentage increases in the black population occurred in New South cities like Birmingham (215 percent) and Atlanta (45 percent)."[14] Furthermore, "According to the census of 1910, two cities, Washington and New York, had over ninety thousand Negroes."[15] While Virginia legislators may not have been concerned over the growing migration of blacks to cities like New York and Birmingham, Washington, D.C., was an entirely different story. Just a few miles away, increases in the black population in the District were likely to spill over into Falls Church, bringing with it a population less tolerant of Jim Crow ideology and practices.

On January 11, 1915, the Falls Church Town Council adopted an ordinance based on the 1912 state law. On June 28, 1915, the council held a special meeting. At this meeting another ordinance was fashioned that determined the boundaries of the area where black residency would be restricted. Creating a map and providing the boundaries of the segregation district was a requirement of the statewide law. In Falls Church, this invisible line included Fairfax Street, Douglass Avenue, and Liberty Avenue. The goal was to ensure that the 1,386 black and white residents living in Falls Church would not live in close proximity to each other, thus preventing social mingling. Consideration was not given to blacks who already owned homes in the newly restricted areas who were expected to relocate. According to the ordinance blacks, who comprised 32 percent of the Falls Church population, would be confined to 5 percent of the land.[16] The proposed legislation meant that 113 blacks would have to relocate. The families of two of the most prominent black citizens in Falls Church, Joseph Tinner and Edwin B. Henderson, were included in the count.[17]

Three council members, Gould, Harmon and Nourse voted against the segregation measure, while two others, Munson and Styles, who had proposed the ordinance, voted in favor of it. Council members favoring the ordinance argued that the state of Virginia had already legalized residential segregation, and that the local ordinance would take effect one year following its passage. Once in place, it was a crime for any black person to rent, purchase, or dwell in a home in the white district; similarly whites could not legally rent, purchase, or occupy a home in the black district.[18]

Refusing to accept laws which consigned them to second-class citizenship, forced them to live in designated spaces, and required that they sell homes they had worked hard to purchase, blacks organized to protest the new legal residential sanctions. Joseph Tinner and Edwin B. Henderson organized the Committee of Nine (which quickly became the Falls Church Colored Citizens Protective League [CCPL] during the early part of 1915) as the first step in protesting the segregation ordinance. On January 20, 1915, Henderson, now secretary of the Committee of Nine, drafted a letter to W. E. B. Du Bois, founding member and director of publicity and research for the National Association for the Advancement of Colored People. He detailed the recent passage of the residential segregation act in the town of Falls Church, Virginia.[19] Henderson also noted that prior to the segregation act of 1915, Falls Church council members elected to forego an optional segregation act passed by the Virginia Assembly in 1912 which gave towns the ability to segregate neighborhoods and communities as they saw fit.[20]

According to the members of the Committee of Nine, the Falls Church Segregation Act of 1915 came as a surprise to the black residents of Falls Church. Attempting to find a possible motive for the passage of the act, Henderson wrote to Du Bois, "The only provocation apparent, is based upon a few incidents in which owners of unimproved or improved property have urged quick sales by threatening to sell to colored people."[21] According to Henderson and other members of the black community, the act was voted upon and passed without public notice. Henderson stated: "We appeared before the Council of the town last Monday night, and made protest, from citizens, and churches. Had we made the same representation before the enactment of such a law, it would probably never have been passed, but like most of these things, the only notice we had was an article appearing in an obscure county paper the week after the Council had voted."[22] He concluded by requesting information from the NAACP regarding other possible efforts in the state of Virginia to protest segregation legislation. Furthermore, he noted the African American community's desire and need to establish an affiliate branch of the organization in Falls Church.

The letter from Henderson was forwarded by Du Bois to the NAACP secretary, Mary Childs Nerney, who responded in February 1915. She advised the committee to seek counsel from a group of prominent black citizens in Richmond, Virginia, who were "contesting the segregation ordinance there. . . . I give below their names and addresses."[23] At the time of Henderson's letter to the NAACP only a single branch of the organization existed in Virginia. Secretary Nerney wrote to Henderson, "We hardly know how to advise you as there is at present no group in Virginia affiliated with this Association excepting a student group in Virginia Union University."[24] Because no other branches of the NAACP existed in the state to provide additional information regarding segregation there, the NAACP appeared hesitant to provide specific advice on how the Committee of Nine should proceed. The Association was aware of other protest efforts in the state, but was less well informed about the particular racial climate that existed in Falls Church. The fact that it was a rural community presented a challenge that the Colored Citizens Protective League perhaps had not anticipated in their efforts to not only seek assistance from the NAACP, but more important to form a branch-level organization.[25] Two of the most significant factors to consider were whether there would be violent retaliation against those joining the NAACP, and whether there was enough community support to sustain a branch.

The potential for vigilante-style violence against blacks openly pushing for racial equality was very real. Those perceived to be too ambitious, independent, and outwardly supportive of racial equality were viewed as uppity, impudent, and a grave threat to the racial status quo.[26] Joining the NAACP, which at the time was considered a radical organization, was cause for alarm among many southern whites who viewed the Association with disdain. Organizing and maintaining a branch further intensified the increasingly hostile racial climate that existed in many southern towns and cities.[27]

Throughout much of the South during the period of World War I, branches of the NAACP were formed, but often quickly became defunct as they were incapable of maintaining active paying membership, and furthermore faced both threatened and actual violence at the hands of local Ku Klux Klan members. The fact that these branches were unable to maintain their viability no doubt impacted upon the ability of blacks living in rural areas such as Falls Church to gain approval for the creation of new chapters.[28] Secretary Nerney informed Henderson that the NAACP was willing to affiliate with the CCPL and establish a local branch if there was enough interest and support among the black citizens of Falls Church. Before the CCPL was granted permission to create a branch they would have to demonstrate their capacity to meet the guidelines established by the national office, which included "the ability to maintain a minimum level of fifty members, to pay an apportionment of at least $50.00, and to carry out a program of activities against racial injustice."[29] Ultimately, branch members served as the eyes, ears, and arms of racial justice in the communities in which they resided. It would be three years after their initial request for affiliation before the Falls Church branch was established. The CCPL was allowed to establish a branch with a membership roster of only thirty-five due to the small number of black residents there.[30]

The passage of the Falls Church Segregation Act served as the backdrop for the formation of the first rural branch of the NAACP in Virginia, located in the community of Tinner Hill in Falls Church. The history of the creation of this branch and the challenges facing the small rural community mirrored those faced by other rural communities in Virginia. Falls Church had a decided advantage over other rural communities in the state because of its progressive and educated black community and its proximity to Washington, D.C. At the same time, color-coded obstacles in the form of Jim Crow laws and practices existed regardless of geographic location within the state. This small community's effort to protest local residential segregation highlights the strength of local activism, while also demonstrating the important role that the NAACP as a national entity played in providing information and protest tactics to African Americans living in rural communities.[31]

In its early years the NAACP strategy for dealing with segregation was the use of test cases as a method of establishing legal precedents.[32] Those living in communities like Falls Church sought information about the outcome of these cases in planning their local protest strategies. Furthermore, they often took their cue from NAACP practices when seeking legal council involving cases that would appear before the local courts.

The year 1915 was important in the civil rights history of Falls Church; more important, on a national level, it was the year that the NAACP instigated a residential segregation case, *Buchanan v. Warley*. This case was touted as the most important civil rights case since the Supreme Court upheld the doctrine of separate but equal in the 1896 *Plessy v. Ferguson* decision. The *Plessy* case all but rendered the Fourteenth Amendment's equal protection clause null and void, thus opening the window of opportunity for more restrictive Jim Crow laws.[33] The *Buchanan v. Warley* case would eventually be heard and decided in the Supreme Court as part of a companion case that included *Harris v. The City of Louisville*. Together these lawsuits served as the NAACP's test case against residential segregation. The circumstances surrounding both cases bore remarkable resemblance to the situation in Falls Church. In both the *Harris* and *Buchanan* cases segregation ordinances were used to restrict black residency to designated spaces. Higginbotham summarizes the Buchanan case in this way:

> Warley, the local president of the NAACP, agreed to buy land on a white block from Buchanan, a white real estate broker who was sympathetic to blacks' efforts to attain equal rights. The terms of the Buchanan-Warley contract stipulated that Warley did not have to deliver the purchase price until he had the right under local, state and federal law to occupy his property as a residence. When Buchanan sought specific performance of the contract, Warley raised the Louisville ordinance as his defense and Buchanan brought suit. The trial court ruled that the Louisville segregation ordinance was invalid and Warley appealed. In reversing the lower court, the Kentucky Court of Appeals in *Harris v. City of Louisville* and *Buchanan v. Warley* upheld the housing segregation legislation and set the stage for the United States Supreme Court to ultimately consider the validity of such racial housing segregation ordinances. The NAACP previously had endeavored to defeat such ordinances in other cities with relatively little success.[34]

While the *Buchanan* decision did not end residential segregation it was no longer sustained by legislative support. Thus future attempts at government sanctioned housing segregation were declared uncon-stitutional if they managed to reach the court.[35]

On January 18, 1915, Edwin Henderson and Joseph Tinner gathered together many of their neighbors—the Costners, Richards, Brices, Powells, Comptons, Pearsons, Carvers, Edwards, Ewings, Joneses, Simmons, Evans, and Carpenters—to hold the first meeting to decide the course of action to be pursued in response to the town's segregation ordinance. A few days later the CCPL led by Joseph Tinner and Edwin Henderson presented the town council with the league's objections to the ordinance. The council did not issue a formal reply but instead passed legislation strengthening the ordinance. The Colored Citizens Protective League used a variety of strategies to fight residential segre-gation in Falls Church. They wrote letters, posted commentary in local papers, appealed to their fellow white citizens in Falls Church, and even-tually sought assistance from the NAACP. It was the belief of Henderson and Tinner, based on conversations with members of their community, that many white residents in Falls Church did not support the segrega-tion ordinance. They therefore gathered the signatures of white citizens willing to sign a petition against the ordinance. They focused their atten-tion on the business community since many local businesses relied heav-ily on the patronage of black citizens.[36]

Realizing that their appeals were being ignored, on June 29, 1915, the CCPL retained the services of District of Columbia attorney T. L. Jones. A suit was filed against the Town of Falls Church. When the case came before the circuit court judge in Fairfax County, he ruled against the town council. In October 1915 council members hired attorney William Ellison to represent their interests. Similar cases were appear-ing in courts throughout Virginia. Eventually the state supreme court weighed in with its decision, ruling that state and local laws could be used to establish and enforce residential segregation.[37]

The efforts of the CCPL were met with threats of violence. Crosses were burned on the property of Henderson and another member of the CCPL. Henderson and Tinner regularly received threatening phone calls and letters like the one below:

> Some night when you are peacefully dreaming . . . of the charm-ing BABOONS you have been instructing, and sniffing in the

delightful odor exuding from their Bodies, you will be rudely awakened by GHOSTS . . . and after you have been gagged, you will be born to a tree nearby, tied, stripped and given thirty lashes on your ETHIOPIAN back, and left to be found by some passer-by. We are for law and order just so long as you aforesaid ETHIOPIANS behave, but when you thrust yourselves on your superiors, the white people, your doom is sealed. . . . A word to the wise is sufficient. [Signed K.K.K.][38]

The period 1915–1925 saw a Klan revival and its membership and activities increased throughout the South.[39] This Klan growth corresponded with the expansion of the NAACP. In Virginia, the heart of the Confederacy, racial tensions grew as blacks pushed for equality. In Fairfax County, in towns such as Falls Church, Ballston, Herndon, and Roslyn, the Klan carried out its ceremonies and initiations in public defiance of any attempts toward racial tolerance and cooperation.[40] In light of such strident resistance to black social, political, and legal equality, Tinner and Henderson eventually concluded that their strategies to end racial oppression must reflect the severity of the problem in their community. As they understood it, theirs was a local problem with national implications. They therefore sought the advice of black leaders with experience and national reputations.

In writing to Du Bois, Henderson hoped to link the CCPL with the NAACP, a strategy that would allow league members to utilize the resources of the national organization to fight their local battle. It was a natural progression for members of the Falls Church Colored Citizens Protective League to seek affiliation with the NAACP. Dr. Henderson was a longtime friend of W. E. B. Du Bois and, perhaps more than most other members of the CCPL, he was aware of the legal strategies used by the NAACP and believed that the best chance for resisting the segregation ordinance was to rely on the court system.[41]

Both Tinner and Henderson's affiliation with the Falls Church community was extensive, and their willingness to organize the protest in spite of potential danger came as no surprise. Joseph Tinner was a longtime resident of Falls Church. He was a stonemason whose skills were recognized and admired throughout Falls Church and the surrounding areas. During the course of his life Tinner managed to establish a successful business for himself and his family. He was responsible for the creation of many stone buildings in the area. His signature arch design was popular. He and his family thrived economically in Falls Church. After purchasing land in 1890, he built a home there that later became known as Tinner Hill. Tinner and his family worked hard to establish a sense of community and cooperation among local residents. They attended the local Methodist church and participated in community activities and events. When the segregation ordinance threatened to dismantle the progress that he and other blacks in Falls Church had made, Tinner began a crusade to end racial discrimination, particularly the kind that infringed upon the livelihood of black residents.[42]

Dr. Edwin B. Henderson was born in Washington, D.C., in 1883. He was keenly aware of the strained race relations in Falls Church because as a child he spent summers there with his grandmother, who owned a small farm and the general store. He therefore had a long-standing commitment to the town and its black residents. Early on he developed an interest in political and social matters. He found the idea that social justice was denied to African Americans because of racial prejudice and bigotry reprehensible and was spurred into action by such matters.[43]

Henderson was also determined that the segregation legislation would not be used to circumscribe the progress of blacks in Falls Church. Prior to his involvement with the segregation ordinance of Falls Church, Henderson experienced firsthand the workings of Jim Crow laws that governed the town. When his father was forcibly removed from a railroad car in Falls Church for refusing to sit in the "negro" section on his way to work, Henderson, with the assistance of Jacob Deuteron (the local white attorney who was present at the time of his father's expulsion), filed a lawsuit in the Falls Church court against the offender. Henderson won the case, and as a result his father was awarded $20.00 plus legal costs.[44] Henderson would fight many more battles in Falls Church.

Even before the *Harris v. Louisville* or *Buchanan v. Warley* cases, the U.S. Supreme Court argued in *Holden v. Hardy* that "Property consists of the free use, enjoyment, and disposal of a person's acquisitions without control or diminution save by the law of the land." The *Holden* case provided local groups and organizations like the CCPL the legal foothold to challenge local residential segregation ordinances and laws.[45]

Enforcement of the segregation ordinance in Falls Church was set to begin January 15, 1916, but the day came and went without incident. The CCPL continued its efforts, circumventing the plans of the council to segregate the town. In November 1917 the United States Supreme Court ruled in *Buchanan v. Warley* that no state or municipality in the United States can create segregation districts. The CCPL managed through legal agitation to curtail efforts to enforce the segregation ordinance until it was no longer legal; however, the ordinance was not rescinded until February 22, 1999, when it was "officially denounced and repudiated."[46]

The CCPL demonstrated through its success in resisting the segregation ordinance that Falls Church had a viable black community—one that was tenacious in its quest for equality. When the league, under the penmanship of Henderson, wrote a letter to the NAACP national office in New York in May 1918 once again requesting the creation of a rural branch of the organization in Falls Church, the petition was approved. The application for charter, dated June 18, 1918, included the names of thirty-five black men and women from the town of Falls Church. Farmers, bricklayers, masons, contractors, ministers, janitors, and a hairdresser were among the first members. Each member paid a one-dollar membership fee, and on July 23, 1918, Falls Church became the first rural branch of the NAACP with Joseph Tinner as its first president and Edwin Henderson as the first secretary.[47]

At the turn of the twentieth century blacks all across America struggled to achieve racial equality and the benefits of full citizenship. Those living in small towns and rural areas like Falls Church faced particular challenges such as active Klan membership within the community and small black populations. The NAACP served as the model for protesting segregation legislation in education, schools, and housing. While black community members in towns like Falls Church relied on the NAACP for information and advice regarding strategies and approaches to combating segregation legislation, it would ultimately fall on the local citizens to protect their economic, social, educational, and political interests within their communities. The NAACP did not have all the answers, but what they offered was a well-educated and informed collective who understood the larger fight for civil rights at the national level and the importance of local cases involving civil rights issues.[48]

The work done by black leaders and community activists in rural towns and communities like Falls Church became the testing ground for other civil rights cases that would gain national attention. In the larger narrative of civil rights history and the NAACP, the segregation ordinance that prompted the black citizens of Falls Church to protest may, at first glance, seem insignificant. Yet it was in this small community that local black leaders were able to establish the first rural branch of the NAACP. After three long years of regular correspondence with the NAACP, the members of the CCPL were finally able to convince the Association that there was sufficient community support to sustain a branch, and furthermore that its members were able to launch and sustain a local protest movement. Members of the CCPL were able to garner support against the segregation ordinance from virtually all levels of the economic spectrum within the black community. The idea of allowing themselves to be corraled into all black districts did not sit well with the black people of Falls Church. They recognized the segregation legislation for what it was: an attempt to turn back the clock on civil rights gains made in the past. Furthermore, they understood that silence and acceptance of the residential segregation ordinance would not only result in segregated housing, but would also impact on public transportation, schools, and other facilities.

Members of the CCPL could proudly proclaim that through their concerted efforts they were able to peacefully stave off the attempts of their local government to violate their civil rights. By the time of the Supreme Court decision in *Buchanan v. Warley* on November 5, 1917, residential segregation had been the law in Falls Church since June 1916, though never enforced, largely due to the efforts of the CCPL. The Supreme Court's decision, of course, nullified the law, but it was not until the late 1990s that the antiquated law was rescinded.

In 1997 community organizers began preserving the activist legacy of Joseph Tinner, Edwin Henderson, and other members of the Falls Church community who fought for civil rights. In 1997 they created the Tinner Hill Heritage Foundation, an organization dedicated to the preservation of civil rights history in Falls Church. Through the work of community activists and local and state leaders, efforts began to create a cultural center to house artifacts, memorabilia, oral history interviews, letters, and other items pertinent to the struggle for racial equality in Falls Church. Every year during the month of June members of the entire Falls Church community come together in order to celebrate their history at the Tinner Hill Festival. They gather in the spirit of cooperation and understanding to remember the past and push forward into the future. Much has changed in Falls Church since the first rural branch of the NAACP was established in 1918, yet a commitment to social equality remains a strong legacy among the residents who live there today.

CHAPTER EIGHT

"To Hope Till Hope Creates"

The NAACP in Alabama, 1913–1945

KEVERN VERNEY

O N THE EVE of the First World War Alabama hardly constituted the most fertile soil for the growth of the early NAACP. A Deep South location and a record of racial violence and discrimination that was matched by few other former Confederate states were formidable obstacles to the organization of branches of the Association. Added to this, Alabama was the adopted home state of the legendary race leader and educator Booker T. Washington, who viewed the Association less as an ally in the struggle against racial injustice than as a rival seeking to undermine his teachings and hard-won personal status.

Nonetheless in 1913 it was in Talladega, fifty miles from Birmingham in the north-central area of the state, that one of the earliest branches of the NAACP in the South was formed. A seemingly unlikely location for such a pioneering initiative the organization of the branch reflected the influence of Talladega College, a black educational institution founded in 1867 by ex-slaves with the support of the Freedmen's Bureau. The college stressed a traditional academic curriculum as opposed to the industrial education associated with Booker T. Washington. William Pickens, the future NAACP field secretary, also worked as an instructor at Talledega from 1904. Typically, Pickens's departure from the institution in 1914 was in part a result of the machinations of Washington, who viewed him as a dangerous demagogue.[1]

The death of the "Wizard of Tuskegee" in 1915, combined with the heightened expectations of African American communities of an improvement in U.S. race relations at the end of the First World War, doubtless contributed to the establishment of NAACP chapters at Montgomery and Selma in 1918, followed by another seven branches in 1919, at Birmingham, Mobile, Ensley, Uniontown, Blocton, Anniston, and Tuscaloosa. During the 1920s the organization of further new branches at Gadsden (1921), Florence (1923), Decatur (1926), and Greensboro (1927) would appear to suggest a gradual consolidation and expansion of NAACP organization in the state.[2]

The reality was more depressing. Established in an initial wave of optimism most of the new branches collapsed within two to three years. In 1919 Tuscaloosa thus boasted 281 members and contributed $176.20 in funds to the NAACP national office in New York. The same year Mobile was able to claim 104 members and contributed $51.00 while Blocton, with 66 members, and Emsley, with 61 members, contributed $32.50 and $30.50, respectively. In 1924 all four branches had their charters revoked, the sanction most commonly applied by the national office in respect to branches that failed to provide annual reports, membership fees, or to respond to repeated requests for information. By 1928–1929 the national office recognized only five branches in the entire state as still being active, at Mobile, Montgomery, Decatur, Selma, and Birmingham. The income from branch memberships received by the New York secretariat in 1928 amounted to just $299.51, of which $239.00 came from Mobile alone.[3]

There were a number of reasons for this dramatic decline. In 1916 the first Amenia conference in New York brought about a reconciliation between the NAACP and supporters of Booker T. Washington. This, combined with the collapse of the Tuskegee machine between 1915 and 1925 and the appointment of former Washingtonian James Weldon Johnson as NAACP secretary in 1920, cleared the way for the expansion of the Association at a national level. In Alabama the situation was different. The interwar years saw improved relations between the national NAACP leadership and Tuskegee Institute when first Robert Russa Moton and later Frederick Patterson succeeded Booker T. Washington as heads of the academic institution. At the same time a sense of mutual distrust continued, reinforced by periodic strains and stresses.

In 1921 the NAACP thus opposed the efforts of Moton to secure the establishment of a segregated hospital for African American war veterans at Tuskegee. When this opposition proved ineffective the Association and the Institute temporarily joined forces to resist a campaign by local whites to ensure the most lucrative jobs at the hospital were reserved for whites, but the truce did not last. In 1924 Moton broke an understanding with the Association to insist on an exclusively African American medical and nursing staff by supporting a compromise settlement by which a small number of white doctors remained in post. The affair soured relations between the NAACP and Tuskegee with the fourteenth annual NAACP report in 1924 claiming that "final victory" in the struggle had been lost as a result of the action of the heads of the Institute.[4] During the 1920s and 1930s the influence of Tuskegee staff helped to discourage the organization of NAACP branches within the state, most particularly in the Montgomery region where the Institute was located.

The Association also suffered from self-inflicted injuries. The recent historiography of the mid-twentieth-century black civil rights struggle has increasingly highlighted the importance of class divisions within African American communities. There has been a tendency to perceive local NAACP branches as being overly cautious and conservative, reflecting middle class anxieties and concerns rather than the aspirations of African American communities as a whole. This has particularly been the case with Alabama.

In his acclaimed study of Alabama communists during the Great Depression Robin D. G. Kelley thus noted that as early as the 1920s NAACP branches in the state declined in part because "the Association's local leadership ignored the problems black working people faced daily." In Birmingham the branch agenda "focused more on the city's black business interests than on racial violence, the denial of civil liberties, and the immediate problems confronting the poor." Consequently, during the 1930s the Communist Party in the state appealed to African Americans because it provided "a working-class alternative to the NAACP."[5] In similar vein Andrew Manis concluded that the outlawing of the NAACP in Alabama between 1956 and 1964, because of the refusal of the NAACP to obey a legal injunction to disclose its membership lists, may have been a disaster for the Association but in a wider context it actually aided the civil rights struggle in Birmingham. The elimination of the NAACP branch in the Magic City cleared the way for the emergence of Reverend Fred Shuttlesworth's Alabama Christian Movement for Human Rights (ACMHR), a more radical working-class-based protest organization.[6]

Albeit harsh, such judgments contain more than an element of truth. Reporting on a visit to Birmingham as early as November 1921 the NAACP national director of branches Robert W. Bagnall bemoaned the fact that the city's 65,000-strong African American community was poorly organized because although the "masses are bold" their leadership was "most timid," despite the fact that "they deny more privileges here than in most places." In particular, "there are a number of cringing servile Negro leaders who are a menace here, and they intimidate and hold back the others."[7]

At the same time, it is easy to place too great an emphasis on the importance of class divisions. The restraining influence of Tuskegee Institute and conservative local leaderships may not have helped the cause of the NAACP but they were only contributory factors to the woes experienced by the Association. More than anything else it was the violent and unrelenting oppression of African American communities by city and state authorities, as well as vigilante organizations, that made NAACP organization in Alabama so difficult during the 1920s. The experience of W. E. Morton, the NAACP branch secretary in Mobile, highlighted the pressures on local Association officials. In May 1921 Morton, a blacksmith, was arrested by a local sheriff and taken to the jailhouse where he was interrogated about the NAACP while a white mob gathered outside. Warned to flee the county on pain of death he was forced to pay a $250.00 fine for incitement to riot to secure his release. Morton left Mobile in 1922 and the local NAACP branch folded.[8]

Writing from the safe environs of the Association's national office in New York it was easy for Robert Bagnall to criticize Birmingham's leadership for excessive timidity. For African Americans who actually lived and worked there the outlook was rather different. In the early 1920s the Magic City became a center of activity for the revived Ku Klux Klan in Alabama. In May 1922 Dr. Charles A. J. MacPherson, NAACP branch secretary in the city, reported that one or two Klan outrages were occurring in Birmingham every week. Moreover, white police officers routinely terrorized the black community to the point where it became an "almost weekly occurance for some Negro to be unmercifully beaten up and killed in this manner. We are helpless and powerless to do anything to change the condition."[9] At the time of its formation in 1919 the Birmingham branch of the NAACP had achieved 985 members and returned $572.65 in membership fees to the national office. Not surprising, by 1924 this had collapsed to just three members and a return of $6.50. By the end of the decade things, if anything, seemed to be even worse. In 1928 McPherson concluded that "general conditions" in Birmingham "so far as Negroes are concerned are deplorable and almost unbearable at times." Reporting on the condition of the local NAACP branch the following year he noted simply that it was "not functioning at all. Birmingham is almost next to impossible when it comes to movements such as the NAACP."[10]

The climate of fear in Alabama during the 1920s was such that in the three most important NAACP branches in the state the work of the Association was kept alive largely as a result of the courage and determination of just three individuals. In Montgomery William G. Porter, a postal worker, combined the offices of secretary and treasurer for most of the 1920s and was still a leading figure in the branch at the end of the Second World War.[11]

In Birmingham Dr. Charles McPherson effectively acted as branch president, secretary and treasurer throughout the 1920s. Born in rural east Alabama in the early post-Reconstruction era McPherson's parents were both teachers who taught in the same schools in which they gained their education. Encouraged by them McPherson went on to study at Atlanta Baptist College in 1897 followed by a course in Classics at Clark University in Atlanta in 1909 before training at Meharry Medical College in Nashville, Tennessee. After qualifying as a doctor, in 1917, he returned to Alabama and established a practice in Birmingham. In 1932 he was awarded the Madame C. J. Walker Gold Medal, an award made annually by the Walker Company to the individual adjudged to have performed outstanding service through the NAACP. He was praised for having shown "exceptional loyalty, devotion and courage in the face of the prejudice, handicaps, and plain dangers of a southern city." McPherson continued to serve as secretary of the Birmingham NAACP during the 1930s and 1940s. Killed in an automobile accident in 1948 he sadly did not live to see the civil rights advances of the 1950s and 1960s. At his funeral service the presiding minister, Dr. H. B. Gibson of St. Paul's Methodist Church, Birmingham aptly noted that McPherson had "held the NAACP together until the rest could wake up to its challenge. He spoke when others were afraid to speak."[12]

In Mobile postal worker John L. LeFlore and insurance manager Wiley Bolden revived the defunct local NAACP branch in 1926. In comparison to its predecessor the new branch was overwhelmingly middle class. In 1919 over half of the forty-nine founding members listed in the application for a branch charter were employed in working-class jobs, such as laborer, plasterer, maid, and car repairer. In the 1926 charter application almost all of the fifty new members had middle-class backgrounds, including twelve postal workers, five insurance workers, three teachers, two dentists, two undertakers, and a physician.[13] Ultimately however, what mattered was not the socioeconomic composition of the new branch but the fact that it endured, whereas its working-class forerunner did not. In the racial climate of 1920s Alabama mere survival was an achievement in itself. The Mobile branch not only succeeded in this objective but in the 1930s and 1940s went on to become one of the most important NAACP branches in the entire South.

This accomplishment owed much to the courage and determination of John L. LeFlore. In terms of the local African American community LeFlore's employment as a letter carrier represented secure middle-class employment, but this concealed a hard early life. Born in Mobile in 1903 LeFlore's father died when he was only nine months old. His mother, Clara, worked hard as a laundress but struggled to support her five children on her wages. Consequently at just five years of age LeFlore took a job selling newspapers to help supplement the family income. His determination to fight racial injustice was influenced by two personal experiences in early adult life. In the first of these, around 1920, he was arrested and imprisoned for refusing to give up his seat to a white passenger on a Mobile streetcar. Two or three years later, in transit to and from a vacation in St Louis, LeFlore and his pregnant wife, Teah, were denied the right to eat in the railway dining car.[14]

Secretary of the Mobile NAACP from 1926 through to the mid-

1950s, LeFlore was clearly the driving force within the branch through-out this period. Undaunted by the outlawing of the NAACP in Alabama in 1956 LeFlore went on to found a new civil rights organization, the Non-Partisan Voters League. Questioning aspiring political officeholders on their views on civil rights issues the league gained considerable influence by distributing fliers, the "pink lists," to African American voters in the city, informing them of the candidates that it recommended. In 1974 LeFlore was elected to the state house of representatives, a position he held until his death in 1976. A committed civil rights campaigner for half a century, LeFlore remains one of the most unjustly neglected figures in the historiography of the twentieth-century black freedom struggle.[15]

Barely able to survive as an organization in the 1920s, during the 1930s the NAACP in Alabama experienced a significant revival in its fortunes. In 1929 the Association had just 275 branch members in the state, a figure that had expanded to 1,784 by 1939.[16] In addition to increasing numerical strength the leading NAACP branches also displayed signs of being more effective in challenging racial injustice, including economic inequalities.

Between 1931 and 1934 the Birmingham branch grew in strength as a result of its involvement in the Willie Peterson case. A "penniless and consumptive Negro" convicted of the double murder of two white women "of which even the jailer and sheriff" did not believe him guilty, Peterson became a rallying point for the city NAACP. By July 1933 a local citizens committee led by branch secretary Charles McPherson had raised $2,475 toward the cost of Peterson's defense. A further $500 was contributed by the Association's national office, which sought to promote the case as the "NAACP's Scottsboro." The campaign achieved partial success in 1934 when Peterson's death sentence was commuted to life imprisonment, though he died in jail only a few years later.[17]

In other initiatives the city branch drafted over one hundred petitions against police brutality in Birmingham and submitted protests against racial discrimination in housing to the city Commission on Interracial Cooperation on Slum Clearance. The branch also campaigned for the creation of a new high school and distributed regular press releases to local newspapers setting out the views of the

Association. In 1935 and 1936 visits by Daisy Lampkin and Juanita Jackson from the Association's national office prompted the formation of a women's auxiliary of the local branch and an NAACP Youth Council in the city. In 1936 the branch also made protests to New Deal officials in Washington about African American women employed in Works Progress Administration projects in the city being compelled to wear heavy overalls and engage in arduous manual labor. By May 1939 paid-up memberships in the city NAACP had risen to 801.[18] Although the tangible gains achieved by the branch over the course of the decade were modest it was nonetheless a major advance on the situation in 1928, when by Secretary McPherson's own admission the branch officers that year did nothing, held no meetings, and sent no memberships, "not even their own."[19]

Inspired by the tireless LeFlore the Mobile NAACP also grew in strength and confidence during the 1930s. In 1931 the branch hosted a visit by African American congressman Oscar DePriest of New York to Mobile, despite the opposition of some conservative black clergy in the city.[20] In 1934 the branch began a sustained campaign against segregation and discrimination on the railways, reflecting Mobile's status as a major railroad terminal in the South. By the end of the decade this had resulted in the desegregation of Pullman dining cars in eight railroad companies that operated in the region. In 1936 the Mobile NAACP initiated an investigation of employment discrimination in the postal service.[21] The same year LeFlore initiated the organization of a Regional Conference of Southern Branches of the Association. First meeting in Mobile on April 25–26 the conference included representatives from NAACP branches in Alabama, Florida, Georgia, Louisiana, and Mississippi. The following year the conference issued a seven-point program to fight against educational inequalities, discrimination on the railroads and in employment, the Democratic Party white primary, police brutality, crime levels within the African American community, and lynching.[22]

In the three leading cities of Alabama it was only in Montgomery that the NAACP struggled to develop an effective organization during the 1930s. In part this may have reflected the continuing negative influence of nearby Tuskegee Institute. NAACP organization in the city also continued to be overly dependent on W. E. Porter, who by the

1930s was appearing to show signs of mental and nervous strain. Porter's belief that he was being targeted for persecution was perhaps more realistic than paranoid. Doubtless there *were* members of Montgomery's white community who were out to get him. However, Porter's perceptions of the forms such persecution might take were, at times, less plausible, most notably his belief that a white doctor was attempting to kill him by the strategic planting of germs.[23]

Despite some problems, either real or imagined, by the end of the 1930s even Montgomery experienced an NAACP revival. The catalyst for this, as in Birmingham, was the coming together of the city's African American community to oppose a blatant miscarriage of justice. In 1938 Dave Canty, a twenty-three-year-old African American, was convicted of murdering a white nurse, despite the fact that the evidence against him rested largely on what appeared to be a confession extracted by use of torture. Although Canty's conviction was overturned by the U.S. Supreme Court he was later retried and sentenced to life imprisonment in Alabama. The Canty case prompted a rebirth of the Montgomery NAACP following a visit by Association leaders from Birmingham. By 1940 the city branch had recruited almost one thousand members.[24]

The NAACP revival in Alabama during the 1930s can be attributed to a number of factors. Nationally the decline of the Ku Klux Klan at the end of the 1920s made the climate of race relations a little less oppressive, even though the Invisible Empire still retained much of its strength in Alabama.[25] This trend was reinforced by the comparatively more enlightened attitudes of the Roosevelt administration on civil rights. Moreover, the impact of the Great Depression and New Deal programs encouraged NAACP branches to place greater emphasis on bread-and-butter economic issues, making the Association more relevant to the daily lives of the majority of African Americans in the state. This greater working-class appeal was further enhanced by a 1938 decision of the Communist Party in Alabama to encourage its members to join the NAACP.[26]

It may also be the case, as Dorothy Autrey has argued, that the NAACP leadership in the state experienced generational change. A number of younger leaders, born in the late nineteenth and early twentieth century, and less conservative than their predecessors, began to emerge.[27] These included John L. LeFlore, the driving force behind the Mobile NAACP and Dr. Earnest Taggart, who became president of the Birmingham branch in 1935. An "energetic social minded dentist," Taggart was viewed as something of a radical by the NAACP's national office. In December 1935 Walter White, the Association's national secretary, thus noted that Taggart's views could be judged by the fact that "for some time" he "was sharply critical of the NAACP because it was not 'more militant' and definitely inclined towards the ILD" (International Labor Defense), the communist-backed organization that supplanted the NAACP as legal counsel in the infamous Scottsboro case.[28]

During the Second World War the Alabama NAACP continued to grow in strength. In 1940 there were eight branches of the Association in the state with a total of 1,717 members. In 1945 there were sixteen branches and 7,244 members, and by 1946 this had risen still further to 25 branches and 14,244 members. Particularly encouraging was the fact that around 60 percent of the new branches were in small towns with a population of fewer than 10,000, suggesting that the organization of the Association was taking root across the state rather than being confined to a few strongholds. At the same time established branches also experienced a sharp rise in membership. The Mobile NAACP thus grew from just a few hundred members in the late 1930s to more than 1,500 by 1944. In Birmingham membership rocketed from 1,010 in 1940 to 8,500 by 1946.[29]

The situation in Alabama reflected the wider experience of the NAACP during the war. In this period the numerical strength of the Association nationally grew from 50,000 members in 1940 to around 500,000 members in 1946.[30] This would suggest that the expansion of the NAACP in Alabama was, at least in part, the result of broader changes in social and political attitudes across the United States. The struggle against the extremes of Nazi racial ideology encouraged black Americans to hope for an improvement in race relations within the United States when the conflict was over. The war years were also marked by the emergence of a heightened civil rights consciousness in African American communities across the nation.

There were also signs of change for the better within the NAACP national office. Traditionally the New York headquarters of the Association had tended to view its local branches as "milk cows" that existed primarily for the purpose of raising funds for centrally directed national campaigns. During the war years there appears to have been some overdue, albeit still tentative, moves toward greater sensitivity. Ella Baker, who was hired as an assistant field secretary in the New York office in December 1940, recalled that it was "a period when there [were] young people who were joining the staff and who were demanding certain kinds of opening up, which meant primarily going down and working with people, not just having a great big mass meeting and collecting the membership."[31]

Committed to the need for greater autonomy and leadership in local branches, as opposed to control by the national office, Baker made Birmingham a testing ground for the introduction of her new philosophy. After making the city the target for her first fieldwork campaign in her own right in 1941 she followed this up by supporting the creation of new "neighborhood units" there in 1942. These acted as extensions of the city branch with their own chairmen and committees. Although they were not involved in policy making the creation of the new units was still a significant development. It meant that, as Baker explained, "you have more people participating in branch work and you are able to contact more persons who perhaps will never get to the general branch meeting but will attend little neighborhood meetings."[32]

Baker's initiative was one of many developments in Alabama that helped boost the strength of the Association in the state. The location for a number of military bases, Alabama experienced an influx of African American servicemen during the war years. Perhaps the best known of these was the famous Tuskegee air base established for the training of black pilots, the presence of which was a key factor in the formation of the first Tuskegee branch of the NAACP in 1944. This advance was somewhat ironic given that the controversy surrounding the existence of the base had marked another low point in the troubled relations between the NAACP national office and the Tuskegee Institute.

In 1941 Frederick Patterson, president of the institute, had vigorously lobbied the War Department for Tuskegee to be selected as the site for the training of black aviators. In contrast the national leadership of the NAACP was strongly opposed to the initiative on grounds of principle, because whatever the location the training provided would be on a segregated basis.[33] The Association's hostility continued undiminished even after the camp had opened. In March 1943 Walter White donated $5.00 to the fund for the erection of the Moton Memorial Gates at the base, but he made it clear that this was solely a mark of his respect for the late Tusgekee principal Dr. Robert Russa Moton. His donation was "not in any way an expression of approval of the segregated Army Primary Flying Field to which the gates give entrance."[34]

The presence of military bases in Alabama clearly constituted a source of potential new members for the NAACP. Recurring conflicts and tensions between African American servicemen and both the military authorities and civilian communities also highlighted the need for an effective local Association organization. In 1942 the NAACP investigated an incident near Tuskegee in which an African American army nurse, Nora Green, was badly beaten and then put in jail by a white policeman. The case was closed when Green was persuaded to drop all charges against the officer in return for an agreement that no further legal action would be taken against her. The army sought to conceal all details of the incident and quickly assigned Green to service overseas.[35] In 1945 reports of the ill treatment of African American servicemen in a military base near Ozark acted as a catalyst for the formation of an NAACP branch in the town.[36]

The worst problems appear to have been at the Brookley Field military base near Mobile. In August 1942 John LeFlore convened an NAACP mass meeting in the local African American community following the murder of a black serviceman stationed at the base, Henry Williams, by a Mobile bus driver. The killing marked the culmination of a series of racial incidents on city bus routes. In an initiative that bore striking similarities to the more-celebrated Montgomery protest thirteen years later Le Flore threatened a bus boycott campaign unless the principal demands made at the meeting were met. These included provisions requiring the immediate disarming of all bus drivers, the employment of African American drivers on predominantly black routes, and a requirement that drivers be required to show equal courtesy to all passengers regardless of race. The situation was defused when the bus company agreed to meet most of these conditions and the threatened boycott was called off.[37]

The peaceful resolution of the 1942 incident notwithstanding, the presence of the Brookley base continued to be a source of racial tensions for the remainder of the war. In 1944 Le Flore reported to the NAACP national office on the "deplorable conditions" endured by African American servicemen at Brookley Field and also wrote letters of complaint to the War Department. The state of affairs at the base became so bad that in one confrontation a gunfight broke out between some thirty African American soldiers and white military police officers. The military authorities hastily intervened to hush up the details of the affair.[38]

The planned bus boycott of 1942 reflected the fact that the NAACP branch in Mobile became increasingly active in areas of concern to the wider black community in this period, including labor-related issues. In 1941 Roosevelt's executive order 8802, creating a federal Fair Employment Practices Committee to counter racial discrimination in the defense industries, ensured that in Alabama, as elsewhere, there was a continuing focus by the NAACP on employment-related issues, despite the winding up of New Deal agencies at the end of the 1930s.

This was particularly the case in Mobile, which became a national center for shipbuilding, holding more than $100 million in defense contracts during the war years, as the city's population rose from 78,720 in 1940 to 125,000 by 1943. Although whites made up most of the newcomers Mobile's black population also rose sharply, from 29,000 in 1940 to around 45,000 by 1950. The local Alabama Dry Dock and Shipbuilding Company grew from being a struggling yard with fewer than 1,000 workers to a major war production plant with a workforce of some 30,000, which included some 7,000 African Americans.[39] This inevitably resulted in racial tensions, even though all the black workers were employed as unskilled labor. In 1941 an unsuccessful Klan-inspired strike at the yard sought to expel all African American employees. In May 1943 the company's upgrading of twelve black workers to welding jobs, in compliance with an FEPC directive, led to a riot at the plant with white employees attacking black coworkers. John LeFlore, as the leading NAACP spokesperson in Mobile, inevitably became involved in such disputes, both as a local mediator and as a reporter for the Association's head office.[40] The expansion of the shipyard also created racial tensions elsewhere in the city, such as in the lack of suitable housing for incoming workers and incidents between whites and blacks on the city's overcrowded public transportation system, particularly on overcrowded buses taking employees of both races to and from work. NAACP intervention in such issues meant that during the war years the local branch of the Association became more actively involved with the daily problems of black workers in the city than had been the case during the 1930s.

There were similar developments elsewhere in the state. In August and September 1941 an investigation by Norman Thomas, president of the Tri-Cities branch of the Association, into discriminatory hiring practices at the Electric Metallurgical Company in Sheffield, Alabama, prompted an FEPC inquiry.[41] In March the same year a protest by the Birmingham NAACP branch at working conditions at the Ingall iron works in the city helped to bring about a new union deal with the management of the plant that brought improvements in wages and job security for both white and black workers.[42]

In May 1941 the Birmingham NAACP was given the prestigious Thalheimer Prize, an annual award made by the Association to "the branch whose program has been most militant and outstanding during the year." In an NAACP press release accompanying the announcement Birmingham was praised for "the intelligent way in which the branch is meeting the challenge of the industrial South, for its splendid work regarding industrial disputes, as well as for its organized action in reducing police brutality" and its efforts in voter registration and increasing branch membership from 603 in 1938 to 1,088 in 1940.[43] By the end of the war even the more conservative Montgomery organization of the Association was showing signs of greater assertiveness following the appointment of Rosa Parks as branch secretary in 1943 and the election of E. D. Nixon as president in 1945.[44]

Unfortunately this growth in NAACP activity in Alabama between 1941 and 1945 was not sustained in the early postwar years. After reaching a peak of 14,244 in 1946 the number of NAACP members in the state had fallen to just 4,795 by 1950 and was still only 7,805 in 1955.[45] This decline can be attributed to a number of factors. In Alabama, as in the nation as a whole, the late 1940s arguably saw a falling away in the earlier levels of wartime optimism and civil rights consciousness that had built up in African American communities. A revival of Klan activity in the state in this period, most especially around Mobile, was a further deterrent to NAACP activity. The running down of the wartime defense industries after 1945 combined with a series of disappointing crop yields in the state provided economic disincentives to NAACP membership, a situation that was not helped by the 1949 decision of the Association's national office to double membership fees from $1.00 to $2.00 a year.[46]

Although motivated by financial need, this decision also reflected the continuing perception in the Association's national office that local branches were little more than sources of revenue. There was a reluctance to delegate responsibility down to the local level and too few staff employed in the New York office to oversee relations with branches. This meant that there were regularly excessive delays in responding to inquiries from local officers of the Association and even in dealing with routine matters, such as the sending out of copies of membership certificates. The changes in approach apparent at the time of Ella Baker's appointment in 1940 proved to be short-lived. Baker herself ended her period of employment in the Association's national office in 1946 disillusioned by the experience.[47]

From 1913 through to 1945 the NAACP in Alabama was marked by dramatic changes in fortune. These ranged from a low point in the mid- to late 1920s, when the organization of the Association in the state almost ceased to exist, through to a peak in the Second World War with the formation of a statewide network of branches and record membership levels. Throughout this period NAACP branches in the state were predominantly middle class but it is a moot point as to whether this should be viewed as a source of weakness.

During the 1920s the Association's flagship branches in the state only survived at all as the result of the courage and dedication of a few individuals, irrespective of their class background. In the period 1930 to 1945 the Association's local leaders remained overwhelmingly middle class, but at the same time they increasingly demonstrated an ability to organize campaigns of relevance to the wider African American community and attracted a larger working-class membership.

The failure to build on this success at the end of the war was more down to external factors—a decline in the wartime levels of optimism and civil rights consciousness in African American communities, police and Klan repression, and economic recession—than a result of class divisions within branches. Admittedly, the periodic claims made by spokespersons in the NAACP's New York office that branch officials in Alabama were timid and conservative were sometimes justified. At the same time the shortcomings in the relationships between the national office and local branches were not one sided. The deficiencies in branch management by the NAACP's New York headquarters were at least as much to blame for the weaknesses of the Association's organization at state level. "My view at the time was that the great weakness of the organization lay in its branch structure—New York didn't pay attention to the branches," national assistant secretary Roy Wilkins reflected on the situation in 1945. "The wartime boom came because enough people had been aroused and wanted to join—and they had the money to join. We had picked up a large membership with relatively small effort, but the situation in the future was bound to be different. Unless we took care of the membership it was sure to melt away." Despite this, at the end of the war, the Association "had only two field workers and a director of branches to handle half a million members; we had four or five major administrative departments and two offices outside New York City, but no real planning or coordination of the NAACP's policy and program." [48]

CHAPTER NINE

"It's Worth One Dollar to Get Rid of Us"

Middle-Class Persistence and the NAACP in Louisiana, 1915–1945

LEE SARTAIN

T HE NAACP HAS been primarily seen as a political and civil rights organization over the century of its existence and, indeed, it has had a remarkably consistent message of equality and integration. However, during the 1920s through to the war years the NAACP underwent an amount of soul searching as to whether it ought to broaden its remit to take into account the economic problems of African Americans in agriculture and industry, or whether to concentrate entirely on full participation in the political process. Various reports, such as the Harris Report, shows that the NAACP believed that it should broaden its appeal to address the economic conditions of the majority of black workers in America. While the NAACP remained by and large with its political message should not cause historians to overlook the fact that an attempt was made to add an economic dimension to its agenda and that its local branches were seen as being instrumental in contributing to this. However, the element that made most NAACP branches exist at all—namely, its middle-class membership—made the development of an economic program difficult to realize in the Deep South.[1]

The most remarkable aspect of the NAACP in Louisiana in the interwar period is that it actually existed at all, particularly outside of

New Orleans. In 1914 a local branch was formed in Shreveport, one of the first NAACP chapters in the Deep South. However, Shreveport was a Ku Klux Klan stronghold and the NAACP failed to survive this threat. The following year in New Orleans another branch emerged and became the longest continuing chapter in the South, although it did occasionally fall from the view of the New York office, who questioned whether it had ceased to exist for national purposes. Elsewhere in Louisiana from the 1920s NAACP branches emerged as small enclaves of enthusiastic supporters and fought the good fight often against improbable odds and the struggle to maintain membership numbers.[2]

A cursory examination of NAACP branch membership lists gives an immediate insight into who these Louisiana activists were. Those most responsive to the NAACP message of civic advancement were from the black elite who had some wealth and status and a tradition of organizing to promote community programs. Indeed the NAACP spoke a bureaucratic language that registered with the black middle classes and reflected their interests in local activism as a technical and professional endeavor. The NAACP was very similar to many of the organizations that they were already involved with, such as Masonic lodges and philanthropic organizations that reflected their professional organizing and their class and status interests, which they also assumed to be the interests of the broader black community.

The influential survey of the black American, *An American Dilemma,* by the Swedish sociologist, Gunnar Myrdal in the early 1940s, highlighted many issues that were to concern civil rights activists throughout the twentieth century, particularly class. While NAACP *Crisis* editor W. E. B. Du Bois had highlighted the issues of race and class and the struggle of being both black and an American, it was with Myrdal's study that white America heard of the wide cultural variations of black America in an academic manner:[3]

> The Negro upper class is most thoroughly assimilated into the national culture, but it is also isolated from the whites. They are the most race conscious. They provide the leadership and often almost the entire membership of the nationally established Negro defense organizations, such as the local branches of the N.A.A.C.P. But they sometimes feel great difficulty in identifying themselves with the Negro masses whose spokesmen they are, although, per-

haps, no more than the white upper class with the white lower class. Their social ambition is to keep up this distinction. In private they are often the severest critics of the Negro masses.[4]

Myrdal questioned the value of a black middle class organizing NAACP branches in the South. He saw such protest groups as having a purely symbolic role as black middle-class organizing was mainly a minimal act in a repressive environment, which could have little serious political impact. In turn such organizing maintained social distinctions in local communities and did little to address working-class and rural poor needs. Thus they forced their political and social agenda on the community as a whole and claimed to be uplifting the race toward greater aspects of group probity. This created unrealistic expectations of the black masses who were deemed inferior for simply not being middle class enough. The aspiration of integrating with white society was seen as a way of furthering black middle-class ambitions and the failure for not achieving this goal, and thus being accepted by white society, was firmly attributed to the moral and intellectual inferiority of the black masses who they believed tainted the entire race in white eyes. Indeed the Association was not interested in the restructuring of the economic system but in a widening of opportunities for black people in their educational and professional capacities and in securing political parity with whites.[5]

A genteel tradition emerged from the black middle classes in such places as New Orleans and Baton Rouge, which had acclimatized to the cultural norms, restraints, and social aspirations of Deep Southern communities. In this way a self-conscious conservatism kept them from identifying with the black masses. Isolated middle-class black groups saw the white American pattern of family life and conventional sexual mores and educational and professional achievement as a model to emulate. The perpetuation and extension of middle-class social and political life throughout all black communities was integral to the NAACP message. Such a dichotomy between leaders and the toiling masses was a simple way of dividing the black community that could make sense in the agricultural South. Indeed outside of New Orleans and Baton Rouge most of Louisiana was seen as a remote and dangerous "hinterland." The Crescent City's NAACP branch president Dr. George W. Lucas stated, "When . . . investigating a . . . case . . . in

New Orleans, I am as safe as I would be in New York. When [I] . . . go into the country, that is another matter. But . . . I go."[6]

In 1927 the director of branches, Robert Bagnall, writing to S. B. Smith of Monroe with regards to setting up a branch, advised that "active" members "may be male or female, white or colored," the only requirement being "that they believe in the principles of the Association." The central premise of such convictions was to procure "the full citizenship and manhood rights of the colored people." Georgia M. Johnson of the Alexandria NAACP branch principally saw this fight for black constitutional rights as an elitist one, that it was the job of a self-selecting social elite, or, in her words, "well thinking educated members of the branch," to work for the liberation of the entire black population. Johnson explained, "Action is paramount. Thinking is in order. Classes should think for the masses, but help by pulling them along and helping them find themselves in this great civilization."[7]

The manner in which NAACP members in Louisiana saw class divisions was exemplified by a short-lived newspaper printed by the New Orleans branch in 1918, the *Vindicator*. The paper gave local and national civil rights and social news that reflected the aspirations and prejudices of activists. The NAACP was "contending for the rights given you by the Constitution of the U.S.," and the exodus of black agricultural laborers from the South was, partly, due to the deprivation of these rights. This was explained in a fanciful evocation:

> The only way to check it is by making conditions in the South better. Not simply higher wages, but better treatment in every respect. The capital or stock in trade in the South consists mainly in her farms and great plantations and as a correlative value or capitol the labor it takes to operate these farms and plantations, the black man . . . [The NAACP] says give us a square deal, make the South fit for the black man to live in and we can honestly tell our people from the pulpit and from the platforms to remain in Dixie and make the cotton fields bloom and the cane fields wave, the factories roar and the gins and steamers whistle as the black man in contentment and satisfaction sings his cornfield songs and plantation melodies, in the balmy breezes of Dixie's Land and under Dixie's blue skies.[8]

This indicated vocational training for large sections of the African American community as, it was perceived, certain black families were not undertaking this important role: "Since the home and the farm and the shop no longer train the children efficiently, there must be a greater call upon the school to take up the work so cast off . . . The proper introduction of manual and industrial training . . . will be the means of keeping larger numbers of boys and girls in the school." By such "manual and industrial" training a true American work ethic could be instilled in the lower orders creating "prosperous and happy" people who were "intelligent, temperate, industrious, skillful, and constantly employed." This was basically Booker T. Washington's concept of industrial training to improve the lot of the African American community as a whole, albeit with political rights in the first instance securing the rights of the race in all other things.

The *Vindicator* became an organ for anti-German sentiment and extolled the virtues of African American wartime patriotism. It also traced the social scene of the Crescent City and detailed the comings and goings of its best citizens, invariably those in the NAACP, and asserted middle-class morality by calling for the suppression of saloons and prohibition of alcohol and eulogizing the sanctity of marriage. The newspaper struggled to reach a wide audience and ceased trading at the end of September 1918. Apparently, there was no mass interest in whether "Sir S. W. Green of New Orleans . . . is looking the picture of health" after his holiday or of being lectured to about working six days a week and keeping Sunday for religion.[9]

Business people were particularly well represented in Louisiana NAACP branches, such as in insurance, real estate, and undertaking that tended to cater exclusively to the black community. For example, Dr. P. H. Dejoie was an NAACP member, along with his wife, Ella Dejoie, who ran the Unity Industrial Life Insurance Company of New Orleans. The president of the company was C. C. Dejoie, whose family also owned the black newspaper *Louisiana Weekly*. Similarly, Mr. and Mrs. L. M. Johnson of Baton Rouge dealt in real estate and were members of the branch regularly from 1929, while undertakers Mr. and Mrs. L. E. Lamothe of Monroe were members from the branch's inception in 1928.[10]

The connection between the middle classes and NAACP membership was essential for a branch to survive in terms of membership numbers and monetary contributions. The Green family in New Orleans is a case in point of middle-class social and professional networking. Mr.

S. W. Green made his fortune as a New Orleans grocer and was president of the Liberty Independent Life Insurance Company. He became supreme chancellor of the Colored Knights of Pythias of the United States in 1908, organizing the building of a Pythian Temple in New Orleans at a cost of $225,000, and the state had nine thousand members and eighty-one lodges. Green was assistant secretary of the New Orleans NAACP in 1920 and on its executive committee throughout the interwar years. His wife was his general office manager and she paralleled her husband's fraternal affiliations as the first worthy counselor of the court of the women's auxiliary of the Knights of Pythias, the Star of Calanthe. Many NAACP meetings were held in the Pythian Temple, and Masonic financial donations kept the New Orleans branch in existence, as well as crossover membership between the groups.[11]

The lack of interest in joining the NAACP by the broader black community was often attributed to a lack of general organizational will. Mrs. D. J. Dupuy, a tireless civil rights activist in Baton Rouge, declared, "If more of our people would realize that just a little willing cooperation on their part would mean so much for our future living we could succeed in a large way. But we have to run the people down and then beg them to pay ... one dollar per year [membership fee] for justice and fairplay." Indeed the Baton Rouge branch president, Benjamin Stanley, reflected the perceived irritation of people accosted on the streets and on their doorsteps by determined NAACP members.[12]

"The fact that we have always responded liberally to calls from the home office and other branches may have given the impression that we have a numerically strong branch," he noted. In reality "we have about 15 or 20 active members. We collected membership from several people who show no interest in our work but give the dollar because we are persistent. It's worth one dollar to get rid of us ... Most people here are afraid to become identified with the N.A.A.C.P."[13]

While specific cases, such as the antilynching campaigns, seemed to cause a flurry of activity, in the canvassing of local people and soliciting funds, there seemed little sustained effort over time that might have created a long-term and popular support for civil rights. Indeed in 1935 the Baton Rouge branch held no mass meetings at all in the city.[14]

The need to take the message beyond the annual membership drive was vital for local NAACP chapters in building up support. This was a difficult task, as acknowledged by the national office when it observed that most members "do not feel inspired to take part in managing the Branch. It is good to get as many as possible out to the business meetings." Yet it was difficult to encourage participation, even of those registered as NAACP members, and public meetings did not always motivate an audience to join. For example, six hundred people, including a white judge of twenty-five years standing, attended the public meeting addressed by William Pickens, NAACP field secretary, in Monroe in May 1932, but the membership levels went below fifty for the first time since the branch's charter.[15]

Furthermore the problems that existed due to an elitist membership with a bureaucratic approach to civil rights meant that it was difficult to translate legal victories into populist achievements that people could comprehend as being meaningful to their everyday lives. Such a "paper victory" was the two-and-a-half-year struggle undertaken by the New Orleans NAACP branch through the legal system that saw the defeat of the residential segregation ordinance in the city. The difficulty of a complex and lengthy legal-oriented campaign was that it only required a minimal reliance upon mass support or a continually high public profile. Sustaining public excitement at this gradualist form of civil rights activism was difficult, and issues such as residential segregation were not a high priority for many black people who may have accepted living separately from potentially hostile whites.[16]

Other groups had much greater appeal to black working classes and agricultural workers in Louisiana. For example, the Universal Negro Improvement Association (UNIA) attracted members of the black community who were receptive to its black nationalism and uplifting racial and economic messages. Membership of the organization in Louisiana had spectacular highs in the 1920s and 1930s and had a distinctively working-class base, with New Orleans UNIA meetings regularly held at the Negro Longshoremen's Hall and at Baptist churches. Founded by Marcus Garvey in 1914 the UNIA was predicated on the ideas of self-help and black pride, including black Americans emigrating to Africa. Indeed the immediate contrast with Louisiana's NAACP chapters and membership is apparent. New Orleans was seen as a "Mecca for Garveyites" and during 1924 there was somewhere in the region of 3,000 members in New Orleans, whilst there were only 206 in the city's

NAACP branch. This included black labor groups, such as the International Longshoremen's Union, joining the UNIA. However, the NAACP only began to approach such unions for membership in the 1930s but with little success.[17]

The UNIA penetrated rural areas that the NAACP could not reach. In 1929 the UNIA had branches in isolated rural areas in Violet (124 members), Algiers (101), White Castle (150), Rosemount (164), and Lockport (192). During 1929 the NAACP could only muster 109 members in New Orleans, one of its main southern branches. Indeed the only other operational branch in the state that year, Baton Rouge, had a mere 67 members. The UNIA held less threat to local white power structures due to its presence as a racially separatist organization and attracted a working-class and rural poor membership base in Louisiana.[18]

The Great Depression, however, was an inescapable issue and the NAACP was forced to confront the possibility of having an economic agenda to make it relevant. Membership levels were affected by the economic downturn but, as in the 1920s, local Associations in Louisiana were sustained by the middle classes. Most of the members were professionals in relatively secure financial situations or were in federal jobs that gave them some security, such as teaching in black schools or the federal postal service. This contrasted sharply with the vast majority of the black population. In the early 1930s half of the southern urban population was on state and federal relief. In New Orleans blacks made up a third of the population yet one-half of them were unemployed, while two-thirds of families were on relief. In the rural areas of the state there were approximately 74,000 black farmers, but only 8,000 of them owned their own land. Meanwhile, white landlords diverted federal aid from their black tenants and kept it for their own purposes.[19]

Local branches had the ideal opportunity to reevaluate their role by lobbying the federal government to implement New Deal initiatives without discrimination. This would have meant that chapters would have had to enlarge their political remit to take on the economic and employment situation of a community. Yet the advent of the New Deal gave local NAACP chapters challenges that led to it being perceived as a bourgeois organization that ignored the situation of the black masses. Indeed the New Deal created a political climate that was suited to the NAACP's chosen strategies—namely, lobbying politicians and publicizing racial injustices. In short the NAACP advocated that politics was the way to attain civil rights and the increase in federal activity affirmed this preferred channel. Besides this broad agenda it would appear that many of Louisiana's urban black middle classes and NAACP members preferred the Republican Party over the New Deal coalition of Franklin D. Roosevelt, and were busy creating the Federation of Civic Leagues to assert black leadership in the state GOP during this period.[20]

However, the New York national office did encourage branches in 1930 to "consider" industrial conditions in their communities, although it did not suggest a next step for them to undertake to improve them. In 1933 Roy Wilkins, NAACP assistant executive secretary, advised a more detailed examination of employment in the regions, particularly relating to New Deal public works agencies, National Recovery Administration (NRA) violations, and the distribution of federal relief. The New Orleans branch looked tentatively into ways of advancing black interests in the Works Projects Administration (WPA) that was set up in response to the unemployment situation and, in this manner, widening access for blacks by government agencies rather than petitioning for specific help. However, this was always secondary to its more traditional NAACP work such as registering to vote.[21]

By 1935 the national office recommended that local branches work with "good unions" (definitely not communist groups) in its civil rights fight. However, union cooperation was a sporadic and sparsely pursued activity in the Louisiana branches. In Baton Rouge the national office had encouraged the Association of Colored Railway Trainmen to organize a branch, or at least to become members at large, but with little success. Similarly, on the insistence of the NAACP attorney Charles Houston, the New Orleans branch sought to procure the support of the International Longshoremen's Union to broaden its public appeal during 1936. By the end of 1937 the branch president, Dr. A. W. Brazier, consulted with the "officers and staff of the Negro Longshoremen's Union" and gained the impression that the 2,200 strong membership would join the city's NAACP. However, this consultation was under the auspices of national field officer William Pickens. The impetus appears to have been from the central Association, rather than initiatives from local officers.[22]

This failure to embrace an economic- or labor-oriented agenda during the 1930s could be seen as surprising considering the areas of industrialization in the state, such as Baton Rouge where oil and chemical factories were increasing the city's population and employment opportunities. It took until the Second World War before the branches in Louisiana embraced their wider role in the economic sphere, and then it tended to be with teachers' salary equalization, which could be seen as an extension of the NAACP educational policy and attacks on Jim Crow rather than a strictly economic agenda. Indeed most of the branches in the state continued their push for political and civil rights and assumed that further opportunities would follow once these were secured.[23]

An exception to this rule was the Louisiana Farm Tenant Security Project. This was an "agricultural infiltration" scheme "for the resettlement of destitute or low-income farm tenant families." The NAACP annual report explained: "In June 1938, colored people in the Transylvania Project were notified that their land, some of which they had occupied since the Civil War, would be allocated to white settlers and that the colored people would be assigned to land in Thomaston thirty miles away. There were about 250 Negro families in the community and more than $6,000 had been invested in a church and school. The colored people also had invested considerable money in improving their property." In 1938 the Transylvania NAACP branch was organized but was not successful in defending the black farmers and "the eviction of the Negro settlers was carried out." The best that the NAACP could do, mainly by instigation of the Washington, D.C., branch, was to mitigate the disaster by revision of the "terms of the removal." In this manner a settled black community was destroyed and NAACP branches were reacting to preserve a rural community from discriminatory implementation of New Deal policies by Louisiana's state officials.[24]

The Monroe branch did endeavor to initiate a strategy that was based on both political and economic rights during the 1930s. The branch had a "live and active Unemployment Committee," which, it claimed, was "doing some tangible work, by which the colored people here are greatly benefited." The actual details remain vague as to what the committee did and it seems either to have been an employment agency of sorts or merely a recording bureau. For example, the branch organized aid with regard to a flood in Ouachita Parish and documented subsequent peonage cases. The Baton Rouge branch had similar concerns for the black situation in agricultural areas: "Especially apropos is the Mississippi Flood Control project fight which we are waging. We are making every effort to get a thorough-going investigation of the exploitation of the Negroes employed in this project, both as to treatment and wages." After the Mississippi River broke its banks in 1927 black sharecroppers were in virtual peonage rebuilding flood controls. The NAACP nationally made propaganda from the fact that federal government organized work was discriminatory toward blacks. It was only in 1933 under the Public Works Administration that black laborers had their hours limited and acquired a wage increase.[25]

The Monroe branch's unemployment committee does not seem to have had a prolonged life and the chapter generally followed conventional NAACP campaigning, such as publicizing local racial injustices and raising funds. However, the idea of a new economic strategy was in the mind of its president, C. H. Myers, who wrote to Walter White in 1935 asking, "what [do] you think about Union labor and the Negro, some thing must be done along those lines." No reply was found on this topic. Louisiana NAACP branches in the 1930s, as a rule, pursued established practices in campaigning and increased their operations on registration drives and in gaining access to the ballot. It was believed that having the vote would increase access to political channels and, in turn, black interests would have to be acknowledged and acted upon. Therefore the ballot would effectively redress racial injustices and give blacks greater influence over New Deal agencies. Radical economic theory was not on the agenda in the NAACP; access and influence to the levers of political power were.[26]

Similarly Mrs. Dupuy of Baton Rouge reported in the early 1940s on an employment campaign to get more blacks employed at "Sears Roe Buck" department store and to secure skilled jobs for carpenters and painters at the local company "Harding Field." It also investigated defense jobs available in the city and reported that with "all these contracts not one of the 14 major industries manufacturing war products . . . will hire skilled negro labor[,] the standard oil Co. included, yet they run public adds [sic] daily, [and] radio programs begging for laborers, skilled . . . [and] semi-skilled." The Alexandria branch also investigated the defense industry for discrimination and potential job opportunities. Chair of the legal redress committee, Georgia Johnson declared that they were examining the defense industries, civil service, and other job opportunities. However, Johnson spent most of her time investigating and defending judicial cases of the civilian and military black population, while the branch's labor and industry committee was inactive by 1944 due to intense factionalism in the organization.[27]

During the Second World War the New Orleans NAACP branch had some success in having its views heard on the Fair Employment Practices Committee. President Roosevelt's Executive Order 8802 in June 1941 directed employers to give "full and equitable participation of all workers in the defense industries without discrimination" and local FEPC offices were organized to investigate and implement the order. Such a directive was fought and evaded by white-owned companies and was not wholly effective although it did become an avenue of official protest for black workers. In New Iberia the president and secretary of the NAACP were run out of town in 1944 for complaining to the FEPC about discrimination in welding training for blacks.[28]

In 1945 the political downgrading of the FEPC saw its office in New Orleans moved to San Antonio, Texas, although the city's NAACP branch did campaign to retain it in Louisiana. Daniel Byrd of the New Orleans branch became secretary of the FEPC, giving the local Association some authority to process claims on to Texas. The usefulness of the FEPC in politicizing black workers throughout Louisiana was not lost on the NAACP, and black labor leaders were regularly invited by the NAACP to advise local black communities on their rights in connection with making complaints before the FEPC.[29]

The historian Adam Fairclough has argued that a mass mobilization occurred in New Orleans during the 1940s due to a mix of wartime mobilization and accelerated militancy in the civil rights cause as well as the development of policies that strengthened and expanded NAACP causes, such as the teachers' equality of pay campaign. A middle-class bias was, however, sustained in the organization, built upon the traditions of the NAACP in the city from the interwar years. In 1944 the familiar pattern persisted of an elite core membership sustaining the branches. This hierarchical command structure was exemplified by a November meeting of the executive committee at the Autocrat Club, "a social and pleasure club house owned by a member of the better class negroes in New Orleans." In 1944 the Federal Bureau of Investigation reported the NAACP as "a large negro group in New Orleans ... [with] membership at the present time ... claimed to be about 5,000. Naturally this is not a closely knit organization and the policies are controlled and dominated by ... a few people namely, the officers and the Executive Committee which is composed of twenty-five members."[30]

Fairclough's examination of New Orleans NAACP factionalism in the early 1940s is instructive of an air of wartime militancy among black activists who were tiring of the gradualism of "racial diplomats." While Fairclough asserts that the move was not exactly revolutionary it was a sign that the old elitist nature of the organization in the city was gradually changing with leaders from the ranks of the federal post office (such as Arthur J. Chapital) and from insurance agency companies (Daniel E. Byrd). This heralded a statewide NAACP organization that pushed the teachers' equality of pay agenda through the state courts, giving example that although the personnel were changing the orientations of the NAACP were built on firm foundations.

Elsewhere in Louisiana, however, there might have been rumblings of discontent but they did not amount to a wholesale overturning of NAACP leaders. In Baton Rouge, businessmen, such as Horatio Thompson, who had helped found the Negro Chamber of Commerce in the city, temporarily took over positions in the local branch, although leaving the presidency to its incumbent, C. H. Myers, and the running of the branch to longtime activist, Mrs. Dupuy. Monroe also remained stable and maintained its 1930s leadership into the war years and beyond. These cities had steady leadership in difficult times and its membership remained quite low, whereas New Orleans underwent massive recruitment due to being perfectly placed as a recipient of wartime militancy. Alexandria saw disruption between a militant group headed by the Methodist minister J. M. Murphy and businesswoman Georgia Johnson, and the old branch hierarchy. This had the effect of destroying the city's NAACP, which was unfortunate because it exemplified many of the wartime issues confronting African Americans as it was surrounded by five military training camps.[31]

What these branches shared was their resolute middle-class core membership through which they remained wedded to the NAACP as a political and civil rights organization, despite personal conflicts and increasing frustration at the pace of change by certain groups. The

NAACP remained purposefully legal and political in its nature in destroying the color line in the United States. It was a long and laborious path to the *Brown* decision and one that flirted with alternative avenues of civil rights activism, notably a more economic-oriented agenda. As Daniel Byrd of the New Orleans NAACP observed, "Only a handful of our people want integration. And it is God's valiant minority who must war on the insidious evil." A portion of the middle classes pushed the agenda for equality and integration in Louisiana and the NAACP was their ideal vehicle of expression.[32]

CHAPTER TEN

"In No Event Shall a Negro Be Eligible"

The NAACP Takes on the Texas All-White Primary, 1923–1944

CHARLES L. ZELDEN

S INCE THE TURN of the twentieth century, Texas blacks had been barred from voting in the Democratic primary by popular consensus, Democratic Party rules, and (from 1923 to 1927) state statutes. The Democratic Party was an organization for whites only. The controlling principle read in part that "in no event shall a Negro be eligible for membership in the Democratic Party and entitled to participate in its deliberations."[1] Given the South's unique political dynamic, this exclusion was significant. In the one-party South, where the Democratic candidate almost always won the election, to be barred from the Democratic primary meant being excluded from the one area where substantive choices as to political leadership was made. The All-White Primary (AWP), in turn, provided for Texas (and the rest of the Deep South) the ultimate and final method of achieving this racial exclusion.

The source of the AWP lay in the unique mix of race hatred that lay at the core of southern social relations, the politics of class as practiced at the end of the nineteenth century, and the negative context of America's built-in historic tendency toward vote denial. In the context of Texas's unique historical and political environment, and given the political realities of the early twentieth century, emphasizing protection of white political power at the primary level made sense. Yet Texas

Democratic politics could be among the most contentious in the South. The combination of Populism's electoral fallout (which in Texas was especially complex) and the need to exclude blacks without filtering out too many easily controlled and managed Mexican American voters in south Texas, dictated the state's reliance on poll taxes and the AWP. So too did rifts within the Democratic Party's established leadership, as some Texas politicians reached out a partial hand of help to the former Populists while others did not. In the end, the application of an extensive and disenfranchising poll tax combined with Populism's political fallout mandated the need for an AWP if white Texans were to maintain political harmony and hegemony.

Ironically, it was these same forces that led the National Association for the Advancement of Colored People to place the AWP at the center of its early efforts to combat the negative effects of Jim Crow segregation. With its explicit focus on race as grounds for vote denial, the AWP simply went too far in excluding blacks from the public realm, and as such it was vulnerable to a litigation-based attack. Defeating the AWP would not prove to be an easy task, however. Begun in the late 1920s, it would not be until 1944's *Smith v. Allwright* that the Texas AWP would finally be put to rest. In the process, the fight against the AWP exposed deep-seated tensions within the NAACP between the national office lawyers and the members of the local branches over the scope and focus and speed of the litigation (and reform) process. It was only when the two sides compromised and agreed on a common litigation approach to defeating the AWP that victory was achieved.[2]

Origins of the All-White Primary

The spark that set off the AWP was Populism. By the late 1890s, trapped in a declining cycle of debt and poverty, half of the state's white farmers, and an even greater percentage of the state's African American farmers, were living under conditions of near peonage (debt slavery). Their response was one of increasing anger and political activism, both of which fueled the rise of Populism and its challenge to the dominance of the traditional political and economic elites who had run Texas since the end of Reconstruction.

Backed largely by poor white and African American votes, the

Populists soon showed remarkable, if not victorious, electoral results. In 1894, the Populist gubernatorial candidate Thomas L. Nugent received over 150,000 votes for governor, losing the race by only 56,000 votes. At the same time, Populist candidates won twenty-two state house of representatives races and two state senate races. In the bitter 1896 gubernatorial election, Jerome J. Kearby, running as a fusion candidate for the Populist and Republican parties, amassed 238,000 votes against Democrat Charles A. Culberson's 298,000, with the Populist electoral share amounting to 44 percent of the vote. On the national scene, the Populist ticket for president, a hybrid with the Democratic Party's candidate, William Jennings Bryan, won 32 percent of the votes cast by Texans.

Bryan's defeat by William McKinley, however, was a high-water mark for Populism, both nationwide and in Texas. Weakened by their merger with the national Democrats, unsuccessful in their reform efforts, and organizationally and emotionally devastated by their defeat in both the presidential and gubernatorial elections, Populists across the state lost interest in politics. Some, disgusted, abandoned politics altogether. Others, mostly upper-working-class whites, confused by the Populists' on again/off again merger with the Democrats, returned to the Democratic fold.[3]

Populism's threat, in turn, deeply shook the leadership of the Texas Democratic Party. They understood how close they had come to losing power. Though separated into many competing and warring factions, in particular a sharp rift between reform and conservative Democrats, the Democratic leadership agreed that the underlying threat posed by Populism, a multiracial, class-based challenge to upper-class white Texans' control of the state's political and social hierarchies, had to be dealt with. The question was how.

It was in this context that Texas turned to the AWP. All factions within the party agreed, whatever their other proposals for change, that some form of disenfranchisement had to be part of the solution. The principal method of this shrinkage was the imposition of an annual, noncumulative poll tax of $1.50 (plus local and/or county surcharges) per voter, the payment of which was a precondition of voting. Though $1.50 was not a huge amount, the extensive poverty of most Texans meant that paying $1.50 or more for the questionable right to vote was a luxury that few could afford. The result was a massive decline in the number of registered voters across the state.

Massive in scope and immediate in its impact, the decline in the size of the electorate had an unintended consequence: the empowerment of black voters. The shrinking of the number of potential voters magnified the influence of small numbers of swing voters on election outcomes, and foremost among the potential swing voters were black Texans. This was especially the case in the all-important Democratic primary (which, since it excluded Republican and third-party voters, had an even smaller pool of potential voters than that found in the general election). As the historian Forrest G. Wood notes, Texas blacks "did not need a numerical majority in order to enjoy a political majority. Rather, if the total number of eligible Negro voters was greater than the difference in the number of votes cast for each [candidate], the Negroes had a 'majority.'" Where elections were tight (as was often the case in Democratic primaries), the candidate reaching out to black voters was usually the winner. This clearly observable result translated to real political clout for the black community, at least so long as their votes were needed. The AWP, in turn, cut this need off at the root.[4]

White Democrats, in other words, turned to the AWP in large part because they could not trust themselves *not* to make use of the forbidden fruit of black votes, at least, when those votes meant the difference between victory and defeat. The AWP, however, removed the temptation by removing the votes. That it also meant that blacks would be denied a voice in the governing process was simply a side benefit.

Implementation of the All-White Primary

The first step in adopting a statewide AWP came in 1903. Leading the call for an AWP was state representative Alexander W. Terrell. An ally of former governor Hogg and his reform Democrats, Terrell had long supported franchise limits. As he explained in 1906, "whether universal manhood suffrage is good for the country depends entirely on the sort of men who vote."[5] Let the wrong type of men vote, "the thriftless, idle and semi-vagrant element of both races," and chaos was the sure result. To Terrell, laws and constitutional provisions that permitted anyone to vote, such as the Fifteenth Amendment, were "the political blunder[s] of the century."[6] To this end, he turned his attention to better regulating primaries.

Proposed in 1902, adopted in 1903 and revised in 1905, the Terrell Election Law, as it came to be known, was a series of related reform measures aimed at the exclusion of poor, and especially minority, voters.[7] Though never directly mentioning blacks, the law's supporters saw it as a direct bar to African American voting in Democratic Party primaries. Their expectation was that local party executives, empowered by this law to "purify" their election procedures, would quickly adopt rules limiting participation in the primary to whites only. This was a correct assumption. While some county executives refused to exclude minority voters, most fell into line, effectively excluding black voters from the Democratic primary in all but a handful of counties.[8]

Yet even this result was not enough for Texas whites. With the end of the First World War, pressure grew for the total exclusion of blacks from the Democratic Party. Though the number of blacks able to vote stood only in the low tens of thousands, and the number of blacks able to vote in Democratic primaries probably stood in the mere hundreds, this was not good enough for white Texans. Exclusion had to be complete.

The result was that in 1923 the Texas legislature revised the state's primary law once again—this time expressly prohibiting, *as a matter of state law*, black voting in the Democratic primaries. As amended, the new statute read in part:

> All qualified voters under the laws and constitution of the State of Texas who are bona fide members of the Democratic party, shall be eligible to participate in any Democratic party primary election, provided such voter complies with all laws and rules governing party primary elections; *however, in no event shall a negro be eligible to participate in a Democratic party primary election held in the State of Texas, and should a negro vote in a Democratic primary election, such ballot shall be void and election officials are herein directed to throw out such ballot and not count the same.* [Emphasis added][9]

With this amendment, the AWP was complete. Texas Democrats were now prohibited from allowing blacks to vote in their primaries as a matter of law and the only potential agency capable of attacking this law was the courts.

What the Court Grants, Texas Democrats Take Away

It was at this juncture that the NAACP entered the picture. As part of their overall litigation strategy in combating the inequities of segregation, the NAACP's lawyers set their sights on the Texas AWP. They chose the AWP for two reasons. First, they recognized the intrinsic importance of voting as a means of enhancing African American civil rights. Give blacks an effective vote and they would have a tool to pry future gains out of reluctant southern governments and the white polities they represented. Second, and more significant, they chose the AWP because they felt that rules excluding *registered* voters were more vulnerable to attack than technically race-neutral statutes and constitutional provisions that "just happened" to disallow black voting.[10]

The NAACP's lawyers, in other words, saw the AWP not only as a perfect vehicle for attacking a clear limit on the civil rights of Texas blacks but also as an instrument by which to intensify, expand, and solidify their wider aims of dismantling all aspects of segregation. In this latter regard, the campaign against the AWP stood hand-in-hand with the NAACP's other assaults on segregated education and the prevailing discriminatory criminal procedures that collectively denied black defendants due process of law. In fact, given the NAACP's commitment to only take on cases that "establish[ed] a precedent which will affect the basic citizenship rights of Negroes and other Americans," it was *mostly* in this light that the NAACP's national leadership viewed the fight against the AWP.[11] Theirs was a big-picture approach to litigation strategy as a means to social reform. The goal was to lay the groundwork for future victories against all forms of segregation, not just to win the right to vote in the Democratic primary for Texas blacks.

This long-term approach gave the NAACP many advantages. Foremost among them was the ability to put together a team of skilled litigators, such as NAACP president Moorfield Storey, NAACP special counsel Charles Hamilton Houston (1935–1940), and Houston's successor, Thurgood Marshall, who understood not only the legal issues at hand but also the politics of using the courts to promote social and political change. As the legal scholar Alan Robert Burch notes, "the Association won victories in the courtroom . . . by exposing how the law discriminated against African-Americans and shaming judges into writing new law." Yet using shame and personal disgust as a motivating tool, or as Thurgood Marshall once put it, making sure that the judges did not "blind themselves as judges to what they know as men," was a tricky procedure. Most judges of the day did not want to "write new law." Overcoming this reluctance took tact and a ready knowledge of which buttons, personal, social, and legal, to push to get these judges to act. Give a judge a loophole, no matter how small, and he was likely to take the opportunity to use it to avoid the substantive issue. The NAACP's lawyers, however, understood these tendencies and thus constructed their legal strategies and arguments to minimize such loopholes and other opportunities for judicial inaction.[12]

Unfortunately, the NAACP's long-term approach also gave rise to many obstacles that would have to be overcome. Foremost among them were the inevitable tensions over questions of strategy and pacing between the NAACP's national leaders and the local black communities they represented in court. The national office lawyers may have taken the lead in litigating, but they were not alone in carrying out the fight. Behind the legal maneuvering lay the concerns, hopes, and dreams of Texas's African American community. At the root, it was *their* fight, and little could have been done to defeat the AWP without the community's general support. As correspondence between the NAACP's national office and leaders of the Texas black community shows, the drive for evermore intense action in attacking the AWP lay in the hands of those directly affected by this discrimination, not national office lawyers. Whereas the lawyers may have *wanted* to act, those denied the vote in Texas *needed* to act, and this difference pushed the lawyers to move faster and to demand more than they might otherwise have wished.[13]

Worse still, such enthusiasm could be as detrimental to careful litigation strategies as they were helpful in generating support for an enfranchisement campaign. The problem was that while the lawyers from the national office might be thinking in big-picture terms, the local chapters of the NAACP and the wider communities that they represented were not. For the local branches, the litigation at hand was the *most* important thing. Winning (judged largely by their ability to vote in the Democratic primary) was the goal, not setting some precedent that might lead to some greater gain in the future. The fight to combat the AWP thus unfolded within the context of an ongoing, complex, and heated debate over objectives and methods between national office lawyers and the membership of the Texas local branches.

It all started in El Paso. At the request of El Paso's NAACP local president, L. W. Washington, Dr. Lawrence Nixon tried to vote in the July 1924 Democratic Primary. Though a personal friend of both of the election judges, C. C. Herndon and Charles Porras, Nixon was turned away under the state's 1923 election law. "Dr. Nixon," Herndon was said to have exclaimed, "you know we can't let you vote." Herndon and Porras even signed a statement declaring that their *only* reason for turning Nixon away from the polls was Nixon's race.[14] Nixon sued, only to lose at the trial court level. Appealed to the U.S. Supreme Court, however, Nixon surprisingly won his case.

Writing for a unanimous Court, Justice Holmes struck down the 1923 Texas voting rights law as a violation of the Fourteenth Amendment. "It seems . . . hard to imagine a more direct and obvious infringement of the Fourteenth Amendment," Holmes wrote. "While states may do a good deal of classifying that is difficult to believe rational, there are limits [to this power], and it is too clear for extended argument that color cannot be made the basis of a statutory classification affecting the right" to vote in a primary election. Holmes's eloquent opinion, however, did not mention the Fifteenth Amendment or its effect on the AWP. In particular, Holmes and the other justices refused to address Nixon's Fifteenth Amendment arguments against the AWP—even though, at the time and in the view of later scholars, they were far stronger than his Fourteenth Amendment arguments, which the Court adopted. Nor did Holmes address the state's argument that elections under the Fifteenth Amendment referred only to general elections, not to primaries.[15]

Holmes's unwillingness to engage the Fifteenth Amendment would prove problematical. His opinion dealt only with the *explicit* prohibition of black voting *by the legislature* as a direct violation of the Fourteenth Amendment's equal protection clauses. Would it make a difference if the legislature were to no longer *impose* the AWP on the

Democrats, but returned merely to *allowing* the party to impose it on itself? This was a question Texas whites quickly asked themselves, and answered in the affirmative. Soon thereafter, Governor Dan Moody called a special session of the state legislature to amend the primary voting law by deleting every provision explicitly barring black voting. The legislature did this on June 7, 1927. Soon thereafter, the Democratic Party Executive Committee resolved that all qualified white Democrats, and none other, would be allowed to participate in Democratic primary elections.[16]

Committed to the cause, Dr. Nixon set out once again to challenge the AWP. Denied access to the polls once again, he filed a fresh lawsuit in March 1929 alleging that the new law had the same flaws as the old one overturned by the Supreme Court. Argued before the High Court in early 1932, Justice Benjamin Cardozo spoke for the majority, which once again ruled in Nixon's favor. The Texas Democratic Party was not a simple voluntary association in primary elections, wrote Cardozo. Its organization and control of these elections derived directly from a "grant of power" from the state, and hence was a prohibited state action" under the Fourteenth Amendment. However, as with Holmes's earlier opinion attacking the Texas white primary, Cardozo left a loophole through which the Texas Democrats could circumvent the High Court's ruling. Cardozo noted that "whatever inherent power a state political party has to determine the content of its membership resides in the state convention." And, as the justice pointed out, this body had never declared its "will to bar negroes of the state from admission to the party ranks."[17]

Responding to this decision, Texas Democrats quickly called a state convention which limited participation in the party to "all-white citizens." Once again, a loophole in the Supreme Court's rulings against the AWP allowed Texas Democrats to ignore the clear intent of the law as handed down by the High Court.

Mixed Agendas and Legal Loopholes

Dejected, as were all Texas blacks, Nixon offered to take up the challenge once again. However, the leadership of the NAACP counseled caution and delay. They feared that as currently made up, the Supreme

Court had gone as far as it would in attacking the AWP. It was time to hold back and take stock of the situation.

Dr. Nixon accepted this advice from the national office lawyers. Others within the Texas black community did not. In Houston, black attorneys Carter Wesley, J. Alston Atkins, and James Nabrit, all of whom had aspirations to be leaders within Houston's black community, called for an immediate attack on this new version of the AWP. They also wanted to be in charge of this effort. Frustrated by the slow pace of change under the NAACP's leadership, and convinced that the cause of this failure was the NAACP's exclusive use of white lawyers to argue their cases, Wesley, Atkins, and Nabrit knew that, given the chance, they could do a better job than the NAACP's lawyers. No white lawyer, Wesley argued in his newspaper, the *Houston Informer,* could "prepare or present Negro cases as well as a trained Negro." More to the point (and this was a point on which all three men agreed), no outsider white lawyer could represent the hopes and dreams of Texas's local black communities.[18]

Convinced that they had both evidence and insight essential to victory, Wesley and Atkins had filed an *amicus curiae* brief with the Supreme Court on their own in *Nixon v. Condon.* This proved to be a dangerous action. The NAACP's brief in this case had been very careful in its wording—each of the NAACP's lawyers, James Marshall and Nathan Margold (both white attorneys from New York City), felt that it was imperative to focus their arguments on a single issue so as to not confuse the Court and thus making it easier for the justices to duck the issues raised by the case. Marshall and Margold saw the danger that the Fourteenth Amendment's "state action" requirement posed to their case. Its equal protection clause was too general to have the sort of direct impact that they hoped a positive ruling in this matter would have. Worse still, it lent itself all too well to an endless debate over the public versus private nature of the Democratic Party, a debate that they hoped they could limit even if they could not avoid it. To win, they were going to have to convince the justices that the Democratic Party was *not* a private agency when it came to primary elections, a goal easier to achieve via the Fifteenth Amendment's more focused reach.[19]

Wesley and Atkins's brief, however, was not so careful. Concerned with winning the case at hand, Wesley and Atkins not only repeated the arguments made by the NAACP lawyers, but added arguments directly attacking the Texas Democratic Party *Executive Committee's* imposition of the AWP. In particular, they argued that the party's capacity to choose its members was distinct from the power of the executive committee to act on behalf of the party. Inasmuch as the current rule imposing the AWP was the result of a ruling by the executive committee, the brief contended that the AWP was invalid and should be overturned.[20]

Although an accurate assessment of the legal situation in Texas, this argument took the focus away from state action and the party's effective role as an agent for the state in running primary elections. In doing so, it opened the door to the ongoing use of the AWP in Texas. Alan Robert Burch notes, "[Atkins's and Wesley's] theory of state action made sense only if the goal was merely to win the case at hand. Atkins and Wesley did not appreciate how much they were conceding to the Party on the continuum of where to draw the line on state action, nor how difficult it would be to win that ground back later."[21] More to the point, their argument gave the justices a loophole by which to avoid bringing the Texas AWP directly under the Fourteenth and Fifteenth amendments. It was a loophole the justices willingly seized—a loophole that allowed the Texas Democrats to, once again, avoid dismantling the AWP.[22]

Wesley and Atkins, however, were unwilling to acknowledge their role in this failure, blaming the NAACP and its reliance on white lawyers to argue their cases for the ambiguous result of the Court's ruling. So when the NAACP counseled caution and delay, Wesley and Atkins disagreed, remaining committed to using the courts to produce change and do it now. Against the explicit advice of the NAACP's lawyers, Wesley and Atkins thus brought another AWP case before the Supreme Court in 1935 on their own. As they perceived the situation, without the power of the vote, Texas blacks would be forever trapped in "poverty and self-hate." The AWP had to go and sooner was better than later.[23]

Their client was a charismatic and politically active Houston barber by the name of Richard Randolph Grovey. Collectively, Grovey, Wesley, and Atkins were (as the historian Darlene Clark Hine put it) "as determined to create a politically unified black community as they were committed to overthrowing the white primary." In fact, they each saw the latter result as the best way to achieve the former goal. To this end, they brought suit in a Houston justice-of-the-peace court against election judge Albert Townshend seeking damages of ten dollars. Since Texas law only allowed appeals of matters with damages valued at twenty dollars or more, this strategy permitted Grovey to appeal his subsequent loss directly to the U.S. Supreme Court and argue his case.

"Argument" turned out to be a relative term in this matter. Neither Texas nor the Democratic Party chose to defend the case. When in March 1935 the Court undertook to decide the case, all the justices had before them were the briefs provided by Grovey and his attorneys and the record of their submissions in oral argument. Yet, despite the advantage such a one-sided debate should have provided, the result in *Grovey v. Townshend* was a devastating loss for the AWP's opponents.

Once again, Wesley and Atkins failed to provide the justices with a narrowly focused argument, instead submitting a broad-based, even scattershot, list of arguments attacking the AWP. And while their claims of constitutional wrong were factually correct, they once again gave the Court the wiggle room it needed to avoid the real underlying issues of inequality and discrimination posed by the AWP.[24]

Writing for a unanimous court, Justice Owen Roberts refused to accept Grovey's argument that Texas's primary elections were by their nature state action because of the state's extensive regulation. Texas's primary elections, Roberts explained, were not "state action." Selectively choosing from Wesley's and Atkins's brief only those examples that best suited his exclusionary intent, Justice Roberts noted that Texas did not pay for the primaries, furnish the ballots, or count the votes. How could the primaries be "state action" when the state failed to control these fundamental functions of an election? More to the point, given that the Texas Supreme Court had determined in *Bell v. Hill* (1934) that the legislature of Texas had not "essayed to interfere, and indeed may not interfere, with the constitutional liberty of citizens to organize a party and to determine the qualifications of its members," how could the Court hold such primaries to be "state action"? "In the light of the principles so announced," Justice Roberts concluded, "we are unable to characterize the managers of the primary election as state officers in such sense that any action taken by them in obedience to the mandate of the state convention respecting eligibility to participate in the organization's deliberations, is state action." Political parties were private voluntary associations; by logical association, their primary elections were private matters also. The AWP was constitutional.[25]

The Pressing Need for Consensus

With these few words, fifteen years of attack on the AWP came to a screeching halt. The AWP was here to stay unless Texas blacks and the NAACP lawyers could find a way to settle their differences and mount a unified and effective campaign against the AWP. The lesson of *Grovey* was the urgent need for unity of effort *and* argument in the fight against the AWP; that defeat was an inevitable result when the AWP's opponents split their efforts. This was a lesson the NAACP took to heart.

In the five years following *Grovey*, the NAACP turned inward on itself. On the national level, its leaders embraced four important truths about the enfranchisement campaign.[26] First, they recognized that, for a litigation-based approach to civil rights reform to work, both dependable legal expertise and consistent legal argument were essential—they were, in fact, intimately related to each other. In practical terms, this recognition meant creating a full-time, in-house legal staff to exercise uniform, centralized control of the campaign against segregation and the AWP. Over time, this commitment to organizational unity resulted in the creation of a separate, fully staffed litigation arm for the Association: the Legal Defense and Educational Fund (LDF), established in March 1940.

Second, legal consistency also meant being more proactive in selecting, organizing, and arguing the NAACP's case against the AWP. As *Grovey* had shown, without careful preparation, dangerous legal and constitutional defects could creep into such improperly prepared cases, defects that later exploded the NAACP lawyers' best efforts in those and future cases. Letting the local branches bring large numbers of hastily prepared suits, or worse, having a case brought independently of the NAACP, as with *Grovey*, was a path to failure. Far better for the NAACP's lawyers to "guide" a case "from its very inception."

Only then, as the Association's executive secretary Walter White noted in 1940, could they ensure that it was "being properly handled."[27]

Third, the NAACP admitted that it had mishandled relations with the local branches, the wider communities they served, and hence the litigation process as a whole. Grassroots support was essential if the campaign against the AWP were to succeed. Unfortunately, as the events surrounding *Grovey* showed, relations between the NAACP and community leaders in Texas were badly strained. At times, arguments between the two camps over issues of pacing and strategy had broken out into open warfare. This had to end.

Finally, the NAACP leadership accepted that its reorganized legal team needed to have black members, and ideally, that it should be headed by a skilled African American lawyer. With an ever-rising number of skilled young black lawyers coming out of such law schools as Washington, D.C.'s Howard University and expressing interest in taking on the fight for equal rights, there was no good reason not to include them, and very good reasons to bring them into the fold. By 1936, an expanded advisory legal committee included large numbers of young, energetic, and committed African American lawyers. Foremost among them was Charles Hamilton Houston, vice dean of Howard University Law School, who joined the NAACP as general counsel in 1935.

The acknowledgment of these truths by the NAACP's leadership, and the acceptance of such reforms by local branches in Texas, redefined the NAACP's fight against AWP. In fact, the need for greater centralized control over the litigation process necessitated a broadening of the membership and leadership of the campaign against the AWP. Without increased centralized control, legal victory was largely unattainable; yet without greater accountability to, and understanding within, the black community, centralized control was a resource beyond the NAACP's grasp. Control though unity was the new watchword, and most of the NAACP's organizational activities throughout the last half of the 1930s sought this end.

Endgame: Smith v. Allwright *and the Defeat of the Texas All-White Primary*

This reorganization took almost five years to complete. By 1940, however, the NAACP was ready to renew the attack on the AWP. Changes in the Supreme Court's make up, along with evolving social perspectives on race, implied that the time was right to act. At the annual meeting of the Texas State Conference of Branches in Corpus Christi in May 1940, Thurgood Marshall, who had just replaced Houston as general counsel, put out a call to arms. Marshall laid out his plan of attack, including his demand for total control of the case from beginning to end. Already anxious to act, conference members welcomed his proposals with open arms. The conference determined that control over the case was, in fact, best left in the hands of Marshall and the LDF. The Texas board also agreed to back a single case of Marshall's choice; after meeting with leading black Texas lawyers, Marshall decided that the case should be filed by the well-funded, aggressive Houston branch.[28]

Following a few false starts, Marshall found his plaintiff in dentist Lonnie Smith, an established and respected member of the community (who also happened to be the second vice president of the Houston chapter of the NAACP). As the polls opened up on July 27, Smith dutifully walked to his local precinct and sought to vote in the Democratic primary. He was, predictably, turned away by the precinct judges. One month later, in the August 24 run-off election, the outcome was the same as Smith was once again denied the ballot.

Argued at both the district and circuit court of appeals levels, where Smith lost, the case finally came before the U.S. Supreme Court on November 12, 1943. At the center of Smith's case was the recently decided *U.S. v. Classic* ruling which held that, in some instances, primary elections were not private affairs; rather where the primary determined who was elected, that primary was a part of the public process of holding an election and thus subject to review by the federal courts under the Fourteenth and Fifteenth Amendments.[29] Marshall's arguments depended on the Court's willingness to extend the *Classic* doctrine to Texas and the AWP. Without *Classic*, Marshall would be sent back to arguing the public versus private nature of the Texas Democratic Party, and the NAACP had been down this road before and lost.

Marshall's primary contention, as set out in Smith's brief to the Court, was that "the Constitution and laws of the United States as construed in *United States v. Classic* prohibit[ed] interference by [either the State or Texas Democrats] with [Smith's] right to vote in Texas

Democratic Primaries." As the brief explained, when properly viewed, there was essentially "no . . . difference between primary elections in Louisiana and in Texas." Both states made "primary elections 'an integral part of the procedure of choice.'" Each had laws mandating that parties choose their candidates by means of a primary election. And, in different ways, each state paid all or part of the costs of running primary elections. More to the point, in both states "the Democratic primary in reality 'effectively control[ed] the choice' of Senators and Representatives." Drawing on the Court's ruling in *Classic,* the brief declared that the obvious "legal consequence" was that "the right to vote in Texas primary elections [was] secured by the Constitution."

Marshall also directly challenged *Grovey.* The brief asserted that in *Grovey* the Court had not "adequately described" the "nature, organization and functioning of the Democratic Party" of Texas. Instead, the justices had relied on "a general conclusion of the Supreme Court of Texas in *Bell v. Hill*" defining the Texas Democratic Party "a voluntary association for political purposes" with the privilege of controlling its membership and hence who can vote in its primary elections. This was a mistake. "This Court was not bound to accept the conclusion of the Supreme Court of Texas as to the legal character of the primary election and the Democratic Party in Texas," Marshall explained, "for it is well settled that where the claim of a constitutional right is involved, this Court will review the record and find the facts independently of the state court."[30]

Arrayed against Smith were the state of Texas and the Texas Democratic Party's executive committee. Texas attorney general Gerald C. Mann argued for the State and the Party. Mann's position was simple. The Texas Democratic primary was a private event. As such, it lay beyond the reach of the Supreme Court to determine its membership or its operating procedures. If Texas Democrats wanted to exclude people from membership, and hence the right to vote in the primary, they had every right to do so. *Grovey* had so ruled and the Court should follow its precedent. As for *Classic,* the factual situation in Texas was different from that of Louisiana, where *Classic* arose. "The facts in the two cases [were simply] so different," concluded Mann, "that the opinion in one [did] not necessarily control the opinion in the other case."[31]

With the argument over, the Court adjourned to decide the case.

The Court's answer was not a foregone conclusion. The *Grovey* precedent permitting the AWP as a private event was only nine years old. Yet, *Classic* raised questions as to the legitimacy of the AWP. After all, in both states, the real winner was chosen at the primary level, not at the general election. Yet did the Court have the authority to act in these matters? Ultimately, in an 8–1 vote the Court decided that *Classic* was the controlling precedent and ruled against the Texas AWP.

Writing for the Court, Justice Stanley Reed explained that "Texas is free to conduct her elections and limit her electorate as she may deem wise, save only as her action may be affected by the prohibitions of the United States Constitution or in conflict with powers delegated to and exercised by the National Government." The question before the Court, therefore, was whether the Texas primary fell under the scope of federal law? In particular, did the exclusion of blacks from the Democratic primaries meet the state action requirements imposed by the Fourteenth and Fifteenth amendments, or was it, as the State argued, merely the private actions of a private association beyond the purview of federal law?

Reed accepted that "when *Grovey v. Townsend* was written, the Court looked upon the denial of a vote in a primary as a mere refusal by a party of party membership," and hence beyond the reach of federal law. Yet he doubted that this was still the case. Since *Grovey* had been decided, other cases relating to these questions had come before the Court. Among these cases was *United States v. Classic,* in which the justices held that "§ 4 of Article I of the Constitution authorized Congress to regulate primary as well as general elections, 'where the primary is by law made an integral part of the election machinery.'" *Classic,* Reed explained, thus changed everything.

"The fusing by the *Classic* case of the primary and general elections into a single instrumentality for choice of officers," Reed wrote for the Court, had "a definite bearing on the permissibility under the Constitution of excluding Negroes from primaries." He continued in uncompromising terms:

> The *Classic* case cuts directly into the rationale of *Grovey v. Townsend* . . . not because exclusion of Negroes from primaries is any more or less state action by reason of the unitary character of the electoral process but because the recognition of the

place of the primary in the electoral scheme makes clear that state delegation to a party of the power to fix the qualifications of primary elections is delegation of a state function that may make the party's action the action of the State.

Given that the "Louisiana statutes for holding primaries are similar to those of Texas," Reed explained, "our ruling in *Classic* as to the unitary character of the electoral process calls for a re-examination as to whether or not the exclusion of Negroes from a Texas party primary was state action." By integrating the Democratic Party into its electoral process, Texas had made this party into a quasi-public agency subject to federal regulations, and federal law prohibited the exclusion of voters on account of race or color. Of what use, asked Reed, was the Constitution's guaranteeing the people "the opportunity for choice" if it could be "nullified by a State through casting its electoral process in a form which permits a private organization to practice racial discrimination in the election?" His answer was none. "Constitutional rights," he concluded, "would be of little value if they could be thus indirectly denied."

"The United States is a constitutional democracy," Reed stressed. "Its organic law grants to all citizens a right to participate in the choice of elected officials without restriction by any State because of race." The party, in turn, "takes its character as a state agency from the duties imposed upon it by state statutes . . . The duties do not become matters of private law because they are performed by a political party." Justice Reed thus concluded: "Here we are applying, contrary to the recent decision in *Grovey v. Townsend,* the well-established principle of the Fifteenth Amendment, forbidding the abridgement by a State of a citizen's right to vote. *Grovey v. Townsend* is overruled." The AWP was unconstitutional.[32]

Conclusion

With these words, Justice Reed ended almost fifty years of race-based exclusion from the voting process in primary elections. True, southern whites were initially unwilling to accept the finality of this ruling. For the next ten years they would attempt to keep the essence of the

AWP intact—only to have the federal courts knock down their efforts.[33] Over time, however, the lesson would sink in, the AWP was unconstitutional and blacks could no longer be excluded from the vote. This was the new law of the land, and the U.S. Supreme Court was ready and willing to enforce this reality.

Marshall and the NAACP would move on to other issues and win other victories against segregation and discrimination, but it was in Texas that Marshall had his first great victory. As he recalled in a 1977 interview, it was *Smith v. Allwright*, and not *Brown v. Board of Education*, that was the greatest victory of his career. Granted, *Brown* was a ruling of clear historic significance; yet it was *Smith* that opened the door to black voting, and as Marshall saw things, the vote was an essential first step to instigating any lasting change.[34] "Without the ballot," Marshall was apt to remind his law clerks, "you have no citizenship, no status, no power in this country."[35] What good were desegregated schools if the newly educated black population could not put its newly acquired education into action? This fact alone, argued Marshall in a 1957 article on the AWP, made the victory in *Smith* "an important and distinct chapter in the story of the Negro's struggle for political equality."[36]

CHAPTER ELEVEN

Tensions in the Relationship between Local and National NAACP Branches

The Example of Detroit, 1919–41

PATRICK FLACK

IN THE SUMMER of 1933, Walter White, then executive secretary of the National Association for the Advancement of Colored People, paid a visit to Detroit, speaking at a meeting sponsored by a senior member of the local NAACP, Snow F. Grigsby.[1] However, this speech was not given to a meeting of the NAACP. Rather it was sponsored by Grigsby's own organization, the Detroit Civic Rights Committee. In the short term, this visit reflected the closeness that had developed between Grigsby and White, who held a similar vision for an activist branch in Detroit, and also their frustration with the less activist established leadership of the branch.[2]

This falling out with the leadership of the local branch also reflected a longer-term tension in the relationship between the national office and the Detroit branch, dating back almost to the establishment of the branch in 1912. This essay will examine the relationship between the national office of the NAACP and the Detroit branch, in the period between the world wars, years that saw a boom in the African American population of Detroit, as workers were drawn to the city by industrial expansion. The national office was naturally anxious that such a large and significant city should have a strong local branch. However, their priorities often did not overlap with those of the local leadership, giving rise to considerable tension.

An examination of the Detroit branch provides an interesting insight into the ways in which the national office related to its affiliates in the interwar period. This is a topic that has not received significant historical attention. Most notable is Beth Tompkins Bates's examination of the NAACP in the 1930s, in which she demonstrates how in this period the branches were a significant source of concern, as the Depression dramatically cut their budgets while simultaneously making them a source of radicalism. As will be shown, this was less true in Detroit, although the city had its radical elements it was not until the 1940s that they entered the ascendancy. Rather, the mismanagement of the local branch by the national office during the 1920s held back the development of an activist branch during the 1930s.[3]

The discussion will encompass four distinct periods. The first, covering the period 1919–1925, will show how tensions developed over the failure of the local branch to contribute significant amounts to national campaigns—despite their hard work at the local level—and examine how this reflected the national office's emphasis on national over grassroots campaigning. The second section will examine what happened when the twin priorities of national and local campaigning collided in the crisis of 1925–1926, most notably in the renowned Sweet case. The third section will examine the period 1926–1935, and suggest that the stifling of initiative at the local level in the earlier period meant that the Detroit branch was unable to respond when the national office became increasingly interested in grassroots activism. Finally, the closing section will consider the presidencies of Louis C. Blount and Dr. James McClendon, in the period 1935–1941, and show how changing pressures at both national and local levels led to a new harmonizing of purpose between the two organizations, and to Detroit becoming the largest and one of the most active branches of the Association in the United States.

The Detroit branch of the NAACP was established in 1912, three years after the foundation of the national Association. However, it only became a significant force in the city in the aftermath of the wave of African American migration that World War I had brought to the city. Detroit's African American population leapt from 5,741 in 1910 to

40,838 in 1920 and was more than 80,000 by 1925.[4] This migration, unfortunately but unsurprisingly, was met with a sharp increase in discrimination in the city. An early report of the Detroit branch noted that "we are sorry to say that discrimination in public places seems to be on the increase in Detroit, due no doubt, to the great number of southern whites who have come to our city along with our southern colored peoples, attracted by the higher wages and the better economic conditions also."[5]

In this early period, the Detroit branch was extremely active at a grassroots level in protesting and fighting against these instances of discrimination. In 1918 their intervention was instrumental in allowing an African American woman, Irene Davis, to take up the position of postal clerk over the protestations of her white colleagues.[6] The following year they protested to the Michigan Central Railway that their Detroit-Cincinnati service was running Jim Crow carriages, prompting an investigation.[7] In 1921 they took action over the case of Miss Catherine Jones, who had been denied access to the Detroit Business Institute and compelled them to admit her.[8]

Perhaps the most significant of these acts of protest concerned the branch's protesting of the showing of D. W. Griffith's *The Birth of a Nation* in Detroit. This film was controversial from the time of its first release, in 1915, and the national office had organized pickets to protest its viciously racist portrayal of the Reconstruction era. When the film was re-released and shown in the new Detroit Opera House in September 1921 the branch threw itself into the fray. A representative of the NAACP, Reverend Robert L. Bradby, of the Second Baptist Church, visited Mayor James Couzens to personally draw his attention to the situation.[9] On September 17 Couzens ordered the police department to block the showing of the film, citing fears that it might stir racial prejudice. The city's police commissioner, James W. Inches, noted that showing the film would "almost certainly lead to serious public disturbances."[10] In his announcement Couzens specifically noted that he made this decision "following protests that were made to me by members of Negro organizations in Detroit," highlighting the crucial role played by the NAACP.[11]

Despite these grassroots successes, the relationship between the Detroit branch and the national office was increasingly fraught as the decade progressed. The main issue between the two was not one of campaigning within Detroit, but rather one of money, and in particular the branch's success in raising money for national campaigns from the city's African American population. As early as February 1925, the director of branches wrote to Fred H. Williams, who had become president of the Detroit branch the previous year, that "it was a disgrace to colored Detroit that the whites of that city should give nearly $1000 towards the work of the Association and the colored people for whom the work is conducted, $50 or $60." If the situation did not improve, he threatened, the national office would be forced to order a reelection of officers and "have the branch reorganised from top to bottom."[12]

When Williams failed to respond in a satisfactory manner, the national office carried out this threat, calling for new elections, which resulted in Reverend Robert Bradby taking over as president. Initially the national office was delighted with this appointment, the director of branches writing to Bradby that "in my opinion you are the key man to make the Association all that it should be in Detroit" and suggesting that "the news of your election is the best that has come from Detroit for many a day."[13] The choice of Bradby is highly significant, as he was well placed to raise the funds the national office was so anxious for. As one of the senior African American ministers in the city he had access to a large congregation and, furthermore, he had close ties to white power structures of Detroit, in particular Henry Ford. Beulah Whitby, a one-time NAACP member, recalled that Bradby was one of those "certain people who had great influence in getting jobs," and in particular that he had "pull" with Ford.[14] One reason that the national office saw him as a "key man" was the possibility of raising money from these sources.

The importance of the financial issue in his appointment is revealed by Bradby's first letter to the national office. In it he outlined a number of possible directions for the Branch—significantly these focused on fund-raising rather than on community activism. For instance, he proposed paying a professional fund-raiser to keep up the Branch's subscriptions, giving them 20 percent of the subscription rate.[15] While the national office rejected this plan, being unwilling to compromise on how much they received per member, Bradby's efforts continued to be focused on fund-raising. In April he organized a baby contest, which the *Detroit Independent* newspaper reported explicitly as being run to raise money to fulfill Detroit's quota obligations.[16] In the short term the reorganization was a great success, in June the director of branches congratulated the branch on exceeding their apportionment of $1,000 by $676.79, the largest excess of any branch.[17]

By intervening in the internal affairs of the Detroit branch, therefore, the national office had sent a very clear message to its senior members. They had firmly established their priority as being fundraising for the purposes of paying for those campaigns which it judged to be of national importance, such as the Washington, D.C., segregation case. Bradby's emphasis on fund-raising in his early weeks in charge showed that he had clearly understood the significance of this message. While the national office continued to stress the importance of campaigning within Detroit itself—in July James Weldon Johnson called on Bradby to take action over the housing situation in the city, —they had made it clear that their priority was action on a national level.[18]

It would not be long after Bradby's appointment, however, that this distinction fell apart as events within Detroit rapidly assumed national significance. Throughout the summer of 1925 racial tensions in the city were escalating and a number of African Americans who had bought homes in "white" districts found themselves driven out by angry mobs. This reached its nadir on Wednesday, September 9, when Dr. Ossian Sweet, a successful African American gynecologist, killed one white man and injured another when they tried to drive him from his home.[19]

The significance of this tragic event for establishing the rights of African Americans to buy property wherever they could afford it and to defend themselves was self-evident. Certainly, when James Weldon Johnson, the national secretary of the NAACP, received newspaper reports of the incident on September 11 he immediately recognized the potential importance of the case and contacted Bradby requesting the "fullest information possible."[20] When Bradby had not responded by the next day, Johnson sent a second telegram to William Hayes McKinney, a member of the local executive committee. McKinney and Moses Walker, the branch's vice president, responded by giving a summary of events and outlining their short-term plans—specifically organizing a mass meeting to raise money for the defense. They noted that one of their key problems was a lack of information about what had actually happened on the evening of the ninth, and that therefore "it will be necessary to have an experienced investigator to secure evidence to aid in the defense of this case. Mr. [Walter] White being the logical man, we are therefore urgently requesting that Mr. White be sent to Detroit immediately, for the above mentioned purpose."[21] Johnson concurred, dispatching Walter White to the city.

Once in Detroit, however, White's role rapidly expanded from that of an investigator. He assumed control of negotiating with the lawyers who had been approached by the defendants and, when it was decided that a white lawyer would be beneficial, took on the task of persuading the lawyers in place to accept this. In a letter back to James Weldon Johnson he reported that he "expressed our insistence on the retaining of the very best lawyer available, doing so as tactfully as I could. I pointed out that this cast no reflections of the colored lawyers, but that it was a question bigger than Detroit or Michigan even for it was the dramatic climax of the nation-wide fight to enforce residential segregation."[22] He also approached potential attorneys; ultimately he was able to secure the services of the renowned criminal lawyer Clarence Darrow.

Although the Detroit Branch had requested that White come to act as an investigator, he told James Weldon Johnson that "I have had no time to do any investigating," instead considering that "getting these other matters untangled is far more important." Meanwhile, the role of the local branch in the case was rapidly downgraded from decision making to fund-raising. Indeed, this proved to be a significant source of friction, as Bradby's frequent appeals for a reduction in Detroit's apportionment obligations in light of their contribution to the Sweet defense fell on deaf ears. As in the period before Bradby's appointment, therefore, the priorities of the national office were clearly set: they would deal with cases of great significance, the local branches would foot the bill.[23]

In the short term, this strategy proved effective, as Darrow's prestige and reputation as a lawyer secured the acquittal of the defendants on all charges. This conclusion vindicated the national office's strategy of micromanaging the case, and it is very questionable whether Dr Sweet and his codefendants would have walked free were it not for the national office. The following years would, however, show that this approach had weaknesses as well as strengths. By stifling local initiative and stressing the importance of fund-raising for national campaigns they had left Detroit without effective leadership for grassroots protest. The years from 1926 to 1941, therefore, saw a reversal of the pre-1925 situation; rather than pressing the local branch for money, the national office was pushing them into a more confrontational stance.

In the immediate aftermath of the Sweet case the future appeared bright for the Detroit NAACP. Certainly, the national office believed that victory in the case was a good springboard to strengthening the branch. In June 1926, only a month after the end of the trial, the director of branches wrote to Bradby urging him to undertake a new membership drive, expressing his confidence that this "would bring in thousands of members, and place Detroit in a most favourable position among the branches of the country."[24] This membership drive would bring in 2,145 new members by December, leading to Detroit being placed on the NAACP's honor roll for 1926.[25]

However, events quickly caused the relationship to sour, not least because the national office became increasingly interested in the importance of small-scale, local campaigning. Through late 1926 and 1927 the national office pressed Bradby to investigate a series of police brutality cases. The issue of police violence against African Americans was a serious and recurring issue in Detroit. In June 1927 Paul Dennie, the chairman of the Constitutional League, another civil rights organization, wrote to the *Detroit Owl* highlighting the fact that "there were 72 Negroes killed by policemen in the City of Detroit during a period of 26 months. Not a single policeman has been tried in the courts, during this carnival of murder."[26] Alarmed by statistics such as these, Walter White wrote to Bradby in January 1927 urging the branch to compile a list of such cases, which could then be taken to the mayor.[27] Bradby failed to do anything so dramatic, preferring instead to rely on his contacts within the city's power structures to obtain investigation of individual cases, with the consequence that no progress was made.[28]

In 1928 the leadership of the Detroit branch changed hands, with Moses Walker taking up the presidency. However, despite his earlier hard work while vice president, the national office lost patience with him as quickly as they had with Bradby. In April the director of branches wrote to him complaining about his failure to reply to letters concerning the 20th Anniversary Campaign. Still receiving no response he contacted Judge Jayne, complaining "that Mr. Walker has been so busy that he has been unable to give the matter his attention."[29] The situation had not improved by 1933, when Walter White wrote a memo which drew attention to the fact that "Mose[s] Walker . . . has either lost interest or has so many irons in the fire that the Branch is not what it ought to be. We have exceedingly great difficulty in even getting responses to our letters."[30]

Their dissatisfaction with the branch was mirrored by the more activist members of Detroit's African American community, most notably Snow F. Grigsby. Grigsby was an employee of the U.S. Postal Service who had migrated to Detroit in 1923 from Chatville, South Carolina.[31] This job gave him a level of security from which he could criticize the established racial norms in Detroit. As Karen Miller has observed, Grigsby was at the forefront of a new wave of criticism of the white establishment, emphasizing that as African Americans were taxpayers they deserved a fair share of jobs and services from the city. In December 1933 he published a pamphlet entitled "An X-Ray Picture of Detroit," which highlighted the small number of policemen, teachers, and other municipal workers who were African American, setting this against the fact that they comprised 7 percent of the city's population.[32]

Grigsby joined the Detroit NAACP in 1931, but quickly became frustrated with what he perceived as a lack of willingness to confront racism in the city. When agitating to end the informal segregation of a swimming pool used by City College he wrote to Walter White to solicit his help, commenting, "Do not think that I am overlooking the branch here [in Detroit], but I am making this request of you as I know we will get immediate action."[33] The two developed a close friendship and shared their criticisms of the local branch with each other. When, in 1933, the executive board rejected a radical plan that Grigsby had submitted reorganizing the Detroit branch, he complained to White that "I regret very much to tell you that . . . executive officials [here] are using the office for personal advancement rather than for the good of the people."[34] By the spring of that year Grigsby was not only bypassing the local office in his contact with White, but doing so in secret, asking that White "not mention my name in any way, as it is a bit antagonistic, due to the fact that I pushed the organisation here to get action."[35]

Such informal contact between White and Grigsby became increasingly significant as both of them loosened their ties to the Detroit branch. As Grigsby's disillusionment and frustration with the Detroit branch increased, he established his own group, the Detroit Civic Rights Committee (DCRC). This organization provided him with a vehicle for furthering his activist career. In 1934 they published a pamphlet entitled "[The] Unfairness of the City Election Commissioners and the Circuit Court Judges in the Employment of Negroes paid out of Public Funds," calculating the small percentage of African Americans employed in these positions.[36] Grigsby and White maintained their informal ties, most notably when White traveled to Detroit to speak at a meeting of the DCRC.[37] Indeed, White came to increasingly treat Grigsby's organization as a de facto local branch, bypassing the official branch entirely. In November 1934, for example, the two corresponded regarding the enrollment of an acquaintance of Grigsby's into the NAACP, the entire exchange being carried out on DCRC-headed paper.[38]

This relationship was more than simply White and Grigsby's personal rapport. In May 1935 field secretary William Pickens, who, as Sheldon Avery observed, had no love for White, reported back to the national office "that the coterie dominating the Branch here is not quite straight . . . They do not want us to reach the people. They have schemes of their own." He went on to praise Grigsby and the DCRC, stating that "Grigsby's organisation is going ahead doing work that the NAACP should do."[39] Both in terms of its activities and its relationship to the national office, therefore, the DCRC had, by the middle of the 1930s, become the de facto Detroit branch of the NAACP. It was only when the national office diverted considerable resources to rebuilding the Detroit branch as an effective campaigning force that it was put back on its feet and again played a major role in the racial politics of Detroit.

The parlous state of the Detroit branch in the middle of the 1930s was a direct consequence of the fraught relationship between it and the national office in the previous decade. It is unsurprising, therefore, that it took the direct intervention of the national office, in particular the field secretaries, to revitalize the branch. They soon saw success in this regard, bringing Detroit's membership numbers up to compete with the largest branches in the nation. However, they faced more significant problems in encouraging the branch to adopt a more confrontational and radical stance to race relations in the city—and in particular with regard to the fraught question of organized labor. To achieve this, the national officers returned to the strategy of the early 1930s, cultivating informal ties to more radical figures in the city in order to encourage the branch to lend its support to the United Automobile Workers' organizing drive in the car factories of the city.[40]

The revitalization of the Detroit branch owed much to the intervention of the national office. Blount had been heavily involved in the ineffectual presidency of Moses Walker—he had been branch secretary for a time in the early 1930s—and little changed immediately after his election. Indeed Walter White continued to maintain his informal connection to Snow Grigsby and the DCRC well into Blount's presidency. When Grigsby wrote to White in November 1936 to let him know that the DCRC had "started out on a crusade" to make the Detroit NAACP branch act to pressure Municipal Hospital to employ African American nurses, White replied that he was "delighted to know that the Branch is working on the City Welfare Commission."[41]

The critical change came with a visit by the national field secretary, Daisy Lampkin, to the city to assist a membership drive in the summer of 1935. It was a mark of how bad relations between the branch and the national office had got that even her visit was controversial—William Pickens complained to White that "we had to contend to get Mrs. Lampkin invited for June campaign . . . [because] they fear that with a national officer on hand, they cannot so easily hold back national office share of funds."[42] However, once there she was able to achieve significant success, writing to White in June that she had raised nearly $1,500.[43] Two months later William Pickens could write with confidence that "the [Detroit] branch has a good membership now." [44]

This limited success in 1935 created significant momentum behind the branch, which the national office sustained both by sending Daisy Lampkin back to the city in 1938 and 1939 and by holding the Association's annual conference for 1937 in the city. In his welcoming address to the conference the branch secretary, Dr. James J. McClendon, was able to boast of a branch with almost three thousand members, and the same year the branch contributed over $2,200 on its apportionment of $1,000.[45]

As much as the conference reflected the progress the branch was making, and the importance of the national office to that renaissance, it also highlighted the significant differences of opinion between the two organizations with regard to strategy. As Meier and Rudwick have observed, by 1937 the national office and Walter White in particular were convinced of the need for African American workers to cooperate with the newly active labor unions.[46] This issue was especially pertinent in Detroit, where the Congress of Industrial Organizations (CIO)-affiliated United Automobile Workers (UAW) was making a concerted effort to mobilize the automobile plants, an objective which would be impossible without the support of African American workers in the industry. To this end, White invited a group of union delegates, including the president of the UAW, Homer Martin, to address the conference. The conservative African American leadership, which still had significant influence over the branch, reacted in anger to the criticism of the automobile manufacturers who, in their eyes, had offered considerable support to the African American community over the years. In advance of the conference at least one minister asked his congregation to boycott the conference because Martin was speaking, and even the moderate Judge Ira Jayne, long an ally of the national office in Detroit, went out of his way in his opening address to praise Henry Ford, suggesting that he "gives employment, I believe, to more Negroes at white man's work, at white man's pay, than any other man in the world."[47]

In the years immediately following the conference the branch continued to go from strength to strength, under the watchful eyes of the national office. Mrs. Lampkin returned to the city for the membership drives of the next two years, bringing in over 3,000 members in the summer of 1938 and over 5,000 in 1939. Such was her success that Walter White wired congratulations to her, telling her "you are indeed a wizard." By the end of 1939 the branch had over 6,000 members and was comfortably the largest and richest branch in the country.[48] This success was also due to the election in December 1937 of a more progressive local board, including Dr. James J. McClendon as president and the old campaigner, Snow F. Grigsby, as a member of the executive committee.[49]

Hand in hand with this revitalized membership and fund-raising came a renewal in the Detroit branch's activism on civil rights issues. In April 1938, the branch supported a benefit dance to fund the distribution of copies of Grigsby's *White Hypocrisy and Black Lethargy* to "every Minister and Religious Worker of the other Group."[50] That this aimed to improve the lot of Detroit's African Americans through appeal to the city's white elites was not unusual. The renewed activism of the mid- to late 1930s was generally limited to traditional strategies of appealing to white elites, rather than organizing mass protests. Through the summer of 1938, for example, the branch held no mass meetings but kept themselves in the public eye by applying pressure on companies to employ African American staff.[51] There were exceptions to this trend, however, which could cause problems for the national office. In April 1938, for example, McClendon had to make an official apology to the national office for participating in an antilynching demonstration sponsored by the radical National Negro Congress, which criticized the Republican senator from Michigan, Arthur H. Vandenberg.[52]

On the key question of labor organizing, however, the ideological tensions continued to be between an increasingly radical national office and a conservative local branch. As Meier and Rudwick have noted, despite his activism in other fields, McClendon was "broadly indifferent" to labor issues and hostile to unions.[53] The national office found an unlikely ally, however, in the form of the city's NAACP youth councils. Chaired by Gloster B. Current, this group had nearly three hundred members in 1937 and expanded rapidly as the decade continued. Furthermore, as early as 1937 they had begun to develop informal ties to the national office that bypassed the local branch. Using language reminiscent of that of Snow Grigsby, Current wrote confidentially to Juanita Jackson, special assistant to Walter White, that "the senior group is practically dead as far as activity is concerned and cannot see any further than their noses."[54]

This informal link would prove invaluable when the UAW's organizing drive at Ford resulted in a major strike at the company's River Rouge plant. In his autobiography, Walter White recalled that the CIO's activity at Ford was the organization's "first real test."[55] With a significant number of plant workers being African Americans it was vital for the union to bring the community to support the union. However, loyalty to Ford and memories of craft union racism made many African Americans suspicious, and when the strike broke approximately 1,500–2,500 African Americans remained at work, compared to only 300 whites.[56] As Walter White negotiated with James McClendon to bring the local branch around, the youth councils took matters into their own hands and secured a sound car to broadcast appeals in the name of the NAACP, urging strikebreakers to leave the plant. The combined actions of the national office and the youth councils were crucial in forcing the adult branch to take a decisive stand, and on Sunday April 6th they distributed ten thousand leaflets urging African Americans not to be used as strikebreakers. This action was an important factor in the victory of the UAW in the National Labor Relations Board (NLRB) elections held shortly afterwards, and helped to cement the union's position as a force for racial equality. This success reflected both the radicalizing journey taken by the local and national offices in the 1930s, and what they could accomplish when they cooperated with each other.[57]

The relationship between the local and national offices was, as we have seen, never simple. While they shared the broad objectives of striving for racial justice and challenging segregation, there were often strong disagreements over the most effective ways to accomplish these ends. In the particular case of Detroit, throughout the interwar period it proved very difficult to strike a balance between fund-raising for campaigns run by the national office and local, grassroots campaigning. This relationship was complicated further by the changing priorities of the national office. Having stressed the importance of fund-raising in the early part of the period, they would later criticize the local leadership for failing to act on local issues. Similarly, the national office's conversion to pro-organized labor policies in the late 1930s clashed with the particular interests of the local officers. In each case the blame for the difficult relationship must sit as much with the national office shifting position as with the local branch's failure to act.

However, the example of Detroit also suggests significant ways in which the national office could overcome these problems. The NAACP's field secretaries and the annual conference could be effective tools to revitalize a torpid branch. In addition to these formal mechanisms, the national office developed informal ties to more activist members of the city's African American community, such as Snow F. Grigsby and Gloster B. Current. These informal connections often bypassed the local branch entirely, but nevertheless provided a way in which officers such as Walter White could ensure their programs were put into effect. Ultimately it would be the actions of the national office that would secure the Detroit branch's greatest successes of the interwar period, in the courtroom in 1926 and on the picket line in 1941.

CHAPTER TWELVE

The Chicago NAACP

A Century of Challenge, Triumph, and Inertia

CHRISTOPHER ROBERT REED

O N THE EVE of the civil rights revolution of the 1960s, the Chicago branch of the NAACP had, by and large, successfully attempted and completed fifty-odd years of essential service to Chicago's African American community and to the cause of civil rights.[1] Recognition of this civic contribution came with its achieving institutional status during the mid-1950s after embarking on a torturous path of commitment to racial egalitarianism in supposedly democratic America. Within several years, its ability to continue to lead the struggle for equal rights had not only been neutralized by the Democratic political machine of Congressman William L. Dawson, but it also began a five-decade journey of inertia and decline that sadly mirrored its initial half-century climb to gain organizational and ideological relevance.[2] It stood on the sidelines when Dr. Martin Luther King Jr. marched in Chicago in protest for open housing in 1966, and today, nearly one hundred years after its birth, it is an organization torn asunder by some of the same forces that hampered its efforts throughout the early twentieth century. Yet, alone out of many local efforts to promote the cause of social justice, it has sustained itself somehow as a part of the quest for equal opportunity to experience the American Dream.

Along the way the branch was required to constantly transform itself, both externally and internally, to overcome obstacles in regard to pervasive racism and of its own making. Struggling against the vestiges of American slavery and the active tenets of twentieth-century American racial supremacy proved challenging while pursuing a goal of egalitarianism. At the same time, various ideological, class, gender, organizational, and indigenous issues emerged as just as formidable challenges, collectively combining to thwart the achievement of the goal of creating a color-blind America.

In this brief essay, major emphasis is placed on the ultimate dichotomy in black urban American life—the contrast between an African American elitist ideology that encompassed an ineluctable belief in the American Dream of racial equality and the various interests of the black middle class and rank-and-file who desired living their lives unfettered from white interference. A 1927 assessment of the organization's chances for acceptance by all classes and groups within black Chicago led to the conclusion that "there are so many diversified interests in Chicago that the N.A.A.C.P. really suffers greatly from the indifference on the part of the people."[3] A decade later, with the ideological climate unchanged, this conclusion was reiterated: "It must be remembered that in Chicago there are a large number of competing interests and an event has to be something that everyone WANTS or is in the nature of a 'natural.' Civil rights are not yet popular like policy or Joe Louis and cannot be considered as a natural drawing card."[4]

As to historical roots, the source of the problem though, ideologically, rested foremost in the relations between the two races that conformed to a superordinate-subordinate arrangement at times approximating, but not constituting, a caste system even in the North. During the Progressive Era, white acceptance of this arrangement easily justified opposition to any demonstration of black racial advancement by denying its possibility, first along theoretical lines and then through the distorted interpretation of observable conditions and facts. "We must not forget," W. E. B. Du Bois wrote in 1903 in *The Souls of Black Folk,* "that most Americans answer all queries regarding the Negro *a priori.*"[5]

Chicago as the locus of this struggle for racial equality had existed as a hotbed of ideological contention throughout its history, bringing in a geographical uniqueness to the discussion.[6] Antislavery, or abolitionist, sentiment occupied center stage during the antebellum period,

CHRISTOPHER ROBERT REED

then yielded to pro-labor agitation in the Gilded Age. Early in the twentieth century, a new age dawned and with it came a near total acceptance of the doctrine of Nordic superiority among whites. Although most blacks rejected this notion of Anglo-Saxon supremacy, from time to time its pervasive influence convinced many of them to challenge their own worth and potential to live and compete as equals with whites. Contrariwise, the raison d'être of the NAACP's existence and mission was embodied in its ideology, which derived its substantive nature from the Declaration of Independence and the Constitution. Formally, it was what, as early as 1912, New York racial egalitarian Joel E. Spingarn referred to as the "New Abolition." In the folksier jargon of the barbershop, street corner, and clubhouse, the slogan "the full loaf or none at all" encapsulated the meaning of the struggle for full realization of equal rights. However, its incorporation into the American way of life depended on the widespread promotion of racial equality as part of a new public policy along with its voluntary adoption among African Americans as a personal attitude and pattern of behavior. The struggle to gain ideological acceptance extended from the dawn of the new century into the World War Two era, when the nation and African Americans finally evinced a change in its attitudes to African Americans that marked a major shift toward more amicable race relations.[7]

During the Progressive Era, whites sometimes endorsed biracialism. This idea demanded that blacks develop a society parallel to that of the dominant culture.[8] Racists within the ranks of the progressives, whether in Chicago or elsewhere within the nation, took great solace in this belief. David Southern thought that "the congenial optimism that progressives had for the common man did not extend to the Negro."[9] In this regard, the historian Dewey R. Grantham concluded that "To liberals the Negro problem posed a challenge, but a challenge that might be rationalized and explained away or evaded . . . To explain the philosophical limitations of the Progressive movement in facing the Negro question in American democracy is more difficult. It would appear paradoxical that a philosophy which emphasized the dignity of man and which laid stress on the democratic process should reveal this blind spot in regard to what was really a complete refutation of its most sacred premises."[10]

The insidious and pervasive influence of this racism was felt to be dangerous and went neither unnoticed nor unchallenged by race egalitarians. Chicago's seemingly placid racial *milieu* degenerated to such an extent in 1910 that renowned black dentist and race equality advocate Dr. Charles E. Bentley became uneasy "in launching any new movement for a cause as unpopular as ours."[11] The threat also alarmed Jane Addams, who observed: "Not only in the South, but everywhere in America, a strong race antagonism is asserting itself, which has modes of lawlessness and insolence. The contemptuous attitude of the so-called superior race toward the inferior results in a social segregation of each race."[12] Her friend, the Reverend Celia Parker Woolley, was equally disturbed and on the occasion of the golden anniversary of the issuance of the Emancipation Proclamation shared her perception that the white race had to "emancipate [it]self from that race arrogance and belief in [its] own inherent superiority and right of rule which is today the greatest obstacle in the Negro's path."[13]

Another dichotomy existed between groups of white and black progressives who advocated racial change, sometimes overtly and, at times, covertly. The distinguishing factor between the groups hinged on their support for either an immediatist or gradualist strategy of racial advancement. In 1917, the influential National Urban League leader and president, L. Hollingsworth Wood, regarded the adherents of immediatism on the issue of racial equality as dreamers of the impractical.[14] What Hollingsworth disdained as theoretical found its expression in "neo-abolitionism." This ideology embraced the idea of a level of equality between the races that was basically economic and political in character and sometimes even social. If acceptance of racial equality was beyond the pale to many white Americans, because of its previous repugnance to American thinking and society, the facts that rendered racial gradualism so acceptable were not. Black subordination because of racial prejudice, discrimination, and segregation had relegated more than eight million Americans to a second-class status. In terms of class status, the bulk of black Chicago's population was working class and suffered under a "job ceiling" that limited their chances for economic advancement. Local custom forced them into low-paid service work as waiters, porters, maids, coachmen, and washerwomen with little hope of entry into the industrial or commercial sectors. Equality in the social sphere stood as the least of their concerns. Their precarious position in the city's labor force and difficulty in attaining a higher quality of life further served as evidence in the racist mind of the validity of the self-fulfilling prophecy of black inferiority. Spatially, their choices of residency were restricted and their demographic presence along South State Street led to the area being euphemistically known as the "Black Belt."

Disparate views among this group of black and white progressives on the appropriateness of turn-of-the-century neo-abolitionism were further illustrated in the famous dispute over tactics and strategy between the immediatists and gradualists, popularly identified with W. E. B. Du Bois of Atlanta University (and later the Niagara and NAACP movements) and Booker T. Washington of Tuskegee Institute. Beyond differences in the style, pace, and methods employed in advocacy, both groups were unified by a binding belief in the need, possibility, and ultimate probability of racial advancement.

Progressivism reached its peak in Chicago between 1907 and 1911.[15] By this time, the enthusiasm for reform created the *milieu* in which neo-abolitionists could adopt the theory of racial equality as a working possibility, confident in the belief that this ideology would liberate both whites and blacks from the shackles of racism. The extent to which this idea gained acceptance was conditioned by the time and place it appeared as much as by the energy expended on its behalf. The time could not have appeared more propitious to progressives of the neo-abolitionist persuasion because the notion of change was pregnant.

Quite often the neo-abolitionists were given to moralistic outbursts and stances that gave their activities the appearance of a crusade. With a moral fervor that bordered on righteousness, this intensity and inclination toward ideological purity became indispensable to the fulfillment of their goals. Given the zealous abolitionist origins of the NAACP ideal, the weight of historical consistency virtually dictated this mode of thought and action. In spring 1912, at the height of Progressivism, Oswald Garrison Villard, a leading spokesman of the NAACP, president of the *New York Evening Post* and the grandson of abolitionist William Lloyd Garrison, addressed the fourth annual conference of the NAACP meeting in Chicago about its mission. At this racially integrated gathering, courageously hosted by Jane Addams, Villard made the following fervent announcement: "Ours . . . is a battle for democracy, pure and undefiled. It is not for us to compromise, however much others feel the necessity for doing so . . . [the NAACP] asks no favors, no privileges, no special advantages for those disadvantaged ones, whose fathers and mothers but fifty years ago were still being sold upon the auction block."[16] Villard rekindled the fervor of neo-abolitionism embodied in the national NAACP's purpose, which sought "to uplift the colored men and women . . . by securing to them the full enjoyment of their rights as citizens, justice in the courts, and equality of opportunity everywhere."[17]

The racial egalitarians of Chicago rarely deviated from this ideological stance, but when they did, it was due to the need to reconcile the pragmatism of American life and thought with the realities of black material deprivation, the existence of a racial caste system, and sometimes their own latent racial inclinations. The Chicago branch's first president, Massachusetts-born Judge Edward Osgood Brown, needed to see black material advancement firsthand on the outskirts of Tuskegee Institute in rural Alabama to revitalize his sometimes wavering ideological commitment.[18] Chicago public schools superintendent Ella Flagg Young also developed deeper appreciation of black people as achievers when she made a trip to Tuskegee as the guest of the renowned Chicago philanthropist, Julius Rosenwald, and of Booker T. Washington. It gave her greater resolve when challenging racial discrimination at the Wendell Phillips High School on the city's South Side, the scene of creeping prejudicial behavior among white students and their parents.[19]

In the eyes of historians two generations removed in time, the triumph of neo-abolitionism in Chicago could be realized only if Booker T. Washington's ideological influence was overcome. Many historians found disagreement among blacks over which strategy should be endorsed for racial advancement. Accordingly, they wrote of the importance of a schism in which a Washington camp competed vigorously for hegemony over the hearts and minds of black Chicagoans with an influential, equally determined Du Bois faction. The concept, however, of divisive ideological warfare in Chicago lacks contemporary evidence to support its existence. While there was disagreement among African Americans, in a population of 30,000 in 1900 and 44,000 in 1910, it never reached the heights presumed and presented by historians and other writers.[20]

Differing views over the best means to advance black racial aspirations persisted for various reasons. First, Booker T. Washington's tenets did, at times, complement the new neo-abolitionist ideology. At a Chicago NAACP meeting in 1914, the peripatetic neo-abolitionist Joel E. Spingarn of New York delivered an unusually incisive explanation to his audience: "Idealism . . . it is the function of the [NAACP] to kindle. Mr. Washington is doing a needed work in making a strong and prosperous people from which the Association may recruit strength. But the two sides of the general movement must thus supplement each other, for together they represent the balance of utilitarianism and idealism which is the characteristic gait of American progress."[21] Further, contemporary editorials in the *Chicago Defender* and the *Chicago Broad-Ax* captured the essence of the black community's feelings on the matter when they explained that Washington's strategy "represented a line of thought that was essential to the masses living under the conditions from which he arose," but that when radical and conservative ideologies were evaluated "both were necessary to complete the armament of this oppressed race . . . [, so] why the hysteria from the advocates of either plan for race advancement; surely both have our interest at heart, and both being earnest and zealous, why let the zeal become embittered . . . ?"[22] As to the *Defender*'s specific stance on, and contribution to, the proper course of race advancement, longtime NAACP stalwart Archie L. Weaver recalled that "our objectives and [its] platform were identical—only [it] was five years ahead of us."[23]

Near midcentury when he wrote his autobiography, militant black clergyman Reverend Reverdy Ransom remembered that while he was in Chicago there were differences but no schism. He recalled that "these two theories of Negro progress were not absolutely contradictory."[24] There was personal animosity in abundance, to be sure, and it was intense, but it existed in Chicago as part of a tactical, or subideological, struggle on how to best assure group racial advancement. Moreover, blacks in Chicago shared a tradition of viewing economics coupled with racial solidarity and self-help as components of their strategy of racial advancement.[25] This arrangement existed before Booker T. Washington made his historic Atlanta Compromise Address in 1895 and established his National Negro Business League in 1900.

The bulk of the black civic leadership living on the periphery of, or outside the Black Belt altogether, seemingly acclimatized itself to whatever furor might have developed deep inside the community. Further, heterogeneity rather than, as often assumed, social un-differentiation, categorized the black rank-and-file. Longtime residents who were a part of the "Old Settlers," short-term residents, attracted by the Columbian Exposition of 1893 and by strikebreaking opportunities at the turn of the century, and newly arrived migrants who came to the city during and after 1915 comprised the mass of ordinary citizens. In the aggregate, the equal rights advocates expected this composite group to constitute its primary base of support in Chicago, which was consis-tent with New York's plan for a national organization. For the most part, the black masses remained aloof from this new ideological thrust that was promoted by the elite. Their primary desire centered around free-dom from white interference in black affairs. With the passage of time in the new century, they found the necessary ingredients for content-ment within the city in the fledgling dream of a self-contained racial enclave under their control, similar to the longings of some of the European immigrant groups.

This pattern reflected the bitter taste left from American race rela-tions from the previous two and one-half centuries wherein black Chicagoans developed a particular northern brand of racial fatalism over time that originated from both their contemporary experiences in Chicago and the subconscious ones they brought from the plantations, small towns, and cities of the South. Much like the situation that devel-oped among Chicago's immigrants, black isolation in American life shaped the attitudes and worldview of African Americans. If an event did not involve members of their group, they ignored it. Accordingly, an incident of international magnitude such as the sinking of the lux-ury liner *Titanic* in 1912 received almost no coverage in the *Defender* and went unreported in the *Broad-Ax*. What concerned the black working class the most were occurrences most relevant to their lives. The reac-tion to pugilist Jack Johnson's pursuit of happiness in his choice of mates, which ran afoul of white psychosexual codes in the city as well as in the nation, assumed importance as a group experience. Blacks sim-ply refused to accept white-set parameters on certain dreams they pursued. [26]

During the "Great Migration" of 1915–1919, newly arrived migrants exhibited an assertiveness consistent with the feelings that originally convinced them to leave their homes in the South to settle in Chicago. Described by the migration historian James R. Grossman as persons who developed a new strategy of racial advancement as part of a new grassroots social movement, they also ignored the Chicago NAACP. Their immediate needs were met as they pursued economic, political, and educational opportunities. In regard to their dreams of their place in the "open" society that Chicago offered, Grossman wrote: "There is little evidence that black southerners coming to Chicago were especially interested in integrating *per se;* most of them were concerned about legal protection, political rights, and access to the paths to security or mobility . . . In some aspects of everyday life, many newcomers looked forward to freedom from whites; they evinced little desire to attend integrated churches or spend leisure time with white people."[27]

Whatever the character of life that blacks carved out for themselves, the acceptability of blacks as political and economic equals in the white mind was directly related to black progress in the areas of community betterment and personal discipline. This became a matter of such importance that various Methodist and Baptist church and civic leaders, such as Ida B. Wells-Barnett and Robert S. Abbott, spent a disproportionate amount of their time involved in improving the quality of community life by raising group standards. When Booker T. Washington came to Chicago in 1910 and 1912, he used this theme as part of his appeal to blacks. Blacks were urged to become more competitive, to assume control over the neighborhoods where they numerically predominated, and to prepare to be criticized for any untoward developments within their communities. He encouraged black Chicagoans by appealing to their sense of racial chauvinism. After observing and meeting with some members of southern Europe's working class, he boasted, "The European thinks slow, moves slow and works slow. The Negro can beat him. But the northern [American] white man thinks fast, moves fast[,] and works fast. Prepare yourself to beat him."[28] And, contrary to what Du Bois wrote in the *Crisis* about Washington's 1912 visit, the Tuskegeean was not demanding any more from blacks than white progressives in Chicago, like Jane Addams and the Reverend Celia Parker Woolley, were asking.[29]

As black Chicago evolved into a somewhat racially isolated society around the First World War, it began to take on the features of the national normative class structure based around socioeconomic interests. The elite constituted the top stratum of an upper and lower middle class positioned above a base of working-class persons divided between industrial laborers in the packing houses and steel mills, and those remaining in the service sector. Beneath them rested the semi-criminal and criminal elements that comprised the undesirables of the lower class. The concept of race equality seemed real and the actualization of a color-blind national society appeared achievable to a portion of the economically well-off upper middle class and their complementary partners, the less well-off cultural elite in the lower middle class. But to the mass of the laboring class, along with business-oriented and political segments of the upper and middle classes, doubt existed as to the efficacy of this goal. And, if the problem of class wasn't severe enough an impediment, the oligarchic structure of branch governance stymied the development of programs relevant to the needs of the people of the Black Metropolis.

Many others favored a belief system that approximated the tenets of Booker T. Washington's accommodationist racial strategy. Many of the 50,000 newly arrived southern migrants who reached Chicago during the "Great Migration," 1916–1918, and the 115,000 who followed in the 1920s often held fatalistic views. Consequently, they remained apathetic to the theoretical promise of racial equality with its commitment to a better tomorrow and sought the practical and the immediate. In the background, the image of thousands of unhooded marching Klansmen along Pennsylvania Avenue in the nation's capital reinforced their doubts. As a result, throughout the history of the city NAACP branch, the perceived pipe dream associated with racial equality met its counterbalance in racial moderation, or even in voluntary separation.

A major ideological strain evolving in the twenties, especially among the business element, but including members of the black political machine under the influence of Edward H. Wright, the "Iron Master," was the "Dream of the Black Metropolis." The racial self-contained enclave of which it boasted embodied varying elements of egalitarianism, militant and moderate, along with black nationalism, depending on its adherents' interpretation. Its appeal was pervasive and across class lines. Meantime, the nationalism of Marcus Garvey's Universal Negro Improvement Association, which sought working-class support, grew as a potent force within the various black neighborhoods throughout Chicago.

Nineteen twenty-five brought the branch to a critical phase in its development—the emergence of a new patriarchy, in which there was exclusive black leadership. This hegemonic change reflected a class shift as biracial, almost exclusively white, upper-class leadership was replaced by an upper-middle-class black professional coterie. Moreover, this development involved generational and ideological change along with racial transformation as the first black president now led the branch. Differences in age and the experiences of black Chicagoans maturing during the "New Negro" era now assumed a greater saliency, prompting an internal NAACP memo at this time to allude to competing, "diversified interests." The new black president of the predominantly African American Chicago NAACP in 1925 was Dr. Carl G. Roberts, a prominent surgeon. A native of neighboring Indiana, Roberts associated with the cause of equal rights on his own volition and was brought to the attention of the Chicago NAACP by chance. The branch secretary and new king maker, Morris Lewis, informed the national office that Roberts was "a thorough N.A.A.C.P. man . . . such talent and enthusiasm [for the equal rights cause] is sorely needed."[30]

In being a "thorough N.A.A.C.P. man," Roberts expressed views that sharply contrasted with the dream of a Black Metropolis, which he equated with racial separation cloaked in the robe of integration. "Biracialism . . . the proposition [that] the Negro should develop his own economic and cultural civilization, separate and apart from the dominant group surrounding him, implies a strong compliment," stated Roberts. His detractors asked "him to do something that no other group in history has successfully accomplished [and that is to survive and thrive in isolation from his fellow men]."[31] That Roberts's view could be counter to what was acceptable in Chicago was explained to him by Robert W. Bagnall, director of branches, in a solicited analysis in 1925, when Bagnall laid emphasis on an evolving "New Negro" personality. "Since the World War, there has been a revolutionary change in the psychology of the Negro. He now will work with whites or permit them to work with him; but he resents it when they work for him—he being their ward. He wants to control to a large degree his own affairs. . . . His racial conscience has been greatly developed. Our trouble in Chicago has been that this has been taken too much into account."[32] What Bagnall recognized was the maturation of a people who were progressing systematically beyond the psychological dependence on whites for guidance imposed upon them by their parents and grandparents or by their own entrenched upper-class leadership.

The black working and emerging middle classes wanted something more closely aligned to what Jesse Binga, the black banker, and Anthony Overton, the black banker-publisher-insurance magnate-manufacturer wanted: tangible success in a locus under their control, in a black city within a city, the Black Metropolis. Whether the latter existed in their minds as a means or end to race advancement, or as a fantasy, it carried relevance to their lives. As late as 1925, race equality was still too theoretical and therefore too much of an intangible for a great many black citizens of the Windy City. White America had not proven itself capable of recognizing the theoretical implications of the American Dream in which "all men were created equal." With this distrust of white intentions, a nationalistic and a particularistic African American version of accommodation sufficed. Within eight months after Roberts had taken office, he resigned from the presidency, probably in disgust with the lack of middle-class and rank-and-file support for the branch's mission and program.

Ideological contention resurfaced in 1933 with the famous "Chicago Revolt," which originated as soon as lower-middle-class control ensued. New branch president A. C. MacNeal assumed power, espousing a level of ideological purity that was euphemistically labeled "the whole loaf or none at all" approach. It was an uncompromising, zealous philosophy that ensured factionalism. MacNeal and his supporters vehemently opposed segregation and even tackled both the concept and existence of the Black Metropolis.[33] In the minds of these advocates of racial equality, there were true believers and traitors, and most of Chicago, the Association, and the nation fell into the latter category. However, MacNeal's ideological purity did not reflect the branch's collective thinking as others questioned his views, seeing little value to combining imprudence with ideological commitment.

MacNeal once wrote that "the only reason that I personally, am ready to abandon everything that is Jim Crow is because it is certainly been [sic] proven that 'we can being separate demonstrate our greatness and break down the barriers' is a washout. It has reinforced the barriers. I am committed to the 'whole loaf or none at all' policy. The half loaf is getting too small via the Jim Crow and separatist route."[34] MacNeal regarded the "Negro National Anthem [also known as "Lift Every Voice and Sing" and written by James Weldon and J. Rosamond Johnson] as a 'Cradle Song' and a hangover of the confused and muddled thinking and approach of the NAACP in its beginning."[35]

As one who was present at the beginning, the venerable W. E. B. Du Bois created a tumult in 1933 and 1934 in a spate of speeches, comments, and editorials in the *Crisis* articulating his misgivings about the economic course that the Association was taking in the middle of a debilitating, worldwide depression. He questioned the organization's longstanding reluctance to tackle economic problems as well as its insistence that all forms of racial separation, forced or voluntary, be opposed.[36] As sexagenarian Du Bois assessed the situation in 1933 he concluded that the economic exigencies of the depression dictated a change in Association policy. The plight of blacks in the aggregate was so severe that he foresaw mass starvation as a real threat. Du Bois, though, was not advocating "a program of complete racial segregation [or] even nationalism among Negroes." On the contrary, he was stressing the real point that "economic discrimination [was] fundamental and advised concentration of planning" as a solution to the black plight during the Depression,[37] something commonly accepted in the Black Metropolis phase of Bronzeville's existence. In the fall of 1933, Du Bois supported a New Deal measure calling for the establishment of a separate federal agency to oversee the social and economic progress of black Americans—something akin to the Bureau of Indian Affairs. MacNeal considered it to be a new "Emperor Jones scheme."[38] To A. Clement MacNeal's and Irvin C. Mollison's ears, Du Bois's pronouncements sounded like apostasy. The emanation of this argument from Chicago in 1934 led Du Bois to dub the assault upon him from within the Association the "Chicago Revolt."[39] William Pickens discovered that some branch leaders considered Du Bois's acceptance of voluntary separation and certain vestiges of segregation as merely a tactical maneuver during an economic crisis. "These leaders do not interpret it as Mollison interpreted it," Pickens wrote. "As one said, we take it that Du Bois means that we should get our team together and smash the opposition with an organized team. At the same time, they believe in the Association's need to stand for equal rights for Negro

Americans."[40] As to the Du Bois affair, it ended in June 1934 as Du Bois resigned from the organization under external pressure and amid some self-generated fanfare.

In the following decade, the attitudes and values of Illinois congressman Arthur W. Mitchell, an Alabaman by birth, self-professed disciple of Booker T. Washington during his youth, and the only sitting African American in the Capitol, exemplified moderation in race relations. By the late 1940s and into the next decade, Mitchell's successor in Congress, another black Democrat, William L. Dawson, acted as the voice of moderation at a time in the city when circumstances dictated immediate changes in race relations. Obviously the political sphere produced no challenge to the racial status quo.

Other ideological influences were important and pervasive. From the right, the influence of Garveyism in the 1920s yielded to the black Islamic chauvinism of the Nation of Islam in the 1950s. A number of blacks supported this ideology because of their longing for an existence free of American racism, separate, if need be. And from the left, communism enjoyed its greatest popularity during the 1930s and remained a major force into the 1950s until the rise of McCarthyism. Socialism emerged during the 1920s as a doctrine of interest and enjoyed a modicum of support through the 1950s as well. By the late 1960s, the rising influence of the Black Panther Party signaled near complete mass discontent with upper- and middle-class leadership, programs, and ideas of racial progress. Economic issues dominated discussions and the intent of street protests.

Just as the advent of the Second World War brought an end to xenophobia from Germany, Italy, and Japan, at home, for the first time in American history, white racial supremacy was on the wane and could be safely assumed to be dissipating as a major belief system. As the branch increased its efforts to eliminate it completely, another internal shift found working-class leaders at the helm, both with a viable program to promote and grow popular support. This transformation brought not only Henry W. McGee, a postal worker and effective labor organizer, into leadership, but also democracy for the first time. With ideological acceptance of the actualization of equal rights and democracy (classlessness) within the leadership and ranks of the Chicago NAACP, programmatic thrust could parallel the journey toward ideological consistency. It was at this juncture that the branch clashed with the desires of Congressman Dawson's machine. Claiming to represent the interests of the working class in meeting their basic, or "welfare needs," in the areas of housing, employment, and education, the Dawson organization competed with the Chicago NAACP's more loftier "status needs" as expressed in its program and ideology.

The branch's attainment of institutional status by midcentury represented the culmination of a process of empowerment of one of the two major countervailing forces in Chicago's black community. One force was the race egalitarian or integrationist movement, which aimed to make the American Dream a reality for black Chicagoans as soon as possible. Its primary vehicle was the Chicago branch of the NAACP and its support from the upper and lower middle class as well as certain segments of organized labor grew impressively. The other power was the black political machine. Led initially by Edward H. Wright and affiliated with Mayor William "Big Bill" Thompson's Republican machine, it functioned well for the select few. In the years and elections after 1933, Democratic mayor Edward Kelly and the Cook County Democratic machine induced the black electorate to abandon its allegiance to, and leadership within, the Republican Party. William L. Dawson led this new Democratic bloc by the late forties and early fifties, aligned with Democratic mayor Richard J. Daley. By midcentury, the simultaneous empowerment of the two movements resulted in conflict and, finally, confrontation. However, the antithetical forces merged by the 1970s and with the election of Harold Washington as Chicago's first African American mayor (1983–1987), civil rights and independent politics were briefly wed. Today, the branch has forgotten its role as the vanguard organization of the civil rights movement in Chicago as has the black public. Without class envy and competition, political domination, gender strife, and ideological conflict to impede its progress, the organization can be said to have weathered the storm but ended up aground.

Dr. Martin Luther King's appearance in Chicago failed to produce the racial utopia of which many dreamed, but it did manage to raise the level of contradictions in the minds of many persons within the masses and left as part of its legacy Operation PUSH—People United to Serve Humanity. Beyond the faded leadership of the Chicago NAACP, such groups, along with many smaller indigenous protest bodies, have carried on the fight until this day.

CHAPTER THIRTEEN

The NAACP in California, 1914–1950

JONATHAN WATSON

W ITHIN FIVE YEARS of its founding, the National Association
for the Advancement of Colored People had established
branches in California. Over the next forty years, and
beyond, these chapters provided an unbroken organizational response
to discrimination and prejudice in the state. The continuity of activism
provided by branches proved of immense value during the period in
which California modernized, industrialized, and integrated into the
fabric of the nation. This essay examines the activities of NAACP
activists in California from the organization's founding through to the
end of the Second World War.

Within the historiography of the NAACP, the work of California
activists during the first half of the twentieth century has been largely
overlooked, featuring little in some of the most recent significant contributions to our understanding of the organization.[1] This omission
is a consequence of a consensus that holds that no nationally significant campaigns or cases originated in the state during this period.
Given the relatively small size of the state's black community prior to
the 1940s, scholars have concluded that, until the mass migration
prompted by war, the west was figuratively "on the periphery of black
America."[2] It has been left to those exploring the development of black
communities in the state to develop our understanding of the
NAACP's contribution to the civil rights struggle in California. Given
this context, much of this work has failed to consider how Californian

NAACP activism contributed to the development of the organization as a whole.[3]

NAACP branches in California played a vital role in stemming Jim Crow in the West during the 1910s and 1920s. In the 1930s, they developed a new research and lobbying agenda to deal with the persistence of discrimination in New Deal welfare agencies. During the Second World War, these branches played a critical role in the battle to desegregate the state's defense industries and labor unions. Outside the workplace they fought to end discrimination in housing and for improved race relations. From the outset, the targets of campaigning and activism reflected the pace of community development and in-migration. The contribution of these branches to the national agenda of the NAACP was also important, acting as an early warning of prejudice in the cinema and supporting national campaigns against federal appointments. From the 1930s, these branches also adopted a model of local research and federal lobbying that became a cornerstone of civil rights activism for much of the rest of the twentieth century. As it is not possible to examine the development of every branch and every campaign in the state, this essay is intended as an outline, charting the creation, development, and maturation of the NAACP in California.

At the start of the twentieth century, black California was relatively small, but growing. Over the first decade, the combined black populations of Los Angeles, Oakland, and San Francisco almost trebled in size to around twelve thousand, the majority based around Los Angeles and Oakland; by contrast, both New York City and Washington, D.C., boasted black populations of over ninety thousand.[4] While California already had established political and economic institutions at the start of the twentieth century, it was not until the 1890s that the infrastructure of transportation, water, power, and public facilities started to be developed across the state; a process that took decades to complete.[5] These factors also affected the emergence of the regional industrial economy, which did not provide African Americans with the same employment prospects of northern industrial cities, such as Chicago or Detroit. As a consequence, black California, while growing, was not a major focus of black in-migration until the 1940s. Of those who did move west, a significant number were relatively affluent, middle class, and professional. It was these people, described by Douglas Flamming as "middle class in spirit and outlook" who formed the core of the NAACP in California during the first half of the twentieth century.[6]

Black Californians had already organized to promote social cohesion, fight for political representation, and protect their civil rights. In 1895 a statewide convention of the Afro-American League had drawn over a hundred delegates. The region was also toured by national black leaders, such as Booker T. Washington, seeking funding and influence.[7] Local churches, masonic lodges, women's clubs, and civic forums reflected the desire of black Californians to forge their own community identities in urban centers across the state. These social organizations were further bolstered by the local black press. By 1910 there were at least seven weekly black newspapers being published across the state, serving as a forum for both news and community affairs. When W. E. B. Du Bois toured the state in 1913 to raise awareness of the NAACP, he was visiting communities already well versed in the civic value of organizations.

During the tour Du Bois jotted details for a report that was later published in the *Crisis*. The article reflected both the positive and negative of the black experience in the sunshine state. Of Los Angeles, he commented, "Nowhere in the United States is the Negro so well and so beautifully housed, nor the average efficiency and intelligence in the colored population so high." In the Bay Area, he was able to stop "in a good hotel" and dine "at first-class restaurants." Pictures of local affluence, such as large suburban homes, and the motorcade that greeted Du Bois in Los Angeles filled other pages of the edition. However, Du Bois also observed the discrimination facing the black Californians. He noted that "the opportunity of the San Francisco Negro to earn a living is very difficult; but he knows this and is beginning to ask why," and that "Los Angeles is not Paradise . . . The Color line is there and it is sharply drawn."[8]

The status of black Californians was indeed mixed. Indicators of affluence showed that, in some cases, black Californians were in a far better position than communities east of the Mississippi. For instance, in 1910, 36.1 percent of black Angelenos owned their own homes, compared to 2.6 percent of black New Yorkers and 11 percent of African Americans in New Orleans.[9] In addition to affluence, the average black

Californian was also relatively well educated: 1910 literacy rates for African Americans in the West as a whole were around 90 percent, double that of their counterparts in the South.[10] However, these communities lived in a state in which attempts to segregate and discriminate had grown in tandem with infrastructure.[11] While blacks could vote, districts were gerrymandered to allow them minimal representation. Intermittent attempts were also made to segregate schooling and housing, which, by the 1940s, had produced embryonic ghettos across the state. Where California's experience differed was that the impact of discrimination was affected in part by the small scale of the black presence and also by the presence of other, larger, nonwhite minorities, notably Asian and Latino in-migrants and their naturalized descendants; antipathy was directed against all those branded nonwhite. So, while black Californians faced significant obstacles to equality, they were not bound into the damaging binary of black/white race relations that typified much of the urban North and the South.

Du Bois's visit energized members of the state's black elite. Within a year, three NAACP branches had become established: Los Angeles, San Diego, and Northern California, a branch that encompassed the Bay Area communities of San Francisco, Oakland, Berkeley, and Alameda County. Established in 1914, the Los Angeles branch was founded and led by John and Vada Somerville, dentists, who were also husband and wife, and attorney E. Burton Ceruti. The branch had a white president for its first few years, yet the post was honorary. Within the Northern California branch, a similar pattern of black leadership quickly emerged. Based in Oakland, the chapter was led by figures such as businessman Walter Butler and attorneys John R. Drake, Tabytha Anderson, Leland Hawkins, and H. L. Richardson.[12] The black leadership of these branches provided a foretaste of developments within the NAACP as a whole. It was not until the early 1920s that critical administrative positions of the national leadership would be occupied by African Americans; in the highest tiers of the Association's management, the process took even longer.

Two campaigns from 1915 highlight the nature of the challenge facing the new NAACP chapters in California. In the first instance, the Los Angeles NAACP joined with local newspapers and other pressure groups to successfully prevent $50,000 being apportioned by the state assembly for the establishment of an industrial school in Allensworth, Tulare County, south of Los Angeles. As Allensworth was an all-black community, it followed that the school would also be all black. NAACP activists felt that to agree to the school's construction was to tacitly approve segregated education.[13] The same year, D. W. Griffith's block-buster *The Birth of a Nation* provoked action from branches across the state. Given an advanced screening in February 1915, appalled branch leaders found the film "designed to (present the) Negro (as) a hideous monster."[14] They wired Association headquarters in New York, giving them time to organize other branches prior to screenings across the nation.[15] After attempts to ban the film being shown in Los Angeles failed, branch attorney E. Burton Ceruti continued to work to prevent any more films that defamed the race reaching the public, securing a citywide ordinance to that effect in 1918.[16]

Other branches met with varying levels of success. In Pasadena, activists succeeded in banning the film outright.[17] The Northern California branch secured cuts to the film in San Francisco, where censors agreed to remove scenes they believed might heighten racial tension. Whether the branch and censors agreed that scenes of interracial contact were inherently offensive is not known, but these were lost in the cut.[18] Similar moves to censor the film later succeeded in New York and Boston, while in Chicago the film received a temporary ban.[19] While failing to remove race prejudice or racial stereotypes from cinema, the campaigns did much to galvanize state branches. They demonstrated how branches could act as early warning for a coming storm and could develop strategies that others within the organization could then adopt.

The campaigns, alongside the fear provoked by the Red summer of 1919 and a tour by field secretary James Weldon Johnson, contributed to increased membership rolls. By 1920, Los Angeles had seven hundred members; Northern California, over a thousand.[20] A further thirteen branches, from Long Beach, San Bernardino, and Vallejo in the South, to Stockton and Sacramento toward the North of the state had been founded by the start of the new decade.[21] In some instances, as elsewhere across the nation these membership figures marked a peak that would not be superseded until the Second World War. This was a consequence of several factors. Competition from other organizations, such as Marcus Garvey's Universal Negro Improvement Association, which, by

1921, had chapters in San Diego, Los Angeles, and San Francisco, was seen by some branches as a drain on membership and unnecessary competition.[22] Yet by 1922, the threat of Garveyism had already peaked and local UNIA activists soon split from Garvey's organization, leading to its presence in the state almost completely dissolving by the end of the decade.

Other barriers to growth included internal splits. In 1923, San Francisco members, disillusioned with the outlook of the Oakland-based Northern California leadership, created their own branch. While this made the organization more locally responsive, concerns persisted in San Francisco, as they did in Los Angeles, that the continued domination by members of the black elite was preventing the organization from achieving mass membership. Of the Los Angeles branch, one black Angeleno later recalled that "the NAACP was run by aristocrats"; in San Francisco, one of the founders of the Northern California branch derided the San Francisco leadership's "high-handed" style for driving away members.[23] Despite these problems, branches continued to pursue local and national campaigns that aimed to benefit the broader black community and not just the middle class.

The reason why such an agenda remained important was the growing segregationist tendency that accompanied the state's extraordinary growth. The opening of the Panama Canal, improved rail routes, such as the Southern Pacific, and highways, all served to integrate the state into the national infrastructure, and cheapen the process of migration. While discrimination in the South began pushing a small but steady stream of black southerners westward, growing oil, shipbuilding, aerospace, agriculture and entertainment industries offered the possibility of work, especially toward southern California. By 1920 Los Angeles's black population had doubled in a decade to over 15,000, twice the size of the combined populations of Oakland and San Francisco.[24] In this context, Anglo-Californians determined to maintain racial supremacy. Examples of the white urge to maintain dominance include the brief boom of the Ku Klux Klan, the state supreme court sanctioning the use of private deeds and covenants allowing whites to proscribe future ownership of property by nonwhites in 1919, and the incorporation of Watts into the city of Los Angeles in 1926 designed to prevent the community succumbing to black domination.[25] Activists were determined to protect the fragile freedoms black Californians possessed, lest the state become "Southernized."

The boldest example of protest during this period was mounted by Los Angeles branch president H. Claude Hudson. Hudson's history was typical of many of those moving west before the Second World War. Born to sharecroppers in Louisiana, Hudson studied dentistry at Howard University and ran an NAACP branch in Louisiana before moving to California. In 1927, he was arrested leading a one-man wade-in on a beach that had been declared white only. The ensuing court case saw Hudson acquitted and the segregated beach ruled illegal. Recognizing the personal risks involved in the case, William Pickens, national field secretary, wrote to Hudson, telling him he was "more than a hero to take *your place* in the line."[26] Through standing against a symbolic act of segregation, Hudson contributed to staunching the westward march of discrimination in public places. In June the following year, Los Angeles became the first city in the Far West to hold the NAACP's annual convention. Branch founder John Somerville built the hundred-room Hotel Somerville to host delegates. The occasion emphasized that the NAACP was a truly national organization.

Californian branches involved themselves in numerous national NAACP campaigns during this period, contributing funds to court cases, antilynching campaigns, and extradition battles. In 1930, they campaigned to block the confirmation of Judge John J. Parker to the U.S. Supreme Court. Citing Parker's past racist comments, the NAACP leadership asked all branches to lobby their local U.S. congressmen to oppose Parker's confirmation.[27] If the congressmen ignored them, the branches were instructed to work for their defeat at the following election. Both the Los Angeles and San Francisco branches lobbied to block Parker. In Los Angeles, the branch helped unseat Senator Sam Shortridge in the 1932 senatorial primary after he backed Parker; his share of the black vote dropped from a previous majority of Negro voters in the state to only a fifth.[28] Through such work California branches demonstrated their ability to deliver the national agenda of the NAACP.

The Great Depression, and the governmental response to it, generated new concerns and opened up new avenues of activism. Criticized by some for failing to develop a response to economic hardships, California branches developed important strategies, reporting on and lobbying federal relief programs. On finding cases of discrimination in works projects, branches passed on information to the national leadership so that federal government officials, more amenable to racial justice than their state counterparts, might reconsider discriminatory policies. The San Francisco and Los Angeles branches were particularly conspicuous in their pursuit of discrimination in welfare projects. In 1934, the San Francisco NAACP investigated discriminatory hiring practices on the construction site of the Boulder Dam, sending a report to the secretary of the interior, which led him to call for more black workers to be hired. Although this was then reneged on, it showed the possibility of local research and national lobbying.[29]

In 1934, The Los Angeles branch placed evidence before a federal grand jury that administrators for the Civil Works Administration (CWA) were guilty of fraud and discriminatory hiring practices. Although the charges were eventually dropped, the model was soon used again.[30] The next year, branch members challenged segregation within the Civilian Conservation Corps (CCC). Black recruits served in internally segregated companies of roughly two hundred men. The new branch president, Thomas Griffith Jr., was concerned that the CCC could be a Trojan horse for Jim Crow in California.[31] The investigation led to an inquiry in the War Department, which was responsible for the CCC. While the protest did not change policy, federal government took the charges seriously. Engaging federal government over local issues offered a foretaste of future tactics within the civil rights struggle; these California activists offer one of the first examples of that strategy in action.

In 1936, the Association restructured its state-level administrative framework. The fourteen California branches met in Los Angeles for three days to hold the first state conference of branches and institute a permanent regional body. This offered the possibility of a more coordinated statewide approach to activism.[32] That move was followed, in some branches, by more restructuring. In 1938, the Los Angeles branch organized new committees focusing on jails and prisons; emergency relief; community betterment; slum clearance and housing; state activities; and complaints and youth problems, reflecting growing local concerns with social and economic issues. [33] In October 1937, branch leaders joined with two local black newspapers and members of the city's small Communist Party in picketing a department store on

Central Avenue in protest at discriminatory employment practices that forced the hiring of black sales staff after a month.[34] Such campaigns and reorganization left state branches ready for the turbulent decade that followed.

The challenges confronting California's black communities as a consequence of the Second World War developed in two phases. First, during the prewar mobilization of 1940 and 1941 and then, after the United States had entered the war, from 1942 to the years immediately after the war's end. During the first of these periods, branches challenged employers' refusal to hire black workers in the state's burgeoning defense industries. In the second phase, branches dealt with issues of employment rights, community race relations, and residential segregation. The response to wartime discrimination by branches depended on the salience of local issues and the nature of local leadership. Many scholars have argued, in line with a wider historiographical current, that the Association was frequently out of step with the needs of the wider black community and the tactics necessary to effect change. Charles Chamberlain has argued that "the workplace served as a key site for the struggle over equality" and that the Los Angeles NAACP, the biggest branch in the state, did little in this area.[35] Yet, taking the efforts of the branches as a whole, it is clear the work of the Association has been undervalued.

Over the first two years of the 1940s, the nation's industrial base mobilized for war. California saw an intensification of its already significant military-industrial development, with over $70 billion being invested in war-related industries in the state.[36] Between 1939 and 1943, southern California, holding a preponderance of aerospace manufacturing in the state, saw a rise in wage and salaried workers from 812,000 to 1,402,000; in the San Francisco Bay Area, the shipbuilding industry grew by over 150,000 jobs between 1940 and 1943.[37] Despite this massive expansion, the region's black workers were initially barred from these new opportunities. Defense contractors recruited only a handful of black workers, reflecting their own prejudice, and that of many in their labor force.[38] NAACP chapters organized to confront this discrimination.

In southern California, attempts to broaden employment opportunities took a number of forms. Los Angeles branch activists picketed and lobbied for jobs and joined local coalitions. They provided support for the United Auto Workers who pushed for an end to employment discrimination in local defense plants. In May–June 1941, the branch joined UAW pickets at North American Aviation as the union sought higher wages and an end to discriminatory hiring practices.[39] Activists also gave evidence to the city's hearings of the president's Fair Employment Practice Committee in October 1941. The testimony presented by the NAACP contributed to the FEPC's damning report on regional hiring practices. Both the witnesses and the committee's findings impressed the national black press. The *Chicago Defender*'s headline trumpeted: "Big Business Trembles During Los Angeles Hearing; coast probe shows bias in defense training."[40] While much scholarship has noted the ineffectiveness of the FEPC in achieving concrete results, the ability of branches to articulate their agenda demonstrated at the outset of the war that local NAACP activists were fully engaged in the struggle for employment opportunity.

After Pearl Harbor, the barriers to employment in some of the state's key defense industries receded. As the war progressed, the number of black workers employed in the state's war industries steadily rose. At its peak, roughly 30,000 African Americans worked in the state's privately owned shipyards.[41] While employment opportunities existed, the struggle for equality within the workplace, and within unions, provided a new challenge. Once a union gained the support of a majority of workers within a yard, it became the sole negotiator on behalf of the workers. In many Californian shipyards, the International Brotherhood of Boilermakers, Iron Shipbuilders and Helpers of America, had struck a "Master Agreement" with management, guaranteeing it as the sole worker's representative; any employee of the shipyard had to be a member of the union. The IBB did not want black workers as equals within the union, either excluding them completely, or, after July 1942, establishing "auxiliary" locals for them. These allowed black workers to pay the same union dues, while receiving no insurance coverage, no transfer rights to other sites, and no right to advance in status.[42] Ultimately, it was activists in the Bay Area, working within the NAACP and through other alliances, that smashed the IBB's Jim Crow practices.[43]

The battle against auxiliary locals was first taken up by independent groups of black workers in a number of the state's shipyards in 1943. Workers in Los Angeles and the Bay Area mounted campaigns for full union rights, refusing to pay union dues and pursuing court action to end the IBB's discriminatory practices.[44] Consequently, in November 1943, the IBB withdrew work permits from a number of protestors at the Marinship yard on the North Bay. The following month, one of those affected, Joseph James, started legal action for himself and fellow black workers' reinstatement and compensation from the IBB in a federal court. Thurgood Marshall deemed the implications of the case for the national future of the Jim Crow auxiliaries as sufficiently important to attend on behalf of the NAACP's Legal Defense Fund.

Marshall wanted to coordinate the case with a similar action being pursued against another IBB local through the NAACP branch in Providence, Rhode Island. When James lost his first hearing, Marshall advised a new plan of attack via state civil rights laws. In February 1944, the state superior court found for James and his colleagues and against Marinship and the IBB. While the IBB prepared its final appeal, James become San Francisco NAACP branch president and was soon exchanging thoughts on the case directly with Thurgood Marshall.[45] The following January the state supreme court confirmed the verdict of *James vs. Marinship,* noting that auxiliary locals were "discriminatory and unequal."[46] The victory smashed a bastion of Jim Crow unionism. If its broader implications were dissipated by layoffs in shipbuilding that followed victory against Japan in August 1945, the history of the struggle against the IBB offers testimony of the NAACP's involvement in the struggle for equal employment rights. In this case, NAACP sponsored litigation was not a conservative alternative to mass action, but an important weapon in striking against bigotry within organized labor. In Richmond, a Bay Area shipbuilding boom town, involvement by shipbuilders led to the creation of a local NAACP branch.[47] Merl Reed has suggested that because of this, the NAACP's role, in conjunction with other organizations in other regions, was "probably the most important black protest activity undertaken during the war years."[48]

Litigation was also a weapon in the NAACP's work against housing segregation. One legacy of increased employment opportunity in California was the rapid increase of black in-migration. Over the decade, the state's black population increased by 272 percent to 338,000, and in every city with a black community, its proportion relative to the total also grew.[49] Across the state, white residents increased their use of private covenants and deeds to prevent any nonwhite from buying, occupying or, by extension, building property on that land. While such efforts stretched back to the start of the century, these private barriers remained semipermeable into the 1930s.[50] However, by the start of the 1940s, white Californians had stepped up the use of legally enforceable race restrictive deeds and covenants. The consequences of the combination of in-migration with covenants, combined with insufficient, substandard public housing, included high rents and mass overcrowding in conditions of squalor.[51]

The response of branches to the housing crisis took a number of forms. Many joined with other groups to push for more public integrated housing projects, with some short-term success. Others provided support for those seeking to hurdle the barriers of residential segregation in private housing markets. As Andrew Wiese has noted, the "housing market was a key area of struggle" in the fight for black equality during the 1940s and 1950s, and California proved a critical battleground.[52] One family of war workers, the Laws, were jailed for contempt of court during their struggle to keep their Los Angeles home in the face of a covenant. Elsewhere, whites resorted to violence and intimidation. On December 3, 1945, an arson attack that killed the Short family in their home in Fontana, near Pasadena, led to an investigation by the San Bernardino and Los Angeles NAACP chapters. In Los Angeles ten black families had burning crosses planted on their property in 1946.[53] Of all those who confronted the menace of covenants, the work of Los Angeles branch attorney Loren Miller proved to be of national significance. Influenced by the tactics of the International Labor Defense lawyers who had used the defense of the Scottsboro Boys to raise more fundamental questions about the relationship between race, society, and the law, Miller took to fighting restrictive deed and covenant cases with a similar vigor.[54]

By 1945, Miller was fighting twenty separate covenant cases in the city, including the "Sugar Hill" case, which threatened the eviction of some of the city's most affluent black residents, such as Oscar-winner Hattie McDaniel.[55] Working with the NAACP-LDF, Miller aimed to shepherd covenant cases to the United States Supreme Court, where a ruling on their unconstitutional nature would strike down covenants everywhere. In 1948, Miller wrote the main NAACP brief (the first sociological argument, or "Brandeis brief," the NAACP deployed) for *Shelley v. Kraemer,* the bundle of covenant cases that the U.S. Supreme Court had agreed to rule on, and represented the plaintiffs in one of the constituent cases.[56] The victory the NAACP secured in these cases only ended one form of private residential segregation, and Miller spent much of the rest of his professional career struggling to end discrimination in private housing markets, public housing, mortgage, and other aspects of the American property system, racking up a number of victories, while never overcoming every aspect of entrenched bigotry. His vital contribution to the victory in *Shelley* does, however, demonstrate how a critical civil rights victory of the era relied on the diligence and determination of activists and lawyers based in California.

Branches also addressed the impact of wartime conditions on community and race relations. As with the violence over housing rights, the determination of some white Californians to maintain the essential whiteness of their communities was also felt on the streets. While California had recent experience of episodes of racial antipathy, such as the incarceration of most of the state's Japanese American population in 1942, the state had not been the site of any major explosion of racial violence in the twentieth century. In 1943, however, Los Angeles erupted in violence as whites and nonwhites fought for control over the city's social space. Here the Los Angeles NAACP demonstrated that the branch could be a force for multiracial justice, and not just a guardian of black equality.

In June 1943 Los Angeles was gripped by ten days of racial violence. Service personnel attacked young Mexican American adolescents, some wearing zoot-suits, beating and stripping them. Violence spread across southern California as mobs broadened their attacks to include African Americans. The riots have long been viewed as a critical moment in the development of Mexican American identity and of broader race relations in southern California.[57] Los Angeles NAACP branch president Thomas Griffith Jr. decried the riots in public meetings, noting the inconsistency of racial violence during a war for democracy. In the days before the riot, as tensions grew, Griffith led a public meeting of 1,500 that included African Americans, Mexican Americans, and union activists from the AFL and CIO. Griffith denounced growing police brutality and argued that racial violence would hamstring the war effort.[58] As the rioting unfolded, the branch dispatched telegrams to both the president and the state governor to protest against discrimination. Griffith testified before a grand jury investigation into the cause of the violence and urged Walter White to pressure federal officials and Governor Earl Warren to curb the military and halt police brutality via pressure from above.[59] Griffith followed up these moves by joining a series of interracial councils, underscoring the new sense of minority unity the violence had created.[60]

Griffith's resolve led to a surge in membership. In the aftermath of the violence, the NAACP recruited 2,000 members in two weeks.[61] By 1945 the Los Angeles branch had increased in size almost seven times in five years, from 1,743 in 1941 to 12,115 in 1945.[62] Griffith was also appointed to a mayoral advisory committee that marked the degree to which the Association was an accepted part of the city's institutional fabric. Beyond that, the branch and the organization's legal team incorporated cases affecting other minorities into its own struggle for justice and equality. In 1946, Loren Miller and Thurgood Marshall wrote a supportive amicus curae brief during the appeal stage of the school desegregation case of *Mendez v. Westminster*. The case, dealing with the separate provision of education for Mexican Americans, provided a foretaste of the arguments that Miller and Marshall would deliver in the *Brown* case ten years later.[63] Miller also helped the American Civil Liberties Union and the Japanese American Citizens League construct legal defenses in cases regarding Asian Americans and restrictive covenants.[64] Miller's ability to tap into a broad range of cases affecting other minority groups proved vital in the development of NAACP case law that would ultimately destroy the legal basis for Jim Crow.

Over the first half of the twentieth century, the NAACP branches of California could boast significant achievements. On a number of occasions they succeeded in preventing the spread of segregation and discrimination in the state. While protecting the rights of black Californians, these branches also filled a pertinent role in the growth and development of the NAACP. Through their presence, the Association earned its credentials as a nationwide organization, and through their work with national leaders, branches, and activists, such as

H. Claude Hudson, Joseph James, and Loren Miller, made important contributions to the development of research, lobbying, and litigation strategies that had national consequences. Their long-term commitment to the fight for black equality also calls on us to reconsider the divisions we place in the history of African American protest. These NAACP branches provide us with a legacy of activism that spans the temporal divide between prewar and post–Pearl Harbor California. By incorporating their work into a broader history of the Association, we can understand more fully how black Californian activism contributed to the development of the NAACP.

CHAPTER FOURTEEN

"Your Work Is the Most Important, but without Branches There Can Be No National Work"

Cleveland's Branch of the NAACP, 1929–1968

ANDREW M. FEARNLEY

O
F THE ONE thousand or so branches that were affiliated with the National Association for the Advancement of Colored People in 1945, Cleveland's might be construed as one of the more curious.[1] Recognized as one of the Association's largest by the postwar years, the branch was regularly mentioned alongside those of Chicago, Detroit, and Baltimore. Unlike branches in those other cities, though, the Cleveland office lacked national prominence. While the branch was regarded as one of the most loyal in supporting the work of the national office—annually sending most of the capital it raised—it was also a leading advocate for greater financial autonomy. Finally, although one might justifiably describe the branch with the well-known criticisms made about the organization as a whole—patrician, aloof, hesitant—it proved at times one of the Association's most radical, joining unions in picketing industry and even petitioning the national office to address the relationship between economic inequality and racial discrimination.[2] As every historian of the Association could testify, there is no such thing as a typical branch.

How to explain these contradictions then? With recourse to a framework of local-national relations so frequently is the answer. This essay opposes such explanations for their reductionism, insisting a more accurate characterization is possible if we first sketch the institutional structures of the Association, and secondly if we replace simplistic references with more fine-grained accounts of members and branch administrators. In the case of the Cleveland branch, it was the arrival of tens of thousands of southern migrants around midcentury that changed both the branch's infrastructure and its political outlook.[3] More than national political shifts, fluctuations in the economy, or the oratory of specific branch leaders, it was demographic movement that led to the branch's greatest transformation, changes that first became noticeable in the period from 1944 to 1948.[4] Increased membership, with the greater financial and administrative burden it brought, renewed discussion over the branch's goals, and more tangibly began the process by which lines of authority and apportionment of resources were reconfigured within the Association. Arguably the most significant change brought about by the increase in membership was the effect it had on sharpening branch officials' sense of duty, making them aware in ways they had previously not been of their accountability to a constituency.

To map these changes, the discussion is divided into three parts. Section 1 shows the many layers of correspondence and connection that bound members to particular parts of the Association. It introduces membership drives and the distribution of members' dues as a first step in breaking down local-national binaries. Section 2 extends this critique by insisting that thinking about local branches can only be done where "local" is taken to mean something more than a spatial connection. Black people who journeyed north remained in touch with those relatives they left in the South, as well as those who moved out west. A rallying article in Cleveland's buoyant *Call and Post* newspaper reminded readers of these bonds when it claimed in September 1948 that "since most of the Negroes in the North are from the South, [the city's NAACP] offers these ex-Southerners a splendid opportunity to contribute something toward the liberation of their own people."[5] The final section traces activists' work in four areas: housing, voting, community-police relations, and the segregation of recreational facilities. It considers how the prosecution of the branch's campaigns changed between 1929 and 1968 under the weight of more, and more diverse, members.

I

According to the records of the NAACP, the history of the Cleveland branch starts with its application for charter on January 25, 1914. It was on this date that with twenty-one members on the rolls the branch organized its first mass meeting, inviting Joel Spingarn to speak to the two thousand assembled guests. To follow this institutional narrative, however, is to avoid the less formal, prior connections that already existed between residents of Cleveland and the fledgling Association. A sharper compass for charting the direction and success of the Association's history can be found in the lives of its members. Take Harry C. Smith, for example: politician, longtime resident of the city, and career editor of a number of black newspapers, as well as a prominent participant in W. E. B. Du Bois's Niagara Movement of 1905, the organizational precursor to the NAACP. Smith's work in these earlier groups would later earn him a nomination to the NAACP's select Committee of One Hundred, at the same time as it starts a different narrative about Cleveland's connections with the Association.[6] In a similar vein, we can perhaps find more exact coordinates for comprehending the relationship between the national executive and the local branch by tracing the Association's financial circuitry. While most accounts either neglect, or at best separate, discussion of membership and money from an assessment of the records of particular branches, this section insists on their centrality.

From the outset, personal ties between members of the Cleveland branch and national officers were close. And they remained so through the branch's first three decades. Searching for a suitable candidate to serve as its executive secretary in November 1919, branch members did not think it inappropriate to mail an invitation to Walter White.[7] Although White turned the offer down, gently telling branch officials that he felt "highly honoured" to be approached, his rejection did not deter further offers from Cleveland executive members.[8] Other national officials, like the Ohioan Robert Bagnell and James Weldon Johnson, similarly interspersed official with personal notes to various Cleveland members.[9] This matrix of personal connections demonstrates that relations between the national office and the localities were anything but bureaucratically straightforward. It also highlights the extent to which the Cleveland branch, especially in the period before the Second World War, depended upon the direction set by the national office. In part such reliance was a result of the branch's limited financial and administrative resources. This only changed as membership grew during the middle years of the 1940s.[10]

For all that has been written about the disputes over strategy and ideology within the NAACP it is the case that the relationship between individual branches and the work of the national office was one deeply influenced by the Association's financial configurations. So crucial was this subject that it is hard to disaggregate it from the daily struggles that took place between officials in New York and in the branches. As Gunnar Myrdal recognized in his midcentury discussion of the Association, the relationship between the national office and the branches was one through which members and money were circularly connected: having more members meant more money for the national office; but recruiting more members required more money for the branches.[11] These were problems that proved central to the realignment of the Cleveland branch, and the emergence of its greater parity with the national office in the postwar years.

Between 1920 and 1942 the Cleveland branch only once managed to send the national office more than $2,000 in members' dues. Commonly, donations amounted to much less.[12] Membership was similarly far from impressive during the branch's first two decades, remaining in the hundreds through the 1920s, rising to the low thousands in the 1930s. These figures placed the office among the top of the Association's middle tier of branches, alongside offices in Birmingham, Alabama, and Boston, Massachusetts.[13] Critically, though, by the immediate postwar period, the Cleveland branch was registering tens of thousands of members, and by the passage of the *Brown* decision in May 1954 was among the Association's three largest branches.

Focusing on the wartime period, it is clear the Cleveland branch underwent three distinct phases in the growth of its membership: first, between 1944 and 1947, when membership annually reached between

8,000–10,000; second, between 1948 and roughly 1952, when figures plummeted to an annual total of 5,000 members or less; and third, to the final decade of interest here—that between 1955 and 1965—when totals once more swelled to between 10,000–14,000 (see Figure 1). These fluctuations were always due to a combination of factors: the branch's organizing efforts; the influx of migrants; Cleveland's social and political *milieu;* and the support and backing the Association enjoyed nationally.

Aside from the effect it had in expanding the branch's administrative tasks, the most notable consequence an increase in members had on the Cleveland office was in encouraging officials to reformulate how they saw their work with the Association. In short, the dramatic increase in members that occurred with the campaign of 1946 directed staff away from an unquestioning support of the national office and more toward the service of its own members. One way in which such changes were manifest was through branch officers' repeated lobbying for a more equitable distribution of the organization's funds. Buoyed by the success of its 1946 campaign, staff in the Cleveland branch swiftly became conscious of their responsibility to

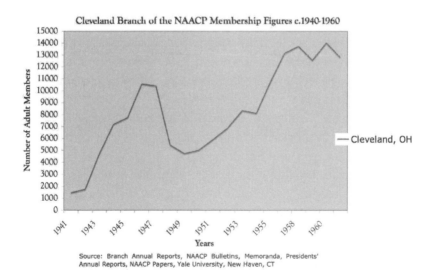

Source: Branch Annual Reports, NAACP Bulletins, Memoranda, Presidents' Annual Reports, NAACP Papers, Yale University, New Haven, CT

FIGURE 1: Adult Membership of the Cleveland Branch of the National Association for the Advancement of Colored People, 1940–1960.

their own members. In the build-up to the ill-fated 1948 campaign, branch executive secretary Charles Lucas requested the national office pay for a greater part of the Cleveland branch's membership campaign on the basis that the city's office needed a bigger budget so as to "adequately serve an increased membership."[14]

If membership figures proved acutely sensitive to the feverish political climate of the immediate postwar period, the branch's success in raising money did not obey such currents. The Cleveland branch's disappointing membership campaign of August 1948, for example, still brought in over $21,000 in dues—some $3,000 more than the previous year—despite registering 60 percent fewer members than in 1947.[15] Such achievements had two opposing consequences: first, they placed branch staff in a stronger position to lobby for a more favorable share of the Association's financial resources; but second, in a period of McCarthyite censure and economic uncertainty, they made executive officials more reliant on the fund-raising efforts of branches like those in Cleveland, Baltimore, Chicago, and Detroit.

II

In his fine history of Cleveland's postwar race politics, Leonard Moore characterized the city's branch of the NAACP as a local branch *par excellence,* writing, "the local branch was perhaps more active than any other branch in addressing local issues."[16] Support for his contention certainly appears in the statements made by prominent members of the branch throughout these four decades. Newly arrived and future branch president Charles White encouraged colleagues in February 1927 to see that "the branch should be responsive to the earnest suggestion that we give more attention to a local program."[17] Other branch officers called attention to such ideas, too. But where did the borders of this locality lie? For to interpret "local" to be an obvious reference to a stable and well-defined space—the city of Cleveland, for example—seems to mistake the demographic fluidity of the United States in these decades. By tracking these processes of migration, and recalling the dense web of formal and personal connections in which this particular branch was suspended, it is possible to challenge scholars' overemphasis on local-national interactions.

Beginning in the mid-1910s, Cleveland's black population grew continuously, though sporadically. Between 1910 and 1920 the number of black residents increased by 325 percent, by far the fastest growth in this period. Slowed temporarily by the Depression of the 1930s, the city's next significant influx of black migrants was concentrated in the 1940s and 1950s, when numbers rose by approximately 170 percent each decade.[18] For the NAACP and the Urban League these changes in the city's racial demography did not pass without comment. Where southern migrants figured in their files, however, it was usually as subjects of their work. Contemporaries were just as likely to recognize migrants' role in raising branch membership, as they were to remark upon the supposedly detrimental effect migrants had on the city's racial climate. Harry C. Smith, the inveterate newspaper editor and long-serving member of the branch, was typical in offering his view that newcomers needed to learn "how to conduct themselves in public places so as to help and not hurt our people of this community."[19] Even branch president Clarence Sharpe's more open-minded 1943 report only mentioned migrants when it called for Association volunteers to provide a "well-rounded program of adult education" to ease migrants' adjustment.[20] But the fact is that migrants were also active in shaping and directing the Cleveland branch: impressing their own concerns upon the branch; challenging where the boundaries of "local" should fall; and reasserting what the branch ought to take as its rightful jurisdiction. If scholars must continue to refer to branches as "local," they must also recognize the complexity of that term.

If residents of Cleveland joined the city's branch of the NAACP, it is important not to forget that they also belonged to a whole host of other social and personal networks. These familial, residential, and business ties remind us that as much as it is important to recapture the conversations that passed between the national office in New York and individual branches around America, a denser web of connections joined each branch of the Association to others nearby, to different organizations, and to varying political currents. Harry E. Davis, a lodestar of the Cleveland branch during the 1920s, and its executive official in the 1930s and 1940s, regularly visited other Association branches in Barberton, Kent, Marietta, and Zanesville, Ohio, for example.[21] Personal ties and local knowledge were also crucial in helping branches like that of Cleveland's in formulating its agenda. Following riots in Detroit in 1943, the branch dispatched two of its members—John O. Holly and the Reverend W. H. McKinney—to investigate and file a report before the mayor's wartime Committee on Democratic Practices. Holly was the president of Cleveland's Future Outlook League (FOL), but also a dues-paying member of the NAACP, and a good choice for the task having spent part of his childhood in the Motor City.[22] Through members' contacts with relatives, friends, and acquaintances, the Cleveland branch also became involved in a number of cases outside the city's boundaries. In May 1931, lawyers from the branch, prompted by neighborhood rumors, visited Mansfield, Ohio, to investigate whether schoolchildren there were being segregated. Two months earlier, in March 1931, members of the branch had lobbied the city's black press to provide coverage of the plight of the Scottsboro boys, mainly because of the city's strong migratory connections with the state of Alabama.[23]

The Cleveland branch's willingness to intervene in similar cases outside of the city's limits was also greatly encouraged institutionally through mechanisms like the Ohio state conference, established in the state in the early 1930s.[24] Created in part as a means of uniting opinion against the election of Senator McCulloch, interactions between the Cleveland branch and the Ohio state conference proved just as regular as those between the branch and the national office, at least through the 1930s. Even more so than the later addition of regional conferences in the 1950s (which often functioned as administrative units), state conferences played a crucial role in the organizational infrastructure of the Association, used initially by individual branches wanting to place their own campaigns before a statewide audience and, ultimately, for the collective petitioning of state legislatures. While the Ohio state conference never attained the same status as that of Texas, for instance, it nevertheless played an important part in building a viable network for grassroots activism.[25] Of course not all interactions between midwestern branches were quite so productive. In the summer of 1932, a dispute broke out at the Ohio state conference over whether the Cleveland branch had exhibited "over-zealousness" in unilaterally investigating charges of discrimination at three penal and correctional institutions in Delaware.[26] Only with the rapid expansion of the Cleveland office in the 1940s did these intraorganizational tensions disappear.[27]

Most histories of the NAACP give short shrift to the influence of broad demographic changes; similarly, studies of the Great Migration seldom mention the role of organizations like the NAACP. In a number of ways, though, these two histories are deeply entwined. For as migrants who traveled North and settled in Cleveland understood, the Association was both a conduit for their journeys, and a means of staying in touch with, and often protecting, those who stayed behind. In 1929, the Cleveland branch provided legal counsel to a Mississippi man threatened with the loss of his farm and crops, because his brother-in-law, a resident of the city, alerted branch officers to his situation.[28] Three decades later, in January 1960, staff investigated the circumstances surrounding the death of one Cleveland woman's nephew at a U.S. Air Force base in Pensacola, Florida.[29] Migrants did not just swell the membership rolls of the city's NAACP; they also helped to graft a grid of new connections onto the Association as a whole.

When southerners packed up their things and moved to the North, it was not just their possessions they took with them. Debts, quarrels, and reputations were equally as likely to accompany them, and frequently it was these that surfaced first when they arrived in the Promised Land. For branches of the NAACP this ultimately meant being drawn into disputes started in places other than where they were based. In the case of the Cleveland branch, the most notable such case occurred in November 1922, when justices from South Carolina attempted to extradite Cleveland resident James Robertson. Robertson, an iron worker at the city's Hardware Company, had been charged "with obtaining money by false pretense," and looked likely to be taken back to the Palmetto State before branch officers intervened to defend him.[30] It was not just for its legal expertise that migrants contacted the Cleveland branch though. As the account of one of the men tried in the Scottsboro case— Clarence Norris—implies, the Association also frequently provided expertise, shelter, and, occasionally, financial resources for those moving about the country. Norris's account is pertinent because following his release in September 1946, he moved—via NAACP branches in Atlanta, Georgia, and New York—to join his family in Cleveland, where his mother worked in a downtown hotel. In the summer of 1948 the branch recorded its only contact with Norris, when it told national officials that Norris had approached them, "seeking some financial assistance due to a severe illness which has prevented him from working the last two months."[31] At no time after the 1930s could it be said the Cleveland branch was solely concerned with events arising in the city's boundaries. Even within the city, more complicated webs of entanglements pulled the branch in directions other than toward New York.

Ever since Beth Tompkins Bates called for historians to "connect . . . the national agenda of the NAACP with local protest networks," scholars have been unflinching in focusing on this axis. Few have stopped to point out the differences and disjunctures that existed between the two realms.[32] One such difference between national officials and local staffers was the salaries of the former and the volunteer status of the latter. William Pickens, the longstanding director of the Association's branches, was told by an exasperated member of the Cleveland branch in 1941 that those who worked in the frontline of the Association "are very busy individuals with a living to make."[33] In 1942, the Cleveland branch reported difficulties in recruiting a president, "because of the heavy volunteer work involved [in the position]."[34] Might it not be the case that salaried officials working for the national office had an alternative set of interests and priorities than the volunteers who ran its branches? One such distinction was the impetus for and implication of working with other organizations.

Unlikely bedfellows were much easier to find within communities than at the national level. And historians must be careful not to mistake tactical differences between local protest groups for a lack of practical cooperation. The relationship between Cleveland's Future Outlook League and the city's branch of the NAACP demonstrates this well. Although the League lost no opportunity to charge that the city's branch of the Association was "conventional" and "conservative," a whiff of collaboration can also be detected between the two groups. When Youngstown police arrested a League member trying to integrate a public swimming pool in July 1940 it was Holly Quick and Charles Quick, an executive secretary with the NAACP, who led investigations. Similarly, when Perry Jackson, a prominent member of the Association stood for municipal judge, League members embraced him as if he were their own.[35] At least at the grassroots level, ideological differences between civil rights groups often dissolved with the practical need to cooperate. The point is not to try and ignore the (occasionally serious) tensions that also defined relations between groups. Rather it is to indicate that historians need a subtly different register for assessing the quality and type of interactions that took place in communities, and within particular branches, and at the level of the Association's national office. What might have seemed detrimental to the interests of the national office could often appear quite differently to the branches, as one wartime example from the Cleveland branch shows.

When national officer Fred Morrow returned from a routine field trip through the state of Ohio, he filed a report in which he claimed, "many of the [state's] branches . . . are in a deplorable condition." Calling for more "agressive [sic] and progressive individuals" to assume leadership of these branches, Morrow hinted to colleagues in New York that he was principally bothered by the fact that those who joined the ranks of competing organizations were "some of our own sympathizers and contributors."[36] That Morrow's discovery shocked him is instructive and illustrative of the disjuncture that could exist between national executives and grassroots activists. He concluded his report by imploring colleagues to "localiz[e] our program," and institute "a miniature of the national program . . . in every local community." Responding to these suggestions, Roy Wilkins explained to the board that Morrow's comments indicated that the "branches are 'sleeping' [on] issues which would not only increase the membership but enhance the prestige of the NAACP." Wilkins's opinion revealed the gap between the outlook of the national office and the branches. While it made sense for a national official to emphasize the role branches assumed in making the Association a household name, it was equally understandable how such concerns might prove lesser priorities for those involved in community organizing.[37]

Collaboration is of course an historical concept, and amid the changed racial politics of postwar America, the timbre of these interactions altered too. Vastly increased membership, particularly after 1953, encouraged staff at the Cleveland office to take a more competitive view of the branch's place in the city's civil-rights sector.[38] But the city's civil-rights profile was affected mostly after the war by the sheer proliferation of civil-rights groups. Two observers writing in the aftermath of the Glenville shoot-out reported that "[b]y 1963 there were some fifty separate civil rights groups in Cleveland."[39] That the city office of the Association moved in spring 1963 to bond these groups more closely together through its formation of the United Freedom Movement should not be simply construed as a shrewd bit of politicking intended to assure the branch's own supremacy however.

III

If Cleveland figures at all in conventional narratives of American race relations, it does so as the first city to elect a black mayor, Carl Stokes. Elected in November 1967, Stokes' victory was augmented the following year when his brother, Louis Stokes, defeated the Republican Charles Lucas for a seat in congress. Explanations of the success all three men enjoyed as black politicians have generally paid reference to each candidate's political sagacity and the region's liberal character. Few have discerned the legislative and political changes that the Cleveland branch of the NAACP brought about which made it possible for black people to harness serious political clout. Only if we link the political victories of the Stokes brothers with the prior court battle Louis fought as head of the Association's legal redress committee is it possible to calculate accurately the branch's political success.

Focusing on four principal campaigns—housing, desegregation of public recreation facilities, relations with the police, and voting—this section examines the shifts that took place in the branch's strategies and priorities between the 1920s and late 1960s. Of course the branch was involved in more than just these four areas. As Roy Wilkins remarked in the Association's 1963 annual bulletin, each branch was always engaged in "struggles too numerous to mention."[40] Education and employment also both occupied the attention of Cleveland members. Speaking before the U.S. Commission on Civil Rights in April 1966, the branch president Reverend Donald Jacobs said it was these two areas, alongside voter registration, that lay at the heart of the branch's program.[41] And while the branch was neither as active as the Future Outlook League had been in the 1930s in securing jobs for black people, nor as vibrant as CORE was in prosecuting a campaign to bring about integration in Cleveland high schools in the 1960s, forays were nevertheless made in both these areas. At the very least, coverage of these two topics can be found elsewhere.[42] My concern here is in fashioning a different way of thinking about political success and in relating that to the Cleveland branch's prosecution of its campaigns.

No issue did more to bring regularity and zeal to the Cleveland branch than the series of antidiscriminatory housing battles it fought during the 1910s and 1920s. Defending black homeowners' rights to buy property and to reside where they chose was not just a principal goal of the branch, it was a branch-making goal. Having largely eschewed the national protests organized by the New York office against *The Birth of a Nation,* the branch's response to attempts by some of the city's residents to maintain the racial exclusivity of their neighborhoods marked its first entry into civil rights activism. The first case that the branch dealt with in which the property of a black couple—Arthur Hill and his wife—was attacked came in June 1924, arguably the first of its kind identified by an NAACP office. Before the infamous case of Ossian Sweet grabbed headlines in Detroit, the Cleveland branch had already responded to a number of similar cases, working to defend the homes of physicians E. A. Bailey and Charles Garvin. And while all three cases provide grisly examples of early resistance to black homeowners' moves into traditionally white neighborhoods, one theme that recurred throughout, and that would recur in later years, was doubt over the protection afforded by the city's police force. In one case, branch officials voiced their opposition to the fact that police were stationed outside one homeowner's property, not to protect its inhabitants but to "search him and his family every time they go in and out as well as any friends who may be visiting them."[43] Revealingly, staff never sought to use any of these cases as a rallying point to increase the profile of the Association, as the Detroit branch would do with the Sweet case in 1925. Indeed, branch officials were restrained in transforming any of those subjected to violence and threats in the course of the 1910s and 1920s into what one scholar has termed "pioneers."[44] Preferring instead to rely on the pressure it could apply in courtrooms and along corridors of power, it was one feature of the Cleveland branch's housing campaign through the 1920s that it avoided drawing mass support. Such tactics would remain fairly continuous throughout these four decades, especially as far as housing was concerned. Only in the mid-1930s did staff begin lobbying on behalf of a broader constituency.

Appeals staff made to those who lived in public or rented accommodation provide one indication of the shifts that took place in the branch's housing policy between the 1920s and the mid-1940s. While the greater emphasis the branch placed on public accommodation owed much to the economic downturn, and subsequent change of personnel on the branch's executive committee, it was a change of emphasis only confirmed when the arrival of tens of thousands of southern migrants fully exposed the city's lack of integrated public accommodation. While branch officials had led tenant strikes in the Mount Pleasant area of the city in the summer of 1931, it was the proliferation of such collective cases in the 1940s that encouraged the branch to focus less on individual plaintiffs than the structural causes of residential segregation.[45] Educated by their experiences dealing with the U.S. Housing Authority, branch members stopped locating discrimination as the outcome of individual events (for example, a prejudiced landlord who refused to rent to a black tenant), and instead acted on the premise that such conditions were the consequences of urban planning (for example, a bank's policy of redlining).[46]

If unscrupulous landlords and white homeowners' associations dominated the branch's housing strategy from 1920 to late 1930, then federal and municipal authorities (and, to a lesser degree, and detrimentally, realty associations) did so between the early 1940s and 1960s. This transition was made most vigorously in the branch's wartime activism. When the House of Representatives baulked at the government's initial attempt to pass the Lanham Defense Housing Bill in late 1939, it was officials from the Cleveland branch who began an intrepid letter-writing campaign to amend the act. "If the bill is passed in its present form," their petition read, "Negroes will not get the protection in these new housing projects that they have received in the past under the USHA."[47] Continuing to adhere to this strategy of revising and refining legislation after the war, branch members won their biggest victory when they were invited to help draft a nondiscriminatory amendment to Cleveland's municipal housing ordinance in late 1949.[48] Similar campaigns occupied branch officials through the 1950s as members worked to replicate the so-called Fair Housing Practices Law that the Association's New York branch had successfully secured the passage of in 1958.[49]

A telling register of the branch's attempts to expand the appeal of its campaigns, redirect the focus of those efforts, and continue the method for their prosecution was the new way in which it created and managed information. Under new bureaucratic procedures introduced gradually by staff through the mid-1940s, surveying and polling of residents became a commonplace activity. One internal memorandum graphically referred to these surveys as "pulse-feeling" techniques. And by the time the branch's Housing Committee had completed its massive "fact-gathering" exercise in 1961, such methods were a routine way in which the branch related to its members. Yet while the postwar decades came to see the branch take its bearings more precisely from the city's population, the marshaling of that information became much more specialized as committees assumed a more formal role in the work of the branch.[50] The consequences of assigning specialized committees to particular campaigns were considerable. It meant that by the 1940s, although the housing committee was operating from a fairly sophisticated understanding of the mechanics of segregation, it was not necessarily working in concert with the branch's other committees. Attempts to integrate the city's schools in the early 1960s were seriously handcuffed, for example, by the branch's failure to prosecute a campaign that meshed an understanding of the city's racial geography with an appreciation of the financial inequalities such urban patterns produced. School superintendent Paul Briggs's contention, made before the 1966 Commission on Civil Rights, that the disparity in Cuyahoga County's tax base was the single greatest reason education provision remained unequal, suggest this was no minor failing.[51]

With all the attention scholars have given to battles over schools, housing, and workplaces, they have generally neglected the frequently poisonous confrontations that took place over public recreation facilities. Yet as the riots that began in a Detroit park in 1943 remind us, recreational facilities—like theme parks, swimming pools, and amusement arcades—were some of the most incendiary spaces in the urban landscape.[52] And Cleveland was of course no exception in the unrest it experienced over such facilities and areas, especially from the 1930s through the mid-1960s. Responding to these events, the city's branch of the NAACP followed a similar campaign strategy to the one it pursued over housing. Again avoiding large-scale picketing and cho-reographed public unrest, and preferring instead to change munici-pal and private statutes through formal political lobbying, the branch's campaign faltered. On a number of occasions through the 1940s the branch was alerted to the segregated use of public and private theaters, ranging from its 1932 investigation of public parks to a 1939 jitterbug dance competition in a public auditorium, as well as the refusal of the city's Cain Parks Theater in 1942 to stage productions by the black company, the Gilpin Players.[53] In all cases the branch responded through private appeals to municipal officials. It was a strategy of moderate success, garnering some improvement with the passage of an antidiscriminatory bill in amusement parks in January 1947. In fail-ing to bring the weight of the thousands of its new members to bear on these problems, however, the branch ultimately missed an oppor-tunity to point out the inequities apparent in the municipal council's provisions. These failings had clear ramifications for the way the branch responded to the Hough Riots of July 1968, a disorder occa-sioned by competing groups' claims to a park and started by provo-cations in a barroom.

Although the official report into the Hough Riots focused atten-tion on the role of black nationalist groups in staging the disturbances, events of July 1968 are in fact better as seen part of the longstanding friction between the city's police force and Hough's residents. While accounts of what started the riots predictably varied, most agreed that the lack of concern shown by city police toward the attacks of two black youths one week prior to the outburst, alongside the death of a twenty-six-year-old black woman, killed on the first day of the riot by police gunfire, were principal irritants. Accounts of the riot recorded by independent observers tend to confirm that residents' principal grievance was with the conduct of the city's police force. These griev-ances were far from new and had long been a rallying point among members of the city's NAACP branch.

Three months before riots broke out in Hough, Clarence Holmes, NAACP branch president from 1960 and 1964, testified before the U.S. Commission on Civil Rights. The core part of Holmes's testimony dealt with the topic of police-community relations, and in particular the abysmal racial profiling police officers carried out on suspected criminals.[54] Between the 1940s and 1960s volunteers at the Cleveland branch worked to correct these practices in two ways: investigating charges of malpractice and heavy-handedness brought against the city's police services; and challenging the stereotypes that associated black people with violence and crime. In 1943, branch members lobbied the editorial staffs of the city's leading papers, demanding descriptions of suspects either carry the person's race for all suspects or for none.[55] Four years later in 1947, following the announcement that the city would establish a super-police force, branch secretary Nathan Christopher led a campaign to ensure officers were given "a thorough course in race relations."[56] Beginning in the late 1950s, the branch intervened in more concrete ways. Following a spate of incidents between 1959 and 1961, in which it was alleged black men had died while being arrested or in police custody, Association members petitioned the state's governor to launch grand jury inquiries.[57] The commitment of staff to this cause culminated in their arguing the *Terry v. Ohio* case (the "stop and frisk" case) before the U.S. Supreme Court. Judging the effectiveness of these various actions is difficult, and perhaps a more tangible index of the impact of court cases can be located in the branch's work with voting registration.

As the New Deal had shown, black political power was a force that could not easily be discounted in the elections of northern cities. To try and weaken the impact of Cleveland's growing black community, the city's political brokers, like others elsewhere, gerrymandered and redrew electoral rolls. Beginning in the immediate postwar years with a series of voter registration drives—usually organized alongside branch membership campaigns—Cleveland NAACP officials attempted to challenge this winnowing of black political power. These efforts peaked in the summer of 1948 when the branch launched its intensive "Register to Vote" campaign. While such campaigns paled in comparison with the later voting drives of the city's branch of the Congress of Racial Equality, they at least indicated an early understanding within the local office that the attainment of political power was a crucial means for eradicating injustice. The emphasis that members continued to place on obtaining public office could be seen most clearly in branch members' tireless commitment to the campaigns of the Stokes brothers in the late 1960s. Following Carl Stokes's successful mayoral bid in fall 1967, some branch members were prompted to note that the victory marked "a new era of political education and voter education" in the city.[58] In other words, the power that Carl Stokes wielded as mayor was taken to be the logical next step in the branch's postwar engagement with direct political activism. In the election of Louis Stokes, the connection between the activism of the city's NAACP branch and the success of a black politician was even more direct. The twenty-first congressional district which Louis came to represent was itself a product of the persistent challenge that the branch had made to the city's gerrymandering. Ensuring these structural changes are not detached from more obvious surface victories is essential when we come to judge the record of such organizations like the NAACP.

IV

Between the 1920s and the late 1960s, the Cleveland branch of the NAACP underwent a series of transformations. The most important of these took place in the mid-1940s, with the spike in membership, and that decade serves as something of a fulcrum: a moment when the increase in members tipped the branch in a new direction. If campaigns waged by the Cleveland branch remained loosely categorized under the same headings throughout this era—"housing" and "voting," for example—marked changes nevertheless followed from the way the branch organized itself, with new methods for filing, arranging, and managing information being gradually instituted.[59] These administrative arrangements, that directed the branch's work through particular committees, in turn shaped how the Association related to its members and clients. Critically, while these bureaucratic changes did not create the disjointed perspective evident in the branch's discrete attempts to address school desegregation, bring about residential integration, and equalize job training, they did entrench such divisions. In spite of these political shortcomings, however, the more aggressive stance taken by the Cleveland branch in the postwar period owed much to the new sense of accountability officials gained from simply having more members. Not only did branch leaders from the late 1930s onward toil on behalf of a wider constituency, their actions also took place under a new ethos. For historians now, just as for contemporaries then, placing the lives of members at the center of our accounts is crucial to explaining the organizational contours and effectiveness of the NAACP.

CHAPTER FIFTEEN

"They Say ... New York Is Not Worth a D—— to Them"

The NAACP in Arkansas, 1918–1971

JOHN A. KIRK

IN 1949, THE fledgling NAACP Arkansas State Conference of branches (ASC), founded just four years earlier, was in crisis. NAACP regional secretary Donald Jones invited the president of the ASC, Pine Bluff attorney William Harold Flowers, to resign or face expulsion because of alleged financial improprieties.[1] But Jones did not count on the angry reaction of the state's membership, many of whom were fiercely loyal to Flowers. Fellow Pine Bluff attorney Wiley Austin Branton led calls for the local NAACP branch to secede from the national organization.[2] The national office responded by wheeling out the big guns, NAACP acting executive secretary Roy Wilkins and former executive secretary Walter White, to plead for unity. Only when Flowers took it upon himself to resign to keep the peace did talk of outright mutiny cease.[3] Nevertheless, discontent among local activists continued to smolder. In 1950, president of the NAACP Texas State Conference of branches, Lulu B. White, reported: "they say the work of the NAACP is in charge of a few favorites in the state, who are Lackies, what ever that is, for New York, and that New York is not worth a D——to them."[4]

The episode summed up the dominant theme of the NAACP in Arkansas between 1918 and 1971: an ongoing struggle between local activists and the NAACP national office to have their agendas, concerns, and needs put first. The ambivalence of Arkansas activists to the national NAACP had deep roots. The first local branch in the state was founded in the state capital of Little Rock in 1918. However, it failed to make any headway in building support in the city, let alone in the surrounding rural areas.[5] This was despite the fact that one of the most celebrated cases of the national NAACP's early history occurred in Arkansas in 1919. The case involved the defense of twelve black prisoners handed the death penalty for their alleged role in a race riot at the town of Elaine, located in the eastern Arkansas Delta, which historically had the highest concentration of the black population in the state. During a lengthy and expensive five years of litigation, the NAACP finally won a reprieve for the convicted men. In the case of *Moore v. Dempsey* (1923), a landmark victory for the organization, the U.S. Supreme Court overruled the sentences of the men on the grounds of improper influence by a hostile courtroom.[6]

The Little Rock NAACP branch secretary, Mrs. H. L. Porter, pinpointed the problem in 1933 when she reported that "the lawyers, Doctors, preachers and businessmen . . . are just a bunch of egoistic discussers and not much on actual doings [*sic*]."[7] Instead of enlisting the help of outside organizations like the NAACP, Little Rock's black leaders proudly boasted that they could best handle racial matters by exerting influence with local white leaders and through a nexus of local black self-help organizations.[8]

Because local leaders and organizations demonstrated little interest in NAACP activities, the NAACP national office, in turn, showed little interest in becoming involved in any initiatives in the state. This was highlighted in 1928 when Little Rock black physician and president of the newly founded Arkansas Negro Democratic Association (ANDA), Dr. John Marshall Robinson, tried to sue white Arkansas Democrats for the right to vote in the party's primary elections. Upon payment of a one dollar poll tax, blacks were allowed to vote in general elections. But since the Democratic Party of Arkansas (DPA) dominated virtually every political office in the state, their primary elections were the true source of political power, and general elections provided for little more than a ratification of a Democratic nominee. DPA regulations forbade black participation in their primary elections, thereby denying blacks any meaningful say in state politics and providing the main source of black disfranchisement in the state.[9]

Requests to the NAACP for help by Robinson and the ANDA met with a cool response.[10] NAACP executive secretary Walter White, in a memo about the lawsuit to NAACP president Arthur Spingarn, declared "[a] reason to feel we should not give much, if anything towards this case . . . [is that] we have never been able to get any considerable support from the state." White concluded that "we send say fifty or one hundred dollars as a contribution [so that if] it turns out to be the one on which we get the definitive decision, we will at least have given something."[11]

On November 27, 1928, Judge Richard M. Mann of the Second Division Circuit Court, sitting in the absence of Chancellor Frank H. Dodge in the Pulaski County Chancery Court, upheld an application by Dr. Robinson et al. for an injunction against the DPA to prevent it from barring black voters from their party primaries. As a precaution, he ordered the separation of black and white ballots in primary elections pending an appeal.[12] On August 30, 1929, Chancellor Dodge, having returned to court, again revoked black voting rights. The ANDA's appeals to the Arkansas and U.S. Supreme Court in *Robinson v. Holman* (1930) both failed to overturn the decision.[13]

During the 1930s and 1940s, a significant shift took place in the balance between local support and outside help in the struggle for black rights. The Depression years crippled many black businesses in Little Rock and other parts of the state. Many successful black enterprises went into terminal decline. At the same time, a new agenda for black advancement was emerging that went beyond the capacity of existing black leaders to handle. The majority of blacks in the state suffered far more at the hands of the Depression than the black elite. Increasingly, they looked to the federal government for help. In return, the government offered a New Deal that brought with it the potential for change, along with a new optimism and raised hopes throughout the state's black population.

While the limited impact of the New Deal on black lives was ultimately ambiguous, and its positive aspects very often undermined by segregation and discrimination, it did provide some hope for blacks. The New Deal meant the construction of more black facilities, such as schools and hospitals, in the 1930s than ever before. It provided more jobs, more training and a greater access to adult education, offering the black population a small glimpse of the potential that the federal government possessed to make a difference in their daily lives. Demographic shifts helped to consolidate black aspirations as the movement of blacks from rural areas to villages, towns, and cities offered a growing base for collective action.[14]

World War II acted as a further catalyst for change. Army bases that located in the South helped its ailing economy, which President Franklin D. Roosevelt recognized as the nation's "number one economic problem," with twelve billion dollars of investment. Encroaching industrialization went hand in hand with further black urbanization. Blacks pushed hard to win their share of wartime prosperity not only in the South but nationwide. The threat of a mass march on Washington by black labor leader A. Philip Randolph led to the formation of the Fair Employment Practice Committee by President Roosevelt to monitor racial discrimination in employment. Even with its shortcomings, the FEPC contributed to a tripling in the federal employment of blacks. Hundreds of thousands of blacks enlisted to help fight in the war for democracy. They did so with the firm intention of winning support for what the *Pittsburgh Courier* termed the "double V"—victory at home for democracy and equality, as well as abroad. Reflecting this growing black militancy, NAACP national membership grew tenfold from 50,000 to 500,000 members between 1940 and 1946. Many of these new members joined burgeoning southern local branches.[15]

Looking to build upon the promise of change that the New Deal had brought and which the United States entry into World War II held the potential to fulfill, there was an ever-growing constituency for mass mobilization in Arkansas. Yet, in spite of this potential base of support, there was still a distinct lack of direction and leadership in the state's black community to foster such a movement. The entrenched conservative elite in Little Rock still wielded considerable influence and still dominated organizational activities. Compounding these problems was the continued lack of NAACP interest in the state that denied Arkansas a possible antidote to the stagnation of local black leadership. By 1940, only six NAACP branches existed in Arkansas.[16]

The implementation of an activist agenda was something that young lawyer William Harold Flowers sought to address. Born in Stamps in southwest Arkansas in 1911, Flowers was the son of an insurance salesman and a schoolteacher. The Flowers family belonged to a small black elite in Stamps and lived in an integrated neighborhood. But rather than sharing a faith in goodwill informal negotiations with whites for racial advancement that other well-to-do blacks did, Flowers's early experiences led him to adopt a more militant stance. Enamored by childhood trips to the courthouse with his father, Flowers finally determined to pursue a legal career after a harrowing and graphic introduction to another side of southern justice. At the age of sixteen, on a visit to Little Rock, he witnessed the burning of lynching victim John Carter on downtown West Ninth Street. It was at this sight, Flowers recalled in later years, that he was "truly converted to be a lawyer."[17]

Flowers had worked his way through law school, taking part-time classes at the Robert H. Terrell School of Law in Washington, D.C., a night school founded by black lawyer George A. Parker in 1931. After graduating, Flowers returned to Arkansas and set up legal practice in Pine Bluff in 1938.[18] Young, eager, and idealistic, with firsthand experiences of southern injustice, from his first days in Pine Bluff Flowers set about trying to use his legal talents to secure black rights. Initially, Flowers looked to the NAACP to help in this ambitious task. In October 1938, he wrote to executive secretary Walter White informing him that Arkansas badly needed organization and leadership and that he wanted to try to provide it, but that he needed financial assistance to do so. As a novice lawyer just starting to build up his business, Flowers explained that he could not afford to take time away from his livelihood without recompense.[19]

Despite these pleadings, no help from the head office was forthcoming. Letters arrived from NAACP special counsel Charles Houston and NAACP assistant special counsel Thurgood Marshall, both offering sympathy but little help.[20] When the NAACP rebuffed his requests for assistance, Flowers decided to take the initiative. On March 10, 1940, at a meeting in Stamps, Flowers launched a Committee on Negro Organizations (CNO) to take on the task of mobilizing the state's black population.[21] Flowers was determined to create a "single organization sufficient to serve the social, civic, political and economic needs of the people." Such an organization would stand up for the rights of blacks to have a say in government, fight "un-American activities . . . enslaving the Negro people," and devise a "system of protest" to remove them.[22]

Flowers subsequently embarked upon a speaking tour of the state to secure support for a coordinated poll-tax purchasing drive. Flowers and the CNO were convinced that if blacks began to purchase poll-tax receipts and to cast their vote at elections, it would prove a vital first step in raising black political consciousness to challenge the all-white DPA primaries.[23] In September 1941, under the direction of the CNO, a physician from the town of Hope, Dr. Roscoe C. Lewis, ran a poll-tax purchasing campaign in southern Arkansas, while an undertaker from Morrillton, W. L. Jarrett, supervised in the north. "Drive to Increase Race Votes Is Successful" headlined the *Arkansas State Press,* the Little Rock–based black newspaper, at the end of the CNO's campaign. It anticipated a record turnout of black voters.[24]

Significantly, the first big legal breakthrough for black Arkansans came in the same year that the *Arkansas State Press* printed Flowers's photograph with a caption acknowledging that "He Founded A Movement."[25] In March 1942, a member of the Little Rock Classroom Teachers' Association (CTA), Sue Morris, sued for the right of black teachers to receive the same salary as white teachers in the city's school system. The case proved to be the first successful attempt by blacks in Arkansas to win equal rights through the courts.[26]

The court victory had a long-term impact on the struggle for black equality in Arkansas. The teachers' salary suit was not only a breakthrough for black Arkansans, but also proved an important national triumph for the national NAACP.[27] The local effort attracted the help of Thurgood Marshall whose presence in Little Rock helped to garner support for the organization there. The NAACP local branch secretary, Mrs. H. L. Porter, reported a surge of new members. Marshall "sure did shoot them some straight dope as to their part and membership to be played in the NAACP cause," Porter declared, adding, "Then and there at that meeting we collected $68.50 in membership."[28] In response to this rising local interest, the NAACP national office began to take more of an interest in the state. In 1945 an NAACP Arkansas State Conference of branches (ASC) was established, with Flowers appointed as its chief recruitment officer.[29]

As the NAACP grew in Arkansas, the groundwork by Flowers and the CNO remained very much apparent. The state organization created the infrastructure, provided the leaders, and ensured the successes that were to follow for the national organization. The year before the ASC came into existence the *Smith v. Allwright* (1944) ruling by the U.S. Supreme Court outlawed the all-white Democratic Party primaries. The work of Flowers and the CNO meant that when blacks could finally reap the benefits of the vote they began to make an immediate impact in significant numbers. In 1940, the number of registered black voters in Arkansas stood at only 4,000. By 1947, that number had increased more than tenfold to 47,000. Through poll-tax drives, voter education rallies, and the general raising of political awareness and activity, Flowers and the CNO made sure that black political organization predated national rulings.[30]

In 1948, Flowers handled the admission of Silas Hunt to the University of Arkansas Law School. Flowers's demands, coupled with national rulings gained by the NAACP Legal Defense and Educational Fund lawyers at the time, finally persuaded white authorities to desegregate without going to court. When Hunt enrolled in February 1948, accompanied by Flowers and Wiley Branton, he became the first black student to attend classes with whites at a southern university since Reconstruction. More black students soon followed his example.[31]

The NAACP national office remained cautious about developments in Arkansas. Though happy to have a more vibrant and active state affiliate, it did not want it to exercise too much independence. Pointedly, when the ASC was set up, Flowers was given the post of chief organizer of branches but the presidency went to the Reverend Marcus Taylor, an older, more conservative, and more pliable figure from Little Rock. Rivalry between the two men quickly developed. Jealous of the support Flowers received, Taylor began to fire accusations of financial misdemeanors at the younger leader. Taylor even went so far as to tell the national office that Flowers was keeping half of the funds collected from the foundation of new branches for himself. Although it was true that funds were slow at making their way from Pine Bluff to New York, an investigation launched into Flowers's activities gave no reason to relieve him of his duties.[32]

In 1948, Flowers ousted Taylor as president of the ASC. By then, even the national office was beginning to come around. "I will admit that I may have underrated Pine Bluff and its leadership," wrote NAACP national membership secretary Lucille Black.[33] When NAACP regional secretary Donald Jones attended the annual ASC meeting that elected Flowers as president in 1948, he reported that spirits were "high and militant," and that "largely responsible for the fine NAACP consciousness in Pine Bluff and the growing consciousness in the state is Attorney Flowers whose . . . tremendous energy ha[s] made him the state's acknowledged leader."[34]

Flowers's election gave heart to other local activists. In Little Rock, Daisy Bates filed an application to form a countywide "Pulaski County Chapter of the NAACP."[35] Daisy Bates and her husband, L. C. Bates, were co-owners of the *Arkansas State Press*. The couple were good friends of Flowers, who wrote for their newspaper using as a pseudonym his grandmother's name, Frances Sampson. By forming a countywide NAACP chapter, Bates hoped to usurp the power-base of older leaders, who still dominated the Little Rock NAACP. In her application for a branch charter Bates included fifty membership subscriptions and a filing fee and nominated herself as president. The response Bates received from the NAACP national office revealed that there were definite limits to the autonomy that the national organization was prepared to grant to local activists. The NAACP director of branches, Gloster B. Current, in a short reply to Bates, pointed out that there was already an NAACP branch in Little Rock and that if people were interested in helping the organization they should join there.[36]

The ultimatum issued to Flowers in 1949, which led to his resignation from office, looked very much like an attempt by the national office to rein in local activists. But with momentum already established, it was only a matter of time before those activists regained control of the state organization. Flowers was initially replaced by an elder statesman, Dr. J. A. White. When White fell ill and resigned from office in 1951, W. L. Jarrett, a veteran of early CNO campaigns, acted as a temporary replacement.[37]

The question over the direction of ASC leadership was finally resolved when Daisy Bates was elected president in 1952. Reporting to the NAACP national office after watching the 1952 convention proceedings, NAACP southwest regional attorney Ulysses Simpson Tate questioned Bates's ability to work with older, more-established leaders in the state. He was also wary of her tendency "to go off the deep end at times" in her forceful pursuit of black advancement. But, Tate concluded, "[although] I am not certain that she was the proper person to be elected . . . there was no one else to be elected who offered any promise of doing anything to further the work of the NAACP in Arkansas."[38]

Daisy Bates's election coincided with a local and national intensification of the black struggle for equality that focused on the testing of segregation statutes in secondary schools. Several suits filed in Arkansas in the late 1940s and early 1950s, both through the offices of the NAACP and independently by Flowers, paved the way for later attacks on segregated education through the courts. Though they met with varying degrees of success, none of them actually won a definitive ruling against discriminatory practices. Events at a national level finally overtook the local challenge to segregation when, on May 17, 1954, the U.S. Supreme Court handed down its ruling in *Brown v. Topeka Board of Education,* which declared an end to segregated schools.[39]

Much of the battle over school desegregation in Arkansas hinged upon what happened in Little Rock, the state's leading community. Daisy Bates's election usefully tied state NAACP leadership to the capital city. Early signs were promising. Little Rock superintendent of schools Virgil T. Blossom quickly announced the formulation of plans for compliance with *Brown.* He subsequently revealed these plans involved building two new schools, in black and white neighborhoods, respectively, ahead of any desegregation taking place. Blossom assured NAACP members that these schools would be desegregated along color-blind lines in September 1957. When the court announced a lenient implementation order for school desegregation in May 1955, which became known as *Brown II,* Blossom introduced modifications to his original plan that further limited the amount of desegregation that would take place.[40]

Blossom's willingness to amend his plans for desegregation without consulting them led to a growing unease among local NAACP branch members.[41] On January 23, 1956, they tested the resolve of Blossom and the school board by assisting thirty-three black students to apply for admission to four different white schools in Little Rock. Their applications were turned down.[42] On February 8, 1956, Wiley Branton, now chair of the ASC's Legal Redress Committee and a local counsel for the NAACP Legal Defense Fund, filed suit in the U.S. District Court against the Little Rock School Board for desegregation on behalf of the thirty-three students under the title of *Aaron v. Cooper*.[43] In preparation for the case, Branton consulted with NAACP special counsel Robert L. Carter and southwest regional attorney Ulysses Simpson Tate.[44]

At the hearing in August 1956, the U.S. District Court backed Blossom's modified school desegregation plan. To a large degree, this reflected conflict within NAACP ranks about the nature of the lawsuit rather than the persuasive arguments of school board attorneys. The Little Rock NAACP built its case on very specific terms that asked only for the enforcement of Blossom's original plan, which despite its limitations still provided for a substantial amount of integration. To reinforce the strength of its argument, branch members went to great pains to select individual examples of students who faced particular hardship under the modified plans.

Tate had different ideas about the case. As previous dealings between the national, regional, and local NAACP revealed, each often had its own agenda of concerns that could cause conflicts of interest and misunderstandings. Tate did not confer with local branch officials before the court met. When he flew into Little Rock the day before the scheduled hearings in the case, he claimed that he was too tired to take instructions and immediately retired to his room to rest. The next morning, Tate ignored the case built by the Little Rock NAACP and proceeded to argue the national NAACP line for the immediate and complete integration of all schools. This was the same line taken by the national organization in all of its other sixty-five integration suits against school boards in the upper South at that time.[45] Since Tate was senior to Branton in the NAACP legal hierarchy, the local lawyer deferred to him.[46]

Tate's line of argument lost the lawsuit by playing straight into the hands of the school board, since he did not demand that it should live up to the promises that it had already made. Rather, by demanding wholesale immediate integration, he allowed school board attorneys to contend that their clients were merely acting in accordance with the guidelines laid down in *Brown II,* which called only for desegregation to take place with "reasonable speed" and did not set limits on when or how much integration needed to take place for compliance with the law. Judge John E. Miller upheld the school board attorneys' argument. Offering a shred of consolation for the local NAACP branch, Miller retained federal jurisdiction in the case to make sure that the school board now carried out the modified school desegregation plans along the lines that it had indicated in court.[47]

In consultation with their lawyer, Wiley Branton, NAACP director-counsel of the Legal Defense Fund, Thurgood Marshall, and NAACP special counsel, Robert L. Carter, the local branch decided to appeal the decision.[48] The appeals court at St. Louis heard arguments in *Aaron v. Cooper* on March 11, 1957. The court again upheld Blossom's modified desegregation plan, stating that it operated within a timetable that was reasonable under the terms of *Brown II.* However, the appeals court also reaffirmed Judge Miller's ruling that the school board was now obliged to carry out its modified plan, beginning with the desegregation of high schools in September 1957.[49]

In the event, it was not Virgil Blossom and the school board but Governor Orval Faubus who proved the main obstacle to desegregation. On the night of September 2, 1957, the day before Central High School was due to desegregate, Faubus, in the name of preventing alleged disorder if integration proceeded, called out the National Guard to prevent the implementation of the court-ordered desegregation plan. Over the following weeks, negotiations took place between Faubus and President Dwight D. Eisenhower that finally led to the withdrawal of National Guard troops. However, when the nine black students that Blossom, after yet more modifications to his desegregation plan, had whittled applicants down to—Minnijean Brown, Elizabeth Eckford, Ernest Green, Thelma Mothershed, Melba Pattillo, Gloria Ray, Terrence Roberts, Jefferson Thomas, and Carlotta Walls—attempted to attend classes on September 23, an unruly white mob caused so much disruption that school officials withdrew them from Central High for their own safety. The scenes of violence finally prompted Eisenhower to intervene in the crisis by sending federal troops to secure the students' safe passage. On September 25, the nine finally completed their first day of classes under armed guard.[50]

Throughout the crisis, and the academic school year that followed,

Daisy Bates acted as mentor to the nine black students. Entry into Central High was, the students soon discovered, not an end to their troubles. Over the ensuing weeks, the students were subject to "threatening notes, verbal insults and threats, crowding, bumping and jostling in the halls."[51] With the battle to keep the nine black students from attending the school lost, segregationists turned their attention to encouraging white students to make life so unbearable inside the school that the black students would be forced to withdraw voluntarily. The director of NAACP branches, Gloster B. Current, had anticipated that "there is possibly going to be a concerted attempt to conduct a war of nerves to force the Negro kids to get out." He warned, "We lose everything we have gained," if that should that happen.[52]

Outside of the school, it was the NAACP, and in particular Daisy and L. C. Bates, that bore the brunt of white hostility. Their home was regularly attacked and crosses were burnt on their lawn. State IRS agents began to take a special interest in their finances. Arkansas attorney general Bruce Bennett applied pressure to try to get Daisy Bates to reveal NAACP membership figures, which she resisted on the basis that members would be targeted for "reprisals, recriminations and unwarranted hardship." The hardest blow segregationists struck was in encouraging a boycott of the *Arkansas State Press* by white advertisers that led to the newspaper's eventual collapse in October 1959.[53]

As the national office strove to give day-to-day assistance to embattled members on the ground, NAACP Legal Defense Fund lawyers continued the struggle in the courts. On February 20, 1958, the Little Rock School Board asked U.S. district court judge Harry J. Lemley for a two-and-half-year delay of their desegregation plan. On June 21, Lemley granted the delay, arguing that the violence witnessed in Little Rock justified a cooling-off period. On August 18, Wiley Branton successfully had the delay overruled on appeal. School board attorneys then indicated that they would take their case to the U.S. Supreme Court. Since the Court did not convene until October 6, it could not hear the appeal until after the Little Rock schools opened, presumably on a segregated basis, in September 1958.[54]

On August 25, U.S. Supreme Court chief justice Earl Warren announced that the Court would meet in a special session on August 28 to hear the Little Rock case. On September 12, in the landmark ruling of *Cooper v. Aaron* (1958), the Court ordered the school board to proceed with their desegregation plan. After over four years of equivocation since the original *Brown* ruling, the Court finally mandated a definite timetable for school desegregation in Little Rock and declared that violence and disruption were not viable reasons for delay. The federal government afterward indicated that it was prepared to enforce the ruling by making plans to support the peaceful opening of integrated schools with the assistance of federal marshals if necessary. Everything appeared to be in place to ensure a smooth and orderly process of desegregation in contrast to the scenes of lawlessness in 1957.[55]

Governor Faubus once again stymied those plans. He called a special session of the Arkansas General Assembly and rushed through a battery of pro-segregation legislation. One bill allowed Faubus to close any school forced to integrate by federal order. With the school closed, voters in the local school district would then participate in a referendum to decide if the school should reopen on an integrated basis. On the day that the Court ordered integration to proceed, Faubus closed all of the city's schools. In the referendum held on September 27, the governor handily stacked the cards in his favor by providing a stark choice between keeping the schools closed or accepting "complete and total integration." By a margin of 19,470 to 7,561 votes, the electorate decided to keep the schools closed.[56]

The morning after the announcement of the referendum result, Faubus pressured the school board into leasing the public schools to a Little Rock Private School Corporation (LRPSC) for private operation. Thurgood Marshall and Wiley Branton later successfully petitioned the appeals court for an injunction against such an action. Faubus then assisted the LRPSC in purchasing private buildings with public funds to operate a school. For one term, the LRPSC provided a limited school service for some of the city's white students before finally going bankrupt.[57]

After the collapse of the LRPSC, white students variously attended private segregated schools, out-of-state schools, or schools in other Arkansas districts, or they took correspondence courses through the University of Arkansas. While the public schools remained closed in Little Rock, most black students attended classes in other Arkansas districts. Those who did not either went to an out-of-state school or took the correspondence course offered by Little Rock's Horace Mann High. The state retained both white and black teachers on full pay to preside over empty classrooms in closed schools.[58]

The state of disarray prompted Little Rock's white elite to mobilize. At the referendum election, a group of influential white women organized the Women's Emergency Committee to Open our Schools (WEC). Though unsuccessful, they continued to pressure white businessmen and professionals to act, not least on the grounds of the negative financial impact events were having on the city. The WEC successfully lobbied for a slate of business candidates to stand against segregationist candidates at the school board elections in December 1958. The results produced a divided board of three segregationists and three business-backed candidates. When, in May 1959, segregationist school board members proposed not to renew the contracts of forty-four employees perceived as unsympathetic to their cause, it triggered a recall election at which business candidates finally wrested control out of their hands. The new board then drew up plans to integrate schools on a token basis in August 1959, when five black students peacefully entered two city schools.

The reopening of integrated schools was a triumph for the NAACP, but it came at a heavy cost. With the immediate crisis over, there was no longer the presence of national-based support from either the NAACP or the federal government to help local blacks. The local NAACP was in a severely weakened state after a campaign of harassment waged by Attorney General Bruce Bennett drained its financial resources and cut its membership rolls. Moreover, in an effort to recoup lost revenue after the demise of the *Arkansas State Press,* Daisy Bates spent much of her time out of the city on speaking engagements and was busy writing her memoir of events.[59]

The vacuum of leadership created by Daisy Bates's absence once again opened up a power struggle within the organization that echoed the circumstances of her election in 1952. One potential new source of leadership was L. C. Bates, who helped to take care of the day-to-day business of the NAACP in his new role as Arkansas's NAACP field secretary. However, without the help of his younger and more dynamic wife, he struggled to make much of an impact.[60] Another potential new source of NAACP leadership in the state was Dr. Jerry Jewell, a dentist, who became president of the Little Rock NAACP branch with the tacit support of Daisy Bates in 1963.[61] A further potential source of new leadership was Pine Bluff lawyer George Howard, who succeeded Daisy Bates as president of the ASC in November 1961. Complicating matters of leadership was the fact that Daisy Bates often revisited Arkansas and still took an active interest in NAACP activities in the state.[62]

One obstacle that all potential new leaders of the NAACP faced was competition from other civil rights organizations operating in the state. In 1962, a group of black professionals in Little Rock founded the Council on Community Affairs (COCA) after disunity among local organizations had led to the failure of the 1960 sit-in movement and the 1961 Freedom Rides in making any impact in the city. The COCA worked closely with the state affiliate of the Atlanta-based Southern Regional Council, the interracial Arkansas Council on Human Relations (ACHR). Both the COCA and the ACHR were instrumental in inviting outside support from the Student Nonviolent Coordinating Committee into the state in late 1962. The SNCC activists successfully helped to mobilize local students to bring an end to segregation at lunch counters and in other public facilities in Little Rock in 1963. The SNCC then began to set up operations in other parts of the state.[63]

As new organizations began to eclipse it, former allies of the NAACP moved on. In June 1962, Wiley Branton headed to Atlanta to coordinate the Voter Education Project (VEP). The VEP was part of a regionwide effort to bolster the black vote across the South in the 1960s, endorsed by all the major national civil rights organizations of the time and run under the tax-exempt auspices of the Southern Regional Council. Alongside this new role, Branton continued to represent plaintiffs in the ongoing Little Rock school desegregation suit. Aware of the problems with the NAACP in Arkansas, Branton encouraged parents to deal directly with the NAACP Legal Defense Fund. Increasingly, his contact point in Little Rock was the COCA rather than the NAACP. Daisy Bates chastised Branton for working with those who did "not feel any moral or financial responsibility to the NAACP," and felt that his actions had "devastating effects" which "added nothing to our campaign for members and funds." Yet in truth Branton was simply being pragmatic about the increasing need to work through a variety of different channels to secure black advancement.[64]

As the SNCC began to dissolve in Arkansas in 1966, when a new black power agenda came to dominate the national organization, it opened the way for the NAACP to reassert its authority in the state. But it was ill equipped to do so. Dissatisfaction with the work of L. C. Bates as Arkansas's NAACP field secretary had been growing for some time. Dr. Jerry Jewell, elected president of the ASC in 1965, felt that Bates's lack of "aggressive activity" had allowed the SNCC to overtake the NAACP in the state. The decline of the NAACP in Little Rock, where the field secretary's office was located, reflected the organization's inactivity statewide. In 1966, the NAACP branch in the state capital reported only seventy-two members. Because of this, by 1969 the ASC was actively pushing for Bates's retirement. Gloster B. Current admitted, "We would be glad to do something along these lines."[65] Finally, in May 1971, the NAACP national office unceremoniously retired the seventy-year-old L. C. Bates against his will.[66]

L. C. Bates's retirement heralded the end of an era for the NAACP in Arkansas. Between the setting up of the ASC in 1945 and the opening of desegregated schools in Little Rock in 1959, the NAACP was the backbone of the civil rights struggle in Arkansas. The organization's slow demise in the 1960s reflected the growing pace of racial change that required multiple organizations working on different fronts and in a variety of different ways to bring about successes. As it had been prior to the 1930s, the NAACP found itself again just one organization among many dedicated to black advancement.

Yet although this marginalized the activities of the NAACP, it did not make it redundant. Dr. Jerry Jewell from the mid-1960s was busy forging new links with other organizations in the state. In 1966, the NAACP joined forces with the COCA and the SNCC in the Arkansas Voter Project, an affiliate of the Voter Education Project. In 1972, Jewell became the first black member of the Arkansas Senate in the twentieth century, by which time over 80 percent of potential black voters in Arkansas were registered to vote, the highest number in any southern state. In 1992, Jewell was elected president *pro tem* of the senate and, in 1993, when Governor Jim Guy Tucker attended the inauguration of Arkansas's former governor, President Bill Clinton, in Washington, D.C., for three days he was the state's first black acting governor. As Jewell's career testified, although the NAACP would never again see the halcyon days of the 1940s and 1950s, it remained an important part of the ongoing struggle for black advancement in the state.[67]

A CHRONOLOGY
OF THE NAACP

1908

August 14, Springfield, Illinois, race riots.

September 3, "The Race War in the North," published in the *Independent* magazine, by William English Walling calling for a biracial national organization to combat the racial divisions.

"The Call" by Mary White Ovington calling for such a national conference.

1909

February 12, National Negro Committee (NNC) founded in New York.

May 31–June 1, first meeting in New York.

1910

May 20, second conference of the NNC.

May 30, officially selected name of the National Association for the Advancement of Colored People.

Moorfield Storey, first president of the NAACP.

Frances Blascoer becomes NAACP secretary.

November 1910, first edition of the NAACP monthly journal the *Crisis: A Record of the Darker Races* published. Its editor is W. E. B. Du Bois.

1911

Mary White Ovington becomes NAACP secretary.

1912

May, Childs Nerney becomes NAACP secretary.

December, The NAACP has 11 branches and 1,100 members.

1913

President Woodrow Wilson officially segregates the federal government.

1915

Guinn v. United States. The U.S. Supreme Court overturned the Oklahoma "grandfather" clause that disfranchised African American voters.

NAACP organizes nationwide protest against D. W. Griffith's film, *The Birth of a Nation,* which depicts blacks in the Reconstruction period in a racially stereotypical way and romanticizes the Ku Klux Klan. The film is temporarily banned in Illinois.

Ernest E. Just awarded the first Spingarn Medal, the Association's highest award conferred annually for outstanding achievement.

1916

August, the first Amenia Conference held on the property of Joel Spingarn in an attempt to bring together African American leaders to unify the movement.

Mary White Ovington briefly becomes acting NAACP secretary.

Royal Freeman Nash becomes NAACP secretary.

1917

Buchanan v. Warley. The U.S. Supreme Court rules that states cannot segregate African Americans into residential districts.

July 28, NAACP silent parade of approximately 15,000 people down New York's Fifth Avenue in support of federal antilynching legislation.

James Weldon Johnson becomes acting NAACP secretary.

1918

John R. Shillady becomes NAACP secretary.

December, The NAACP has 65 branches in 38 states and 43,994 members.

1919

Thirty Years of Lynching in the United States, 1898–1918, published in New York by the NAACP.

Shillady badly beaten in a visit to Texas and never fully recovers.

December, The NAACP has 310 branches and 91,203 members. For the first time membership in the South exceeds that in the North.

1920

NAACP annual conference held in the South for the first time, in Atlanta, one of the most active areas of Ku Klux Klan activity.

James Weldon Johnson appointed as NAACP secretary and Walter White as assistant secretary.

1922

NAACP campaigns for the passage of the Dyer antilynching bill in Congress. It passes the House of Representatives but is filibustered in the Senate.

1923

Moore v. Dempsey. The U.S. Supreme Court rules that federal courts can intervene to protect procedural rights of defendants who were tried in mob dominated areas.

1930

The NAACP and the American Federation of Labor (AFL) successfully protest against the Supreme Court justice nominee John J. Parker of North Carolina, who had publicly supported the political disfranchisement of African Americans.

Joel Spingarn becomes NAACP president.

1931

Scottsboro case. The Scottsboro defendants (nine black men and boys aged between twelve and twenty) are falsely convicted of raping two white women in Alabama and sentenced to be executed. The NAACP initially represents the accused but cedes control of the case to the communist International Labor Defense (ILD). Walter White becomes NAACP secretary.

1932

Nixon v. Condon. A "white primary" case. The U.S. Supreme Court rules that the exclusion of African Americans from voting in the Texas Democratic primary is unconstitutional.

Second Amenia Conference to discuss the NAACP's response to the economic plight of African Americans during the Great Depression.

1934

Charles Hamilton Houston, dean of Howard Law School, appointed as the NAACP's first full-time legal counselor.

W. E. B. Du Bois resigns as editor of the *Crisis* over controversial editorial endorsing racial self-segregation, contrary to NAACP official policy.

Abram L. Harris chairs an NAACP commission that urges the Association to be more involved in economic issues affecting the African American community.

1935

Gaines v. University of Maryland. Charles Houston and Thurgood Marshall win legal battle to admit a black student to the University of Maryland Law School, or alternatively the state must provide a comparable "separate and equal" institution.

Roy Wilkins becomes editor of the *Crisis.*

1937

Another antilynching bill passed the House of Representatives only to be filibustered in the Senate.

1939

After the Daughters of the Revolution prevent African American soprano Marian Anderson from performing at their Constitution Hall, the NAACP moved the concert to the Lincoln Memorial, Washington, D.C.

Marian Anderson awarded the Spingarn Medal.

NAACP Legal Defense and Educational Fund established.

1940

A third antilynching bill passed the House of Representatives and again filibustered in the Senate.

Arthur B. Spingarn becomes NAACP president.

NAACP membership stands at 50,000.

1941

The wartime Fair Employment Practices Committee formed after pressure from African American labor leader A. Philip Randolph's March on Washington Movement forces President Franklin D. Roosevelt to sign Executive Order 8802 to improve employment opportunities for African Americans in the defense industries.

1943

Opening of NAACP's Washington Bureau, Washington D.C.

1944

Recorded 430,000 memberships.

W. E. B. Du Bois rejoins the national staff of the NAACP as director of special research.

NAACP Veterans Affairs office opened in Washington, D.C.

Smith v. Allwright. The U.S. Supreme Court rules that the Texas all-white primary is unconstitutional.

Walter White begins a tour of European and Pacific theaters of war that extends into 1945.

December, NAACP membership reaches 430,000.

1945

NAACP campaigns when Congress refuses to fund the creation of a permanent FEPC.

Lobbies the newly established United Nations with *An Appeal to the World: A Statement of the Denial of Human Rights of Minorities in the Case of Citizens of Negro Descent in the United States of America.*

Walter White publishes *A Rising Wind,* an account of his European and Pacific tours.

NAACP national office moved from Fifth Avenue to West Fortieth Street, New York.

December, NAACP membership exceeds 500,000 for the first time in the Association's history.

1946

Morgan v. Virginia. The U.S. Supreme Court bans states from having laws that sanction segregated facilities in interstate travel.

NAACP Labor Department established.

1947

NAACP Church Department established.

1948

President Harry S. Truman signs Executive Order 9981 banning segregation in the U.S. armed forces.

W. E. B. Du Bois dismissed from the NAACP.

Sipuel v. Board of Regents. The U.S. Supreme Court declares that segregated educational facilities for African Americans must be genuinely equal to those available to whites. Failing this, states must provide integrated facilities. As a result of the case Ada Sipuel is admitted to the University of Oklahoma Law School.

1949

James W. Ivy becomes editor of the *Crisis.*

Roy Wilkins becomes acting NAACP secretary.

1950

Sweatt v. Painter. The U.S. Supreme Court orders the University of
Texas to admit black applicant, Herman Sweatt.

Clarence M. Mitchell Jr. appointed head of the NAACP's
Washington Bureau, Washington, D.C.

1954

Brown v. the Board of Education. NAACP special counsel Thurgood
Marshall wins historic case before the U.S. Supreme Court. In
a unanimous decision the Court rules that segregation in public schools is unconstitutional.

1955

Rosa Parks is arrested for refusing to give up her seat on a segregated
bus in Montgomery, Alabama. Parks is secretary of the
Montgomery branch of the NAACP. Her protest leads to the
Montgomery Bus Boycott in which local civil rights campaign-
ers unite under the Montgomery Improvement Association
(MIA) with the twenty-six-year-old Martin Luther King Jr. as
its president.

Walter White dies and Roy Wilkins becomes NAACP executive
director.

1956

The NAACP is outlawed by state courts in Alabama for refusing to
publish its membership lists.

1957

Daisy Bates, president of the Little Rock, Arkansas, branch of the
NAACP, campaigns to get nine African American high school
children admitted into the Little Rock High School.

Martin Luther King Jr. receives Spingarn Medal.

1960

Greensboro, North Carolina, members of the NAACP Youth
Council support nonviolent sit-ins at segregated lunch
counters.

1963

Medgar Evers, NAACP field director, assassinated at his home in Jackson, Mississippi.

NAACP campaigns for the passage of the Equal Employment Opportunity Act.

March on Washington for Jobs and Freedom.

Council of Federated Organizations (COFO) created to coordinate united action by civil rights organizations to register black voters in Mississippi.

1964

Civil Rights Act passed by Congress.

1965

Voting Rights Act passed by Congress.

1966

Henry Lee Moon appointed editor of the *Crisis*.

Kivie Kaplan becomes NAACP president.

1971

NAACP National Housing Corporation established through which local branches sponsor nonprofit-making housing programs.

1975

Warren Marr II becomes editor of the *Crisis*.

1976

W. Montague Cobb becomes NAACP president.

1977

Benjamin L. Hooks Jr. becomes NAACP executive director and CEO.

1978

Regents of University of California v. Bakke decision. The U.S. Supreme Court placed limits on affirmative action or positive discrimination programs, requiring the University of California to admit *Bakke,* a white student previously rejected for admission.

1979

Ex-convict Leroy Mobley appointed NAACP director of prison programs.

1981

NAACP leads a successful campaign to renew the Voting Rights Act and initiates the "Fair Share Program" to work with business corporations to promote black economic empowerment.

Eight people arrested in an alleged conspiracy to bomb NAACP headquarters in Baltimore, Maryland.

1982

NAACP successfully campaigns to prevent President Ronald Reagan from giving a tax break to the racially segregated Bob Jones University.

NAACP national headquarters moved to Brooklyn, New York.

1983

James Kemp becomes NAACP president.

1984

Enolia P. McMillan becomes NAACP president.

1985

NAACP leads rally against apartheid in South Africa in New York City.

1986

NAACP national headquarters moved back to Baltimore, Maryland.

1987

NAACP successfully campaigns to defeat the nomination of Judge Robert Bork to the Supreme Court.

1989

Jesse Jackson receives the Spingarn Medal.

Hazel N. Dukes becomes NAACP president.

1991

NAACP undertakes a voter registration campaign in Louisiana that garners a 76 percent black turnout to prevent the election of former Klan leader David Duke to the United States Senate.

1993

Benjamin F. Chavis Jr. becomes NAACP executive director and CEO.

1994

NAACP almost $4 million in debt.

Earl T. Shinhaster appointed acting NAACP executive director and CEO after Benjamin Chavis is dismissed by the board of directors following allegations of sexual harassment and financial impropriety.

1995

Myrlie Evers-Williams, widow of Medgar Evers, elected chair of the NAACP's board of directors.

1996

Kweisi Mfume becomes NAACP president and CEO.

NAACP pays off $3.8 million debt.

1997

NAACP launches the "Economic Reciprocity Program" in response to anti-affirmative action legislation across the states.

1998

Julian Bond elected as chair of the NAACP board of directors.

2000

NAACP's National Voter Fund helps to achieve the largest African American voter turnout for twenty years at presidential election.

2001

NAACP v. Harris. Supreme Court rules that the state of Florida did not violate the Voting Rights Act of 1965 and the U.S. Constitution's Equal Protection Amendments during the 2000 presidential elections.

2004

George W. Bush becomes the first sitting president since Herbert Hoover not to address the NAACP's annual conference.

Kweisi Mfume resigns as NAACP president and CEO.

2005

January–July, Dennis C. Hayes becomes acting NAACP president and CEO.

August, Bruce S. Gordon appointed NAACP president and CEO.

2007

Gordon resigns as NAACP president and CEO.

Dennis C. Hayes becomes acting president and CEO.

2008

July, Barack Obama, the first African American to be selected as a presidential candidate by either the Democratic or Republican parties, addresses the NAACP annual conference.

November, Benjamin T. Jealous becomes NAACP president and CEO. Obama succeeds in his bid to become the first African American to be elected president of the United States.

2009

January, President Barack Obama takes office.

The NAACP celebrates its centenary year.

July, Obama addresses NAACP centenary dinner. Although acknowledging the continuing "pain of discrimination" he calls for a "new mindset, a new set of attitudes" by which African Americans should take responsibility for their own destiny.

NOTES

Kevern Verney and Lee Sartain,
The NAACP in Historiographical Perspective

1. Ulrich Bonnell Phillips, *American Negro Slavery: A Survey of the Supply, Employment and Control of Negro Labor as Determined by the Plantation Regime* (New York: D. Appleton and Company, 1918). Carter Woodson quoted in August Meier and Elliott Rudwick, *Black History and the Historical Profession, 1915–1980* (Urbana: University of Illinois Press, 1986), 4.

2. W. E. B. Du Bois, *Darkwater: Voices From Within The Veil* (New York: Harcourt, Brace and Howe, 1920); W. E. B. Du Bois, *Dusk of Dawn: An Essay Toward an Autobiography of a Race Concept* (New York: Harcourt, Brace, 1940); James Weldon Johnson, *Along This Way* (New York: Viking Penguin, 1933), Mary White Ovington, *The Walls Came Tumbling Down, The Autobiography of Mary White Ovington: The Story of the National Association for the Advancement of Colored People Told by One of its Founders* (New York: Harcourt, Brace and Company, 1947); Walter White, *A Man Called White* (New York: Viking Press, 1948).

3. Peter Ling in discussion with the editors during the preparation of the essays for this volume.

4. August Meier, *A White Scholar and the Black Community, 1945–1965: Essays and Reflections* (Amherst: University of Massachusetts Press, 1992), 3–38.

5. Charles W. Eagles, "Toward New Histories of the Civil Rights Era," *Journal of Southern History* 66, no. 4 (November 2000): 819–21.

6. Rodney Hilton, *Bond Men Made Free: Medieval Peasant Movements and the English Rising of 1381* (London: Maurice Temple Smith Limited, 1973); Christopher Hill, *The World Turned Upside Down: Radical Ideas during the English Revolution* (Harmondsworth: Penguin, 1972); E. P. Thomson, *The Making of the English Working Class* (London: Victor Gollancz, 1963).

7. Kenneth M. Stampp, *The Peculiar Institution: Slavery in the Ante-Bellum South* (New York: Alfred A. Knopf, 1956); John Blassingame, *The Slave Community: Plantation Life in the Antebellum South* (New York: Oxford University Press, 1972); Herbert Gutman, *The Black Family in Slavery and Freedom, 1750–1925* (Oxford: Oxford University Press, 1976); George Rawick, *From Sundown to Sunup: The Making of the Black Community* (Westport, Conn.: Greenwood Press, 1972); Eugene Genovese, *Roll, Jordan, Roll: The World the Slaves Made* (New York: Vintage Books, 1974).

8. Eagles, "Toward New Histories of the Civil Rights Era," 822. See also

Steven F. Lawson, "Freedom Then, Freedom Now: The Historiography of the Civil Rights Movement," *American Historical Review* 96, no. 2 (April 1991): 456–57; Kevern Verney, *The Debate on Black Civil Rights in America* (Manchester: Manchester University Press, 2006), 91–92.

    9. Francis Broderick, *W. E. B. Du Bois: Negro Leader in Time of Crisis* (Stanford, Calif.: Stanford University Press, 1959); Elliott Rudwick, *W. E. B. Du Bois: A Study in Minority Group Leadership* (Philadelphia: University of Pennsylvania Press, 1960); W. E. B. Du Bois, *The Autobiography of W. E. B. Du Bois: A Soliloquy on Viewing My Life from the Last Decade of Its First Century* (New York: International Publishers, 1968). In this, his last work, Du Bois was more candid about his relationship with the NAACP, most notably in his scathing assessment of the leadership of Walter White from the 1920s through to the 1950s. From a charitable perspective it might be concluded that this was because the events in question had long since passed and the Association would suffer little or no harm from their being discussed. More cynically, it might be noted that White, now deceased, was not in a position to exercise the right of reply or instigate a defamation lawsuit.

    10. Walter B. Hixson, *Moorfield Storey and the Abolitionist Tradition* (New York: Oxford University Press, 1972); B. Joyce Ross, *J. E. Spingarn and the Rise of the NAACP* (New York: Atheneum, 1972); Eugene Levy, *James Weldon Johnson: Black Leader, Black Voice* (Chicago: University of Chicago Press, 1973).

    11. Clement E. Vose, *Caucasians Only: The Supreme Court, the NAACP and the Restrictive Covenant Cases* (Berkeley and Los Angeles: University of California Press, 1967); Charles Flint Kellogg, *NAACP: A History of the National Association for the Advancement of Colored People, Volume I, 1909–1920* (Baltimore: Johns Hopkins University Press, 1967); Elliottt Rudwick and August Meier, "The Rise of the Black Secretariat in the NAACP, 1909–35," and August Meier and Elliott Rudwick, "Attorneys Black and White: A Case Study of Race Relations within the NAACP," both in August Meier and Elliott Rudwick, *Along the Color Line: Explorations in the Black Experience* (Urbana: University of Illinois Press, 1976), 97–127, 128–73.

    12. Mark Robert Schneider, *"We Return Fighting": The Civil Rights Movement in the Jazz Age* (Boston: Northeastern University Press, 2002), 45, 48; Manfred Berg, *"The Ticket to Freedom": The NAACP and the Struggle for Black Political Integration* (Gainesville: University Press of Florida, 2005), 20.

    13. See essays by Verney, Zelden, Flack, Fearnley, and Kirk, this volume.

    14. Roy Wilkins and Tom Mathews, *Standing Fast: The Autobiography of Roy Wilkins* (New York: Viking, 1982).

    15. Genna Rae McNeil, *Groundwork: Charles Hamilton Houston and the Struggle for Civil Rights* (Philadelphia: University of Pennsylvania Press, 1983); Sheldon Avery, *Up from Washington: William Pickens and the Negro Struggle for Equality, 1900–1954* (Newark: University of Delaware Press, 1988); Manning Marable, *W. E. B. Du Bois: Black Radical Democrat* (Boston: Twayne, 1986); David Levering Lewis, *W. E. B. Du Bois: Biography of a Race, 1868–1919* (New York: Henry Holt, 1993); David Levering Lewis, *W. E. B. Du Bois: The Fight for Equality and the American Century, 1919–1963* (New York: Henry Holt, 2000).

    16. Carolyn Wedin, *Inheritors of the Spirit: Mary White Ovington and the Founding of the NAACP* (New York: John Wiley and Sons, 1998); Schneider, *"We Return Fighting"*; Kenneth Robert Janken, *White: The Biography of Walter White, Mr. NAACP* (New York: New Press, 2003).

17. August Meier et al. (eds.), *The NAACP Papers* (University Publications of America, 1982–).

18. The Booker T. Washington Papers, also housed in the Library of Congress and containing more than a million items, is perhaps the only African American archival collection to match the completeness, diversity, and scale of the information contained in the NAACP Papers.

19. Robert L. Zangrando, *The NAACP Crusade against Lynching, 1909–1950* (Philadelphia: Temple University Press, 1980); Dan T. Carter, *Scottsboro: A Tragedy of the American South* (Baton Rouge: Louisiana State University Press, 1979); Robert Cortner, *A Mob Intent on Death: The NAACP and the Arkansas Riot Cases* (Middletown, Conn.: Wesleyan University Press, 1988); Kenneth W. Goings, *The NAACP Comes of Age: The Defeat of John J. Parker* (Bloomington: Indiana University Press, 1990); Grif Stockley, *Blood in Their Eyes: The Elaine Race Massacres of 1919* (Fayetteville: University of Arkansas Press, 2001).

20. Denton L. Watson, *Lion in the Lobby: Clarence Mitchell, Jr.'s Struggle for the Passage of Civil Rights Laws* (New York: Morrow, 1990); Jack Greenberg, *Crusaders in the Courts: How a Dedicated Band of Lawyers Fought for the Civil Rights Revolution* (New York: Basic Books, 1994); Mark V. Tushnet, *The NAACP's Legal Strategy against Segregated Education, 1925–1950* (Chapel Hill: University of North Carolina Press, 1987), Mark V. Tushnet, *Making Civil Rights Law: Thurgood Marshall and the Supreme Court, 1936–1961* (New York: Oxford University Press, 1994); Mark V. Tushnet, *Making Constitutional Law: Thurgood Marshall and the Supreme Court, 1962–1991* (New York: Oxford University Press, 1997); Charles Zelden, *The Battle for the Black Ballot: Smith v. Allwright and the Defeat of the Texas All-White Primary* (Lawrence: University Press of Kansas, 2004); Manfred Berg, *"The Ticket to Freedom."*

21. Beth T. Bates, "A New Crowd Challenges the Agenda of the Old Guard in the NAACP, 1933–1941," *American Historical Review* 102, no. 2 (April 1997): 340–77; Christopher Robert Reed, *The Chicago NAACP and the Rise of Black Professional Leadership, 1910–1966* (Bloomington: Indiana University Press, 1997); Aaron Henry, *The Fire Ever Burning* (Jackson: University Press of Mississippi, 2000); Ben Green, *Before His Time: The Untold Story of Harry T. Moore, America's First Civil Rights Martyr* (New York: Free Press, 1999); Merline Pitre, *In Struggle against Jim Crow: Lulu B. White and the NAACP, 1900–1957* (College Station: Texas A & M University Press, 1999).

22. Wedin, *Inheritors of the Spirit;* Barbara Ransby, *Ella Baker and the Black Freedom Movement: A Radical Democratic Vision* (Chapel Hill: University of North Carolina Press, 2003).

23. Lee Sartain, *Invisible Activists: Women of the Louisiana NAACP and the Struggle for Civil Rights, 1915–1945* (Baton Rouge: Louisiana State University Press, 2007).

24. Gilbert Jonas, *Freedom's Sword: The NAACP and the Struggle against Racism in America, 1909–1969* (New York: Routledge, 2005).

25. August Meier and John H. Bracey, "The NAACP as a Reform Movement, 1909–1965: 'To Reach the Conscience of America,'" *Journal of Southern History* 59 (February 1993): 3–30.

26. Richard M. Dalfiume, "The 'Forgotten Years' of the Negro Revolution," *Journal of American History* 55, no. 1 (June 1968): 90–106.

27. Wilkins and Mathews, *Standing Fast,* 190; Adam Fairclough, *Race and Democracy: The Civil Rights Struggle in Louisiana, 1915–1972* (Athens: University of Georgia Press, 1995), 48, 50.

28. Walter White, *A Rising Wind* (Westport, Conn.: Negro Universities Press, 1945).

29. Bates, "A New Crowd Challenges the Agenda," 343.

30. Robin D. G. Kelley, *Hammer and Hoe: Alabama Communists during the Great Depression* (Chapel Hill: University of North Carolina Press, 1990); Andrew M. Manis, *A Fire You Can't Put Out: The Civil Rights Life of Birmingham's Reverend Fred Shuttlesworth* (Tuscaloosa: University of Alabama Press, 1999).

1. Simon Topping, "All Shadows Are Dark": Walter White, Racial Identity, and National Politics

1. Many thanks to Harry Bennett of the University of Plymouth and Kristofer Allerfeldt of the University of Exeter for their input. *Chicago Defender,* April 2, 1955, 10.

2. Leo E. Grove, Oxford University Press, New York, to Thurgood Marshall, March 25, 1955. NAACP Papers, part 17, reel 9, frame 621 (henceforth NAACP, pt17, r9, f621). For Universal Studios' approach to Poppy Cannon and Henry Lee Moon, see George Gregory Jr. to William Gordon, June 28, 1955. NAACP, pt. 17, r9, f708. Cannon was reportedly keen on the idea.

3. See, for example, Nancy Weiss, *Farewell to the Party of Lincoln: Black Politics in the Age of FDR* (Princeton, N.J.: Princeton University Press, 1983); Harvard Sitkoff, *A New Deal for Blacks: The Emergence of Civil Rights as a National Issue* (New York: Oxford University Press, 1978); and Robert Zangrando, *The NAACP Crusade against Lynching, 1909–1950* (Philadelphia: Temple University Press, 1980).

4. See, for example, John White, *Black Leadership in America from Booker T. Washington to Jesse Jackson* (Edinburgh: Pearson Education, 1990), and Henry Louis Gates Jr. and Cornell West, *The African American Century* (New York: Simon and Schuster, 2000).

5. *Chicago Defender,* April 2, 1955, 35; Kenneth Robert Janken, *White: The Biography of Walter White, Mr. NAACP* (New York: New Press, 2003).

6. *Time,* April 4, 1955, 18–19.

7. W. E. B. Du Bois, *The Autobiography of W. E. B. Du Bois* (New York: International Publishers, 1968), 293.

8. *Crisis,* April 1934, 115.

9. Walter White, *A Rising Wind* (New York: Doubleday, Doran and Company, 1945), 54.

10. *Chicago Defender,* April 9, 1955, 10.

11. Walter White, *How Far the Promised Land?* (New York: Viking Press, 1955), 10.

12. White, *A Man Called White: The Autobiography of Walter White* (Athens, Ga.: Thrasher Books, 1948), 3. For a good example of White's sense of his own identity, see "Why I Remain a Negro," published in the *Saturday Review of Literature,* October 11, 1947, and the *Reader's Digest,* January 1948, vol. 52, no. 309. The title of this article suggests that there was an element of choice involved in how White defined himself.

13. White, *A Man Called White*, 366. White was, in fact, descended from President William Henry Harrison. White, *A Man Called White*, 3.

14. White, *A Man Called White*, 11; Janken, *White*, 17–19.

15. Janken, *White*, 328–29.

16. Janken, *White*, 338.

17. Helen Martin to White, May 20, 1949. Janken, *White*, 338.

18. Carl Murphy to Palmer Weber, August 31, 1949. NAACP, pt17, r23, f925–26. See also Alfred Baker Lewis to Carl Murphy, August 30, 1949. NAACP, pt17, r23, f922.

19. *Washington Afro-American*, July 30, 1949, cited in Janken, *White*, 339. Chairman of the NAACP Board, Louis T. Wright was highly critical of the *Afro-American*'s coverage of White. Louis T. Wright to Carl Murphy, September 23, 1949. NAACP, pt17, r23, f953–54. Murphy to Wright, September 28, 1949. NAACP, pt17, r23, f952. Roy Wilkins, the acting secretary, took P. B. Young of the *Guide* to task over its editorial policy on White. Wilkins to P. B. Young, August 18, 1949. NAACP, pt17, r23, f921.

20. *Chicago Defender*, September 3, 1949, 1, cited in Janken, *White*, 340.

21. *Charlotte Post*, July 30, 1949. NAACP, pt17, r24, f101. For similar comments, see the *Chicago Defender*, September 3, 1949. NAACP, pt17, r24, f123.

22. *Los Angeles Sentinel*, undated. NAACP, pt17, r24, f153.

23. *Look*, August 30, 1949, 94–95, cited in Janken, *White*, 341–42.

24. *Afro-American*, May 6, 1950. NAACP, pt17, r24, f003–005.

25. Janken, *White*, 344.

26. Memorandum, Moon to White, September 20, 1949. NAACP, pt17, r23, f931. See also, memorandum, White to Moon, Hicks, Walker, and Booker, September 22, 1949. NAACP, pt17, r23, f939. For the minutes of White's press conference of September 22, 1949, see NAACP, pt17, r23, f940–41. *Black No More* was Schuyler's satirical novel, published in 1931, about a skin-lightening chemical that turned African Americans white.

27. Poppy Cannon, *A Gentle Knight: My Husband, Walter White* (New York: Popular Library, 1956), 18.

28. Cannon, *A Gentle Knight*, 102.

29. Janken, *White*, 351–53. Eleanor Roosevelt threatened to resign if White was not retained.

30. Cannon, *A Gentle Knight*, 32.

31. White, *A Man Called White*, 36.

32. White, *A Man Called White*, 277–87; Janken, *White*, 293–94.

33. Janken, *White*, 295.

34. See Zangrando, *NAACP Crusade*; Philip Dray, *At the Hands of Persons Unknown: The Lynching of Black America* (New York: Modern Library, 2003); Weiss, *Farewell to the Party of Lincoln*, 97–119.

35. Janken, *White*, 2.

36. White, *A Man Called White*, 50–51. Janken, as ever, offers a more sober account of the incident. Janken, *White*, 52–55.

37. Robert Zangrando, "The NAACP and a Federal Anti-lynching Bill, 1934–1940," *Journal of Negro History* 50 (April 1965): 107.

38. Stewart E. Tolney and E. M. Beck, *A Festival of Violence: An Analysis of Southern Lynching, 1882–1930* (Urbana: University of Illinois Press, 1992), 256.

39. Walter White, *Rope and Faggot: A Biography of Judge Lynch* (New York: Alfred A. Knopf, 1929), 11–12.

40. *Time,* April 4, 1955, 18–19. NAACP, pt17, r19, f670–71.

41. *New York Times,* January 1, 1935, 14.

42. Raymond Wolters, *Negroes and the Great Depression: The Problem of Economic Relief* (Westport, Conn.: Greenwood Publishing, 1970), 302–52; Janken, *White,* 180–84.

43. Janken, *White,* 183–84.

44. Wolters, *Negroes and the Great Depression,* 340–41.

45. White to Charles Studin, March 26, 1928, cited in Weiss, *Farewell to the Party of Lincoln,* 7.

46. White confirmed to the *Saturday Review of Literature* that he had voted for Roosevelt in 1936 and would do so again in 1940. NAACP, pt18, C, 23, f0095–0096.

47. Weiss, *Farewell to the Party of Lincoln,* 7–9; Janken, *White,* 127–35; White, *A Man Called White,* 99–101.

48. Beth Tompkins Bates, "A New Crowd Challenges the Agenda of the Old Guard in the NAACP, 1933–1941," *American Historical Review* 102, no. 2 (April 1997): 367.

49. Dray, *At the Hands of Persons Unknown,* 342.

50. Janken, *White,* 226.

51. John B. Kirby, *Black Americans in the Roosevelt Era: Liberalism and Race* (Knoxville: University of Tennessee Press, 1980), 183–84.

52. Kirby, *Black Americans in the Roosevelt Era,* 185.

53. Weiss, *Farewell to the Party of Lincoln,* 34 and 119.

54. Cannon, *A Gentle Knight,* 31; White regarded the PCCR as one of his greatest achievements. Janken, *White,* 367. Zangrando argues that "To Secure These Rights," became "thereafter the American civil rights agenda at all levels." Zangrando, *NAACP Crusade,* 175; Mary Ellison, *The Black Experience: American Blacks since 1865* (London: B. T. Batsford, 1974), 176.

55. White to Pearl Mitchell, October 1, 1940. NAACP, pt18, C, 15, f0685.

56. Janken, *White,* 70; Zangrando, *NAACP Crusade,* 154; *Topeka Plaindealer,* October 18, 1940, 2.

57. Kenneth W. Goings, *"The NAACP Comes of Age": The Defeat of Judge John J. Parker* (Bloomington: Indiana University Press, 1990), 27.

58. *Chicago Defender,* May 31, 1930. Herbert Hoover Presidential Papers, Secretary's File, box 430. White would have challenged whoever Hoover nominated to the Supreme Court. Janken, *White,* 137.

59. *Crisis,* 40, December 1934, 364; NAACP Press Release May 15, 1936. NAACP, pt11, B, r24, f124; Topping, "The Republican Party and Civil Rights, 1928–1948" (Unpublished Ph.D. thesis, University of Hull, 2002), 67–70.

60. J. L. LeFlore, of the Mobile, Alabama, NAACP to White, August 12, 1937, NAACP, pt11, A, r9, f470.

61. Telegram, White to Franklin Roosevelt, September 16, 1937, NAACP, pt11, A, r9, f510; NAACP press release dated September 17, 1937, NAACP, pt11, A, r9, f511–12.

62. White to Rev. John Haynes Holmes, August 25, 1937, NAACP, pt11, A, r9, f491; White to Branches, September 16, 1937, NAACP, pt11, A, r9, f519–21, and White to Rev. John Haynes Holmes, September 20, 1937, NAACP, pt11, A, r9, f532–33.

63. White to Black, May 5, 1937. NAACP, pt11, A, r9, f468; White, *A Man Called White*, 179.

64. White, *A Man Called White*, 179.

65. Du Bois, *Autobiography*, 293.

66. Janken, *White*, 310.

67. Janken, *White*, 356; August Meier and Elliott Rudwick, *Along the Color Line: Explorations in the Black Experience* (Chicago: University of Illinois Press, 1976), 113.

68. Walter White, *Crisis*, 44, February 1936, 46–47; *Time*, August 17, 1936, 10; Paul W. Ward, *The Nation*, 143, no. 5, August 1, 1936, 119–20; Henry Lee Moon, *New York Times*, October 18, 1936, iv, 7.

69. Topping, "'Never argue with the Gallup Poll': Thomas Dewey, Civil Rights and the Election of 1948," *Journal of American Studies* 38, no. 2 (August 2004): 179–99.

70. White to Cannon, January 25, 1949. Janken, *White*, 333.

71. "Supplement to Survey of the Negro Vote in the 1952 Presidential Election." NAACP pt18, B, r17, f652–56; "The 1952 Elections, A Statistical Analysis," October 1953, 30, Papers of the Republican Party, Part II, Reports and Memoranda of the Research Division of the Headquarters of the Republican National Committee, 1938–1980.

72. Janken, *White*, 148–55 and 158–60; Dray, *At the Hands of Persons Unknown*, 307–17.

73. See, for example, Memorandum by Walter White, August 29, 1950, NAACP Records II A 369. Cited in Manfred Berg, *"The Ticket to Freedom": The NAACP and the Struggle for Black Political Integration* (Gainesville: University Press of Florida, 2005), 132–33.

74. Meier and Rudwick, *Beyond the Color Line*, 94–128.

75. *New York Times*, March 22, 1955, 31.

2. Jenny Woodley, In Harlem and Hollywood: The NAACP's Cultural Campaigns, 1910–1950

1. Press Release, January 24, 1925. Papers of the NAACP on microfilm (hereafter NAACP/MF): Part 1, Reel 1.

2. W. E. B. Du Bois, "Criteria of Negro Art," *Crisis*, October 1926, 290.

3. For a discussion of the NAACP's connection to the Renaissance, see David Levering Lewis, *When Harlem Was in Vogue* (New York: Penguin, 1997; original 1981); George Hutchinson, *The Harlem Renaissance in Black and White* (Cambridge, Mass.: Belknap Press, 1995); Nathan Huggins, *Harlem Renaissance* (Oxford: Oxford University Press, 2007; original 1971); Charles Flint Kellogg, *NAACP: A History of the National Association for the Advancement of Colored People, Volume 1, 1909–1920* (Baltimore: Johns Hopkins University Press, 1967); Mark Robert Schneider, *"We Return Fighting": The Civil Rights Movement in the Jazz Age* (Boston: Northeastern University Press, 2002); David Levering Lewis, *W. E. B. Du Bois: The Fight for Equality and the American Century, 1919–1963* (New York: Henry Holt and Co., 2000); Kenneth Robert Janken, *Walter White: Mr. NAACP* (Chapel Hill: University of North Carolina Press, 2006); Eugene Levy, *James Weldon Johnson: Black Leader,*

Black Voice (Chicago: University of Chicago Press, 1973). Thomas Cripps discusses the NAACP and the film industry in *Slow Fade to Black: The Negro in American Film, 1900–1942* (Oxford: Oxford University Press, 1977) and *Making Movies Black: The Hollywood Message Movie from World War II to the Civil Rights Era* (Oxford: Oxford University Press, 1993). The only work to focus primarily on the NAACP's cultural work is Leonard C. Arthur, *Black Images in the American Theatre: NAACP Protests Campaigns—Stage, Screen, Radio and Television* (New York: Pageant-Poseidon, 1973). However the book is greatly flawed because Arthur does not use the NAACP's extensive papers in his research.

4. August Meier and John Bracey Jr., "The NAACP as a Reform Movement, 1909–1965: 'To Reach the Conscience of America,'" *Journal of Southern History* 59, no. 1 (February 1993): 4.

5. James Weldon Johnson, *The Book of American Negro Poetry* (New York: Harcourt, Brace and World, 1958; original 1922), 9.

6. Johnson, *American Negro Poetry*, 9.

7. Lewis, *Fight for Equality*, ch. 5.

8. Fauset's contribution to the Renaissance and the *Crisis* is often overlooked. See Carolyn Wedin Sylvander, *Jessie Redmon Fauset, Black American Writer* (Troy, N.Y.: Whitston, 1981).

9. Jean Fagan Yellin, "An Index of Literary Materials in the *Crisis*, 1910–1934: Articles, Belles Lettres and Book Reviews," *CLA Journal* (December 1971): 197.

10. It is estimated that in 1916 80 percent of its readers were African American. Kellogg, *NAACP*, 150.

11. "Editorial," *Crisis*, September 1916, 217.

12. "Postscript," *Crisis*, April 1927, 70.

13. Du Bois, "Criteria of Negro Art," 297.

14. Lewis, *Fight for Equality*, 180.

15. "The Browsing Reader," *Crisis*, June 1928, 202.

16. Du Bois, "Criteria of Negro Art," 296.

17. See Lewis, *Fight for Equality*, 156.

18. Donald Bogle, *Toms, Coons, Mulattoes, Mammies and Bucks: An Interpretive History of Blacks in American Film* (New York: Continuum, 2002).

19. Walter White, *A Man Called White* (New York: Viking Press, 1948), 199.

20. White to David Selznick, June 26, 1938. Papers of the NAACP at the Library of Congress, followed by Group, Series and Box (hereafter NAACP/LC):II-L-15.

21. White to Editor of *PM*, September 23, 1942. NAACP/LC: II-A-275.

22. "Editorial," *Crisis*, May 1915, 33.

23. Local NAACP branches were more active in this campaign than in any of the Association's other cultural work. The national office called on branches to organize boycotts and protests against *The Birth of a Nation* in their area and many branches took the lead in the fight against the film. For a discussion of the NAACP's campaign, see Melvyn Stokes, *D. W. Griffith's* The Birth of a Nation*: A History of the Most Controversial Motion Picture of All Time* (Oxford: Oxford University Press, 2007), 129–70.

24. White to Bloomington Branch, April 22, 1924. NAACP/MF: Part 11A, Reel 34.

25. For a discussion of the impact of the war on Hollywood and depictions of race, see Cripps, *Making Movies*, and Clayton Koppes and Gregory Black,

Hollywood Goes to War: How Politics, Profits and Propaganda Shaped World War II Movies (London: I. B. Tauris, 1988).

26. Press Release, July 27, 1942. NAACP/LC: II-A-275.

27. White to Sara Boynoff, March 12, 1942. NAACP/LC: II-A-274.

28. Press Release, July 27, 1942.

29. Press Release, August 21, 1942; Press Release, July 27, 1942. NAACP/LC: II-A-275.

30. These films showed blacks participating in the war as equals. See Cripps, *Making Movies,* ch. 3.

31. White to NAACP members, December 26, 1945. NAACP/LC: II-A-275.

32. The NAACP would eventually open a Hollywood Bureau in 2002. See Thomas Cripps, "'Walter's Thing': The NAACP's Hollywood Bureau of 1946—a cautionary tale," *Journal of Popular Film and Television* 33, no. 2 (Summer 2005): 116–25.

33. During the 1950s the NAACP also became alert to the possible dangers of television. See Melvin Patrick Ely, *The Adventures of Amos 'n' Andy: A Social History of an American Phenomenon* (Charlottesville: University Press of Virginia, 2001).

34. Megan E. Williams, "The *Crisis* Cover Girl: Lena Horne, the NAACP, and Representations of African American Femininity, 1941–1945," *American Periodicals* 16, no. 2 (2006): 201.

35. E. Franklin Frazier, *Black Bourgeoisie: The Rise of a New Middle Class in the United States* (New York: Collier, 1962), 23.

36. David Levering Lewis, "Parallels and Divergences: Assimilationist Strategies of Afro-American and Jewish Elites from 1910 to the Early 1930s," *Journal of American History* 71, no. 3 (December 1984): 543.

37. White to Edwin Embree, March 4, 1943. NAACP/LC: II-A-279. Examples of successful all-black Hollywood films from the era include *Cabin in the Sky* and *Stormy Weather* (both 1943).

38. White, February 18, 1946. NAACP/LC: II-A-277.

39. See Jill Watts, *Hattie McDaniel: Black Ambition, White Hollywood* (New York: Harper Collins, 2005), chs. 9 and 10.

40. "Negroes Ask for Better Shade in Pix: Lawyers too," *Variety,* June 17, 1942. NAACP/LC: II-A-275.

41. Huggins, *Harlem Renaissance,* 151.

42. Johnson, *American Negro Poetry,* 9.

43. James Weldon Johnson, ed., *The Book of American Negro Spirituals* (New York: Viking Press, 1925).

44. Amy Helene Kirschke, *Aaron Douglas: Art, Race and the Harlem Renaissance* (Jackson: University Press of Mississippi, 1995), ch. 3.

45. Harold Cruse, *The Crisis of the Negro Intellectual* (New York: New York Review Books, 2005; original 1967), 33–38, 83–84.

46. Henry Louis Gates Jr., "The Trope of a New Negro and the Reconstruction of the Image of the Black," *Representations* 24 (Autumn 1988): 147–48.

47. Huggins, *Harlem Renaissance,* 90, 145.

48. Joe Street, *The Culture War in the Civil Rights Movement* (Gainesville: University of Florida Press, 2007).

49. Du Bois, "Criteria of Negro Art," 294.

50. "NAACP Leaders Speak Out against Racist Comments Aimed at Rutgers University Team," April 9, 2007. http://www.naacp.org/news/press/2007–04–09.

3. George Lewis, "A Gigantic Battle to Win Men's Minds": The NAACP's Public Relations Department and Post-*Brown* Propaganda

1. For a full transcript of Huntley's remarks, see "Editorial Comment: Mr. Huntley's Astounding Proposal," *Journal of Negro Education* 28, no. 2 (Spring 1959): 85–91.

2. Edward Bliss Jr., *Now the News: The Story of Broadcast Journalism* (New York: Columbia University Press, 1991), 304; Gilbert Jonas, *Freedom's Sword: The NAACP and the Struggle against Racism in America, 1909–1969* (New York: Routledge, 2007), 382.

3. See, for example, Amzie Moore interview in Howell Raines (ed.), *My Soul Is Rested: The Story of the Civil Rights Movement in the Deep South* (New York: Penguin, 1983), 234, 235–36; Clayborne Carson, *In Struggle: SNCC and the Black Awakening of the 1960s*, 2nd ed. (Cambridge, Mass.: Harvard University Press, 1995), 26 and 136–37.

4. "REPORT OF THE DEPARTMENT OF PUBLIC RELATIONS, February 1959," in Papers of the National Association for the Advancement of Colored People, ed. August Meier, microfilm, 28 parts (Frederick, Md.: University Publications of America, 1982), Part 24, "Special Subjects 1956–1965," Series C "Life Memberships—Zangrando" (hereafter NAACP Special Subjects Papers), reel 19, frames 978–81.

5. "REPORT OF THE DEPARTMENT OF PUBLIC RELATIONS, March 1959," NAACP Special Subject Papers, reel 19, frames 982–84.

6. There is no mention of the Huntley episode, for example, in the most recent histories of the NAACP, such as Manfred Berg, *"The Ticket to Freedom": The NAACP and the Struggle for Black Political Integration* (Gainesville: University Press of Florida, 2005), or Jonas, *Freedom's Sword*; historians of southern segregation have also ignored it despite the presence of Waring, such as Numan V. Bartley, *The Rise of Massive Resistance: Race and Politics in the South during the 1950s* (Baton Rouge: Louisiana State University Press, 1969); and there is no mention in either the growing volume of work on television, the media, and civil rights, such as Allison Graham, *Framing the South: Hollywood, Television, and Race during the Civil Rights Struggle* (Baltimore: Johns Hopkins University Press, 2001), or more general works on televised news programs, such as Bliss, *Now the News*, or J. Fred MacDonald, *One Nation Under Television: The Rise and Demise of Network TV*, 2nd ed. (Chicago: Nelson-Hall, 1994).

7. "Chronology of a Crusade: The Story of the NAACP, 1909–1959," NAACP Special Subject Papers, reel 19, frames 0324–44.

8. On the subject of finances, Manfred Berg, for example, has calculated that between 1948 and 1952 the NAACP ran at an annual deficit of roughly $37,000. Berg, *The Ticket to Freedom*, 152. Walter White, "Some Tactics Which Should Supplement Resort to the Courts in Achieving Racial Integration in Education,"

Journal of Negro Education 21, no. 3 (Summer 1952): 342; J. H. Calhoun letter to Roy Wilkins, October 10, 1956, and Wilkins reply to Calhoun, November 5, 1956, in Papers of the NAACP Part 20, "White Resistance and Reprisals, 1956–1965" (hereafter NAACP White Reprisals Papers), reel 8, frames 685 and 684, respectively; "REPORT OF THE DEPARTMENT OF PUBLIC RELATIONS, March 1960," NAACP Special Subject Papers, reel 19, frames 996–1000.

9. "Discussion by Gloster B. Current at the Leadership Training Workshop, Thursday, October 6 [1960], 8:00p.m." NAACP Special Subjects Papers, reel 19, frames 406–10.

10. Julian Bond, for example, a noted political and civil rights activist who assumed the chair of the NAACP board of directors in February 1998, has written that "there has been vast documentation of the NAACP. Printed works about discrete chapters in its history constitute a small library." Bond introduction to Jonas, *Freedom's Sword,* xiv. There is, however, no systematic analysis of the role of the Department of PR, which continues to be ignored by many historians. For the most recent examples, see Berg, *The Ticket to Freedom,* and Jonas, *Freedom's Sword,* but see also older works such as Langston Hughes, *Fight for Freedom: The Story of the NAACP* (New York: W. W. Norton, 1962), and August Meier and John Bracey Jr., "The NAACP as a Reform Movement, 1909–1965: 'To Reach the Conscience of America,'" *Journal of Southern History* 59, no. 1 (February 1993): 3–30. Similarly, Gilbert Ware has noted of the NAACP that "although its most spectacular activity has occurred in the courts, the true measure of its efforts is not to be found exclusively in the favorable decisions secured." In seeking to redress that imbalance, however, Ware focuses only on the extent to which "the NAACP has sought to influence the formulation and execution of policy in all government arenas" by lobbying. Gilbert Ware, "Lobbying as a Means of Protest: The NAACP as an Agent of Equality," *Journal of Negro Education* 33, no. 2 (Spring 1964): 103–10, quotation from 103. For studies that ably draw attention to the importance of the NAACP's radio work to the black cause, see Brian Ward, *Radio and the Struggle for Civil Rights in the South* (Gainesville: University Press of Florida, 2004); Stephen R. J. Walsh, "Black-Oriented Radio and the Campaign for Civil Rights in the United States, 1945–1975" (Ph.D. dissertation, University of Newcastle-upon-Tyne, 1997); and in the early postwar period, Barbara D. Savage, *Broadcasting Freedom: Radio, War and the Politics of Race, 1938–1948* (Chapel Hill: University of North Carolina Press, 1999).

11. "REPORT OF THE DEPARTMENT OF PUBLIC RELATIONS, February 1957" and "REPORT OF THE DEPARTMENT OF PUBLIC RELATIONS, June–August, 1962," both in NAACP Special Subject Papers, reel 19, frames 936–37 and 1001–3, respectively.

12. "REPORT OF THE DEPARTMENT OF PUBLIC RELATIONS, November 1959," NAACP Special Subject Papers, reel 19, frames 993–95.

13. Memorandum to Moon from Julia E. Baxter, April 30, 1957, frame 940, NAACP Special Subject Papers, reel 19.

14. In purely numerical terms, there were 39.4 million television sets in the United States by 1955. MacDonald, *One Nation under Television,* 60.

15. In June 1963, for example, John A. Morsell appeared on WNDT-TV and WOR; Roy Wilkins on CBS-TV; Jesse DeVore on WOR; Gloster B. Current on WMCA; Herbert Hill on WNDT-TV; Robert L. Carter on NBC-TV; and June

Shagaloff and Charles Evers appeared together on WNDT-TV. "REPORT OF THE DEPARTMENT OF PUBLIC RELATIONS, June, July, August, 1963," NAACP Special Subject Papers, reel 19, frames 1003–5.

16. "Rough Draft of Manual for NAACP Branch PR Chairmen," NAACP Special Subject Papers, reel 19, frames 367–87.

17. The majority of the PR Department's monthly reports include some reference to this routine act of dissemination. This particular quotation from "REPORT OF THE DEPARTMENT OF PUBLIC RELATIONS, April, 1958," NAACP Special Subject Papers, reel 19, frames 963–65.

18. Moon quoted in "REPORT OF THE DEPARTMENT OF PUBLIC RELATIONS, September 1957," NAACP Special Subject Papers, reel 19, frames 941–42.

19. Hodding Carter quoted in George Lewis, *Massive Resistance: The White Response to the Civil Rights Movement* (London: Hodder, 2006), 41.

20. See, for example, "New South Notes" and "South Increases Propaganda" in *New South* 14, no. 5 (May 1959): 2 and 3, respectively.

21. "Rough Draft of Manual for NAACP Branch PR Chairmen," NAACP Special Subject Papers, reel 19, frames 367–87.

22. For contemporary accounts of the organization of Citizens' Councils as a counter to the perceived threat of the NAACP, see, for example, David Halberstam, "The White Citizens' Councils: Respectable Means for Unrespectable Ends," *Commentary* 22, no. 4 (October 1956); Stan Opotowsky, *Dixie Dynamite: The Inside Story of the White Citizens' Councils* (New York: National Association for the Advancement of Colored People, n.d.). For a later historian's account, see Neil R. McMillen, *The Citizens' Council: Organized Resistance to the Second Reconstruction*, Illini Book Edition (Urbana: University of Illinois Press, 1994), esp. ch. 2.

23. "Rough Draft of Manual for NAACP Branch PR Chairmen," NAACP Special Subject Papers, reel 19, frames 367–87.

24. For a recent work that seeks to downplay the traditional view that the NAACP's radicalism was neutered by the expulsion of suspected communists in the early cold war years, see Manfred Berg, "Black Civil Rights and Liberal Anticommunism: The NAACP in the Early Cold War," *Journal of American History* 94, no. 1 (June 2007): 75–96. For the clearest exposition of the traditional view, see Gerald Horne, *Black and Red: W. E. B. Du Bois and the Afro-American Response to the Cold War, 1944–1963,* SUNY Series in Afro-American Society (Albany: State University of New York Press, 1986), esp. ch. 7. Eugene Cook, *The Ugly Truth about the NAACP* (Greenwood, Miss.: Lawrence Printing, 1955); M. J. Heale, *McCarthy's Americans: Red Scare Politics in State and Nation, 1935–1965* (Athens: University of Georgia Press, 1998), 250–53. Jeff Woods, *Black Struggle, Red Scare: Segregation and Anti-Communism in the South, 1948–1968 (*Baton Rouge: Louisiana State University Press, 2004), esp. 57–91, quotation 59. For a copy of Cook's address reprinted and distributed by a Citizens' Council, in this case the Patriots of North Carolina, Inc., see box 115, Wesley Critz George Papers, Southern Historical Collection, Wilson Library, University of North Carolina at Chapel Hill.

25. See, for example, Woods, *Black Struggle, Red Scare,* 61–62.

26. *The Truth Versus Ugly Lies about the NAACP* (New York: NAACP, 1957), copy in box 7, Virginia Council on Human Relations Papers, Albert H. Small Special Collections Library, University of Virginia. The NAACP pamphlet followed

the error-strewn "Answer Rebuttal to Georgia's Atty. General Eugene Cook's Attack on The NAACP," which first appeared as an article by Charles R. Graggs in the Dallas *Star Post* in August 1956, and later appeared in pamphlet form. Copy in NAACP White Reprisals Papers, reel 8, frames 780–84.

27. Erle Johnston, who served both as director of the Mississippi State Sovereignty Commission and as Eastland's "publicity manager," recalls that the senator was such a popular totem of resistance that a speech he made opposing *Brown* on the floor of the Senate on May 27, 1954, received so many requests for copies that he had 135,000 printed as pamphlets, of which 100,000 were sent to Mississippians and 35,000 to those from "other sections of the country." Erle Johnston, *Mississippi's Defiant Years, 1953–1973: An Interpretive Documentary with Personal Experience* (Forest, Miss.: Lake Harbor, 1990), 17.

28. Copies of the pamphlet were widely circulated, and exist in a number of southern archives. There are also a number of copies, many with handwritten remarks, in the NAACP's own papers. See, for example, NAACP White Reprisals Papers, reel 9, frames 909–13.

29. Replies to the Eastland pamphlet and Wilkins's note include those from John W. Curran, professor of law, De Paul University, frame 146; Herschel C. Loveless, Governor of Iowa, frame 147; James A. MacLachlan, Law School of Harvard, frame 172; all NAACP White Resistance Papers, reel 10; W. H. Adams III letter to President of the United States, January 22, 1957, frame 846, and Robert P. Bender letter to Dwite [sic] W. Eisenhower, February 20, 1957, frame 863, both in NAACP White Resistance Papers, reel 9.

30. For a copy of the form letter sent with enclosures to each of the twenty-one editors, see Roy Wilkins letter to Charles Mitchell, October 2, 1956, NAACP White Reprisals Papers, reel 2, frames 929–30.

31. *M is for Mississippi and Murder,* 2nd ed. (New York: National Association for the Advancement of Colored People, 1956), frames 655–59; Press release, "Mississippi Congressman Riled by NAACP Pamphlet," February 2, 1956, frame 691; J. F. Hulse letter to Wilkins, March 7, 1956, frame 752; all in NAACP White Reprisals Papers, reel 2.

32. William B. Rotch letter to Wilkins, November 1, 1956, NAACP White Reprisals Papers, reel 2, frame 977.

33. Richard P. Lewis, editor of the *Journal-Transcript* of Franklin, New Hampshire, quoted in Lewis, *Massive Resistance,* 109.

34. Wilkins letter to Prattis, March 11, 1959, NACP White Reprisals Papers, reel 21, frame 185; Moon was so concerned with the way in which the NAACP presented itself that he traveled down to New Orleans to oversee the first program in person. "REPORT OF THE DEPARTMENT OF PUBLIC RELATIONS, February 1958," NAACP Special Subject Papers, reel 19, frames 952–55; "NAACP Memorandum on Advertisement of the Joint Legislative Committee, State of Louisiana, Published in the New York *Herald Tribune,* February 17, 1958," frames 566–69; while Moon compiled the memo, others thought it salient to write to the *Herald Tribune,* including Wilkins, who noted dryly that Rainach's outlook on life strongly suggested "that Negroes are not the only ones who have been damaged by segregation." Wilkins letter to the Editor, *Herald Tribune,* February 18, 1958, frames 552–53; all NAACP Special Subject Papers, reel 9.

35. Moon letter to George A. Cornish, Executive Director, *New York Herald & Tribune,* August 2, 1957, frame 048; Cornish reply to Moon, August 8, 1957, frame 0403, both in NAACP Special Subject Papers, reel 21.

4. Yvonne Ryan, Leading from the Back: Roy Wilkins's Leadership of the NAACP

1. Although Manfred Berg frames his thesis around the NAACP's battle to secure the right to vote, he takes a broader view of the organizational structure of the group and its national agenda in his book, *The Ticket to Freedom: The NAACP and the Struggle for Black Political Integration* (Gainesville: University of Florida Press, 2005). Kenneth Robert Janken's book, *White: The Biography of Walter White, Mr. NAACP* (New York: New Press, 2003), also explores the strategy and agenda of the Association from the perspective of its national executive.

2. Review by August Meier, "Standing Fast, The Autobiography of Roy Wilkins," *Journal of Southern History* 49, no. 2 (May 1983): 326–27.

3. Aspects of the Association's work on a local level have been examined in several local studies. Nationally, each of the Association's main areas of legal focus has been the subject of scholarly studies although a study of the organization's national agenda remains to be written.

4. Charles L. Sanders, "A Frank Interview with Roy Wilkins," *Ebony,* 1972. Two other profiles of Wilkins also provide a picture of Wilkins's personal life: "Roy Wilkins, Columnist," published in *Tuesday* magazine in September 1966 examined Wilkins's editorial career, while "Wilkins: The NAACPs Top Man," published in *Ebony* in July 1955, introduced the new NAACP to a wider audience.

5. Martin Arnold, "There is no Rest for Roy Wilkins," *New York Times,* September 28, 1969, SM40; Interview with Roger Wilkins, August 16, 2006, Washington, D.C.

6. Arnold, "There is no Rest for Roy Wilkins," SM40.

7. Roy Wilkins with Tom Mathews, *Standing Fast: The Autobiography of Roy Wilkins* (New York: Penguin Books, 1984), 30.

8. Albin Krebs, "Roy Wilkins, 50-Year Veteran Of Civil Rights Fight, Is Dead," *New York Times,* September 9, 1981.

9. Wilkins and Mathews, *Standing Fast,* 36, 53.

10. Letter from Roy Wilkins to Walter White, April 13, 1931 ("for the formal consideration of the board"); Letter from Roy Wilkins to Walter White, April 13, 1931 ("an informal aside"); Letter from Roy Wilkins to Walter White, April 20, 1931. NAACP Papers, Manuscript Division, Library of Congress, Washington, D.C.

11. Wilkins and Mathews, *Standing Fast,* 116.

12. Memo to the Board of Directors from W. E. B. Du Bois, Herbert J. Seligman, William Pickens, Robert M. Bagnall, Roy Wilkins, December 1931. W. E. B. Du Bois Papers, Reel 35, frames 0458–60.

13. See also Janken, *White,* for more on the relations between White and Wilkins.

14. NAACP Annual Reports for 1943 and 1947, NAACP Papers, Part 2, Box K1. Figures on the exponential regional growth of the NAACP are cited in Janken,

White, 262, and Adam Fairclough, *Better Day Coming: Blacks and Equality,*
1890–2000 (London: Penguin Books, 2001), 184.

15. Fairclough, *Better Day Coming,* 184.

16. Wilkins and Mathews, *Standing Fast,* 189. Wilkins made an almost identical comment at the time in two memoranda to Walter White, March 7, 1946, and October 6, 1946. Roy Wilkins Papers, Box 2.

17. Memorandum from Roy Wilkins to Walter White, March 7, 1946; Roy Wilkins Papers, Box 2.

18. Letter from Roy Wilkins to Walter White, September 25, 1941, NAACP Papers, Part 17, Reel 29, fo190–92.

19. The *Afro-American,* dated May 6, 1950, NAACP Papers, Part 17, Reel 24, fo004; New York *Amsterdam News,* February 18, 1950, NAACP Papers, Part 17, Reel 24, fo007.

20. Wilkins and Mathews, *Standing Fast,* 210.

21. The resolution was passed by a vote of 309 to 57. Memo from Roy Wilkins to Walter White, July 21, 1950, Roy Wilkins Papers, Box 22.

22. Statement from Roy Wilkins to the Board of Directors, June 22, 1950, Roy Wilkins Papers, Box 22.

23. Wilkins with Mathews, *Standing Fast,* 214.

24. Adam Fairclough, *Race and Democracy: The Civil Rights Struggle in Louisiana, 1915–1971* (Athens: University of Georgia Press, 1995), 196–233.

25. Brief History of the National Association for the Advancement of Colored People, 1909–1959, to be included in the Subcommittee Hearing minutes (Part 3, Box A73).

26. Wilkins had, to all intents and purposes, been running the Association since Walter White's leave of absence in 1949. Despite White's return to the NAACP the following year, Wilkins's role as administrator placed much of the day-to-day running of the organization in his hands.

27. Gilbert Jonas, *Freedom's Sword: The NAACP and the Struggle against Racism in America, 1909–1969* (New York: Routledge, 2005), 305.

28. In his initial reorganization plan presented to the NAACP's board in September 1955, Wilkins requested that Marshall, "with whom the Secretary frequently confers," be named assistant executive secretary. Juan Williams, *Thurgood Marshall: American Revolutionary* (New York: Times Books, 1998), 244. When Marshall married Cecile Suyat in December 1955, Wilkins gave the bride away, and was named godfather to Marshall's first son the following year. Williams writes that Wilkins and Marshall were "firm friends" during the 1940s, united in part by a "common distaste" for Walter White. Williams, *Thurgood Marshall,* 250, 190.

29. Mitchell's biographer, Denton Watson, cites several instances during White's leave of absence in 1950 where Wilkins disregarded Mitchell and instead deferred to Leslie Perry, the administrative assistant for the Washington Bureau, as his representative in the capital, Denton L. Watson, *The Lion in the Lobby: Clarence Mitchell Jr.'s Struggle for the Passage of Civil Rights Laws* (New York: Morrow, 1990), 184–85, 273–74.

30. Wilkins and Mathews, *Standing Fast,* 222.

31. Memorandum from Roy Wilkins to the Board of Directors, September 12, 1955, Roy Wilkins Papers, Box 29.

32. Wilkins and Mathews, *Standing Fast,* 221.

33. Telegram from Roy Wilkins to branch leaders, February 23, 1955, NAACP Papers, Part 3, Box A175.

34. Letter from Roy Wilkins to Martin Luther King, March 8, 1956, NAACP Papers, Part 3, Box A273.

35. Letter from Roy Wilkins to James Peck, February 4, 1958, NAACP Papers, Part 3, Box A317.

36. Letter from Roy Wilkins to Alex Bradford, March 27, 1956, NAACP Papers, Part 3, Box A275.

37. Wilkins and Mathews, *Standing Fast,* 237–38.

38. Letter from Roy Wilkins to Alex Bradford, March 27, 1956, NAACP Papers, Part 3, Box A275.

39. Letter from Stanley Levison to Roy Wilkins, September 1958.

40. Paul Jacobs, "The NAACP's New Direction," *New Republic,* July 16, 1956, 9–11.

41. "NAACP Opens 47th Meeting," *Washington Post and Times Herald,* June 27, 1956, 32.

42. Uptown Lowdown with Jimmy Booker, *New York Amsterdam News,* May 12, 1956, NAACP Papers, Part 3, Box A317.

43. Uptown Lowdown with Jimmy Booker, *New York Amsterdam News,* May 12, 1956, NAACP Papers, Part 3, Box A317.

44. Wilkins and Mathews, *Standing Fast,* 238.

45. Claude Lewis, "Wilkins, Master Rights Strategist," *New York Times,* March 28, 1965, NAACP Papers, Part 3, Box A318, cited later in Martin Arnold, "No Rest for Roy Wilkins," *New York Times,* September 28, 1969, SM40.

46. Watson, *Lion in the Lobby,* 606.

47. Meeting on February 3, 1961; Roy Wilkins Oral History for the JFK Library, August 13, 1964.

48. Memo from Louis Martin to Kenneth O'Donnell, June 20, 1961.

49. Memo dated May 5, 1961, from Frank Reeves to Kenneth O'Donnell re: meetings with Civil Rights leaders; fo110. (The same arguments are presented in an earlier memo dated March 22, 1961.)

50. Wilkins and Mathews, *Standing Fast,* 289.

51. In an oral history interview for the LBJ Library Wilkins said that there was dismay among black Americans when Johnson was selected as the vice presidential candidate and that, at that time, Wilkins himself would acknowledge only his knowledge of government not his attitude toward race relations. Transcript, Roy Wilkins Oral History Interview I, April 1, 1969, by Thomas H. Baker.

52. Interview between Althea Simmons and Sam Rose, December 18–19, 1963. Roy Wilkins Papers, Box 29, Library of Congress.

53. Note to Vice President Johnson from Jack Valenti, November 13, 1964, WHCF, Named file, Roy Wilkins, LBJ Library.

54. Watson, *Lion in the Lobby,* 620; Wilkins and Mathews, *Standing Fast,* 302.

55. Keynote address by Roy Wilkins to the 56th National Convention of the National Association for the Advancement of Colored People, June 28, 1965; Part 3, Box A20, NAACP Papers.

56. Jack Tanner, head of the NAACP's Northwest Conference of Branches and a

leader of the "Young Turks" group that challenged Wilkins in the mid-1960s, was quoted by one newspaper as saying, "The job of the NAACP is to intensify the heat on all fronts in all parts of the country and not to play around with the Government." M. S. Handler, "NAACP to Help Implement Laws," *New York Times,* July 4, 1965.

57. Simon Hall interview with Herbert Hill, August 9, 2000, cited with the kind permission of Simon Hall.

58. Kevin L Yuill, "The 1966 White House Conference on Civil Rights," *Historical Journal* 41, no. 1 (March 1998): 259.

59. Wilkins and Mathews, *Standing Fast,* 315.

60. The episode is recounted in several histories, including Clayborne Carson, *In Struggle: SNCC and the Black Awakening of the 1960s* (Cambridge, Mass.: Harvard University Press, 1995), 207; Adam Fairclough, *To Redeem the South of America: The Southern Christian Leadership Conference and Martin Luther King, Jr.* (Athens: University of Georgia Press, 2001), 314; and David Garrow, *Bearing the Cross: Martin Luther King Jr., and the Southern Christian Leadership Conference* (New York: Quill, 1986), 476–77.

61. Memorandum from Roy Wilkins to delegates to the 57th annual NAACP convention, July 5, 1966, NAACP Papers, Part 4, A81.

62. Memorandum from Roy Wilkins to delegates to the 57th annual NAACP convention, July 5, 1966, NAACP Papers, Part 4, A81.

63. Kwame Ture and Charles V. Hamilton, *Black Power: The Politics of Liberation* (New York: Vintage Books, 1992), 44–46.

64. Roy Wilkins keynote address to the 57th NAACP Annual Convention, Los Angeles, July 5, 1966. NAACP Papers, Part 4, Box A3.

65. Roy Wilkins keynote address to the 57th NAACP Annual Convention, Los Angeles, July 5, 1966. NAACP Papers, Part 4, Box A3.

66. Manfred Berg, "*Guns, Butter and Civil Rights,*" in *Aspects of War in American History,* ed. David K. Adams and Cornelis A. Van Minnen (Keele: Keele University Press, 1997), 231. The NAACP Papers show a significant amount of correspondence, particularly during 1967, from members protesting about its stance on the war in Vietnam.

67. Jacqueline Trescott, "End of an Epoch," *Washington Post,* June 29, 1977, C1.

68. Melvin Drimmer, "Roy Wilkins and the American Dream: A Review Essay," *Phylon* (1984): 160.

5. Peter J. Ling, Uneasy Alliance: The NAACP and Martin Luther King

1. Roy Wilkins and Tom Mathews, *Standing Fast* (New York: Da Capo Press, 1994), 226.

2. Memo to field staff, August 23, 1957, which includes *Courier* editorial to be published the next day, cited by Manfred Berg, "*The Ticket to Freedom*": *The NAACP and the Struggle for Black Political Integration* (Gainesville: University Press of Florida, 2005), 169.

3. Barbara Ransby, *Ella Baker and the Black Freedom Movement: A Radical Democratic Vision* (Chapel Hill: University of North Carolina Press, 2003), 147, 149, 154.

4. Clayborne Carson et al., eds., *Threshold of a New Decade, January 1959–December 1960, Papers of Martin Luther King Jr.*, vol. 5 (Berkeley and Los Angeles: University of California Press, 2005), 312.

5. Berg, *"The Ticket to Freedom,"* 176.

6. Carson et al., eds., *Threshold of a New Decade*, 445 n. 3.

7. Wilkins, *Standing Fast*, 269.

8. Carson et al., *Threshold of a New Decade*, 434.

9. Carson et al., *Threshold of a New Decade*, 445; Wilkins and Mathews, *Standing Fast*, 269.

10. Wilkins and Mathews, *Standing Fast*, 270.

11. Quoted in David Garrow, "FBI Political Harassment and FBI Historiography: Analyzing Informants and Measuring the Effects," *Public Historian* 10, no. 4 (Autumn 1988): 12–13.

12. Cited by Steven E. Barkan, "Legal Control of the Southern Civil Rights Movement," *American Sociological Review* 49, no. 4 (August 1984): 557.

13. Wilkins and Mathews, *Standing Fast*, 237.

14. Quoted in Taylor Branch, *Parting the Water: America in the King Years* (New York: Simon and Schuster, 1988), 625.

15. James Farmer, *Lay Bare the Heart* (New York: Arbor House, 1985), 194–95.

16. Branch, *Parting the Waters*, 816.

17. Wilkins and Mathews, *Standing Fast*, 287–89, quotation 289.

18. Wilkins and Mathews, *Standing Fast*, 291.

19. David Colburn, *Racial Change and Community Crisis: St. Augustine Florida, 1877–1980* (Gainesville: University of Florida Press, 1991), 35, 56–63, 209–10.

20. Wilkins and Mathews, *Standing Fast*, 314.

21. Matthew J. Countryman, "From Protest to Politics: Community Control and Black Independent Politics in Philadelphia 1965–1984," *Journal of Urban History* 32, no. 6 (2006): 813–61; Gerald L. Early, *This is Where I Came In: Black America in the 1960s* (Lincoln: University of Nebraska Press, 2003), 67–130.

22. John L. Rury, "Race, Space, and the Politics of Chicago Public Schools: Benjamin Willis and the Tragedy of Urban Education," *History of Education Quarterly* 39, no. 2 (1999): 117–42.

23. Simon Hall, "The NAACP, Black Power, and the African American Freedom Struggle, 1966–1969," *Historian* 69, no. 1 (Spring 2007): 49–82; quotations 58–61.

6. Simon Hall, The NAACP and the Challenges of 1960s Radicalism

1. For histories of the NAACP, see, in particular, August Meier and John H. Bracey Jr., "The NAACP as a Reform Movement, 1909–1965: 'To Reach the Conscience of America,'" *Journal of Southern History* 59, no. 1 (February 1993); Manfred Berg, *"The Ticket to Freedom": The NAACP and the Struggle for Black Political Integration* (Gainesville: University Press of Florida, 2005); and Gilbert Jonas, *Freedom's Sword: The NAACP and the Struggle against Racism in America, 1909–1969* (New York: Routledge, 2005).

2. For Thompson quote, see http://www.nytimes.com/books/01/07/01/reviews/010701.01bellt.html on July 15, 2005.

3. For a comprehensive history of the relationship between opposition to the war in Vietnam and the civil rights movement, see Simon Hall, *Peace and Freedom: The Civil Rights and Antiwar Movements in the 1960s* (Philadelphia: University of Pennsylvania Press, 2005).

4. The SNCC statement against the war in Vietnam, January 6, 1966, is printed in James Forman, *The Making of Black Revolutionaries* (Washington, D.C.: Open Hand Publishing, 1985), 445–46.

5. *National Guardian*, July 16, 1966, 5.

6. David J. Garrow, *Bearing the Cross: Martin Luther King, Jr. and the Southern Christian Leadership Conference* (London: Vintage, 1993), 552–53.

7. For a fuller treatment of this subject, see Manfred Berg, "Guns, Butter, and Civil Rights: The National Association for the Advancement of Colored People and the Vietnam War, 1964–1968," in *Aspects of War in American History*, ed. David K. Adams and Cornelius A. van Minnen (Keele: Keele University Press, 1997); and Simon Hall, "The Response of the Moderate Wing of the Civil Rights Movement to the War in Vietnam," *Historical Journal* 46, no. 3 (2003).

8. Letter from Roy Wilkins to Joseph Stern, March 17, 1966, in NAACP Papers, Group IV, Box A86, folder "Vietnam Correspondence, 1966," Library of Congress (LC).

9. Roy Wilkins, "Sidetrack," *New York Post*, July 18, 1965, Roy Wilkins Papers, Box 39, folder "newspaper column clippings, 1964–65," LC.

10. Garrow, *Bearing the Cross*, 555, and Berg, "Guns, Butter, and Civil Rights," 223.

11. Roy Wilkins, "LBJ's Programs Would Aid Negro," *Detroit News*, August 26, 1967, Office Files of Frederick Panzer, Box 331, Folder—Civil Rights 1967–1968, Lyndon Baines Johnson Presidential Library; Austin, Texas (LBJ).

12. See also Simon Hall, "The NAACP, Black Power, and the African American Freedom Struggle, 1966–1969," *Historian* 69, no. 1 (Spring 2007).

13. John Dittmer, *Local People: The Struggle for Civil Rights in Mississippi* (Urbana: University of Illinois Press, 1994), 396, and Cleveland Sellers with Robert Terrell, "From Black Consciousness to Black Power," in *The Eyes on the Prize Civil Rights Reader*, ed. Clayborne Carson et al. (New York: Penguin, 1991), 281.

14. Orrin Evans, "Roy Wilkins Warns NAACP of Extremists," July 7, 1966, in Records of the NAACP, Part 4, Box A18—NAACP Administration, 1966–; General Office File, Folder "Black Power 1966–69," LC, and Keynote Address of Roy Wilkins, 1–2 in NAACP Records, Part 4, Box A3, NAACP Administration, 1966–, Annual Conference File, Folder "Speeches, 1966," LC.

15. Leonard H. Carter, "A Years End Message," NAACP—the *Western Messenger*, December 1968, in NAACP, Part 6, Box C174, NAACP Branch Dept. Newsletters, Folder "West Coast Regional Office, 1968"; Roy Wilkins, "Segregation Disaster," *Daytona Journal Herald*, March 29, 1969, in NAACP Records, Part 4, Box A18—NAACP Administration, 1966–; General Office File, Folder "Black Power 1966–69"; and Emil Dansker, "War on Separatism Vowed by Top NAACP Official," *Dayton Daily News*, March 30, 1969, in NAACP Records, Part 4, Box A18—NAACP Administration, 1966–; General Office File, Folder "Black Power 1966–69," LC. See also Roy Wilkins, "Integration," *Ebony* (August 1970), and "Black Nonsense," *Crisis*, April 1971, 78.

16. Hasan Kwame Jeffries, "SNCC, Black Power, and Independent Political Party Organizing in Alabama, 1964–1966," *Journal of African American History* 91, no. 2 (April 2006): 176. Tim Tyson has done much to draw attention to the importance of armed self-defense and independent political organizing among black southerners. See Timothy B, Tyson, "Robert F. Williams, 'Black Power,' and the Roots of the African American Freedom Struggle," *Journal of American History* 85, no. 2 (September 1998).

17. Bob Moses quoted in Charles M. Payne, *I've Got the Light of Freedom: The Organizing Tradition and the Mississippi Freedom Struggle* (Berkeley and Los Angeles: University of California Press, 1997), 204.

18. Bruce Hartford interview with Jean Wiley, October 26, 2001, on http:// www.crmvet.org/nars/wiley1.htm (accessed June 4, 2008). I am deeply grateful to David Choy, one of my undergraduate students, for bringing this to my attention. See David M. Choy, "Hold the front page! A critical study of mainstream press coverage during the civil rights movement, 1955–70" (B.A. history dissertation, University of Leeds, 2008), 29.

19. Clayborne Carson, *In Struggle: SNCC and the Black Awakening of the 1960s* (Cambridge, Mass.: Harvard University Press, 1981), 162–66.

20. Jeffries, "SNCC, Black Power," 172.

21. For the MFDP, see especially Kay Mills, *This Little Light of Mine: The Life of Fannie Lou Hamer* (New York: Plume Books, 1994). Dittmer, *Local People*, 302, and Hall, *Peace and Freedom*, 17–18.

22. Comments made by Zoharah Simmons at "The Ongoing Radicalization of SNCC and the Movement," a panel session at "We Who Believe in Freedom Cannot Rest": Miss Ella J. Baker and the Birth of SNCC, National Conference, April 13–16, 2000, Shaw University, Raleigh, North Carolina. Transcription and tape of this session in author's possession.

23. See Clayborne Carson, *In Struggle*, 42, and Forman, *The Making of Black Revolutionaries*, 395–96.

24. On the radicalization of the grassroots, see Carson, *In Struggle*, esp. 111–29; Hall, *Peace and Freedom*, 13–22; and Doug McAdam, *Freedom Summer* (New York: Oxford University Press, 1988). See also Anne Braden, "The SNCC Trends: Challenge to White America," *Southern Patriot*, May 1966, 2.

25. Howard Zinn, unpublished article, winter 1965, in Howard Zinn Papers, Box 3, Folder 5, Wisconsin Historical Society (WHS).

26. SNCC Statement on the War in Vietnam, January 6, 1966, in Massimo Teodori, *The New Left: A Documentary History* (London: Jonathan Cape, 1970), 251.

27. Howard Zinn, unpublished article, Winter 1965, in Howard Zinn Papers, Box 3, Folder 5, WHS.

28. Hall, *Peace and Freedom*, 53–54, 57–58. See also Akinyele O. Omoja, "1964: The Beginning of the End of Nonviolence in the Mississippi Freedom Movement," *Radical History Review* 85 (Winter 2003), and Simon Wendt, "God, Gandhi, and Guns: The African American Freedom Struggle in Tuscaloosa, Alabama, 1964–1965," *Journal of African American History* 89, no. 1 (Winter 2004).

29. Carmichael, "What We Want," *New York Review of Books*, September 22, 1966 in Henry Steele Commager, ed., *The Struggle for Racial Equality* (New York: Harper Torchbooks, 1967), 255.

30. Carson et al., eds., *The Eyes on the Prize Civil Rights Reader,* 244. See also Hall, *Peace and Freedom,* esp. chapter 1, and William L. Van Deburg, *New Day in Babylon: The Black Power Movement and American Culture, 1965–1975* (Chicago: University of Chicago Press, 1992), 40–43.

31. Transcript, Roy Wilkins Oral History Interview I, April 1, 1969, by Thomas H. Baker, Internet Copy, LBJ, 14.

32. Adam Fairclough, *Race and Democracy: The Civil Rights Struggle in Louisiana, 1915–1972* (Athens: University of Georgia Press, 1995), 283.

33. Berg, "Guns, Butter, and Civil Rights," and Denton L. Watson, "Reassessing the Role of the NAACP in the Civil Rights Movement," *Historian* 55 (Spring 1993): 453–68, and Denton L. Watson, "The Papers of the '101st Senator': Clarence Mitchell Jr. and Civil Rights," *Historian* 63 (Spring–Summer 2002): 623–41.

34. See Van Deburg, *New Day in Babylon,* 167. For the rise of the New Right, see Mary C. Brennan, *Turning Right in the Sixties: The Conservative Capture of the GOP* (Chapel Hill: University of North Carolina Press, 1995); Dan T. Carter, *The Politics of Rage: George Wallace, the Origins of the New Conservatism, and the Transformation of American Politics* (Baton Rouge: Louisiana State University Press, 2000); Godfrey Hodgson, *The World Turned Right Side Up: A History of the Conservative Ascendancy in America* (Boston: Houghton Mifflin, 1996); Rebecca E. Klatch, *A Generation Divided: The New Left, the New Right, and the 1960s* (Berkeley and Los Angeles: University of California Press, 1999), and Lisa McGirr, *Suburban Warriors: The Origins of the New American Right* (Princeton, N.J.: Princeton University Press, 2001).

35. Of course, they ran the risk of cutting themselves off from lucrative sources of outside funding, too. While those groups associated with black militancy, such as the SNCC, saw their finances collapse in the mid-1960s, the NAACP and the Urban League, widely viewed as moderate, enjoyed significant increases in income. The NAACP's outside income rose from $388,077 in 1965 to $2,418,000 in 1968. The same period saw SNCC's income fall from $637,736 to $150,000. See Herbert H. Haines, "Black Radicalization and the Funding of Civil Rights: 1957–1970," *Social Problems* 32, no. 1 (October 1984): 36.

36. For a fuller discussion of this, see Hall, "The Response of the Moderate Wing of the Civil Rights Movement to the War in Vietnam," and Bayard Rustin, "From Protest to Politics: The Future of the Civil Rights Movement," in *Down the Line: The Collected Writings of Bayard Rustin.* Introduction by C. Vann Woodward (Chicago: Quadrangle Books, 1971).

37. Author's interview with Herbert Hill, May 16, 2000, and August 9, 2000.

38. Author's interview with Herbert Hill, May 16, 2000.

39. See, for example, Julius Lester, "To Hell With Protest," *New South Student* 5 (February 1968).

40. Marisa Chappell, Jenny Hutchinson, and Brian Ward, "'Dress modestly, neatly . . . as if you were going to church': Respectability, Class and Gender in the Montgomery Bus Boycott and the Early Civil Rights Movement," in Peter Ling and Sharon Monteith, eds., *Gender in the Civil Rights Movement* (New York: Garland, 1999), 70, 73.

41. Nathan Blumberg, "Misreporting the Peace Movement," *Columbia Journalism Review* 9 (Winter 1970–1971): 30–32. For media distortion of the peace

movement, see Todd Gitlin, *The Whole World Is Watching: Mass Media in the Making and Unmaking of the New Left* (Berkeley and Los Angeles: University of California Press, 1980), and Melvin Small, *Covering Dissent: The Media and the Anti-Vietnam War Movement* (New Brunswick, N.J.: Rutgers University Press, 1994).

42. Simon Hall, "Marching on Washington: The Civil Rights and Anti-War Movements of the 1960s," in *The Street as Stage: Public Demonstrations and Protest Marches since the Nineteenth Century,* ed. Matthias Reiss (Oxford: Oxford University Press, 2007).

43. Roy Wilkins, "Negroes and the Draft," *New York Post,* August 20, 1965, in Roy Wilkins Papers, Box 39, Folder "Newspaper Column Clippings 1964–65," LC.

44. Roy Wilkins, "SNCC's Foreign Policy," January 16, 1966, in Roy Wilkins Papers, Box 39, Folder "Newspaper Column Clippings 1966," LC.

45. "Wilkins Raps King's Civil Rights Policy," *Worcester Sunday Telegram,* April 19, 1967, NAACP Papers, Group IV, Box A86, folder "Vietnam Correspondence, 1967–68," LC.

46. Author's interview with Herbert Hill, May 16, 2000.

47. Letter, John Morsell to Henry Wallace, January 10, 1966, 1–2, NAACP Papers, Group IV, Box A86, Folder "Vietnam Correspondence 1966," LC.

48. Memo from Gloster Current to NAACP staff, April 22, 1965, NAACP Records, Group III, Box A328, Folder "Vietnam War, 1964–65," Library of Congress. See also Berg, "Guns, Butter, and Civil Rights," 215.

49. Roy Wilkins, "Sidetrack," *New York Post,* July 18, 1965, Roy Wilkins Papers, Box 39, Folder "Newspaper Column Clippings, 1964–65," LC.

50. NAACP Annual Report, 1969, 155, and VMC Records, Box 4, Folder 6, "National Youth Leaders Endorse Moratorium," press release, October 11, 1969, WHS.

51. Manfred Berg has argued that the NAACP "perceived a genuine ideological gap between its own long-standing goals and values and those of 'Black Power,'" and that the conflict between the Association and Black Power was over "fundamentally different visions." See Berg, "*The Ticket to Freedom,*" 236–37.

52. See Berg, "*The Ticket to Freedom,*" 231–33.

53. Letter, John Morsell to Michael G. Bradley, September 6, 1966, in NAACP Records, Part 4, Box A18—NAACP Administration, 1966–; General Office File, Folder "Black Power 1966–69," LC.

54. Letter, John Morsell to Charles A. Pine, November 3, 1966, in NAACP Records, Part 4, Box A18—NAACP Administration, 1966–; General Office File, Folder "Black Power 1966–69," LC.

55. Van Deburg, *New Day in Babylon,* 32, and Adam Fairclough, *Better Day Coming: Blacks and Equality, 1890–2000* (New York: Penguin, 2002), 315.

56. McKissick quoted in Van Deburg, *New Day in Babylon,* 12.

57. Van Deburg, *New Day in Babylon,* 19.

58. Letter, John Morsell to Charles A. Pine, November 3, 1966, in NAACP Records, Part 4, Box A18—NAACP Administration, 1966–; General Office File, Folder "Black Power 1966–69," LC. My emphasis.

59. "Wilkins vs. 'Black Power,'" *Rocky Mountain News,* July 9, 1966, 42, and Letter, John Morsell to Charles A. Pine, November 3, 1966, in NAACP Records, Part 4, Box A18—NAACP Administration, 1966–; General Office File, Folder "Black Power 1966–69," LC.

60. Letter, John Morsell to Charles A. Pine, November 3, 1966, in NAACP Records, Part 4, Box A18—NAACP Administration, 1966–; General Office File, Folder "Black Power 1966–69," LC.

61. This chapter has focused on the response of the NAACP leadership. However, although support for antiwar stands and Black Power appears to have only ever constituted a minority within the Association and could thus be relatively easily contained by the national office, there was much diversity of opinion within the Association's many hundreds of branches. For more on views at the grassroots, see Hall, "The Response of the Moderate Wing of the Civil Rights Movement to the War in Vietnam," 690–93, and Hall, "The NAACP, Black Power, and the African American Freedom Struggle, 1966–1969," 71–79.

62. Author's interview with Herbert Hill, May 16, 2000.

63. "Negroes and the Draft," *New York Post*, August 29, 1965, Roy Wilkins Papers, Box 39, Folder "Newspaper Clippings, 1964–65," LC.

64. Hall, "The Response of the Moderate Wing," 692–93, and Hall, "The NAACP, Black Power, and the African American Freedom Struggle, 1966–1969," 72–74.

65. Meier and Bracey, "The NAACP as a Reform Movement," 29, and Berg, "*The Ticket to Freedom*," 232, 240.

66. There is some evidence that the NAACP leadership sought to use the Black Power controversy to cement their organizational preeminence. Gloster Current argued that the SNCC's adoption of Black Power would "undoubtedly cause some defections in their ranks" and that "where likely prospects for NAACP recruitment appear among the mature and balanced young people associated with the student group an effort should be made to recruit them into NAACP ranks." Memorandum from Gloster Current to Branch Department Staff, May 31, 1966, NAACP Papers, Group IV, Box A50, "SNCC 1966–67," LC.

7. Beverly Bunch-Lyons and Nakeina Douglas, The Falls Church Colored Citizens Protective League and the Establishment of Virginia's First Rural Branch of the NAACP

1. U.S. Census Bureau, 2000 Decennial Census.

2. For a discussion of Black Codes and Jim Crow laws in Virginia, see Peter Wallenstein, *Blue Laws and Black Codes: Conflict, Courts, and Change in 20th-Century Virginia* (Charlottesville: University of Virginia Press, 2004); Steven J. Hoffman, *Race, Class and Power in the Building of Richmond, 1870–1920* (Jefferson, N.C.: McFarland and Company, 2004); Lewis A. Randolph, *Rights for a Season: The Politics of Race, Class, and Gender in Richmond, Virginia* (Knoxville: University of Tennessee Press, 2003); Nan Netherton, Donald Sweig, Janice Artemel, Patricia Hickin, and Patrick Reed, *Fairfax County, Virginia: A History* (Fairfax, Va.: Fairfax County Board of Supervisors, 1978), 270.

3. The Tinner Hill Heritage Foundation has compiled news clippings, letters, fliers, and other information related to the Colored Citizens Protective League in Falls Church, and the NAACP. These sources are not catalogued and are in the possession of the foundation's current president. Subsequent reference to these sources will be cited as THHF files. When available, additional information will be provided. Jim Kelly, "A Time to Remove the Barriers," *The Connection*, no date, THHF files.

4. Melvin Lee Steadman Jr., *Falls Church by Fence and Fireside* (Annandale, Va.: Turnpike Press, 1964), 206.

5. Netherton et al., *Fairfax County, Virginia,* 508.

6. Netherton et al., *Fairfax County, Virginia,* 538.

7. It was rumored that the local sheriff, Howard Field, was heard saying that he "hit Sandy James with a Blackjack in the head over 25 times, and it did not seem to faze him." James was never found, but locals speculated that he was murdered. *Fairfax Herald,* November 25, 1904; January 18, 1907; June 1907.

8. Leon Higginbotham, "De Jure Housing Segregation in the US and South Africa: The Difficult Pursuit for Racial Justice," *University of Illinois Law Review* (1990): 763–877.

9. Roger L. Rice, "Residential Segregation by Law, 1910–1917," *Journal of Southern History* 34, no. 2 (May 1968): 179–99.

10. Rice, "Residential Segregation by Law."

11. Higginbotham, "De Jure Housing Segregation."

12. Higginbotham, "De Jure Housing Segregation."

13. Higginbotham, "De Jure Housing Segregation."

14. August Meier and Elliott Rudwick, *From Plantation to Ghetto,* 3rd ed. (New York: Hill and Wang, 1990), 234–35; For other discussions of the Great Migration, see also, Malaika Adero, ed., *Up South: Stories, Studies and Letters of This Century's African-American Migrations* (New York: New Press, 1993); Beverly Bunch-Lyons, *Contested Terrain: African American Women Migrate from the South to Cincinnati, Ohio, 1900–1950* (New York: Routledge Press, 2002); Elizabeth Clark-Lewis, *Living In, Living Out: African American Domestics and the Great Migration* (New York: Kodansha International, 1996); William Cohen, *At Freedom's Edge: Black Mobility and the Southern White Quest for Racial Control, 1861–1915* (Baton Rouge: Louisiana State University Press, 1991); Peter Gottlieb, *Making Their Own Way: Southern Blacks' Migration to Pittsburg, 1916–30* (Urbana: University of Illinois Press, 1987); Farah Jasmine Griffin, *"Who set you flowin'?" The African-American Migration Narrative* (New York: Oxford University Press, 1995); James R. Grossman, *Land of Hope: Chicago, Black Southerners, and the Great Migration* (Chicago: University of Chicago Press, 1989); Kenneth L. Kusmer, *A Ghetto Takes Shape: Black Cleveland, 1870–1930* (Urbana: University of Illinois Press, 1978); Gretchen Lemke-Santangelo, *Abiding Courage: African American Migrant Women and the East Bay Community* (Chapel Hill: University of North Carolina Press, 1996); Gilbert Osofsky, *Harlem: The Making of a Ghetto: Negro New York, 1890–1930* (Chicago: Ivan R. Dee Publisher, 1966); Joe William Trotter Jr., ed., *The Great Migration in Historical Perspective* (Bloomington: Indiana University Press, 1991).

15. Meier and Rudwick, *From Plantation to Ghetto,* 234–35.

16. THHF Files.

17. THHF Files.

18. "Tinners Hill Celebrates Civil Rights History," THHF files; Higginbotham, "De Jure Housing Segregation."

19. The Committee of Nine eventually becomes known as the Colored Citizens Protective League, or the CCPL.

20. Edwin B. Henderson to W. E. B. Du Bois, January 20, 1915, NAACP Branch Files, Virginia, Box I-G207, Folder 3, Library of Congress (hereafter cited as NAACP Branch Files, Falls Church, Virginia).

21. Edwin B. Henderson to W. B. Du Bois, January 20, 1915, NAACP Branch Files, Falls Church, Virginia.

22. Edwin B. Henderson to W. B. Du Bois, January 20, 1915, NAACP Branch Files, Falls Church, Virginia.

23. NAACP Secretary to E. B. Henderson, February 1, 1915, NAACP Branch Files, Falls Church, Virginia.

24. NAACP Secretary to E. B. Henderson, February 1, 1915, NAACP Branch Files, Falls Church, Virginia.

25. THHF Files.

26. Leon F. Litwack, *Trouble in Mind: Black Southerners in the Age of Jim Crow* (New York: Vintage Books, 1999).

27. Dorothy Autrey, "'Can These Bones Live?': The National Association for the Advancement of Colored People in Alabama, 1918–1930," *Journal of Negro History* 82, no. 1 (1997): 6–7.

28. Autrey, "'Can These Bones Live?'" 1–12.

29. Autrey, "'Can These Bones Live?'" 5.

30. NAACP Branch Files, Falls Church, Virginia.

31. E. Nakashima, "History Echoes through the Hill," *Washington Post,* June 6, 1996, Virginia Section.

32. Susan D. Carle, "Race, Class, and Legal Ethics in the Early NAACP, 1910–1920," *Law and History Review* 20, no. 1 (Spring 2002): 97–146.

33. Charles D. Lowery and John F. Marszalek, *Encyclopedia of African-American Civil Rights: From Emancipation to the Present* (New York: Greenwood Press, 1992). See also, Mark V. Tushnet, *Making Civil Rights Law: Thurgood Marshall and the Supreme Court, 1956–1961* (New York: Oxford University Press, 1994).

34. Higginbotham, "De Jure Housing Segregation."

35. Rice, "Residential Segregation by Law."

36. THHF Files.

37. THHF Files.

38. NAACP Branch Files, Falls Church, Virginia.

39. David M. Chalmers, *Hooded Americanism: The First Century of the Ku Klux Klan, 1865–1965* (Garden City, N.J.: F. Watts Publisher, 1966), 28–33, 38, 291–306.

40. Netherton et al., *Fairfax County, Virginia,* 536–37; E. B. Henderson (as told to Edith Hussey), *History of the Fairfax County Branch of the NAACP* (Fairfax, Va.: 1965) (hereinafter referred to as Henderson, NAACP); THHF files; Jonas Gilbert, *Freedom's Sword: The NAACP and the Struggle against Racism in America, 1909–1969* (New York: Routledge Press, 2005); Michael J. Klarman, *From Jim Crow to Civil Rights: The Supreme Court and the Struggle for Racial Equality* (New York: Oxford University Press, 2004); National Association for the Advancement of Colored People, *Highlights of NAACP History, 1909–1979* (New York: NAACP, 1979).

41. THHF Files.

42. S. Moreno, "Falls Church Recalls Role in NAACP History," *Washington Post,* B3; R. White, "Grounded in Racial History: Falls Church Hopes to Buy Land for Civil Rights Museum," *Fairfax Journal,* A1, THHF Files.

43. THHF Files.

44. Henderson, NAACP; Michael H. Bassert, *The Role of Citizen Participatory Groups in the Decision-Making Process in Falls Church, Virginia: A Perspective on the*

Conflicts of Interest about Growth and Development, 1968–1974" (Falls Church, Va.: Falls Church Historical Commission, 1977).

45. See http://supreme.justia.com/us/169/366/case.html.

46. J. D. Kelly, "A Time to Remove the Barriers," *The Connection,* 20, THHF Files.

47. THHF Files.

48. Carle, "Race, Class, and Legal Ethics in the Early NAACP, 1910–1920."

8. Kevern Verney, "To Hope Till Hope Creates": The NAACP in Alabama, 1913–1945

1. Sheldon Avery, *Up from Washington: William Pickens and the Negro Struggle for Equality, 1900–1954* (Newark: University of Delaware Press, 1989), 33–34.

2. Dorothy A. Autrey, "The National Association for the Advancement of Colored People in Alabama, 1913–1952" (Unpublished Ph.D. dissertation, University of Notre Dame, 1985), 13–14; Dorothy Autrey, "'Can These Bones Live?': The National Association for the Advancement of Colored People in Alabama, 1918–1930," *Journal of Negro History* 82, no. 1 (Winter 1997): 1.

3. Autrey, "The NAACP in Alabama, 1913–1952," 25–26, 41–42.

4. *Papers of the NAACP, Part 11. Special Subject Files, 1912–1939, Series B: Harding, Warren G. through YMCA* (Microfilm, University Publications of America, 1982–), r30, f583–85, 658–59, 669–70. See also Pete Daniel, "Black Power in the 1920s: The Case of Tuskegee Veterans Hospital," *Journal of Southern History* 36, no. 3 (August 1970): 368–88; Robert J. Norrell, *Reaping the Whirlwind: The Civil Rights Movement in Tuskegee* (New York: Vintage Books, 1985), 27–30.

5. Robin D. G. Kelley, *Hammer and Hoe: Alabama Communists during the Great Depression* (Chapel Hill: University of North Carolina Press, 1990), xii, 8–9.

6. Andrew M. Manis, *A Fire You Can't Put Out: The Civil Rights Life of Birmingham's Reverend Fred Shuttlesworth* (Tuscaloosa: The University of Alabama Press, 1999), 92–96.

7. *Papers of the NAACP, Part 1, 1909–1950: Special Correspondence, 1910–1939,* r15, f269.

8. *Papers of the NAACP, Part 12, Selected Branch Files, 1913–1939, Series A: The South,* r3, f10–11, 26.

9. *Papers of the NAACP, Part 12, Series A,* r1, f253, 357–61. On the Klan in Alabama in the 1920s, see William R. Snell, "Masked Men in the Magic City: Activities of the Revised Klan in Birmingham, 1916–1940," *Alabama Historical Quarterly* 34 (Fall and Winter 1972): 206–27; Glen Feldman, *Politics, Society, and the Klan in Alabama, 1915–1949* (Tuscaloosa: The University of Alabama Press, 1999), 21–192.

10. Autrey, "The NAACP in Alabama, 1913–1952," 63; *Papers of the NAACP, Part 12, Series A,* r1, f357–61, 445.

11. Autrey, "The NAACP in Alabama, 1913–1952," 100, 103–4, 171, 246.

12. *Papers of the NAACP, Part 11, Special Subject Files, 1912–1939, Series A: Africa through Garvey, Marcus,* r6, f879, 915–16; *Birmingham World,* November 30, 1948, 1, December 7, 1948, 1.

13. Applications for Charter of Mobile, Alabama Branch of the National Association for the Advancement of Colored People, April–May 1919 and August–September 1926, Mobile Public Library.

14. "John L. LeFlore, Biographical Information," John L. LeFlore Papers, University of South Alabama, Box 8A—Personal Records, microfilm r12, sections 75–76.

15. "John L. LeFlore, Biographical Information."

16. Autrey, "The NAACP in Alabama, 1913–1952," 115.

17. *Papers of the NAACP, Part 16, Board of Directors, Correspondence and Committee Materials, Series A: 1919–1939*, r3, f786, 790–91; Autrey, "The NAACP in Alabama, 1913–1952," 134–35.

18. *Papers of the NAACP, Part 12, Series A*, r2, f142–43, 376–77, 573, 593, 632, 889, 922–24.

19. *Papers of the NAACP, Part 12, Series A*, r1, f 339.

20. *Papers of the NAACP, Part 12, Series A*, r3, f379; *Papers of the NAACP, Part 26, Selected Branch Files, 1940–1955, Series A: The South*, r2, f197.

21. *Papers of the NAACP, Part 26, Series A*, r2, f197.

22. *Papers of the NAACP, Part 12, Series A*, r1, f2, 69.

23. Autrey, "The NAACP in Alabama, 1913–1952," 171.

24. Autrey, "The NAACP in Alabama, 1913–1952," 173–74; *Papers of the NAACP, Part 17, National Staff Files, 1940–1955*, r11, f282.

25. Feldman, *The Klan in Alabama*, 219–84.

26. Kelley, *Hammer and Hoe*, 181.

27. Autrey, "The NAACP in Alabama, 1913–1952," 139.

28. *Birmingham World*, June 17, 1941, 1: *Papers of the NAACP, Part 12, Series A*, r2, f404.

29. Autrey, "The NAACP in Alabama, 1913–1952," 179–80; Bruce Nelson, "Organized Labor and the Struggle for Black Equality in Mobile during World War II," *Journal of American History* 80, no. 3 (December 1993): 963.

30. *Papers of the NAACP, Part 1, Minutes of the Board of Directors, Records of Annual Conferences, Major Speeches and Special Reports, 1909–1950*, r14, f756–57; Roy Wilkins with Tom Mathews, *Standing Fast: The Autobiography of Roy Wilkins* (New York: Da Capo Press, 1994), 190.

31. Barbara Ransby, *Ella Baker and the Black Freedom Movement: A Radical Democratic Vision* (Chapel Hill: University of North Carolina Press, 2003), 108.

32. Ransby, *Ella Baker*, 138.

33. Norrell, *Reaping the Whirlwind*, 47–48.

34. *Papers of the NAACP, Part 9, Discrimination in the U.S. Armed Forces, 1918–1955, Series B: Armed Forces' Legal Files, 1940–1950*, r25, f574, 576. Given White's clearly stated position it is difficult to comprehend the claim made by Gilbert Jonas that "the experiment known as the Tuskegee Airman" was a result of "constant NAACP pressure." Gilbert Jonas, *Freedom's Sword: The NAACP and the Struggle against Racism in America, 1909–1969* (New York: Routledge, 2005), 153.

35. *Papers of the NAACP, Part 9, Series B*, r25, f610, 612–13, 634.

36. Autrey, "The NAACP in Alabama, 1913–1952," 186.

37. Autrey, "The NAACP in Alabama, 1913–1952," 231; Nelson, "Mobile during World War II," 967–69.

38. John L. LeFlore to Hon. Truman K. Gibson, Civilan Aide to the Secretary of War, June 15 and 28, 1944, The John L. LeFlore Papers, University of South Alabama, r4, sections 44–45.

39. *Papers of the NAACP, Part 13, NAACP and Labor, 1940–1955, Series A: Subject Files on Labor Conditions and Employment Discrimination, 1940–1955*, r1, f36–37; Nelson, "Mobile during World War II," 952, 956–57.

40. *Papers of the NAACP, Part 13, Series A,* r1, f53, 361–63, 393–404.

41. *Papers of the NAACP, Part 13, Series A,* r1, f38–41.

42. *Papers of the NAACP, Part 13, series A,* r1, f52.

43. *Papers of the NAACP, Part 26, Selected Branch Files, 1940–1955, Series A: the South,* r1, f102.

44. Autrey, "The NAACP in Alabama, 1913–1952," 245; Douglas Brinkley, *Rosa Parks* (New York: Lipper Viking, 2000), 48; *Papers of the NAACP, Part 26, Series A,* r2, f882.

45. Autrey, "The NAACP in Alabama, 1913–1952," 180, 251; *Papers of the NAACP, Part 26, Series A,* r3, f792.

46. Autrey, "The NAACP in Alabama, 1913–1952," 195–96.

47. *Papers of the NAACP, Part 17,* r1, f256, 409, 432; Ransby, *Ella Baker,* 146.

48. Wilkins and Mathews, *Standing Fast,* 190.

9. Lee Sartain, "It's Worth One Dollar to Get Rid of Us": Middle-Class Persistence and the NAACP in Louisiana, 1915–1945

1. The cultural background of Louisiana, with its blend of French, Spanish, and American history, gave its black population a unique standpoint in the United States that affected the racial environment throughout the nineteenth and twentieth centuries. However, there has been much academic debate regarding the cultural differences between ex-slaves (who were perceived as *Americanized,* Protestant, and English-speaking) and creoles of color, who were said to have an interracial background and were generally not slaves before the Civil War (and were of French or Spanish ancestry and Catholic). The supposed maintenance of a three-caste system has been seen as dividing the twentieth-century civil rights crusade by class and intricate racial differences, although this analysis has not been without its critics; see Joseph G. Tregle, *Louisiana in the Age of Jackson: A Clash of Cultures and Personalities* (Baton Rouge: Louisiana States University Press, 1999), 116. The issue of ethnic differences affecting the African American community in the twentieth century, especially with regard to civil rights, has, according to Adam Fairclough, been overstated by academics and a common oppression based on race overshadowed other differences, except that of class, and these were inevitably based on cultural backgrounds of various groups; Adam Fairclough, *Race and Democracy: The Civil Rights Struggle in Louisiana, 1915–1972* (Athens: University of Georgia Press, 1995), 2–5, 15–17.

2. NAACP Branch Files, Louisiana, Selected Branch Files, 1913–1939, Part 12 Series A: The South, Reel 13, Papers of the NAACP, microfilm, Cambridge University Library, England (hereafter cited as Papers of the NAACP); Fairclough, *Race and Democracy,* 8.

3. W. E. B. Du Bois, *The Philadelphia Negro: A Social Study* (New York: Schocken Books, 1971)

4. Gunnar Myrdal, *An American Dilemma, vol. II, The Negro Problem, and Modern Democracy* (London: Transaction Press, 1944), 703.

5. Myrdal, *An American Dilemma,* 2:776.

6. Fairclough, *Race and Democracy,* 17–18, 48; George W. Lucas, New Orleans branch president, cited in Mary White Ovington, *The Walls Come Tumbling Down* (New York: Arno Press, 1969), 227.

7. Robert Bagnall, director of branches, to S. B. Smith, March 14, 1927, Selected Branch Files, 1913–1939, Reel 13, Papers of the NAACP; "Protest," Alexandria NAACP Branch to the National Executive Committee of the NAACP, January 3, 1945, A. P. Tureaud Papers, Amistad Research Center, Tulane University, New Orleans, LA, Roll 7; "Alexandria Branch N.A.A.C.P.," undated letter circa 1941 by Georgia Johnson, chair of legal redress committee (addressee unknown), Selected Branch Files, 1940–1950, Reel 17, Papers of the NAACP.

8. "Excerpts from the President's Address," *Vindicator,* August 20, 1918, vol. 1, no. 2, 1, Selected Branch Files, 1913–1939, Reel 14, Papers of the NAACP.

9. "The present necessity of vocational training," *Vindicator,* August 20, 1918, 2; "How You Can Help Win the War," *Vindicator,* August 20, 1918, 1; "Society Notes," *Vindicator,* September 12, 1918, 3.

10. A. E. Perkins, ed., *Who's Who in Colored Louisiana* (Baton Rouge: Douglas Loan Co., 1930), 136; New Orleans, Baton Rouge, Monroe, Papers of the NAACP: Part 12: Selected Branch Files, 1913–1939, Series A: The South, Reels 13–15; Papers of the NAACP: Part 16: Selected Branch Files, 1940–55, Series B: The South, Louisiana; Fairclough, *Race and Democracy,* 15, 42.

11. "New Orleans Number," *Crisis,* February 1916, 169, 171; Joseph J. Boris, ed., *Who's Who in Colored America: A Biographical Dictionary of Notable Living Persons of Negro Descent in America, vol. 1: 1927* (New York: Who's Who in Colored America Corp., 1927), 79; New Orleans, NAACP Branch Files, Papers of the NAACP; Perkins, *Who's Who in Colored Louisiana,* 141.

12. Unsigned letter, "Another year has passed into history," November 15, 1927, Tureaud Papers, NAACP Correspondence, 1926–1929, Roll 8; Mrs. D. J. Dupuy, Baton Rouge NAACP branch secretary, to Walter White, NAACP executive secretary, July 6, 1937, Selected Branch Files, 1913–1939, Part 12, Series A: The South, Reel 13, Papers of the NAACP.

13. B. J. Stanley, Baton Rouge branch president, to Walter White, NAACP executive secretary, June 12, 1936, Part 8, Series A: Legal 1910–55, Reel 8, Papers of the NAACP.

14. P. A. Washington, Baton Rouge branch treasurer, to national office, New York, March 1935, Part 8, Series A: Legal 1910–55, Reel 8, Papers of the NAACP; B. J. Stanley, Baton Rouge branch president, to Walter White, NAACP executive secretary, November 12, 1935, Part 8, Series A: Legal 1910–55, Reel 8, Papers of the NAACP; Baton Rouge Mass Meeting, January 1936, Part 8, Series A: Legal 1910–55, Reel 8, Papers of the NAACP.

15. William Pickens, field secretary, to Dr. A. W. Brazier, New Orleans branch president, January 16, 1939, Selected Branch Files, 1913–1939, Part 12, Series A: The South, Reel 15, Papers of the NAACP; C. H. Myers, Monroe branch president, to

Robert Bagnall, director of branches, May 17, 1932, Selected Branch Files, 1913–1939, Part 12, Series A: The South, Reel 13, Papers of the NAACP.

16. Unsigned letter, November 15, 1927, Tureaud Papers; Mark V. Tushnet, *The NAACP's Legal Strategy against Segregated Education, 1925–50* (Chapel Hill: University of North Carolina Press, 1987), 99; Roy Wilkins and Tom Mathews, *Standing Fast: The Autobiography of Roy Wilkins* (New York: Da Capo Press, 1994), 147.

17. Report by Bureau Agent Harry D. Gulley, January 16, 1923, New Orleans, in Robert A. Hill, ed., *The Marcus Garvey and Universal Negro Improvement Association Papers,* vol. 5 (Berkeley and Los Angeles: University of California Press, 1990), September 1922–August 1924, 178; Report by UNIA secretary general Henrietta V. Davis in the *Negro World,* August 1929, *Garvey Papers* vol. VII, November 1927–August 1940, 404; New Orleans, NAACP Branch Files, Selected Branch Files, 1913–1939, Part 12, Series A: The South, Reels 14 and 15, Papers of the NAACP.

18. Report by UNIA secretary general Henrietta V. Davis in the *Negro World,* August 1929, *Garvey Papers,* vol. VII, November 1927–August 1940, 404; Report of Activities in UNIA Divisions and Garvey Clubs by Samuel A. Haynes, *Negro World,* August 1929, *Garvey Papers,* vol. VII, November 1927–August 1940, 671.

19. Fairclough, *Race and Democracy,* 42–43; Wilkins and Mathews, *Standing Fast,* 127; C. H. Myers, Monroe NAACP branch president, to William Bagnall, director of branches, May 17, 1932, Selected Branch Files, 1913–1939, Part 12, Series A: The South, Reel 13, Papers of the NAACP.

20. Harvard Sitkoff, *A New Deal for Blacks: The Emergence of Civil Rights as a National Issue, Vol. 1: The Depression Decade* (New York: Oxford University Press, 1978), 250; Fairclough, *Race and Democracy,* 18, 23, 44; "Civic Leagues," *Louisiana Weekly,* June 30, 1934; Program of the New Orleans Federation of Civic Leagues, February 19, 1933, Tureaud Papers, Roll 15.

21. Wilkins and Mathews, *Standing Fast,* 147.

22. William Pickens, field secretary, to D. J. Guidry, New Orleans branch secretary, October 29, 1930, Selected Branch Files, 1913–1939, Part 12, Series A: The South, Reel 14, Papers of the NAACP; Letter to all branch officers from Roy Wilkins, NAACP assistant executive secretary, October 11, 1933, Tureaud Papers, Roll 8; James Gayle, New Orleans branch president, to Walter White, NAACP executive secretary, July 16, 1937, Selected Branch Files, 1913–1939, Part 12, Series A: The South, Reel 15, Papers of the NAACP; "Program Book for NAACP branches: Education for Negroes," 1935, Tureaud Papers, Roll 10; Robert Bagnall, director of branches, to H. O. Gair, Association of Colored Railway Trainmen, Baton Rouge, February 21, 1928, Selected Branch Files, 1913–1939, Part 12, Series A: The South, Reel 13, Papers of the NAACP; Charles Houston, NAACP special counsel, to James Gayle, New Orleans branch president, March 10, 1936, Selected Branch Files, 1913–1939, Part 12, Series A: The South, Reel 15, Papers of the NAACP; Pickens to national office, December 15, 1937, Selected Branch Files, 1913–1939, Part 12, Series A: The South, Reel 15, Papers of the NAACP.

23. Hebert, "Beyond Black and White," 1–2.

24. Twenty-ninth Annual Report of the NAACP, 1938, 14; John H. Scott with Cleo Scott Brown, *Witness to the Truth: My Struggle for Human Rights in Louisiana* (Columbia: University of South Carolina Press, 2003), 81–93, 102.

25. C. H. Myers, Monroe branch president, to Robert Bagnall, director of

branches, February 19, 1932, Selected Branch Files, 1913–1939, Part 12, Series A: The South, Reel 13, Papers of the NAACP; Bagnall to H. E. Carter, November 26, 1932, Selected Branch Files, 1913–1939, Part 12, Series A: The South, Reel 13, Papers of the NAACP; John M. Barry, *Rising Tide: The Great Mississippi Flood of 1927 and How It Changed America* (New York: Simon and Schuster, 1997), 313, 315, 320, 325, 328; Wilkins and Mathews, *Standing Fast*, 119–25.

26. C. H. Myers, Monroe branch president, to Walter White, NAACP executive secretary, December 4, 1935, Selected Branch Files, 1913–1939, Part 12, Series A: The South, Reel 13, Papers of the NAACP.

27. Annual Report of Branch Activities, Alexandria, 1944, Branch Department Files, Part 25, Series A, Regional Files, 1941–55, Reel 17, Papers of the NAACP; Georgia Johnson, chair of legal redress committee, to A. P. Tureaud, New Orleans attorney, August 1, 1943, Tureaud Papers, Roll 8; Tureaud to Johnson, August 3, 1943, Annual Report of Branch Activities, Alexandria, 1944, Branch Department Files, Part 25, Series A, Regional Files, 1941–55, Reel 17, Papers of the NAACP; Johnson to National Legal Committee, New York, May 19, 1944, Discrimination in the Criminal Justice System, 1910–1955, Part 8, Series B, Legal Department and Central Office Records, Reel 1, Papers of the NAACP; Annual Report of Branch Activities, Baton Rouge, 1941, Selected Branch Files, 1913–1939, Part 12, Series A: The South, Reel 17, Papers of the NAACP; 34th Annual Report of the NAACP, 1943, 34.

28. Robert Korstad and Nelson Lichtenstein, "Opportunities Found and Lost: Labor, Radicals, and the Early Civil Rights Movement," *Journal of American Studies* 75 (December 1988): 788; Harvard Sitkoff, "Racial Militancy and Interracial Violence in the Second World War," *Journal of American History* (December 1971): 666, 672, 676; Risa L. Goluboff, *The Lost Promise of Civil Rights* (Cambridge, Mass.: Harvard University Press, 2007), 204–5.

29. Annual Report of Branch Activities, New Orleans, August 1945, Tureaud Papers, Roll 10; FBI Report on the New Orleans branch of the NAACP, February 7, 1945, FBI Files on the NAACP, 1941–57, African American Resource Center, New Orleans Public Library.

30. FBI Report on the New Orleans Branch of the NAACP, February 7, 1945; November 11, 1944; Annual Reports of Branch Activities, New Orleans, 1942–1943, Tureaud Papers, Roll 10.

31. Fairclough, *Race and Democracy*, 56–60; Daniel Byrd, president of Louisiana state conference, to Georgia Johnson, chair of legal redress committee, October 12, 1947, Legal Department Files, 1940–55, Part 15, Series A, Reel 2, Papers of the NAACP; Donald Jones, regional secretary, to Reverend J. M. Murphy, Alexandria branch president, December 1, 1947, Legal Department Files, 1940–55, Part 15, Series A, Reel 2, Papers of the NAACP.

32. Daniel E. Byrd, assistant field secretary, to Viola Johnson, Maharry Medical College, Nashville, Tennessee, February 3, 1948, Tureaud Papers, Roll 50.

10. Charles L. Zelden, "In No Event Shall a Negro Be Eligible": The NAACP Takes on the Texas All-White Primary, 1923–1944

1. *General Laws of the State of Texas* (1923), 74–74.
2. For a history of this effort, see Charles L. Zelden, *The Battle for the Black*

Ballot: Smith v. Allwright *and the Defeat of the Texas All White Primary* (Lawrence: University Press of Kansas, 2004), and Darlene Clark Hine, *Black Victory: The Rise and Fall of the White Primary in Texas* (Millwood, N.Y.: KTO Press, 1979).

3. On the rise and fall of Populism in Texas, see Alwyn Barr, *Reconstruction to Reform: Texas Politics, 1876–1906* (Austin: University of Texas Press, 1971); Gregg Cantrell and D. Scott Barton, "Texas Populists and the Failure of Biracial Politics," *Journal of Southern History* 55 (November 1989): 659–92; Lawrence C. Goodwyn, "Populists Dreams and Negro Rights: East Texas as a Case Study," *American Historical Review* 76 (December 1971): 1435–56; Forrest G. Wood, "On Revising Reconstruction History, Negro Suffrage, White Disenfranchisement, and Common Sense," *Journal of Negro History* 51 (April 1966): 98–113.

4. On the unintended consequences of disenfranchisement, see William J. Brophy, "The Black Texan, 1900–1950: A Quantitative History" (Ph.D. dissertation, Vanderbilt University, 1974), 303. See also generally, Michael Perman, *Struggle for Mastery: Disfranchisement in the South, 1888–1908* (Chapel Hill: University of North Carolina Press, 2001); J. Morgan Kousser, *The Shaping of Southern Politics: Suffrage Restriction and the Establishment of the One-Party South, 1880–1910* (New Haven, Conn.: Yale University Press, 1974)

5. Quoted in Hine, *Black Victory,* p. 26.

6. Quoted in Chandler Davidson, "Negro Politics and the Rise of the Civil Rights Movement in Houston, Texas" (Ph.D. dissertation, Princeton University, 1968), 21.

7. *General Laws of the State of Texas* (1903), 148–52.

8. See Hine, *Black Victory,* 40; Alwyn Barr, *Black Texans: A History of Negroes in Texas, 1528–1971* (Austin, Tex.: Pemberton Press, 1973), 201: David Montejano, *Anglos and Mexicans in the Making of Texas, 1836–1986* (Austin: University of Texas Press, 1987), 143.

9. *General Laws of the State of Texas* (1923), 74–74.

10. As NAACP lawyer, federal judge, and former dean of Howard University Law School, William Henry Hastie explained in a 1973 interview to the historian Darlene Clark Hine: "We all felt then that the things we were doing in education or housing or residential segregation and so on, would not amount to much unless the blacks in the South were effectively franchised . . . even though the courts may decide in our favor on any number of those basic and important rights. Unless blacks had the power as voters to influence their local governments, the enforcement of these other rights would be so unsatisfactory that we wouldn't have gained very much by winning those battles." Hine, *Black Victory,* 66–67.

11. Walter White, the NAACP's executive secretary of the NAACP from 1931 to 1955, quoted in Alan Robert Burch, "Charles Hamilton Houston, the Texas White Primary, and Centralization of the NAACP's Litigation Strategy," *Thurgood Marshall Law Review* 21 (Fall 1995): 113.

12. Burch, "Charles Hamilton Houston," 95.

13. Correspondence between the NAACP head office and the Texas branches can be found at the Manuscripts Division of the Library of Congress. They are also available on microfilm from the University Publications of America under the title, *Papers of the NAACP: Part 4. The Voting Rights Campaign, 1916–1950.* In particular, see correspondence in Group B/Series B, "Legal File: Wesley, Carter—Houston Informer, 1940–1941."

14. Quoted in Hine, *Black Victory,* 75. See also, Conrey Bryson, *Dr. Lawrence A. Nixon and the White Primary,* rev. ed. (El Paso: Texas Western Press, 1992 [orig. pub. 1974]).

15. *Nixon v. Herndon,* 273 U.S. 536 (1927).

16. This chain of events is described in detail in Robert Wendell Hainsworth, "The Negro and the Texas Primaries," *Journal of Negro History* 18 (October 1933): 177–78.

17. *Nixon v. Condon,* 286 U.S. 73 (1934), quote at 84.

18. *Houston Informer,* July 16, 1932; Robert V. Haynes, "Black Houstonians and the White Democratic Primary, 1920–1945," in *Black Dixie: Afro-Texan History and Culture in Houston,* ed. Howard Beeth and Cary D. Wintz (College Station: Texas A & M University Press, 1992), 192–210, quote at 199.

19. See Burch, "Charles Hamilton Houston," 101–6, for a summary of Marshall's and Margold's arguments.

20. See Burch, "Charles Hamilton Houston," 106–9, for a summary of Wesley's and Atkins's arguments.

21. Burch, "Charles Hamilton Houston," 107.

22. In this case, the AWP was continued by the simple expedient of having the general assembly of the Texas Democratic Party vote to maintain the AWP.

23. Quoted in Haynes, "Black Houstonians and the White Democratic Primary," 201. On the NAACP national office's advice in this matter, see Hine, *Black Victory,* 168.

24. Grovey's arguments are summarized by Justice Roberts in his opinion for the Court. *Grovey v. Townsend,* 295 U.S. 45.

25. *Grovey v. Townsend,* 295 U.S. 45 (quote at 53).

26. On these points generally, see Burch, "Charles Hamilton Houston," 133–44.

27. Quoted in Michael Lowery Gillette, "The NAACP in Texas, 1937–1957" (Ph.D. dissertation, University of Texas at Austin, 1984), 17.

28. This meeting is described in Hine, *Black Victory,* 198–201.

29. *United States v. Classic,* 313 U.S. 299 (1941).

30. "Complainant's Brief," reprinted in Philip Kurland and Gerhard Casper, eds., *Landmark briefs and arguments of the Supreme Court of the United States,* Vol. 41 (Washington, D.C.: University Publications of America, 1975).

31. "Respondent's Brief," reprinted in Philip Kurland and Gerhard Casper, eds., *Landmark briefs and arguments of the Supreme Court of the United States,* Vol. 41 (Washington, D.C.: University Publications of America, 1975).

32. *Smith v. Allwright,* 321 U.S. 649 (1944).

33. For a discussion of the white primary cases that followed *Smith v. Allwright,* see Michael J. Klarman, "The White Primary Rulings: A Case Study in the Consequences of Supreme Court Decision Making," *Florida State University Law Review* 29 (Fall 2001): 55–107; Pauline Yelderman, *The Jaybird Democratic Association of Fort Bend County: A White Man's Union* (Waco, Tex.: Texian Press, 1979); C. Calvin Smith, "The Politics of Evasion: Arkansas' Reaction to *Smith v. Allwright,* 1944," *Journal of Negro History* 67 (Spring 1982): 40–51; Charles D. Farris, "The Re-Enfranchisement of Negroes in Florida," *Journal of Negro History* 39 (October 1954): 259–83; David W. Southern, "Beyond Jim Crow Liberalism: Judge Waring's Fight against Segregation in South Carolina, 1942–52," *Journal of Negro*

History 66 (Autumn 1981): 209–27; Tinsley E. Yarbrough, *A Passion for Justice: J. Waties Waring and Civil Rights* (New York: Oxford University Press, 1987).

34. A full transcript of Marshall's 1977 oral history interview for the Columbia University Oral History Research Office is reprinted in Mark V. Tushnet, *Thurgood Marshall: His Speeches, Writings, Arguments, Opinions, and Reminiscences* (Chicago: Lawrence Hill Books, 2001).

35. James O. Freedman, "The Tyrrell Williams Memorial Lecture: Thurgood Marshall: Man of Character," *Washington University Law Quarterly* 72 (1994): 1498.

36. Thurgood Marshall, "The Rise and Collapse of the 'White Democratic Primary,'" *Journal of Negro Education* 26 (Summer 1957): 249–54.

11. Patrick Flack, Tensions in the Relationship between Local and National NAACP Branches: The Example of Detroit, 1919–1941

1. An early draft of this chapter was given as a paper at the Annual Conference of the British Association for American Studies in April 2007 at the University of Leicester. I would like to thank the conference organizers for the opportunity and all who attended the panel for their very helpful comments.

2. Snow F. Grigsby to Walter White, June 29, 1933, Papers of the NAACP on Microfilm, Part 12: Selected Branch Files, 1913–39, Series C: The Midwest, Reel 13, Frame 411. Kenneth Robert Janken, *White: The Biography of Walter White, Mr. NAACP* (New York: New Press, 2003).

3. Beth Tompkins Bates, "A New Crowd Challenges the Agenda of the Old Guard in the NAACP, 1933–41," *AHR* 102, no. 2 (April 1997): 340–77.

4. J. R. Grossman, *Land of Hope* (Urbana: University of Illinois Press, 1989), 4. David Allan Levine, *Internal Combustion: The Races in Detroit, 1915–26* (Westport, Conn.: Greenwood Press, 1976), 1.

5. Detroit Branch Report for 1919, Papers of the NAACP, Part 12, Series C, Reel 11, 701.

6. *Detroit Leader,* May 24, 1918.

7. Undated memo, 1919, Papers of the NAACP, Part 12, Series C, Reel 11, 704.

8. Undated bulletin, 1921, Papers of the NAACP, Part 12, Series C, Reel 11, 719.

9. Lillian Johnson to Secretary of national office, September 23, 1921, Papers of the NAACP, Part 12, Series C, Reel 11, 777.

10. "Clansmen Film Gets Court OK," 3, *Detroit Free Press,* September 24.

11. "Mayor Forbids Ku Klux Klan Movie," 1, *Detroit Free Press,* September 18; see also K. Miller, "The Color of Citizenship: Race in Politics in Detroit, 1916–1940" (Ph.D. dissertation, University of Michigan 2004), 78.

12. Director of Branches to Fred H. Williams, February 6, 1925, Papers of the NAACP, Part 12, Series C, Reel 12, 2–3.

13. Director of Branches to Rev. Robert Bradby, March 4, 1925, Papers of the NAACP, Part 12, Series C, Reel 12, 13.

14. Interview of Beulah Whitby by Jim Keeney and Roberta McBride on September 16, 1969. Oral History Transcripts, Reuther Library.

15. Rev. Robert Bradby to Director of Branches, March 4, 1925, Papers of the NAACP, Part 12, Series C, Reel 12, 17.

16. *Detroit Independent,* April 10, 1925.

17. Director of Branches to Beulah Young, June 24, 1925, Papers of the NAACP, Part 12, Series C, Reel 12, 67.

18. James Weldon Johnson to Rev. Robert Brady, July 22, 1925, Papers of the NAACP, Part 12, Series C, Reel 12, 78.

19. The most recent, and most complete, narrative of the Sweet case and the events building up to it is Kevin Boyle's *Arc of Justice: A Saga of Race, Civil Rights, and Murder in the Jazz Age* (New York: Henry Holt, 2004). See also David Allan Levine *Internal Combustion;* Arthur G. Hays, *Let Freedom Ring* (Horace Liverlight, 1928); Irving Stone, *Clarence Darrow for the Defense* (New York: Doubleday, 1941); A. and L. Weinberg, *Clarence Darrow: A Sentimental Rebel* (New York: G. P. Putnam's Sons, 1980); and Wolcott, *Remaking Respectability: African American Women in Inter-War Detroit* (Chapel Hill: University of North Carolina Press, 2001).

20. James Weldon Johnson to Rev. Robert Bradby, September 11, 1925, Papers of the NAACP on Microfilm, Part 5: The Campaign Against Residential Segregation, 1914–1955, Reel 2, Frame 929.

21. Moses Walker and W. Hayes McKinney to James Weldon Johnson, September 12, 1925, Papers of the NAACP, Part 5, Reel 2, 931–32.

22. Walter White to James Weldon Johnson, September 16, 1925, Papers of the NAACP on Microfilm, Part 5, Reel 2, 943–46.

23. Walter White to James Weldon Johnson, September 17, 1925, Papers of the NAACP, Part 5, Reel 2, 1031–32.

24. Director of Branches to Rev. Robert Brady, July 17, 1926, Papers of the NAACP, Part 12, Series C, Reel 12, 244.

25. Director of Branches to Moses Walker, December 31, 1926, Papers of the NAACP, Part 12, Series C, Reel 12, 289.

26. Letters, *Detroit Owl,* June 3, 1927, 4. I would like to express my sincere thanks to Mr. Arthur LaBrew for allowing me access to copies of the *Detroit Owl* in his possession.

27. Walter White to Rev. Robert Bradby, January 25, 1927, Papers of the NAACP, Part 12, Series C, Reel 12, 315–16.

28. Miller, *The Color of Citizenship,* 249.

29. Director of Branches to Moses Walker, April 12, 1929, Papers of the NAACP, Part 12, Series C, Reel 12, 483. Director of Branches to Hon. Ira W. Jayne, April 12, 1929, Papers of the NAACP, Part 12, Series C, Reel 12, 515.

30. Memo, Walter White to William Pickens and Ray Wilkins, January 21, 1933, Papers of the NAACP, Part 12, Series C, Reel 13, 119.

31. Page 1, Interview of Mr. Snow F. Grigsby by Roberta McBride on March 12, 1967. Oral History Transcripts, Reuther Library.

32. *An X-Ray Picture of Detroit,* Pamphlet by Snow F. Grigsby, Papers of the NAACP, Part 12, Series C, Reel 13, 295–303; Miller, *The Color of Citizenship,* 253–88.

33. Snow F. Grigsby to Walter White, October 16, 1931, Papers of the NAACP, Part 12, Series C, Reel 12, 898–99.

34. Snow F. Grigsby to Walter White, January 19, 1932, Papers of the NAACP, Part 12, Series C, Reel 13, 124.

35. Snow F. Grigsby to Walter White, April 7, 1932, Papers of the NAACP, Part 12, Series C, Reel 13, 213.

36. *Unfairness of the City Election Commissioners and the Circuit Court Judges in the Employment of Negroes paid out of Public Funds,* Pamphlet published by the Detroit Civic Rights Committee, Papers of the NAACP, Part 12, Series C, Reel 13, 451.

37. Snow F. Grigsby to Walter White, June 29, 1934, Papers of the NAACP, Part 12, Series C, Reel 13, 411.

38. Snow F. Grigsby to Walter White, November 27, 1934, Papers of the NAACP, Part 12, Series C, Reel 13, 470.

39. William Pickens to Walter White, May 20, 1935, Papers of the NAACP, Part 12, Series C, Reel 13, 546. For a full discussion of the relationship between Pickens and White, see Sheldon Avery *Up from Washington: William Pickens and the Negro Struggle for Equality, 1900–1954* (Newark: University of Delaware Press, 1989).

40. A full discussion of the relationship between the UAW and the African American community in this period can be found in August Meier and Elliott Rudwick, *Black Detroit and the Rise of the UAW* (Oxford: Oxford University Press, 1979).

41. Walter White to Snow F. Grigsby, November 17, 1936, and Grigsby's reply to White, November 20, 1936, Papers of the NAACP, Part 12, Series C, Reel 13, 797–98.

42. William Pickens to Walter White, May 20, 1935, Papers of the NAACP, Part 12, Series C, Reel 13, 546.

43. Daisy Lampkin to William Pickens, June 17, 1935, Papers of the NAACP, Part 12, Series C, Reel 13, 555.

44. William Pickens to Charles R. Perkins, August 13, 1935, Papers of the NAACP, Part 12, Series C, Reel 13, 663.

45. Welcome address on behalf of the Detroit Branch, Dr. James McClendon, June 29, 1937, Papers of the NAACP on Microfilm, Part 1: Meetings of the Board of Directors, Records of Annual Conferences, etc., Reel 9, 1087. William Pickens to Dr. James McClendon, February 17, 1938, Papers of the NAACP, Part 12, Series C, Reel 14, 9.

46. Meier and Rudwick, *Black Detroit.*

47. Address of welcome by Hon. Ira W. Jayne, June 29, 1937, Papers of the NAACP, Part 1, Reel 9, 1089. Press release, July 2, 1937, Papers of the NAACP, Part 1, Reel 9, 1239. In his autobiography, Walter White recalled being "confronted by an angry and belligerent delegation of Negro ministers" who threatened to boycott the conference if Martin was allowed to speak. White, *A Man Called White,* 212.

48. Memo, Walter White to Executive Staff, June 18, 1938, Papers of the NAACP, Part 12, Series C, Reel 14, 34. Daisy Lampkin to Walter White, June 20, 1939, Papers of the NAACP, Part 12, Series C, Reel 14, 303. Meier and Rudwick, *Black Detroit,* 78–79.

49. Report of Election of Officers from December 13 election, Papers of the NAACP, Part 12, Series C, Reel 14, 8.

50. Report of Election of Officers from December 13 election, Papers of the NAACP, Part 12, Series C, Reel 14, 8.

51. Advertising pamphlet, Papers of the NAACP, Part 12, Series C, Reel 14, 26.

52. Dr. James McClendon to Walter White, April 11, 1938, Papers of the NAACP, Part 12, Series C, Reel 14, 17–18. The fact that this was an NNC-sponsored march is significant, as Beth Tompkins Bates has suggested that the Congress was formed in

late 1935 by activists frustrated with the conservatism of the NAACP. See Beth Tompkins Bates, "A New Crowd," and Meier and Rudwick, *Black Detroit*, 29–33.

53. Meier and Rudwick, *Black Detroit*, 78.

54. Gloster B. Current to Juanita E. Jackson, January 16, 1937, Papers of the NAACP, Part 12, Series C, Reel 14, 626–7.

55. White, *A Man Called White*, 211.

56. Meier and Rudwick, *Black Detroit*, 87–88.

57. White, *A Man Called White*, 215. Meier and Rudwick argue that the sound car action was ineffective in getting African American workers to leave the plant, but that it was successful in weakening the rival AFL-UAW's "back-to-work" campaign. Meier and Rudwick, *Black Detroit*, 91–97.

12. Christopher Robert Reed, The Chicago NAACP: A Century of Challenge, Triumph, and Inertia

1. The complete saga is recounted and analyzed in Christopher Robert Reed, *The Chicago NAACP and the Rise of Black Professional Leadership, 1910–1966* (Bloomington: Indiana University Press, 1997).

2. James R. Ralph Jr., *Northern Protest: Martin Luther King, Jr., Chicago, and the Civil Rights Movement* (Cambridge, Mass.; Harvard University Press, 1993), 10, 12, 22, 79.

3. MEMO, TO THE NAACP CONFERENCE, June 22, 1927, NAACP Papers, Branch Files, the Library of Congress (hereafter referred to as NAACP MSS., Branch Files).

4. MacNeal to White, June 1, 1937, NAACP MSS., Branch Files.

5. *The Souls of Black Folk* (New York: 1903; reprint, Greenwich, Conn.: Fawcett Publishing, 1961), 81.

6. As E. Franklin Frazier wrote, most cities have the capacity to possess a uniqueness to their character: "Cities have personalities." See "The New Frontage on American Life," in *The New Negro*, ed. Alain Locke (New York: Boni, 1925; reprint, New York: 1968), 288, 9. Also, for Detroit, see August Meier and Elliott Rudwick, *Black Detroit and the Rise of the UAW* (New York: Oxford University Press, 1979), and Thomas J. Sugrue, *Origins of the Urban Crisis: Race and Equality in Post-War Detroit* (Princeton, N.J.: Princeton University Press, 1996), 170–76; for Buffalo, New York, see Lillian Serece Williams, *Strangers in the Land of Paradise: The Creation of an African American Community, Buffalo, New York, 1900–1940* (Bloomington: Indiana University Press, 1999), 153–78; and, for San Francisco, see Albert S. Broussard, *Black San Francisco: The Struggle for Racial Equality in the West, 1900–1954* (Lawrence: University Press of Kansas, 1993), 75–91.

7. St. Clair Drake and Horace R. Cayton, *Black Metropolis: A Study of Negro Life in a Northern City* (New York: Harcourt, Brace and World, 1945), 763, as part of chapter 24, "Of Things to Come."

8. Undated article entitled "A New Account in Negro Progress," in an unidentified Chicago newspaper, in the Blaine MSS., NAACP File, part of the Cyrus McCormick Papers, State Historical Society of Wisconsin and B. Joyce Ross, *J. E. Spingarn and the Rise of the NAACP, 1911–1939* (New York: Atheneum, 1972), 31.

9. David W. Southern, *The Malignant Heritage: Yankee Progressives and the Negro Question, 1901–1914* (Chicago: Loyola University Press, 1968), 32. Also see Steven J. Diner, "Chicago Social Workers and Blacks in the Progressive Era," *Social Service Review* 44 (December 1984): 393–410.

10. Dewey R. Grantham, "The Progressive Movement and the Negro," *South Atlantic Quarterly* 54 (October 1955): 473. Also see Avery, *Up from Washington*, 23.

11. Charles E. Bentley to Frances Blascoer, June 24, 1910, NAACP MSS., Branch Files.

12. Jane Addams, *Social Control* (New York: NAACP Publications, 1911), 1, in Blaine Papers, a part of the Cyrus McCormick Papers, the State Historical Society of Wisconsin, Madison (hereafter referred to as Blaine MSS., NAACP File).

13. Diner, "Chicago Social Workers," 404.

14. L. Hollingsworth Wood to William C. Graves, September 27, 1917, Julius Rosenwald Papers, Chicago Urban League File, Regenstein Library, the University of Chicago.

15. Edward R. Kantowicz, "Carter H. Harrison II: The Politics of Balance," in *The Mayors: The Chicago Political Tradition*, ed. Paul M. Green and Melvin G. Holli (Carbondale: Southern Illinois University Press, 1987), 28.

16. Oswald Garrison Villard, "The Objects of the National Association for the Advancement of Colored People," *Crisis*, May 1912, 81, 82.

17. First Annual Report, NAACP, January 1, 1911, Blaine MSS., NAACP File.

18. *Chicago Defender*, March 13, 1915, 4. At this point in his life, Judge Brown blamed his pessimism on the horrific war being waged in Europe.

19. *Chicago Tribune*, January 16, 1915, 1 as well as *Chicago Defender*, January 16, 1915, 4 and April 17, 1915, 1.

20. See Allan H. Spear, *Black Chicago: The Making of a Negro Ghetto, 1890–1920* (Chicago: University of Chicago Press, 1967), 84f. and Arvarh E. Strickland, *History of the Chicago Urban League* (Urbana: University of Illinois Press, 1966), 34f, for views that support the belief that a split among the black elite existed and was of great importance in black Chicago. For an interpretation that holds that the split was of major importance on a national scale, see the definitive work on the subject by August Meier, *Negro Thought in America, 1880–1915: Racial Ideologies in the Age of Booker T. Washington* (Ann Arbor: University of Michigan Press, 1963), especially chapter 10, "Radicals and Conservatives."

21. "Opinion," *Crisis*, March 1914, 227. The view of Spingarn as the uncompromising champion of egalitarianism and carrier of the torch of "New Abolitionism" is best described in Ross, *Spingarn*, 21–48.

22. *Chicago Defender*, January 10, 1914, 4, and *Chicago Broad-Ax*, September 7, 1912, 1.

23. Archie L. Weaver to A. L. Foster, September 18, 1953, NAACP MSS., Branch Files.

24. Reverdy C. Ransom, *The Pilgrimage of Harriet Ransom's Son* (Nashville, Tenn.: Sunday School Union, 1947), 164. St. Clair Drake's study of African American churches and voluntary associations which was completed in 1940 corroborated this view. See *Churches and Voluntary Associations in the Chicago Negro Community* (Chicago: Works Projects Administration, 1940), 125. In addition, longtime NAACP egalitarian stalwart, Attorney Earl B. Dickerson, who devoted two-thirds of his

ninety-five years in the service of the movement under both the branch and national banners, reflected in 1984 that there never appeared to be any sense of urgency among Chicagoans to choose between the two ideologies. Dickerson knew both Washington and Du Bois, having taught at Tuskegee in 1914 and having interacted with Du Bois as a fellow NAACP supporter. Dickerson led the Legal Redress Committee of the Chicago branch between 1930 and 1933, led the legal team that prepared the groundbreaking *Hansberry v. Lee* case (1940), and served the NAACP on the board of directors for over three decades. (Source: Interview with Mr. Earl B. Dickerson in his corporate office on March 21, 1984, in Chicago.) Recently, the Booker T. Washington biographer Louis R. Harlan assessed the national situation as being one that fell far short of a total ideological split. See *Booker T. Washington: The Wizard of Tuskegee, 1901–1915* (New York: Oxford University Press, 1983), 359–78, 427, 435–37. The complexity of the disagreement was such that matters of personality could overshadow differences of principle, tactics, and strategy.

25. Spear, *Black Chicago*, 60.

26. While investigating housing conditions on the West Side and the South Side, a University of Chicago researcher found blacks unwilling to accept white standards as to how they should live in Chicago. "Some of this overcrowding would be unnecessary," he observed, "if the colored people were willing to follow the customs of other nationalities and use all of the room in their apartments as sleeping-rooms. . . . This means that unlike the immigrant, even the poor colored people like to keep a kitchen and 'parlor' and occasionally a dining room, distinctly as such and not crowded with beds." The researcher encountered an aversion to anything that stamped the black family as unusual and inferior and went on to conclude that "the Negro, with a weekly wage no larger, and usually smaller, than that of his immigrant neighbor, endeavors to maintain a standard of living more similar to that of the native-born white citizen than does the immigrant." Alzada Comstock, "Chicago Housing Conditions, IV: The Problem of the Negro," *American Journal of Sociology* 18 (September 1912): 250, 257.

27. James R. Grossman, *Land of Hope: Chicago, Black Southerners, and the Great Migration* (Chicago: University of Chicago Press, 1989), 161.

28. *Chicago Broad-Ax*, October 26, 1912, 1, 2. Also, see Louis R. Harlan, *Booker T. Washington: The Wizard of Tuskegee*, 290–94, for information surrounding his trip to Europe in 1910.

29. *Chicago Broad-Ax*, August 24, 1912, 2.

30. Lewis to Bagnall, April 20, 1923, NAACP MSS., Branch Files.

31. *Chicago Defender*, February 22, 1930, 16.

32. Robert W. Bagnall to Carl G. Roberts, March 31, 1925, NAACP MSS., Branch Files.

33. A. C. MacNeal was a Yale University graduate who served as editor of the militant *Chicago Whip* newspaper, which is credited with initiating the "Don't Spend Your Money Where You Can't Work" campaign in 1929–39.

34. MacNeal to White, April 28, 1934, NAACP MSS., Branch Files.

35. MacNeal to White, April 24, 1936, NAACP MSS., Branch Files.

36. MacNeal to White, October 20, 1933, NAACP MSS., Branch Files. Also, *Chicago Defender*, March 31, 1934, 24, and April 14, 1934, 10.

37. W. E. B. Du Bois, *Dusk of Dawn* (New York: Schocken Books, 1970), 197f.

38. MacNeal to White, October 20, 1933, and April 28, 1934, as well as MacNeal to Mary White Ovington, May 12, 1934, all in NAACP MSS., Branch Files.

39. Wilkins to MacNeal, May 2, 1934, NAACP MSS., Branch Files.

40. Pickens to White, June 8, 1934, NAACP MSS., Branch Files.

13. Jonathan Watson, The NAACP in California, 1914–1950

1. Manfred Berg, *"The Ticket to Freedom": The NAACP and the Struggle for Black Political Integration* (Gainesville: University Press of Florida, 2005); Kenneth W. Goings, *"The NAACP Comes of Age": The Defeat of Judge John J. Parker* (Bloomington: Indiana University Press, 1990); Langston Hughes, *Fight for Freedom: The Story of the NAACP* (New York: Berkeley Publishing Corporation, 1962); Gilbert Jonas, *Freedom's Sword: The NAACP and the Struggle against Racism in America, 1909–1969* (New York: Routledge, 2005); Mark Robert Schneider, *"We Return Fighting": The Civil Rights Movement in the Jazz Age* (Boston: Northeastern University Press, 2002).

2. Walter Nugent, *Into the West: The Story of Its People* (New York: Alfred A. Knopf, 1999), 211; Douglas Flamming, "African Americans in the Twentieth-Century West," in *A Companion to the American West*, ed. William Deverell (Oxford: Blackwell, 2004), 221.

3. Important community studies include Albert S. Broussard, *Black San Francisco: The Struggle for Racial Equality in the West, 1900–1954* (Lawrence: University Press of Kansas, 1993); Douglas Flamming, *Bound for Freedom: Black Los Angeles in Jim Crow America* (Berkeley and Los Angeles: University of California Press, 2005); Gretchen Lemke-Santangelo, *Abiding Courage: African American Migrant Women and the East Bay Community* (Chapel Hill: University of North Carolina Press, 1996); Shirley Ann Wilson Moore, *To Place Our Deeds: The African American Community in Richmond, California, 1910–1963* (Berkeley and Los Angeles: University of California Press, 2000); Josh Sides, *L. A. City Limits: African American Los Angeles from the Great Depression to the Present* (Berkeley and Los Angeles: University of California Press, 2003). Articles include Lonnie G. Bunch, "A Past Not Necessarily Prologue: The Afro-American in Los Angeles," in *20th Century Los Angeles: Power, Promotion and Social Conflict*, ed. Norman M. Klein and Martin J. Schiesl (Claremont, Calif.: Regina Books, 1990), 101–30; Lawrence B. De Graaf, "Significant Steps on an Arduous Path: The Impact of World War II on Discrimination against African Americans in the West," *Journal of the West* 35, no. 1 (1996): 24–33; Kevin Allen Leonard, "'In the Interest of All Races': African Americans and Interracial Cooperation in Los Angeles during and after the World War Two," in *Seeking El Dorado: African Americans in California*, ed. Laurence B. De Graaf, Kevin Mulroy, and Quintard Taylor (Seattle: University of Washington Press, 2001), 309–40; Kevin Allen Leonard, "'Brothers under the Skin?': African Americans, Mexican Americans and World War II in California," in *The Way We Really Were: The Golden States in the Second Great War*, ed. Roger Lotchin (Urbana: University of Illinois Press, 2000), 187–214; Kevin Allen Leonard, "Federal Power and Racial Politics in Los Angeles during World War Two," in *Power and Place in the North American West*, ed. Richard White and John M. Findlay (Seattle: University of Washington Press, 1999), 87–116; Rick Moss, "Not Quite Paradise: The Development

of the African American Community in Los Angeles through 1950," *California History* (Fall 1996): 222–35; Josh Sides, "Battle on the Home Front: African American Shipyard Workers in World War II Los Angeles," *California History* no. 75 (1996): 250–63; Alonzo Smith, "Blacks and the Los Angeles Municipal Transit System, 1941–1945,"*Urbanism Past and Present* 11 (Winter–Spring 1980–81): 25–31; Paul R. Spickard, "Fire in the Night: A 1945 Southern California Hate Crime and Historical Memory," *Southern California Quarterly* 82, no. 3 (2000): 291–304; Paul R. Spickard, "Work and Hope: African American Women in Southern California during World War II," *Journal of the West* 32, no. 3 (1993): 70–79; Charles Wollenberg, "*James vs. Marinship:* Trouble on the New Black Frontier," *California History* 60, no. 3 (1981): 262–79. No study has examined the work of the NAACP in San Diego. A valuable overview of the black West, which notes the work of the NAACP, is Quintard Taylor, *In Search of the Racial Frontier: African-Americans in the American West 1528–1990* (New York: W. W. Norton and Company, 1998).

4. Taylor, *In Search of the Racial Frontier,* 193; Emma Lou Thornbrough, "American Negro Newspapers, 1880–1914," *Business History Review* 40, no. 4 (1966): 470.

5. Kevin Starr, *California: A History* (New York: Modern Library, 2005), 166.

6. Broussard, *Black San Francisco,* 20–23; Flamming, *Bound for Freedom,* 35–55.

7. Rudolph M. Lapp, *Afro-Americans in California,* 2nd ed. (San Francisco: Boyd and Fraser Co., 1987), 35–36.

8. W. E. B. Du Bois, "Colored California," *Crisis,* September 1913, 192–96.

9. Bunch, "A Past Not Necessarily Prologue," 103–4.

10. Gayle K. Berardi and Thomas W. Segady, "The Development of African-American Newspapers in the American West: A Sociohistorical Perspective," *Journal of Negro History* 75, no. 3/4 (1990): 105.

11. Bunch, "A Past Not Necessarily Prologue," 106.

12. Delilah L. Beasley, *The Negro Trail Blazers of California* (Fairfield, Calif.: James Stevenson Publisher, 2004), 189–90.

13. James A. Fisher, "The Political Development of the Black Community in California, 1850–1950," *California Historical Quarterly* 50, no. 3 (1971): 261; Flamming, *Bound for Freedom,* 146.

14. Flamming, *Bound for Freedom,* 88.

15. David Levering Lewis, *W. E. B. Du Bois: Biography of a Race, 1868–1919* (New York: Henry Holt and Co., 1993), 506.

16. Flamming, *Bound for Freedom,* 87–90, 146–47, 199–200.

17. Lewis, *Biography of a Race,* 507.

18. Broussard, *Black San Francisco,* 77–78.

19. Lewis, *Biography of a Race,* 507–8.

20. Flamming, *Bound for Freedom,* 152; Broussard, *Black San Francisco,* 76.

21. The *Crisis,* August 1920, 181.

22. Emory J. Tolbert, *The UNIA and Black Los Angeles: Ideology and Community in the American Garvey Movement* (Los Angeles: Center for Afro-American Studies, 1980), 7–14; Taylor, *In Search of the Racial Frontier,* 240.

23. Shirley Ann Wilson Moore, "'Your Life Is Really Not Your Own': African

American Women in Twentieth-Century California," in De Graaf, Mulroy, and Taylor, *Seeking El Dorado*, 219; Broussard, *Black San Francisco*, 83.

24. Nugent, *Into the West*, 218–26; Taylor, *In Search of the Racial Frontier*, 223.

25. Nugent, *Into the West*, 213.

26. William Pickens, letter to H. Claude Hudson, August 11, 1927, in Folder: "Los Angeles, California 1927," Box G16, Group One, Records of the National Association for the Advancement of Colored People, Library of Congress, Washington, D.C. (hereafter referred to as NAACP Records).

27. Goings, *"The NAACP Comes of Age."*

28. H. C. Hudson, letter to Walter White, September 1, 1932, in Box G16, Group One, "Los Angeles Branch 1931–1935," NAACP Records.

29. Broussard, *Black San Francisco*, 128.

30. *California Eagle*, January 12, 1934, 1a; January 19, 1934, 1a; April 27, 1934, 1a; November 16, 1934, 1a.

31. Thomas L. Griffith Jr. to Walter White, August 6, 1935 in Folder: "Los Angeles Branch 1931–1935," Box G17, Group 1 NAACP Records; *California Eagle*, August 9, 1935.

32. *California Eagle*, July 17, 1936, 1.

33. *California Eagle*, November 3, 1938, 6B.

34. *California Eagle*, September 30, 1–5A; October 7, 1937, 1A-2B.

35. Charles Chamberlain, *Victory at Home: Manpower and Race in the American South during World War Two* (Athens: University of Georgia Press, 2003), 107. The analysis is supported by E. Frederick Anderson, *The Development of Leadership and Organization Building in the Black Community of Los Angeles from 1900 through World War II* (Saratoga, Calif.: Century Twenty One Publishing, 1980); Keith E. Collins, *Black Los Angeles: The Maturing of the Ghetto, 1940–1950* (Saratoga, Calif.: Century Twenty One Publishing, 1980); De Graaf, "Significant Steps on an Arduous Path"; Sides, "Battle on the Home Front"; Sides, *L. A. City Limits;* Smith, "Blacks and the Los Angeles Municipal Transit System"; Alonzo Smith and Quintard Taylor, "Racial Discrimination in the Workplace: A Study of Two West Coast Cities during the 1940s," *Journal of Ethnic Studies* 8, no. 1 (1980): 35–54; Spickard, "Work and Hope."

36. On the long-term relationship between the U.S. military and the state of California, see Roger Lotchin, *Fortress California 1910–1961: From Warfare to Welfare* (Urbana: University of Illinois Press, 2002); Gretchen Lemke-Santangelo, *Abiding Courage: African American Migrant Women and the East Bay Community* (Chapel Hill: University of North Carolina Press, 1996), 50.

37. John H. M. Laslett, "Historical Perspectives: Immigration and the Rise of a Distinctive Urban Region, 1900–1970," in *Ethnic Los Angeles*, ed. Roger Waldinger and Mehdi Bozorgmehr (New York: Russell Sage Foundation Press, 1996), 54; Broussard, *Black San Francisco*, 145.

38. Leonard, "'In the Interest of All Races,'" 311; *California Eagle*, October 9, 1941, 3A.

39. *California Eagle*, May 29, 1941, 1.

40. Merl E. Reed, *Seedtime for the Modern Civil Rights Movement: The President's Committee on Fair Employment Practice, 1941–1946* (Baton Rouge: Louisiana State University Press, 1991), 38–39.

41. Chamberlain, *Victory at Home,* 114.

42. Reed, *Seedtime,* 268.

43. Joseph James, Letter to the Labor Editor of the *San Francisco Examiner* (undated), Box 5, Group 2, NAACP Records.

44. Sides, "Battle on the Home Front," 260.

45. Thurgood Marshall to Joseph James, March 22, 1944; Joseph James to Thurgood Marshall, March 24, 1944, in Box 5, Group 2, NAACP Records.

46. Wollenberg, "James vs. Marinship," 274.

47. Moore, *To Place Our Deeds,* 62.

48. Reed, *Seedtime,* 315.

49. Taylor, *In Search of the Racial Frontier,* 251.

50. Broussard, *Black San Francisco,* 34–35; Flamming, *Bound for Freedom,* 261–62.

51. Johnson, *The Second Gold Rush,* 93; Broussard, *Black San Francisco,* 174; Lawrence B. De Graaf, *Negro Migration to Los Angeles, 1930 to 1950* (Ph.D. dissertation, University of California, Los Angeles, 1962), 199, 201.

52. Andrew Wiese, *Places of Their Own: African American Suburbanization in the Twentieth Century* (Chicago: University of Chicago Press, 2005), 126, 127.

53. *California Eagle,* May 23, 1946, 1; Carey McWilliams, "The House on 92nd Street," *Nation,* 162 (1946): 691–92; Spickard, "Fire in the Night," 291–304; "The Ku Klux Klan in California," Council for Civic Unity Press Release, June 1946 in "The Ku Klux Klan in California" Folder, Los Angeles, California Race Question Box, California Ephemera Collection, Department of Special Collections, Young Research Library, University of California, Los Angeles.

54. Kenneth W. Mack, "Law and Mass Politics in the Making of the Civil Rights Lawyer, 1931–1941," *Journal of American History* 93, no. 1 (2006): 37–63.

55. Clement Vose, *Caucasians Only: The Supreme Court, the NAACP and the Restrictive Covenant Cases* (Berkeley and Los Angeles: University of California Press, 1959), 62.

56. Mark Tushnet, *Making Civil Rights Law: Thurgood Marshall and the Supreme Court, 1936–1961* (New York: Oxford University Press, 1994), 88; Vose, *Caucasians Only,* 58.

57. Mauricio Mazon, *The Zoot-Suit Riots: The Psychology of Symbolic Annihilation* (Austin: University of Texas Press, 1984); Eduardo Obregon Pagan, *Murder at the Sleepy Lagoon: Zoot Suits, Race, and Riot in Wartime L.A.* (Chapel Hill: University of North Carolina Press, 2006); Edward Escobar, *Race, Police and the Making of a Political Identity: Mexican Americans and the Los Angeles Police Department, 1900–1945* (Berkeley and Los Angeles: University of California Press, 1999); George Sanchez, *Becoming Mexican American: Ethnicity Culture and Identity in Chicano Los Angeles, 1900–1945* (Oxford: Oxford University Press, 1993); Leonard, *The Battle for Los Angeles;* Leonard, "'In the Interest of All Races'"; Leonard, "Brothers under the Skin?"

58. *California Eagle,* June 3, 1943, 1a.

59. Leonard, "'In the Interest of All Races,'" 320–24; Thomas L. Griffith Jr. to Walter White, June 9, 1943, "Zoot-Suit Riots 1943–44," Box A676, Group Two, NAACP Records.

60. Leonard, "'In the Interest of All Races,'" 326–27.

61. *California Eagle,* June 17, 1943, 4a.

62. De Graaf, "Significant Steps on an Arduous Path," 31.

63. For an outline of the case, see Charles Wollenberg, *All Deliberate Speed: Segregation and Exclusion in California Schools, 1855–1975* (Berkeley and Los Angeles: University of California Press, 1976), 125–32.

64. Greg Robinson and Toni Robinson, "Korematsu and Beyond: Japanese Americans and the Origins of Strict Scrutiny," *Law & Contemporary Problems* 68 (Spring 2005): 29–55.

14. Andrew M. Fearnley, "Your Work is the Most Important, but without Branches There Can Be No National Work": Cleveland's Branch of the NAACP, 1929–1968

1. L. Pearl Mitchell to Roy Wilkins, December 28, 1944, NAACP Papers, Part 26, Series C, Reel 11.

2. For membership figures, see Richard Dalfiume, "The 'Forgotten Years' of the Negro Revolution," *Journal of American History* 55, no. 1 (June 1968): 100.

3. See Michael Denning, *The Cultural Front: The Laboring of American Culture in the Twentieth Century* (New York: Verso, 1997).

4. Alternative views can be found in Kenneth Kusmer, *A Ghetto Takes Shape: Black Cleveland, 1870–1930* (Urbana: University of Illinois Press, 1976), 261–65; Christopher Robert Reed, *The Chicago NAACP and the Rise of Black Professional Leadership, 1910–1966* (Bloomington: Indiana University Press, 1997), iv and 160–62. Reed ascribes the militancy of the late 1950s Chicago branch to its charismatic president, Willoughby Abner, for instance.

5. Clipping, *Cleveland Call and Post,* September 25, 1948, NAACP Papers, Part 26, Series C, Reel 12. These sentiments were not unique to Cleveland. See Matthew Countryman, *Up South: Civil Rights and Black Power in Philadelphia* (Philadelphia: University of Pennsylvania Press, 2007); Glenda Gilmore, *Defying Dixie: The Radical Roots of the Civil Rights Movement* (New York: W. W. Norton, 2008).

6. On Harry Smith, see Kusmer, *A Ghetto Takes Shape,* 132.

7. Harry Davis to Walter White, November 24, 1919, NAACP Papers, Part 12, Series C, Reel 22.

8. Walter White to Harry Davis, November 28, 1919, NAACP Papers, Part 12, Series C, Reel 22.

9. See Robert Bagnell to David H. Pierce, September 2, 1932, Group 1, Folder 4, Container G-159, NAACP Files, Manuscript Division, Library of Congress, Washington, D.C. (hereafter LOC).

10. See also Lee Sartain, *Invisible Activists: Women of the Louisiana NAACP and the Struggle for Civil Rights, 1915–1945* (Baton Rouge: Louisiana State University Press, 2007).

11. Gunnar Myrdal, *An American Dilemma: The Negro Problem and Modern Democracy* (New York: Harper & Brothers Publishers, 1944), 1406.

12. Walter White to Gordon Simpson, January 13, 1933, Group 1, Folder 8, Container G-159, LOC.

13. See *NAACP Bulletins,* Beinecke Library, Yale University, New Haven, Connecticut.

14. Charles P. Lucas to Gloster Current, July 29, 1948, NAACP Papers, Part 26, Series C, Reel 12.

15. See "Report: 1949 NAACP Membership Campaign in Comparison to 1948," NAACP Papers, Series C, Reel 12.

16. Leonard N. Moore, *Carl B. Stokes and the Rise of Black Political Power* (Urbana: University of Illinois Press, 2002), 24.

17. Charles White, "Communication to Executive Committee," February 14, 1927, NAACP Papers, Part 12, Series C, Reel 22.

18. Author's own calculation from data printed in *Hearing Before the U.S. Commission on Civil Rights, Hearing Held in Cleveland, Ohio, April 1–7 1966* (Washington, D.C.: U.S. Government Printing Office, 1967), 645–46.

19. Harry C. Smith, *The Gazette,* in Kusmer, *A Ghetto Takes Shape,* 253.

20. *Annual Report of the President of the Cleveland Branch of the NAACP,* December 12, 1943, NAACP Papers, Part 25, Series A, Reel 21.

21. Robert Bagnell to Harry E. Davis, February 23, 1926, NAACP Papers, Part 12, Series C, Reel 22.

22. Philips fails to mention Holly's membership in the NAACP. See Kimberly Philips, *AlabamaNorth: African American Migrants, Community and Working Class Activism in Cleveland, 1915–1945 (Urbana: University of Illinois Press, 1999).*

23. C. E. Dickinson to William Andrews, January 15, 1931, NAACP Papers, Part 12, Series C, Reel 18; Felecia G. Jones Ross, "Mobilizing the Masses: The *Cleveland Call and Post* and the Scottsboro Incident," *Journal of Negro History* 84, no. 1 (Winter 1999), 48–60.

24. Robert Bagnell to Charles W. White, December 2, 1929, NAACP Papers, Part 12, Series C, Reel 23.

25. See Michael Lowery Gillette, "The NAACP in Texas, 1937–1957" (Ph.D. dissertation, University of Texas, 1984), vii.

26. L. Pearl Mitchell to C. E. Dickinson, July 15, 1932, NAACP Papers, Part 12, Series C, Reel 23.

27. "Report: Ohio State Annual Conference," April 22, 1966, Part 29, Section C, Reel 4, NAACP Papers, Yale University, New Haven, Connecticut.

28. Charles White, "Annual Report: 1929," November 21, 1929, NAACP Papers, Part 12, Series C, Reel 23.

29. Robert Saunders and Roy Wilkins to Harold Williams, January 5, 1960, NAACP Papers, Part 27, Series C, Reel 11.

30. Harry Davis to Walter White, November 15, 1922, Folder 2, Box 1, Cleveland NAACP Branch Files, 1913–1923, Mss.4475, Western Reserve Historical Society, Cleveland, Ohio (hereafter WRHS). See also Kusmer, *A Ghetto Takes Shape,* 264–65.

31. Clarence Norris and Sybil Washington, *The Last of the Scottsboro Boys: An Autobiography* (New York: G. P. Putnam's Sons, 1979), 210; Charles Lucas to Roy Wilkins, October 13, 1948, NAACP Papers, Part 26, Series C, Reel 12.

32. Beth Tompkins Bates, "A New Crowd Challenges the Agenda of the Old Guard in the NAACP, 1933–1941," *American Historical Review* 102, no. 2 (April 1997): 340–77, quotation at 343.

33. William Pickens to L. Pearl Mitchell, January 14, 1941, NAACP Papers, Part 26, Series C, Reel 11.

34. L. Pearl Mitchell and L. O. Baumgardner to Walter White, April 10, 1942,

NAACP Papers, Part 26, Series C, Reel 11. Activists' economic self-sufficiency is discussed in Darlene Clark Hine, "Black Professionals and Race Consciousness: Origins of the Civil Rights Movement, 1890–1950," *Journal of American History* 89, no. 4 (March 2003): 1279–94.

35. Charles H. Loeb, *The Future Is Yours: The History of the Future Outlook League, 1935–1946* (Cleveland: Future Outlook League, 1947), 103.

36. Memorandum: E. Frederick Morrow to The Executive Staff, October 28, 1941, NAACP Papers, Part 26, Series C, Reel 12.

37. Morrow to Executive Staff, October 28, 1941; Memorandum: Roy Wilkins to Walter White, October 29, 1941, NAACP Papers, Part 26, Series C, Reel 12. When the Chicago branch joined a "Don't Buy Where You Can't Work" boycott, Walter White praised the action for enhancing the "prestige for the Chicago Branch and the Association as a whole." Quoted in Bates, "A New Crowd Challenges the Agenda," 349.

38. Ralph Findley and Charles Lucas to Gloster Current, May 3, 1950, NAACP Papers, Series C, Reel 12.

39. Louis Masotti and Jerome Corsi, *Shoot-Out in Cleveland: Black Militants and the Police: July 23, 1968 A Report Submitted to the National Commission on the Causes and Prevention of Violence* (New York: Bantam Book, 1969), 6.

40. Roy Wilkins in Langston Hughes, *Fight for Freedom: The Story of the NAACP* (New York: W. W. Norton & Company, 1962), 171.

41. "Testimony of the Reverend Donald Jacobs, Cleveland, OH," *Hearing Before the U.S. Commission on Civil Rights, Hearing Held in Cleveland, Ohio, April 1–7, 1966* (Washington, D.C.: U.S. Government Printing Office, 1967), 640.

42. See Philips, *AlabamaNorth*; August Meier and Elliot Rudwick, *CORE: A Study in the Civil Rights Movement, 1942–1968* (New York: Oxford University Press, 1973).

43. Clayborne George to Robert Bagnell, October 13, 1925, NAACP Papers, Part 12, Series C, Reel 22.

44. Wiese, *Places of Their Own*, 130.

45. Clipping, "Recent Activities of Cleveland Branch, NAACP," n.d. . NAACP Papers, Part 12, Series C, Reel 23.

46. See also Christopher Wye, "The New Deal and the Negro Community: Toward a Broader Conceptualization," *Journal of American History* 59, no. 3 (December 1972): 621–39, quotation at 625.

47. "Re: Lanham Defense Housing Bill (H.R. 6128)," NAACP Papers, Part 26, Series C, Reel 11.

48. Ralph Findley and Charles Lucas to Gloster Current, December 27, 1949, NAACP Papers, Part 26, Series C, Reel 12.

49. See "You Can Outlaw HATE in Housing, 1957," New York City Branch of the NAACP, NAACP Papers, Part 27, Series C, Reel 10.

50. See *New Release #48*, October 13, 1947, NAACP Papers, Part 26, Series C, Reel 12; *Annual Report for 1961*, NAACP Papers, Part 27, Series C, Reel 11. See also Sarah Igo, *The Averaged American: Surveys, Citizens, and the Making of a Mass Public* (Cambridge, Mass.: Harvard University Press, 2007).

51. "Statement of Paul W. Briggs, Superintendent of Schools, Cleveland, Ohio, 5 April 1966," in *Hearing before the U.S. Commission on Civil Rights*, 766–68. See also

Robert O. Self, *American Babylon: Race and the Struggle for Postwar Oakland* (Princeton, N.J.: Princeton University Press, 2003).

52. Victoria Wolcott, "Recreation and Race in the Postwar City: Buffalo's 1956 Crystal Beach Riot," *Journal of American History* 93, no. 1 (June 2006): 63–90; Jeff Wiltse, *Contested Waters: A Social History of Swimming Pools in America* (Chapel Hill: University of North Carolina Press, 2007), chs. 5–6.

53. Note [from David Pierce] to Roy Wilkins, July 9, 1932, "Recent Activities of the Cleveland Branch N.A.A.C.P.," Group 1, Box G-159, Folder 3, LOC; Reverend Grant Reynold to Herbert Buckman, October 11, 1939, Folder 1, Box 62, NAACP Papers, Series I, Mss. 3520, WRHS; Rowena Jelliffe to Langston Hughes, April 22, 1942, Folder 1675, Box 88, Langston Hughes Collection, Beinecke Library, Yale, New Haven, Connecticut.

54. "Testimony of Clarence Holmes, April 7, 1966," in *Hearing before the U.S. Commission on Civil Rights*, 513–14.

55. *Report of the President of the Cleveland Branch of the NAACP*, December 12, 1943, NAACP Papers, Part 25, Series A, Reel 21.

56. New Release #48, October 13, 1947, NAACP Papers, Part 26, Series C, Reel 12.

57. *Annual Report for 1962*, NAACP Papers, Part 27, Series C, Reel 11.

58. *Ohio State Conference Annual Report for 1966*, NAACP Papers, Part 29, Reel 4.

59. See Membership Department to the Cleveland Branch, August 1947, NAACP Papers, Part 26, Series C, The Midwest, Reel 12.

15. John Kirk, "They Say . . . New York Is Not Worth a D—— to Them": The NAACP in Arkansas, 1918–1971

1. Donald Jones to Gloster B. Current, February 24, 1949, group II, series C, container 10, folder "Arkansas State Conference 1949–1950," National Association for the Advancement for Colored People Papers. Library of Congress, Manuscripts Division, Washington, D.C. (hereafter cited as NAACP Papers [Washington, D.C.]).

2. "Resolution," September 3, 1949, group II, series C, container 10, folder "Pine Bluff, Ark., 1948–1955," NAACP Papers (Washington, D.C.).

3. Walter White to Pine Bluff NAACP, February 25, 1949; Roy Wilkins to Arkansas Branches of the NAACP, May 10, 1949, group II, series C, container 10, folder "Pine Bluff, Ark., 1948–1955," NAACP Papers (Washington, D.C.).

4. Lulu B. White to Gloster B. Current, November 1, 1950, group II, series C, container 11, folder "Arkansas State Conference 1949–1950," NAACP Papers (Washington, D.C.).

5. "Application for Charter and Official Authorization," reel 4, frames 0785–87, National Association for the Advancement of Colored People Papers, Microfilm, University Publications of America, Bethesda, Maryland, 1991 (hereafter cited as NAACP Papers [Microfilm, Maryland]).

6. August Meier and John Bracey Jr., "The NAACP as a Reform Movement 1909–1965: 'To Reach the Conscience of America,'" *Journal of Southern History* 59 (February 1993): 3–30. For a more detailed account of the Elaine riot cases, see Richard C. Cortner, *A Mob Intent on Death: The NAACP and the Arkansas Riot Cases* (Middletown: University of Connecticut Press, 1988).

7. Mrs. H. L. Porter to Roy Wilkins, November 14, 1933, reel 5, frames 0039–0041, NAACP Papers (Microfilm, Maryland).

8. On the black elite in Little Rock and Arkansas, see Willard B. Gatewood, *Aristocrats of Color: The Black Elite, 1880–1920* (Bloomington: Indiana University Press, 1990); John William Graves, *Town and Country: Race Relations in an Urban/Rural Context, Arkansas, 1865–1905* (Fayetteville: University of Arkansas Press, 1990); Fon Louise Gordon, *Caste and Class: The Black Experience in Arkansas, 1880–1920* (Athens: University of Georgia Press, 1995); Tom Dillard, "Perseverance: Black History in Pulaski County, Arkansas—An Excerpt," *Pulaski County Historical Review* 31 (Winter 1983): 62–73.

9. On politics in Arkansas in the 1940s, see V. O. Key Jr., *Southern Politics in State and Nation* (New York: Alfred A. Knopf, 1949).

10. John A. Hibbler to William T. Andrews, September 27, 1929; William T. Andrews to John A. Hibbler, June 12, 1930, both in group I, series D, container 44, folder "Cases Supported—Arkansas Primary Case 1928–1929," NAACP Papers (Washington, D.C.).

11. Walter White to Arthur Spingarn, November 7, 1929, miscellaneous correspondence, 1917–25, 1928–32, National Association for the Advancement of Colored People (Arkansas) Papers, Microfilm, Special Collections Division, University of Arkansas Libraries, Fayetteville (hereafter cited as NAACP Papers [Microfilm, Fayetteville]).

12. *Arkansas Gazette,* November 27, 1928.

13. William T. Andrews to John A. Hibbler, July 19, 1930, group I, series D, container 44, folder "Cases Supported—Arkansas Primary Case 1928–1929," NAACP Papers (Washington, D.C.); Darlene Clark Hine, *Black Victory: The Rise and Fall of the White Primary in Texas* (Millwood, N.Y.: KTO Press, 1979), 115; John A. Kirk, "Dr. John Marshall Robinson, the Arkansas Negro Democratic Association, and Black Politics in Little Rock, 1928–1952," in *Beyond Little Rock: The Origins and Legacies of the Central High Crisis* (Fayetteville: University of Arkansas Press, 2007), 35–54.

14. On blacks and the New Deal, see Allen Kiefer, "The Negro under the New Deal" (Unpublished Ph.D. dissertation, University of Wisconsin, 1961); Barton J. Bernstein, "The New Deal: The Conservative Achievements of Liberal Reform," in *Towards a New Past: Dissenting Essays in American History,* ed. Baton J. Bernstein (New York: Pantheon Books, 1968), 263–88 (quoted page 279); Bernard Sternsher, ed., *The Negro in Depression and War: Prelude to Revolution, 1930–1945* (Chicago: Quadrangle Books, 1969); Raymond Wolters, *Negroes and the Great Depression: The Problem of Economic Recovery* (Westport, Conn.: Greenwood, 1970); Christopher G. Wye, "The New Deal and the Negro Community: Toward a Broader Conceptualization," *Journal of American History* (December 1972): 621–39; Ralph J. Bunche, *The Political Status of the Negro in the Age of FDR* (Chicago: University of Chicago Press, 1973); Harvard Sitkoff, *A New Deal for Blacks: The Emergence of Civil Rights as a National Issue: Volume 1: The Depression Decade* (New York: Oxford University Press, 1978); John B. Kirby, *Black Americans in the Roosevelt Era: Liberalism and Race* (Knoxville: Tennessee University Press, 1980); Nancy J. Weiss, *Farewell to the Party of Lincoln: Black Politics in the Age of FDR* (Princeton, N.J.: Princeton University Press, 1983); Patricia Sullivan, *Days of Hope: Race and Democracy in the New Deal Era* (Chapel Hill: University of North Carolina Press, 1996); and Kevin J. McMahon,

Reconsidering Roosevelt on Race: How the Presidency Paved the Road to Brown (Chicago: University of Chicago Press, 2003).

15. On blacks and World War II, see Harvard Sitkoff, "Racial Militancy and Interracial Violence in the Second World War," *Journal of American History* 58 (June 1971): 661–81; John Morton Blum, *V Was for Victory: Politics and American Culture during World War II* (New York: Harcourt Brace Jovanovich, 1976); Richard M. Dalfumie, *Desegregation of the U.S. Armed Forces: Fighting on Two Fronts, 1939–1953* (Columbia: University of Missouri Press, 1969); Merle E. Reed, *Seedtime for the Modern Civil Rights Movement: The President's Committee on Fair Employment Practice, 1941–1946* (Baton Rouge: Louisiana State University Press, 1991); and Neil A. Wynn, *The Afro-American and the Second World War* (London: Paul Elek, 1976).

16. William Pickens to W. H. Flowers, May 10, 1940, group II, series C, container 10, folder "Pine Bluff, Ark., 1940–1947," NAACP Papers (Washington, D.C.).

17. Maya Angelou, *I Know Why the Caged Bird Sings* (New York: Random House, 1969), 47; *Arkansas Gazette*, July 31, 1988.

18. *Arkansas Gazette*, July 31, 1988. For a portrait of black Pine Bluff in the age of segregation, see George Lipsitz, *Ivory Perry and the Culture of Opposition* (Philadelphia: Temple University Press, 1988), 15–38.

19. W. H. Flowers to Walter White, October 31, 1938, William Harold Flowers Papers, privately held in possession of Stephanie Flowers, Pine Bluff, Arkansas (hereafter cited as Flowers Papers).

20. Charles Houston to W. H. Flowers, November 22, 1938, Thurgood Marshall to W. H. Flowers, April 14, 1939, both in Flowers Papers.

21. Press Release, n.d., Flowers Papers.

22. *The CNO Spectator*, July 1, 1940, Flowers Papers.

23. *The CNO Spectator*, July 1, 1940, Flowers Papers.

24. *Arkansas State Press*, September 19, 1941.

25. *Arkansas State Press*, March 6, 1942.

26. Thomas E. Patterson, *History of the Arkansas Teachers Association* (Washington, D.C.: National Education Association, 1981), 89–91.

27. On teachers' salary suits, see Mark Tushnet, *The NAACP's Legal Strategy against Segregated Education, 1925–1950* (Chapel Hill: University of North Carolina Press, 1987), chs. 4–7; Mark Tushnet, *Making Civil Rights Law: Thurgood Marshall and the Supreme Court, 1936–1961* (New York: Oxford University Press, 1994), ch. 8.

28. Mrs. H. L. Porter to William Pickens, June 9, 1940, group II, series C, container 9, folder "Little Rock, Arkansas, 1940–1947," NAACP Papers (Washington, D.C.).

29. W. H. Flowers to Ella Baker, August 18, 1945, group II, series C, container 11, folder "Arkansas State Conference, April 1945–December 1948," NAACP Papers (Washington, D.C.).

30. Manfred Berg, *"The Ticket to Freedom": The NAACP and the Struggle for Black Political Integration* (Gainesville: University Press of Florida, 2005), 141.

31. Guerdon D. Nichols, "Breaking the Color Barrier at the University of Arkansas," *Arkansas Historical Quarterly* 27 (Spring 1968): 3–21.

32. Rev. Marcus Taylor to Ella Baker, December 4, 1945, group II, series C, container 9, folder "Little Rock, Arkansas, 1940–1947," NAACP Papers (Washington, D.C.).

33. Lucille Black to W. H. Flowers, January 15, 1948, group II, series C, container 10, folder "Pine Bluff, Ark., 1948–1955," NAACP Papers (Washington, D.C.).

34. Donald Jones to Gloster B. Current (memorandum, n.d.), group II, series C, container 11, folder "Arkansas State Conference, April 1945–December 1948," NAACP Papers (Washington, D.C.).

35. Mrs. L. C. Bates to Miss Mary W. Ovington, December 9, 1948, group II, series C, container 10, folder "Little Rock, Ark., 1948–1955," NAACP Papers (Washington, D.C.).

36. Gloster B. Current to Mrs. L. C. Bates, January 19, 1949, group II, series C, container 10, folder "Little Rock, Ark., 1948–1955," NAACP Papers (Washington, D.C.).

37. "Memorandum to the Staff, Branches and Regional Offices" from Gloster B. Current, August 7, 1951, group II, series C, container 11, folder "Arkansas State Conference 1951–1952," NAACP Papers (Washington, D.C.).

38. U. Simpson Tate to Gloster B. Current, August 20, 1952, group II, series C, container 11, folder "Arkansas State Conference 1951–1952," NAACP Papers (Washington, D.C.).

39. For an extensive account of the background to *Brown v. Board of Education*, see Richard Kluger, *Simple Justice: The History of* Brown v. Board of Education *and Black America's Struggle for Equality* (New York: Alfred A. Knopf, 1976).

40. On Blossom's plans for school desegregation, see John A. Kirk, "Massive Resistance and Minimum Compliance: The Origins of the 1957 Little Rock Crisis and the Failure of School Desegregation in the South," in *Beyond Little Rock*, 94–115.

41. Georg. C. Iggers, "An Arkansas Professor: The NAACP and the Grass Roots," 288–89, in *Little Rock, U.S.A.*, ed. Wilson Record and Jane Cassels Record (San Francisco: Chandler Publishing Co., 1960).

42. *Southern School News*, February 1956, 11.

43. *Southern School News*, March 1956, 4; Wiley A. Branton, "Little Rock Revisited: Desegregation to Resegregation," *Journal of Negro Education* 52 (Summer 1983): 253.

44. Branton, "Little Rock Revisited," 254.

45. Iggers, "An Arkansas Professor," 290.

46. Tony Freyer, *The Little Rock Crisis: A Constitutional Interpretation* (Westport, Conn.: Greenwood Press, 1984), 52.

47. Branton, "Little Rock Revisited," 254; Freyer, *The Little Rock Crisis*, 56–58.

48. "Our Reason for Appeal," Rev. J. C. Crenchaw, n.d., box 4, folder 10, Daisy Bates Papers, State Historical Society of Wisconsin, Madison (hereafter cited as Bates Papers [Madison]); Branton, "Little Rock Revisited," 255–56.

49. *Southern School News*, May 1957, 2; Branton, "Little Rock Revisited," 255–56.

50. On the Little Rock crisis, see John A. Kirk, *Redefining the Color Line: Black Activism in Little Rock, Arkansas, 1940–1970* (Gainesville: University Press of Florida, 2002), ch. 5.

51. Statement by Clarence Laws, November 13, 1957, box 5, folder 2, Bates Papers (Madison).

52. Transcript of telephone conversation between Gloster Current, Daisy Bates, and Clarence Laws, Wednesday, October 2, 1957, box 5, folder 2, Bates Papers (Madison).

53. Daisy Bates to Bruce Bennett, September 13, 1957, box 6, folder 4, 1957, Bates Papers (Madison); *Arkansas Gazette*, September 17, 1957. See also Kirk, *Redefining the Color Line*, 123–29.

54. *Southern School News*, March 1958, 2–3; July 1958, 3–4; August 1958, 6; September 1958, 2; Branton, "Little Rock Revisited," 265–66; J. W. Peltason, *Fifty-eight Lonely Men: Southern Federal Judges and School Desegregation* (Urbana: University of Illinois Press, 1971), 183–87; Corrine Silverman, *The Little Rock Story* (Tuscaloosa: University of Alabama Press, 1958), 17–19.

55. *Southern School News*, September 1958, 2; Peltason, *Fifty-eight Lonely Men*, 189–90, 192; Silverman, *The Little Rock Story*, 21, 24–25, 27; Tushnet, *Making Civil Rights Law*, 261–63.

56. *Southern School News*, October 1958, 5, 7; November 1958, 9; Branton, "Little Rock Revisited," 266–67; Freyer, *The Little Rock Crisis*, 156; Peltason, *Fifty-eight Lonely Men*, 187, 196; Roy Reed, *Faubus: The Life and Times of an American Prodigal* (Fayetteville: University of Arkansas Press, 1997), 245; Silverman *The Little Rock Story*, 21–22, 28.

57. *Southern School News*, November 1958, 8; Peltason, *Fifty-eight Lonely Men*, 198–202; Freyer, *The Little Rock Crisis*, 155–57.

58. *Southern School News*, May 1959, 6.

59. Kirk, *Redefining the Color Line*, 135–38.

60. Daisy Bates to Roy Wilkins, January 30, 1956; Daisy Bates to Roy Wilkins, November 8, 1956; J. C. Crenchaw to Frank Smith, April 11, 1957, all in group III, series C, container 4, folder "Arkansas State Conference, 1956–57," NAACP Papers (Washington, D.C.); *Arkansas Gazette*, August 24, 26, 28, October 19, 1980.

61. Daisy Bates to Dr. Jerry Jewell, September 3, 1966, group IV, series C, container 2, folder "Little Rock, Ark, 1966–67," NAACP Papers (Washington, D.C.); Dr. Jerry Jewell interview with John A. Kirk, April 19, 1993, Little Rock, Arkansas, deposited in the Pryor Center for Arkansas Oral and Visual History, Special Collections, University of Arkansas, Fayetteville.

62. *Southern School News*, March 1959, 2, December 1961, 12; George Howard interview with John A. Kirk, April 13, 1993, Little Rock, Arkansas, deposited in the Pryor Center for Arkansas Oral and Visual History, Special Collections, University of Arkansas, Fayetteville.

63. Kirk, *Redefining the Color Line*, chapter 6; John A. Kirk, "The Southern Regional Council and the Arkansas Council on Human Relations, 1954–1974," in *Beyond Little Rock*, 116–38.

64. *Arkansas Gazette*, June 3, 1962; Daisy Bates to Wiley Branton, August 28, 1962, series 1, box 1, folder 2, Bates Papers (Fayetteville).

65. Memorandum to the files from Mr. Current, December 17, 1965, group III, series C, container 5, folder "Arkansas State Conference, 1961–65"; Gloster B. Current to L. C. Bates, March 13, 1967; Gloster B. Current to Dr. George Flemmings, January 7, 1969, group IV, series C, container 2, folder "Arkansas State Conference, 1966–70," all in NAACP Papers (Washington, D.C.).

66. L. C. Bates to Dr. John A. Morsell, May 17, 1971, series 2, box 5, folder 3, Daisy Bates Papers, Special Collections Division, University of Arkansas Libraries, Fayetteville.

67. Jewell interview; Berg, *"Ticket to Freedom,"* 189.

CONTRIBUTORS

BEVERLY BUNCH-LYONS is an associate professor of history at Virginia Polytechnic Institute and State University, National Capital Region. She is the author of *Contested Terrain,* and her articles have appeared in the *Journal of American History,* the *International Journal of the Humanities,* the *Magazine of History,* and the *Encyclopedia of Civil Rights in America.*

NAKEINA DOUGLAS is assistant professor at the Grace E. Harris Leadership Institute, Virginia Commonwealth University. She is a doctoral candidate at the Center for Public Administration and Policy at Virginia Polytechnic Institute and State University and a graduate research assistant at the Virginia Tech Race and Social Policy Research Center.

ADAM FAIRCLOUGH is a professor of American history at the University of Leiden. He has many highly acclaimed publications in the field of African American history. They include *To Redeem the Soul of America: The Southern Christian Leadership Conference and Martin Luther King, Jr.; Race and Democracy: The Civil Rights Struggle in Louisiana, 1915–1972; Teaching Equality: Black Schools in the Age of Jim Crow; Better Day Coming: Blacks and Equality, 1890–2000;* and *A Class of Their Own: Black Teachers in the Segregated South.*

ANDREW M. FEARNLEY is a lecturer at the University of Groningen in the Netherlands. His doctoral thesis looks at how the discipline of American psychiatry conceptualized the issue of race and more broadly plots a history of racial thought within the country's biological and human sciences. He wrote his M.Phil. on the Cleveland branch of the NAACP.

PATRICK FLACK is a graduate of Cambridge University, where he is currently studying for a Ph.D. under the supervision of Professor Tony Badger. His research topic is racial identity and racial conflict in interwar Detroit.

SIMON HALL is a senior lecturer in American history at the University of Leeds. He is the author of *Peace and Freedom: The Civil Rights and Antiwar Movements in the 1960s*. He has published numerous essays and journal articles on the civil rights movement, Black Power, and student radicalism in America during the 1960s. Simon is currently writing a book on popular protest and political dissent in the United States since the mid-1970s.

JOHN A. KIRK is a professor in American history at Royal Holloway, University of London. He is author of *Redefining the Color Line: Black Activism in Little Rock, Arkansas, 1940–1970*, which was awarded the 2003 J. G. Ragsdale Book Award from the Arkansas Historical Association; *Martin Luther King, Jr.;* and *Beyond Little Rock: The Origins and Legacies of the Central High Crisis.* He has also edited two books: *Martin Luther King, Jr. and the Civil Rights Movement: Controversies and Debates* and *An Epitaph for Little Rock: A Fiftieth Anniversary Retrospective on the Central High Crisis.*

GEORGE LEWIS is a reader in American history at the University of Leicester. He is author of *The White South and the Red Menace: Segregationists, Anticommunism and Massive Resistance, 1945–1965* and *Massive Resistance: White Resistance to the Civil Rights Movement.* Other recent publications include articles in the *Journal of Southern History,* the *Journal of American Studies,* and the *Virginia Magazine of History and Biography.*

PETER J. LING is a professor in American studies at the University of Nottingham. He is the author of *Martin Luther King, Jr.* and coeditor of *Gender and the Civil Rights Movement.* He has conducted research at the King Center, Howard University, and other Movement archives, and is currently completing an essay collection, *King in Comparative Perspective,* and beginning a new research project on social capital and the civil rights movement.

CHRISTOPHER R. REED is professor emeritus of American history in the Department of History, Art History and Philosophy, Roosevelt University, Chicago. He is author of *The Chicago NAACP and the Rise of Black Professional Leadership, 1910–1966*, the only known complete history of a branch; *All the World Is Here; The Black Presence at White City, Black Chicago's First Century, 1833–1900*, and *Black Chicago's Second Century, 1901–1933*.

YVONNE RYAN is a Ph.D. candidate working with Professor Adam Fairclough at the University of Leiden. Her thesis on the leadership of Roy Wilkins will be completed in 2009. She holds an M.A. in United States Studies from the Institute of U.S. Studies, University of London.

LEE SARTAIN is a senior lecturer in American history at the University of Portsmouth. His first book, *Invisible Activists: Women of the Louisiana NAACP and the Struggle for Civil Rights, 1915–1945* was awarded the Landry Prize for the best book on the history of the American South to be published by Louisiana State University Press in 2007.

SIMON TOPPING is a lecturer in American history and subject leader for American studies at the University of Plymouth. He is the author of *Lincoln's Lost Legacy: The Republican Party and the African American Vote, 1928–1952*. He has published articles in a number of journals, including the *Journal of African American History* and the *Journal of American Studies*, and has begun work on a book about the early civil rights movement.

KEVERN VERNEY is a professor in American history and associate head of the Department of English and History at Edge Hill University. His publications include *Black Civil Rights in America, The Art of the Possible: Booker T. Washington and Black Leadership in the United States, 1881–1925, African Americans and U.S. Popular Culture,* and *The Debate on Black Civil Rights in America*. He is currently working on a book on the NAACP in Alabama, 1913–1956.

JONATHAN WATSON is a lecturer in American history at the University of Reading. He is currently completing research for an article on the lawyer/journalist/activist Loren Miller and a book on the branch history of the Los Angeles NAACP.

JENNY WOODLEY is a Ph.D. student working with Professors Peter Ling and Richard King at the University of Nottingham. She is writing her thesis on the cultural work of the NAACP during the first half of the twentieth century. She was the recipient of a Library of Congress–AHRC scholarship to the Kluge Center to carry out research using the NAACP Papers.

CHARLES L. ZELDEN is professor of history at Nova Southeastern University in Fort Lauderdale, Florida. He is the author of *Battle for the Black Ballot: Smith v. Allwright and the Defeat of the Texas All White Primary* and *Bush v. Gore: Exposing the Hidden Crisis in American Democracy.*

INDEX

Abbott, Robert S., 177
abolitionist movement, ix, xi, 170, 173;
    "new abolition," 171–75 passim
Adams, W. H., III, 37
Addams, Jane, 172–73 passim, 177
AFL, 198, 237, 283n57. *See also* CIO;
    labor unions
African American women, vii, xxiv,
    xxv, 6, 27, 101, 112, 126, 172, 174, 187.
    See also occupations; teachers
Alabama, x, xxvii, 12, 47, 53, 58, 61, 64, 67,
    78, 105–20, 174, 182, 204, 208, 238, 241;
    A. G. Gaston, 67; Birmingham, 44,
    53, 58, 67–68, 69, 93, 105–12 passim,
    113–15 passim, 118, 204; Mobile
    NAACP branch, 64, 106, 108, 110, 112,
    114, 117, 118; NAACP branches, 114;
    NAACP outlawed in state, 107, 111,
    241; Talladega NAACP branch, 105;
    Tuscaloosa NAACP branch, 106;
    Tuskegee air base, 115, Tuskegee
    NAACP branch, 115. *See also*
    Alabama Christian Movement for
    Human Rights; LeFlore, John L.;
    Parks, Rosa; Shuttleworth, Rev. Fred
Alabama Christian Movement for
    Human Rights, 67, 108. *See also*
    Alabama
Allen, Henry, (senator, Kansas), 11
American Civil Liberties Union, 198
Amsterdam News, 46, 50. *See also*
    Wilkins, Roy
Anderson, Marian, 239
Anderson, William, 65
annual convention, 47, 50, 55–57 pas-
    sim, 71, 77, 82, 191
anti-communism, 35, 47, 72, 82, 84
anti-lynching campaign, ix, xi, xxiii, 3,

4, 8–9, 10, 15, 26, 112, 126, 166, 191,
    236–39 passim; Dyer anti-lynching
    bill, 11, 237
Arkansas, xxvii, 33, 34, 219–34, 241;
    Aaron v. Cooper, 228, 229; *Arkansas
    State Press,* 224, 226, 230, 232;
    Arkansas Negro Democratic
    Association, 220; Arkansas Voter
    Project, 234; L. C. Bates, 226, 230,
    232, 234; Bruce Bennett, 230, 232;
    Virgil T. Blossom, 227–29 passim;
    Committee on Negro Organi-
    zations, 223; Elaine, 8, 220, Little
    Rock, 33, 220–28 passim, 230–34
    passim, 241; poll tax, 220, 224, 225;
    Stamps, 223; teachers equal pay
    case, 109, 130, 224, 232; University of
    Arkansas Law School, 225; Orval
    Faubus, 33, 229, 231; Jim Guy
    Tucker, 234. *See also* Flowers,
    William Harold; Little Rock Nine;
    Moore v. Dempsey; white primary
Astor, Viscountess Nancy Witcher, 5
Atlanta, ix, xviii, 5, 59, 93, 109, 173, 209,
    233, 237. *See also* Georgia
Autrey, Dorothy, 113
Avery, Sheldon, xxii, 163

Bagnall, Robert W., 108, 124, 179–80
Baker, Ella, xxiv, 61, 63, 115, 119
Baltimore, Maryland, 201, 206, 243;
    desegregation protests, xvii. *See also*
    Gaines v. University of Maryland
Baltimore Afro-American, 6–7. *See also*
    Murphy, Carl
Bataan, 22. *See also* Hollywood
Bates, Beth Tompkins, xxiv, xxvi, 10,
    156, 210, 282n52

303

civil rights movement, xiii, xiv, xviii,
xix, xxvii, 4, 26, 43–44 passim,
51–52, 56, 72–73 passim, 75–76, 78,
80–82, 85; Albany campaign, 64–67;
Birmingham campaign, 44, 53, 58,
67–68, 69; Selma campaign, xviii,
44, 58; sit-in demonstrations, 51,
62–63 passim, 66, 69, 233, 241. *See
also* Civil Rights Act; King, Martin
Luther, Jr.; Voting Rights Act
Civil War, vii–viii, xv, 9, 91, 130, 274n1
class tensions, xiv, xxi, xxiv,
xxvii–xxviii, 17, 23, 25, 45–46, 67,
107–8, 110, 119, 122–25, 127, 170,
177–80, 182, 183, 274n1. *See also*
Frazier, E. Franklin
Cleveland, 30, 206–7, 209, 213, 217;
NAACP branch, xxvii, 201–18;
Future Outlook League, 208, 210,
212. *See also* Ohio
Clinton, William Jefferson, 234
Cobb, W. Montague, 242
Colburn, David, 69
Cold War, 14, 35, 47, 72, 82, 258n24. *See
also* House Un-American Activities
Committee
colonialism, xxv
communism, xiv, 13–14, 59, 82, 107,
113–14 passim, 129, 182, 192, 238;
NAACP accused of, 35–36, 47, 82,
258n24
Communist Party, 47, 107, 113, 192–93;
International Labor Defense, 114,
196, 238. *See also* communism
Confederacy, viii, 99, 105
Congress, vii, ix, xi, xiii, 9, 13, 47–48
passim, 50–55 passim, 67, 80, 151,
182, 191, 212, 237, 240, 242
Congress of Racial Equality (CORE),
xviii, 55, 62, 64, 66, 71–72, 76–77, 79,
83, 213; Freedom Rides, 62, 66, 233.
See also civil rights movement;
Farmer, James; McKissick, Floyd
Connor, Eugene "Bull," 67
Constitution (U.S.), vii, x, xi, xiii, 92,
124, 149–52 passim; 13th
Amendment, vii; 14th Amendment,

vii, 16, 97, 142–45 passim, 149, 151;
15th Amendment, vii, 16, 139, 142,
144, 145, 149, 151–52 passim
Cortner, Robert, xxiii
Crash Dive, 22. *See also* Hollywood
Crisis, ix, xvi, 5, 17–18, 24, 122, 177, 181,
187, 235, 238, 240, 242; jazz, 17;
Warren Marr II, 242. *See also* Du
Bois, W. E. B.; Fauset, Jessie
critics of NAACP, xiii–xiv, xxiii, 5, 43,
50, 55, 114, 191–92, 201; too conservative, xxii, xxv, xxvii–xxviii, 14, 57, 63,
75, 107–8, 120. *See also* black nationalists; Garvey, Marcus; Malcolm X
Cruse, Harold, 25
Cullen, Countee, 17. *See also* Harlem
Renaissance
cultural program, xii, xxvi, 15–27, 171,
179, 254n23
Current, Gloster B., 31, 61, 72, 77, 82,
166, 168, 226, 230, 234, 269n66;
NAACP Leadership Training
Workshops, 31

Daley, Mayor Richard J., Sr., 70–71, 183.
See also Chicago
Dalfiume, Richard, xxv
Darrow, Clarence, 160. *See also* lawyers
Dawson, William L., 70, 169, 182–83
Deacons for Defense, 55
Deburg, William Van, 83
DeCell, Hal C., 38. *See also* Mississippi
Declaration of Independence, 171
Democratic Party, viii, 9, 72, 78, 112,
135–37, 139, 143–46, 149, 150, 169, 183,
220, 225, 245
DePriest, Oscar, 112
Detroit, 68, 159, 186, 208, 215; Detroit
Civic Rights Committee, 155, 163;
Detroit NAACP branch, xxvii, 46,
70, 155–68, 201, 206, 213; *Detroit
Owl*, 161; Ossian Sweet, 156, 159–61,
213; police violence, 161. *See also*
Ford, Henry; labor unions
disfranchisement, viii, xi, 93, 221, 236,
237. *See also Guinn v. United States*,
voting

Dixiecrats, 13. *See also* political parties

Douglas, Aaron, 17, 24. *See also* Harlem Renaissance

Douglas, Nakeina, xxvi

Douglass, Frederick, 3

Dray, Philip, 10

Du Bois, W. E. B., ix–x, xvii, xix, xxii, xxvii–xxviii, 3, 5, 11–12, 15, 17–19, 23, 26, 46, 59, 94–95, 99, 170, 173–74, 177, 181–82, 187–88, 203, 239–40 passim, 285n24; *A Soliloquy on Viewing My Life from the Last Decade of Its First Century,* xix; *Darkwater,* xvi; *Dusk of Dawn,* xvi; editor of *Crisis,* xvi, 17, 122, 181, 235, 238; *Souls of Black Folk,* 170. *See also Crisis*

DuVore, Jesse, 32. *See also* Moon, Henry Lee

Eagles, Charles, xix

Eastland, James O., 36–37, 42, 259n27

economic program, xiv, xxi, xxvii, 9, 58, 111, 113, 121, 128, 129–30, 134, 181–82, 192, 201, 238, 243; fair employment, 3, 70, 131, 162, 193, 212, 222, 242; Harris Report, 121. *See also* Harris, Abram L.

education policy, xi, 26, 101, 112, 130, 153, 177, 198, 227; desegregation, 3, 29, 33–34, 37, 60–61, 153, 198, 227–34; teachers equal pay, xii, 132–33; University of Mississippi, 53. *See also Brown v. Board of Education; Regents of University of California v. Bakke; Sipuel v. Board of Regents; Sweatt v. Painter*

Eisenhower, Dwight D., 36–37 passim, 48, 50, 60, 65, 229

Emancipation Proclamation, 172

Evers, Medgar, 68–69, 242

Evers-Williams, Myrlie, 244

Fairclough, Adam, 132–33, 274n1; foreword, vii–xiv

Fair Employment Practices Commission (FEPC), 10–11, 117–18, 132, 194, 222, 239–40

Falls Church NAACP branch, 89–104; Sandy James, 91; Lee Gaskins, 91; residential segregation campaign, 91–92, 94, 96–98, 100, 102. *See also* Virginia

Farmer, James, 62, 66. *See also* Congress of Racial Equality

Faubus, Orval, 33, 229, 231. *See also* Arkansas; Little Rock Nine

Fauset, Jessie, 17, 254n8. *See also Crisis*

Fearnley, Andrew, xxvii–xxviii

Federal Bureau of Investigation (FBI), 64, 66. *See also* Hoover, J. Edgar

Fellowship of Reconciliation (FOR), 30

Flack, Patrick, xxvii

Florida, xxiv, 37, 54, 209; *NAACP v. Harris,* 245; Robert Hayling, 69; St Augustine campaign, 60, 69

Flowers, William Harold, 219, 223–27. *See also* Arkansas

Ford, Henry, 158, 165, 166–67. *See also* Detroit

Franklin, John Hope, xvii

Frazier, E. Franklin, 23, 283n6

Freedmen's Bureau, 105

Gaines v. University of Maryland, 238. *See also* education policy

Gandhi, Mohandas Karamchand, 49, 65

Garrison, William Lloyd, 173

Garvey, Marcus, xii, xiv, xx, 3, 59, 127, 178, 182, 189, 190. *See also* Universal Negro Improvement Association

Gates, Henry Louis, Jr., 25

Genovese, Eugene, xviii

Georgia, 64, 112, 209; Albany, 65–67; Eugene Cook, 35–36. *See also* Atlanta; Pritchett, Laurie

Gilded Age, 171

Goings, Kenneth, xxiii

Gordon, Bruce S., 245

Grantham, Dewey R., 171

Great Depression, xvii, xxi, 3, 9, 13, 47, 107, 113, 128, 156, 181, 191, 207, 221, 238

Great Migration, xxviii, 92–93, 156–57, 176–77, 178, 185–86, 195, 209

Green, Ben, xxiv

Kellogg, Charles Flint, xx
Kemp, Jack, 243
Kennedy, John F., xix, 52–55, 67–68
Kennedy, Robert. F., xix, 66
King, Martin Luther, Jr., xiv, xviii, xix,
    xxiii, xxvi, 8, 49, 50–51, 54–56, 59–74,
    76, 169, 183, 241. *See also* civil rights
    movement; Montgomery
    Improvement Association;
    Southern Christian Leadership
    Conference
Kirk, John, xxvii
Korean war, 69
Ku Klux Klan, 12, 69, 96, 108, 113, 122,
    190, 236–37 passim
Kweisi, Mfume, 244–45 passim

labor unions, viii, xi–xiii passim, 10,
    128–29, 131, 165, 166–67, 186, 194–95,
    197–98, 201; International
    Brotherhood of Boilermakers, 194;
    Iron Shipbuilders and Helpers of
    America, 194; International
    Longshoremen's Union, 128–29 pas-
    sim; United Automobile Workers,
    164–65 passim. *See also* AFL; CIO
Lampkin, Daisy, xxv, 112, 164–65
Laws, Clarence, 34
Lawson, James, 62–63. *See also* Student
    Nonviolent Coordinating
    Committee
lawyers, xi, 20, 23, 74, 136, 140, 141–42,
    144–45, 147–49, 160, 197, 208, 220,
    225; T. L. Jones, 98; Ulysses Simpson
    Tate, 226, 228. *See also* Darrow,
    Clarence; Houston, Charles
    Hamilton; Legal Defense and
    Education Fund; Margold, Nathan;
    Marshall, James; Marshall,
    Thurgood; Miller, Loren; Mitchell,
    Clarence
LeFlore, John L., 110–12, 114, 116–17;
    Non-Partisan Voters League, 111. *See
    also* Alabama
Legal Defense and Education Fund, 62,
    147, 225, 239. *See also* lawyers
Levison, Stanley, 50, 66, 68

Levy, Eugene, xx
Lewis, David Levering, xxii, 17, 23
Lewis, George, xxvi
Ling, Peter, xvii, xxvi
Little Rock Nine, 229; Classroom
    Teachers' Association; Council on
    Community Affairs, 224; Private
    School Corporation, 231; Women's
    Emergency Committee to Open
    Our Schools, 232. *See also* Arkansas;
    Bates, Daisy; education program
Look, 6–7
Los Angeles Sentinel, 6
Los Angeles, 46, 57, 77, 186–87 passim,
    189, 194, 196; Rev. James E. Jones, 71;
    NAACP branch, 20, 70, 188, 190–93
    passim, 197–98; Watts riot, 70. *See
    also* California
Louisiana, 47, 112, 121–23, 125, 191, 244,
    274n1; Alexandria NAACP branch,
    124, 131, 133; Baton Rouge NAACP
    branch, 125–26, 128–29, 130–31, 133;
    Joint Legislative Committee to
    Maintain Segregation, 40;
    Louisiana Farm Tenant Security
    Project, 130; Monroe NAACP
    branch, 124–25, 127, 130–31, 133;
    New Iberia NAACP branch, 132;
    Shreveport NAACP branch, 84, 122;
    Transylvania NAACP branch, 130;
    UNIA, 127–28; White Citizens'
    Councils, 40; white primary, 150,
    152. *See also Louisiana Weekly*; New
    Orleans
Louisiana Weekly, 125

Malcolm X, xiii, xix, 59. *See also* Nation
    of Islam
Manis, Andrew, xxvii, 107
Marable, Manning, xxii
March on Washington Movement, 10,
    59, 68, 222, 239, 242. *See also* King,
    Martin Luther, Jr.; Randolph, A.
    Philip
Margold, Nathan, 144
Marshall, James, 144
Marshall, Thurgood, 13, 36, 48, 62,

internal divisions, xii–xiii, xvii, 37, 132–33, 137, 174, 180, 190; Madam C. J. Walker medal, 109; *NAACP Papers* xxiii; objectives, 48, 82, 140, 167; pamphlets, 31–32, 35–39, 258n26, 259n27; STOP, 27. *See also* African American women; Alabama; annual convention; Arkansas; Bagnall, Robert; Baker, Ella; Bates, Daisy; *Brown v. Board of Education; Brown II;* California; campaigns; Chicago; civil rights movement; class tensions; *Crisis;* critics of NAACP; Detroit; Du Bois, W. E. B.; Florida; Georgia; Hollywood; Johnson, James Weldon; Lampkin, Daisy; Legal Defense and Education Fund; Louisiana; Marshall, Thurgood; membership; Mississippi; Nerney, Mary Childs; New York; North Carolina; occupations; Ohio; Ovington, Mary White; Philadelphia NAACP branch; Pickens; William; Scottsboro case; South Carolina; Spingarn, Arthur; Spingarn, Joel E.; state conferences; teachers; tensions (local-national); Texas; Virginia; voting; white primary; White, Walter; Wilkins, Roy; women's auxiliary; youth councils

Nash, Roy Freeman, 236
National Baptist Convention, 69
National Urban League. *See* Urban League
Nation of Islam, 59, 182. *See also* Malcolm X
Nerney, Mary Childs, 95–96, 236
New Deal, 4, 10, 12, 14, 112–13, 117, 128–29, 130–31, 181, 186, 217, 221–22. *See also* Fair Employment Practices Commission
New Orleans, 121–24, 128–29, 132–33, 187; Federation of Civic Leagues, 129; NAACP branch, 41, 122, 126–29 passim, 132; residential segregation ordinance, 127; *Vindicator,* 124–25. *See also* Louisiana

News and Courier, 30, 41. *See also* Waring, Thomas R.
New York, vii, 5, 30, 32, 41, 61, 70, 76, 93, 124, 144, 171, 175, 186–87, 189, 235–37 passim, 240, 243; Fair Housing Practices Law, 214; New York City NAACP branch, 47, 61, 70, 72, 209, 215
New York Times, 32, 51, 63
Niagara Movement, 173, 203. *See also* Du Bois, W. E. B.
Nix, Robert, 70
Nixon E. D., 61, 118
Nixon v. Condon, 144, 238; Lawrence Nixon, 142–44. *See also* white primary
North Carolina, 11, 51; Greensboro, 241; Monroe NAACP branch, 60; Pollocksville, 37; Raleigh, 62;

Obama, Barack, 245–46
occupations (NAACP members), viii, ix, xxviii, 23–23, 70, 92, 107, 110, 117–18, 128, 131–32, 162, 172, 193, 218, 220; banker, 180; barber, 145, 171; blacksmith, 108; business, 17, 20, 67, 99, 125, 133, 188; dentists, 69, 110, 114, 149, 172, 188, 191, 232; insurance, 110, 125–26, 133, 180, 223; laundress, 110; newspaper owners/editors, 6, 30, 41, 46, 203, 207; postal worker, viii, 109, 110–12, 128, 157, 162, 182; physicians, 110, 213, 220, 224; preachers, 59, 63, 76, 108, 157–58, 208, 212, 225; real estate, 125; undertaking, 110, 125, 224. *See also* African American women; lawyers; teachers
Ohio, 11, 203, 207–8 passim, 211; *Terry v. Ohio,* 217. *See also* Cleveland
Ovington, Mary White, xvi–xviii passim, xxii, xxiv, 235–36 passim
Oxford University Press, 3

Page, Marion, 65
Panama Canal, 190
Parker, John J., 11–12, 191, 237
Parks, Rosa, 48–49, 60–61, 118, 241. *See*

South Africa, 30, 243
South Carolina, 30, 46, 162, 209;
    Columbia NAACP branch, 64
Southern Christian Leadership
    Conference (SCLC), xxvi, 47, 61–66,
    69; Crusade for Citizenship, 61. *See
    also* King, Martin Luther, Jr.
Southern Regional Council (SRC), 34
Spingarn, Arthur, 221, 239
Spingarn, Joel E., xx, 171, 175, 203, 237
Spingarn medal, 59, 236, 239, 241, 244
Stampp, Kenneth, xviii
state conferences: Arkansas, 34, 219,
    224; California, 192; New York, 84;
    Ohio, 208; Texas, 149, 219
Stockley, Grif, xxiii
Stokes, Carl, 212, 217–18
Stokes, Louis, 212, 218
Storey, Moorfield, xx, 140, 235
Street, Joe, 26
Student Nonviolent Coordinating
    Committee (SNCC), xviii, 55–56,
    62–65, 67, 71–72, 76–80, 85, 233–34,
    267n35, 269n66; Ed King, 62;
    Lowndes County Freedom Party,
    78. *See also* civil rights movement;
    Lawson, James
Supreme Court, viii, xi, xii, 12, 34, 36,
    37, 47, 51, 97, 100–101, 102, 113,
    142–46 passim, 149–50, 153, 191,
    196–97, 217, 220–21, 225, 227, 230,
    236–41 passim, 243–45 passim;
    Robert Bork, 244; Earl Warren, 230.
    *See also Brown v. Board of
    Education;* Parker, John J.
Sweatt v. Painter, 241. *See also* educa-
    tion policy

teachers, ix, 20, 109, 110, 162, 223; equal-
    ization of salaries, xii, 130, 132–33,
    224, 232. *See also* education policy
television, xix, 27, 31, 33–34, 40, 53, 54,
    81, 255n33; NBC-TV, 29–30. *See also*
    Huntley, Chester "Chet"; White,
    Walter
tensions (local-national), xii, xxi,

xxvi–xxvii, 64, 72, 114, 119, 136, 141,
    155–68, 204
Texas, xxv, 54, 80, 132, 237; *Bell v. Hill,*
    146, 150; El Paso NAACP branch,
    142; *Houston Informer,* 144;
    Houston NAACP branch, 149
Thomson, E. P., xviii
Thurman, Wallace, 19. *See also* Harlem
    Renaissance
Till, Emmett, 39. *See also* Mississippi
Time, 9, 66
Tobias, Channing, 31
Toomer, Jean, 17. *See also* Harlem
    Renaissance
Topping, Simon, xxii, xxv
Truman, Harry S., 11, 13, 240; *To Secure
    These Rights,* 11
Tushnet, Mark, xxiv
Tuskegee Institute, x, 106–8, 112, 115–16,
    173, 174; Frederick Patterson, 106,
    115. *See also* Alabama; Moton,
    Robert Russa; Washington,
    Booker T.
Twentieth Century Fox, 21. *See also*
    Hollywood; Willkie, Wendell

Universal Negro Improvement
    Association (UNIA), xx, 127–28,
    190. *See also* Garvey, Marcus
Universal Studios, 3. *See also*
    Hollywood
Urban League, 53, 71, 172, 207, 262n35;
    L. Hollingsworth Wood, 172. *See
    also* Young, Whitney

Variety, 24. *See also* Hollywood
Vechten, Carl Van, 24
Verney, Kevern, xxvi–xxvii passim; his-
    toriographical introduction
    xv–xxviii
Vietnam conflict, 55–56, 57, 60, 72,
    75–82, 84, 85; Operation Rolling
    Thunder, 75. *See also* peace
    movement
Villard, Oswald Garrison, x, 173–74;
    New York Evening Post, 173

KEVERN VERNEY is associate head of the department of English and history at Edge Hill University, England. He is the author of *The Debate on Black Civil Rights in America; African Americans and U.S. Popular Culture; The Art of the Possible: Booker T. Washington and Black Leadership in the United States, 1881–1925;* and *Black Civil Rights in America.*

LEE SARTAIN is senior lecturer in American studies at the University of Portsmouth, England, and the author of *Invisible Activists: Women of the Louisiana NAACP and the Struggle for Civil Rights, 1915–1945.*

ADAM FAIRCLOUGH is the Raymond and Beverly Sackler Professor of American History at Leiden University, Netherlands, and the author of many books, including, most recently, *Race and Democracy: The Civil Rights Struggle in Louisiana, 1915–1972* and *A Class of Their Own: Black Teachers in the Segregated South.*